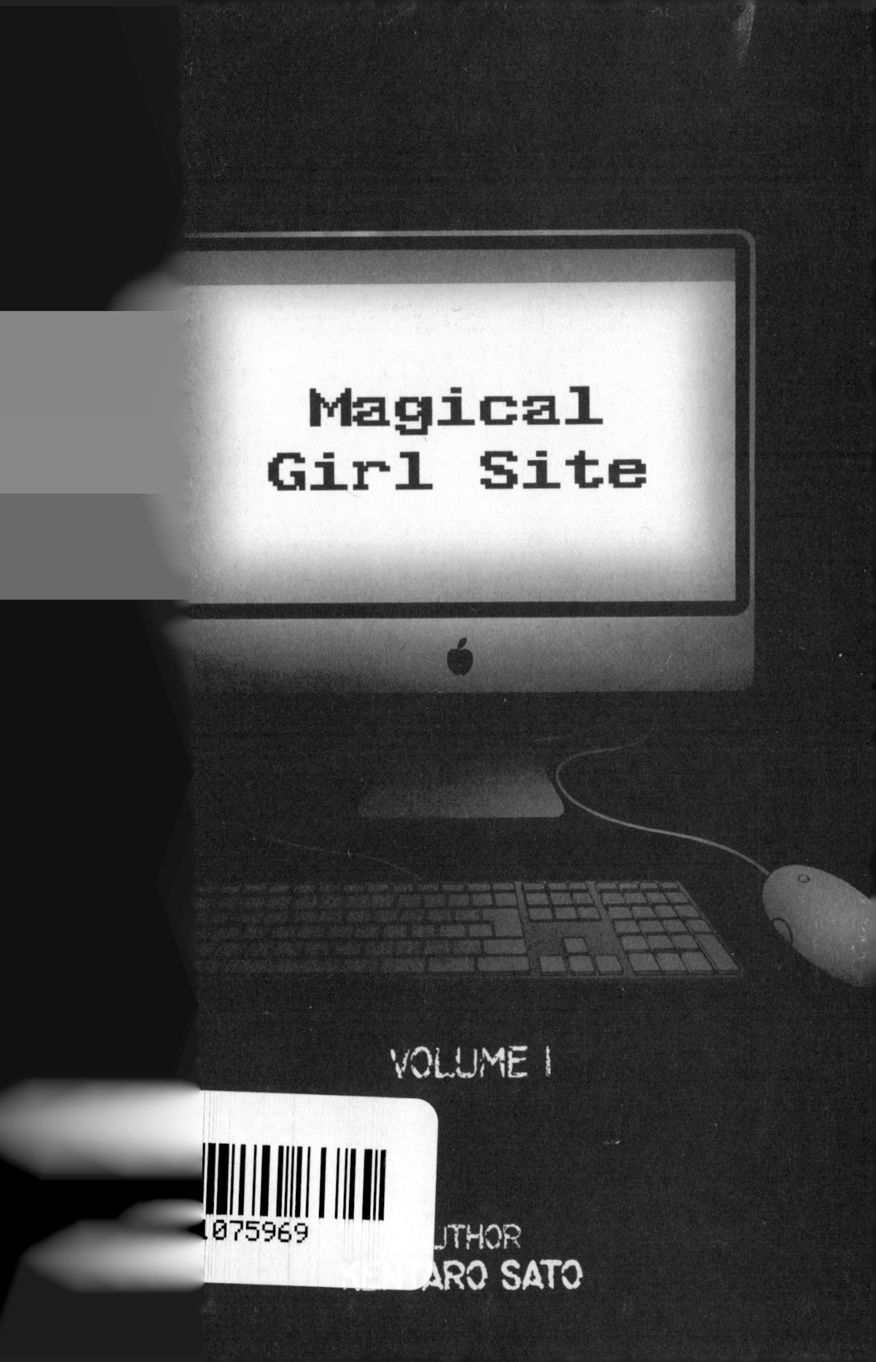
Magical
Girl Site
VOLUME 1
UTHOR
ARO SATO

SEVEN SEAS ENTERTAINMENT PRESENTS

MAGICAL GIRL SITE

story and art by KENTARO SATO

VOLUME 1

TRANSLATION
Wesley Bridges

ADAPTATION
Janet Houck

LETTERING AND LAYOUT
Meaghan Tucker

LOGO DESIGN
Karis Page

COVER DESIGN
Nicky Lim

PROOFREADER
Shanti Whitesides

PRODUCTION MANAGER
Lissa Pattillo

EDITOR-IN-CHIEF
Adam Arnold

PUBLISHER
Jason DeAngelis

MAHO SYOJYO SITE Volume 1
© Kentaro Sato 2014
Originally published in Japan in 2014 by Akita Publishing Co., Ltd..
English translation rights arranged with Akita Publishing Co., Ltd. through
TOHAN CORPORATION, Tokyo.

Seven Seas books may be purchased in bulk for promotional, educational, or
business use. Please contact your local bookseller or the Macmillan Corporate
and Premium Sales Department at 1-800-221-7945, extension 5442, or by
e-mail at MacmillanSpecialMarkets@macmillan.com.

ISBN: 978-1-626924-76-5

Printed in Canada

First Printing: February 2017

10 9 8 7 6 5 4 3 2 1

FOLLOW US ONLINE: *www.gomanga.com*

READING DIRECTIONS

This book reads from *right to left*, Japanese style.
If this is your first time reading manga, you start
reading from the top right panel on each page and
take it from there. If you get lost, just follow the
numbered diagram here. It may seem backwards at
first, but you'll get the hang of it! Have fun!!

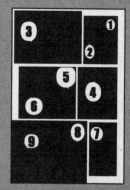

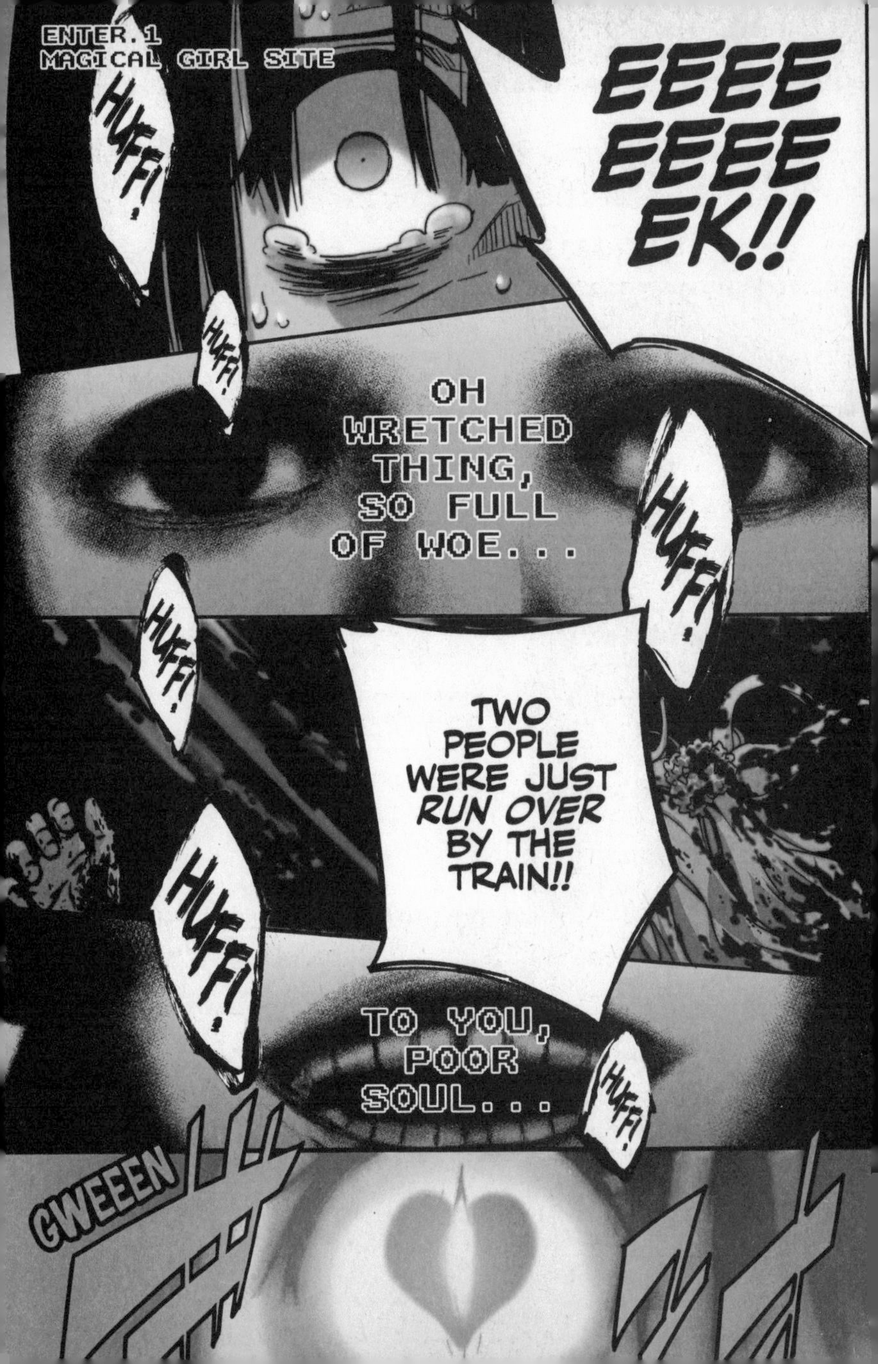
ENTER. 1
MAGICAL GIRL SITE
EEEEEEEEEK!!
HUFF!
HUFF!
HUFF!
OH WRETCHED THING, SO FULL OF WOE...
HUFF!
TWO PEOPLE WERE JUST RUN OVER BY THE TRAIN!!
HUFF!
TO YOU, POOR SOUL...
HUFF!
GWEEEN

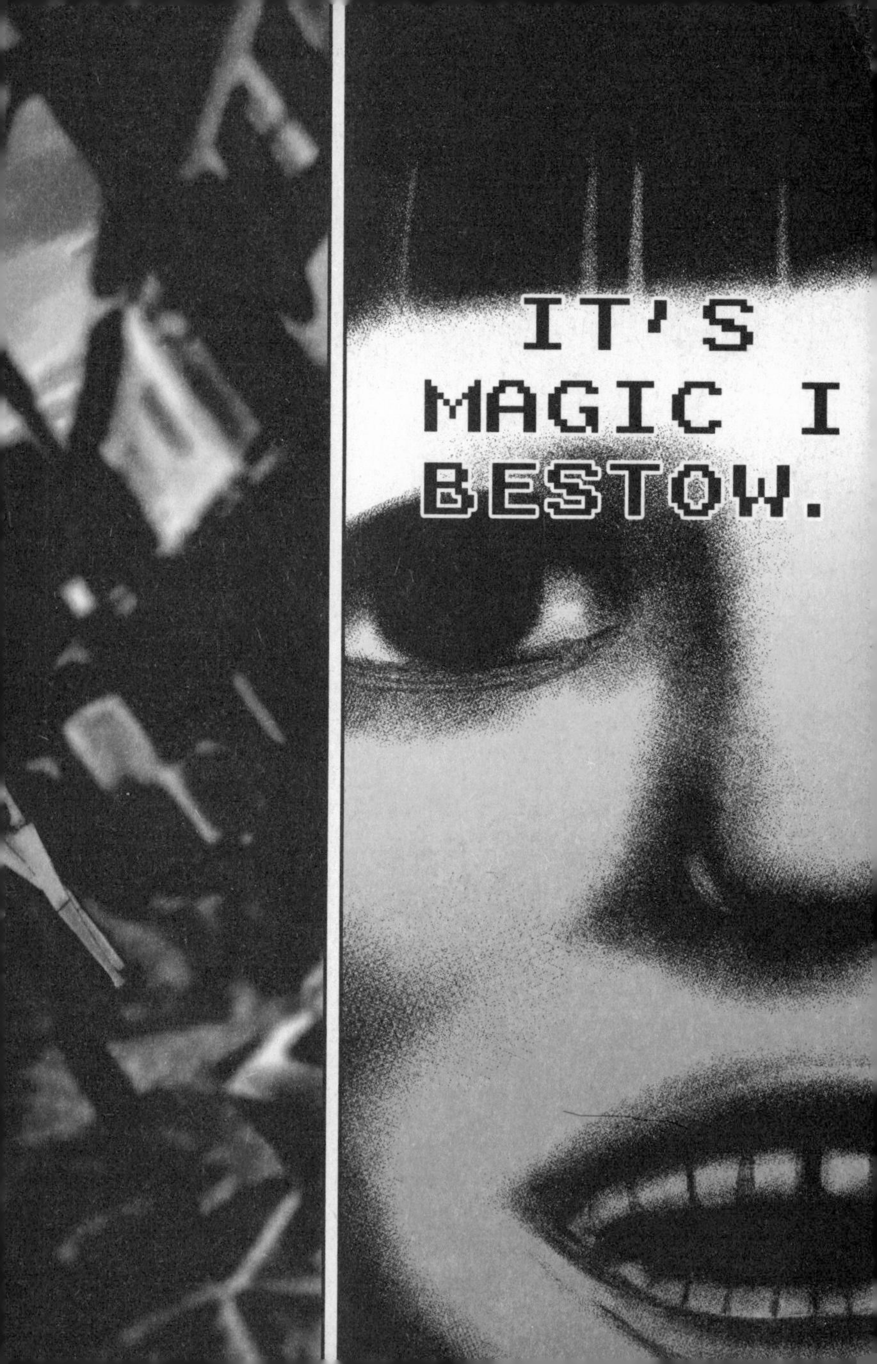
IT'S MAGIC I BESTOW.

ENTER.1
MAGICAL GIRL SITE

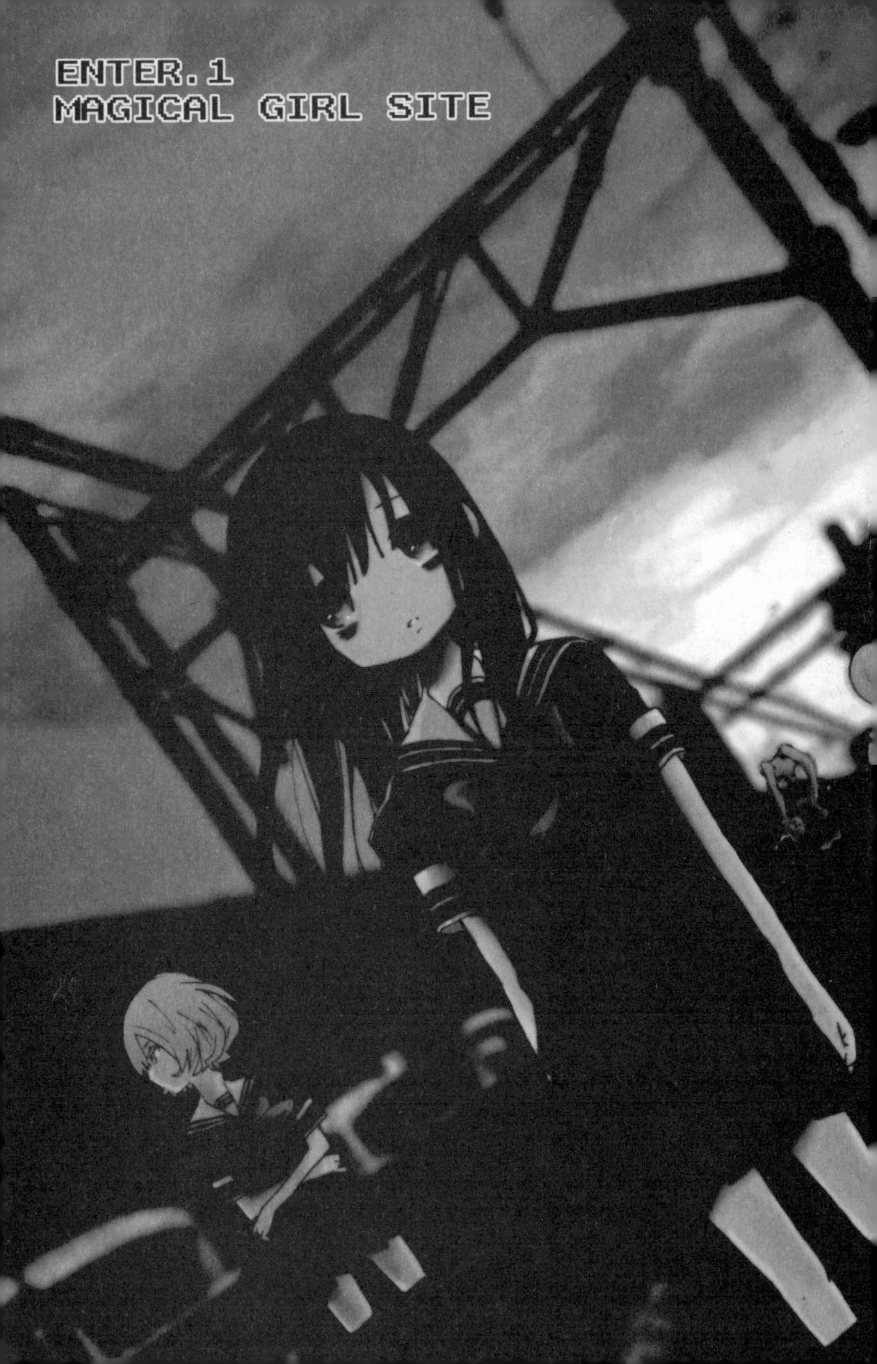

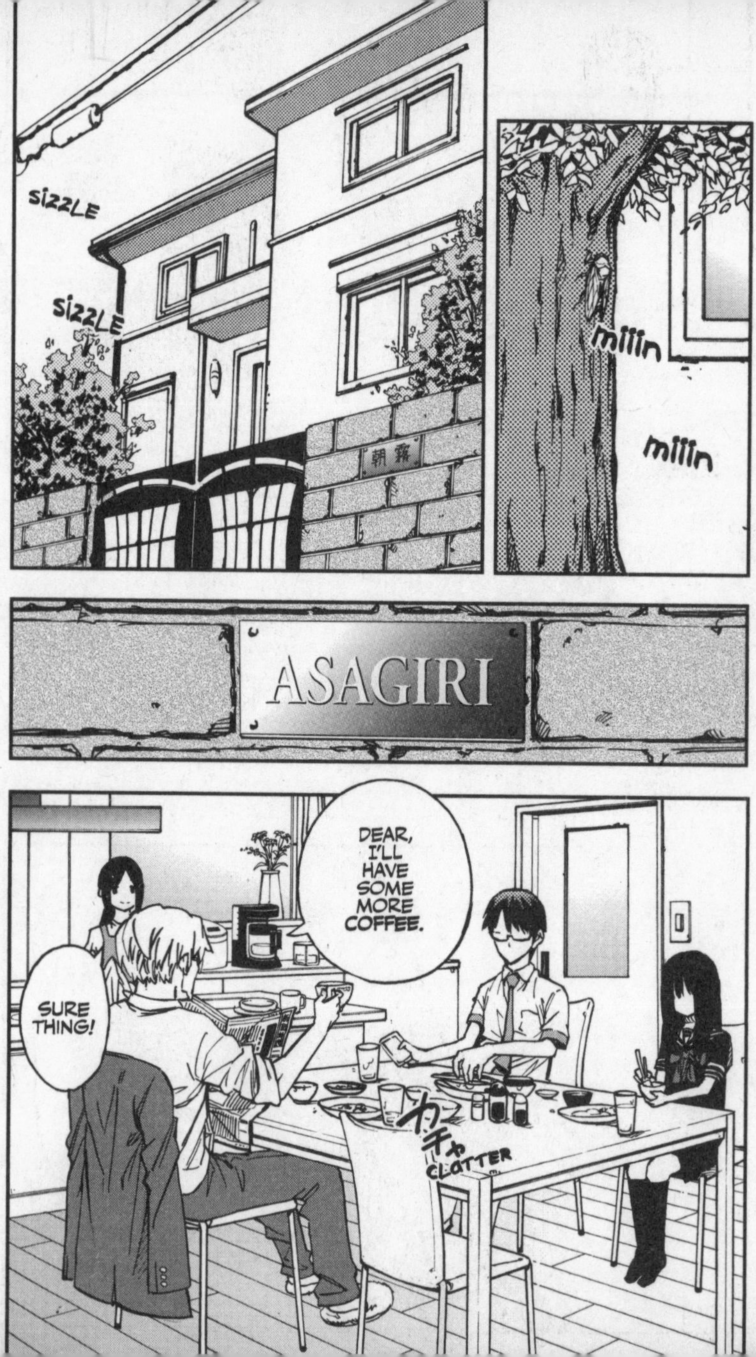
miiin
miiin
sizzle
sizzle
朝霧
ASAGIRI
DEAR, I'LL HAVE SOME MORE COFFEE.
SURE THING!
カチャ
CLATTER

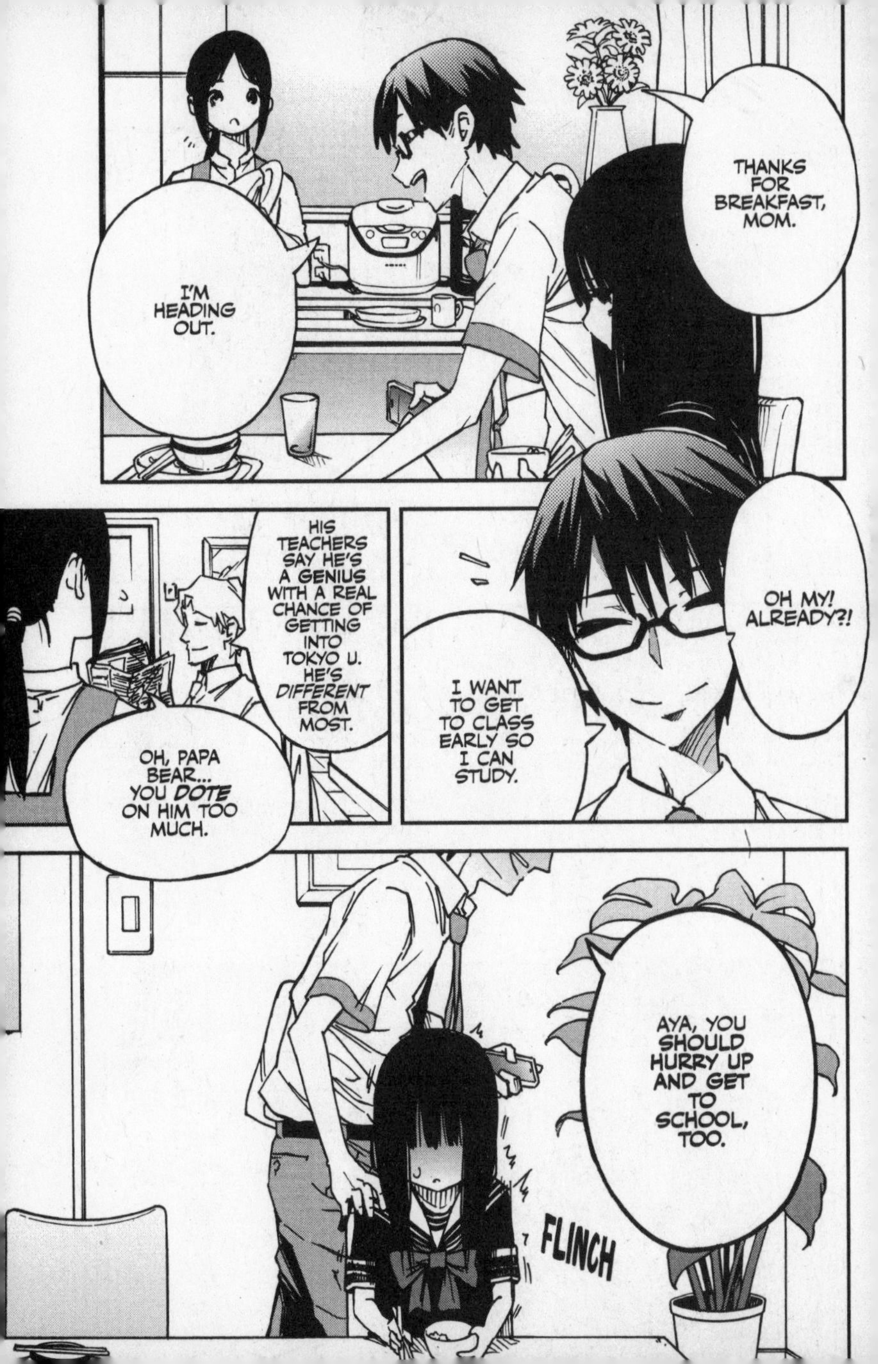
THANKS FOR BREAKFAST, MOM.
I'M HEADING OUT.
OH MY! ALREADY?!
I WANT TO GET TO CLASS EARLY SO I CAN STUDY.
HIS TEACHERS SAY HE'S A GENIUS WITH A REAL CHANCE OF GETTING INTO TOKYO U. HE'S *DIFFERENT* FROM MOST.
OH, PAPA BEAR... YOU *DOTE* ON HIM TOO MUCH.
AYA, YOU SHOULD HURRY UP AND GET TO SCHOOL, TOO.
FLINCH

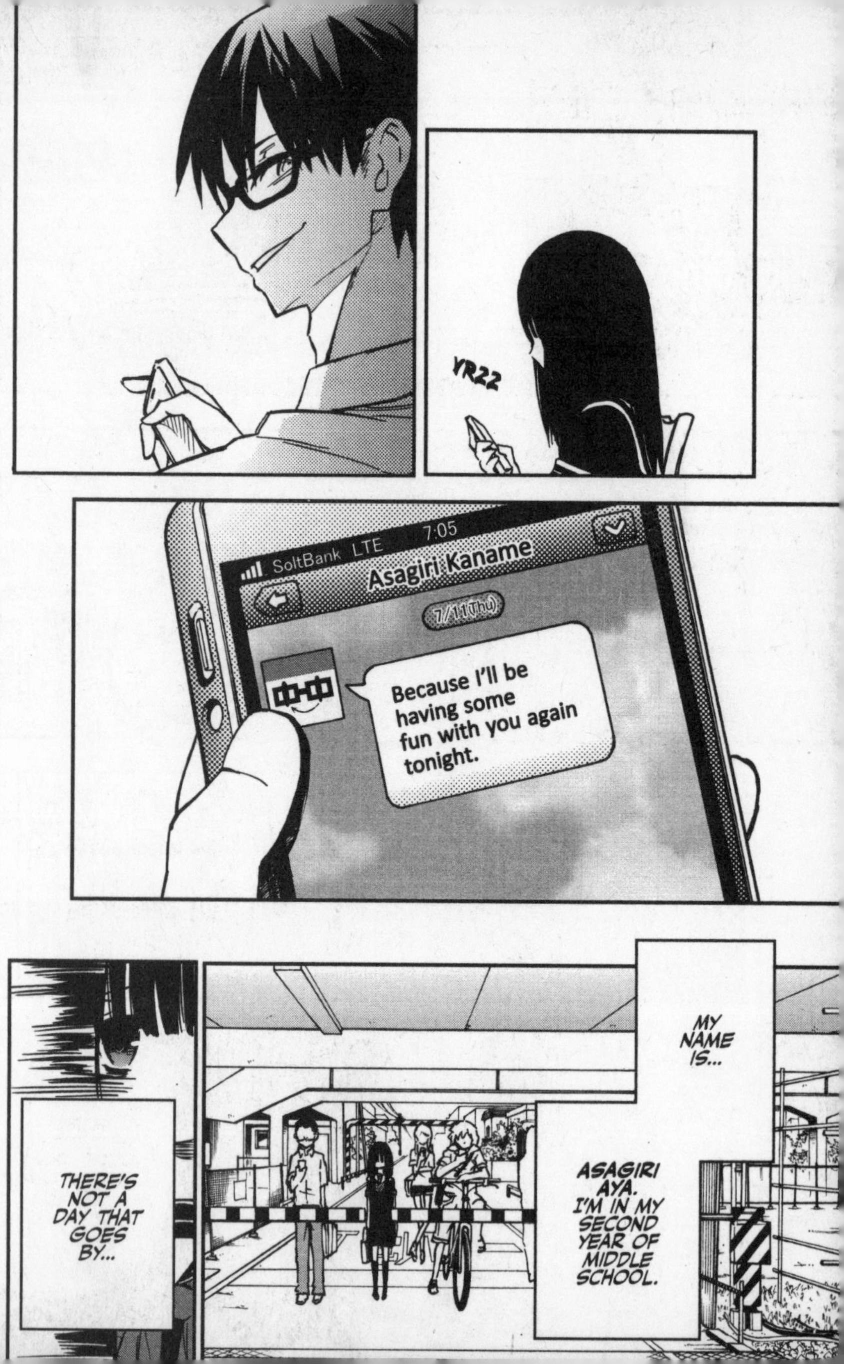
YR22
SoltBank LTE 7:05
Asagiri Kaname
7/11(Thu)
Because I'll be having some fun with you again tonight.
MY NAME IS...
ASAGIRI AYA. I'M IN MY SECOND YEAR OF MIDDLE SCHOOL.
THERE'S NOT A DAY THAT GOES BY...

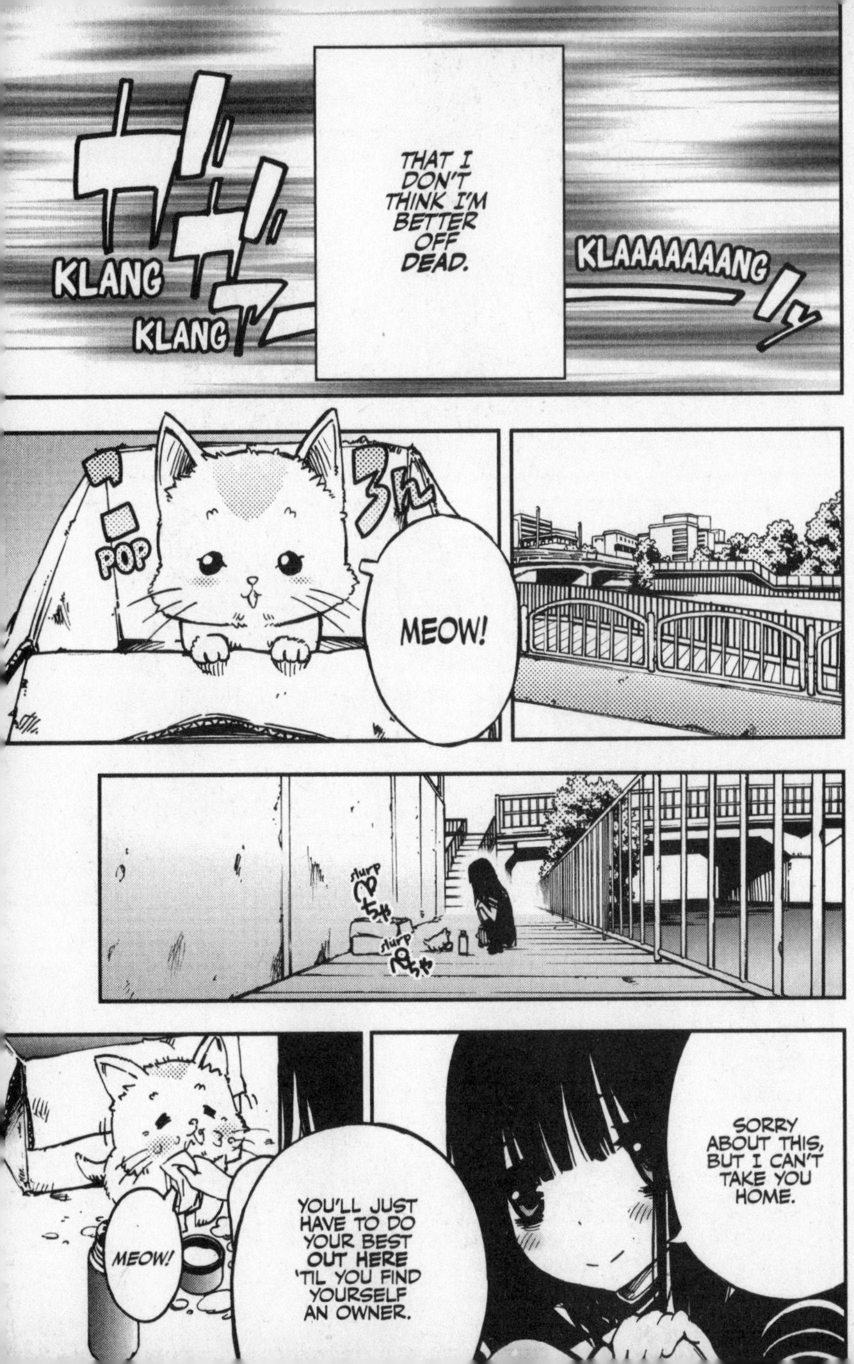
THAT I DON'T THINK I'M BETTER OFF DEAD.
KLAAAAAAANG
KLANG
KLANG
MEOW!
POP
slurp
slurp
SORRY ABOUT THIS, BUT I CAN'T TAKE YOU HOME.
YOU'LL JUST HAVE TO DO YOUR BEST OUT HERE 'TIL YOU FIND YOURSELF AN OWNER.
MEOW!

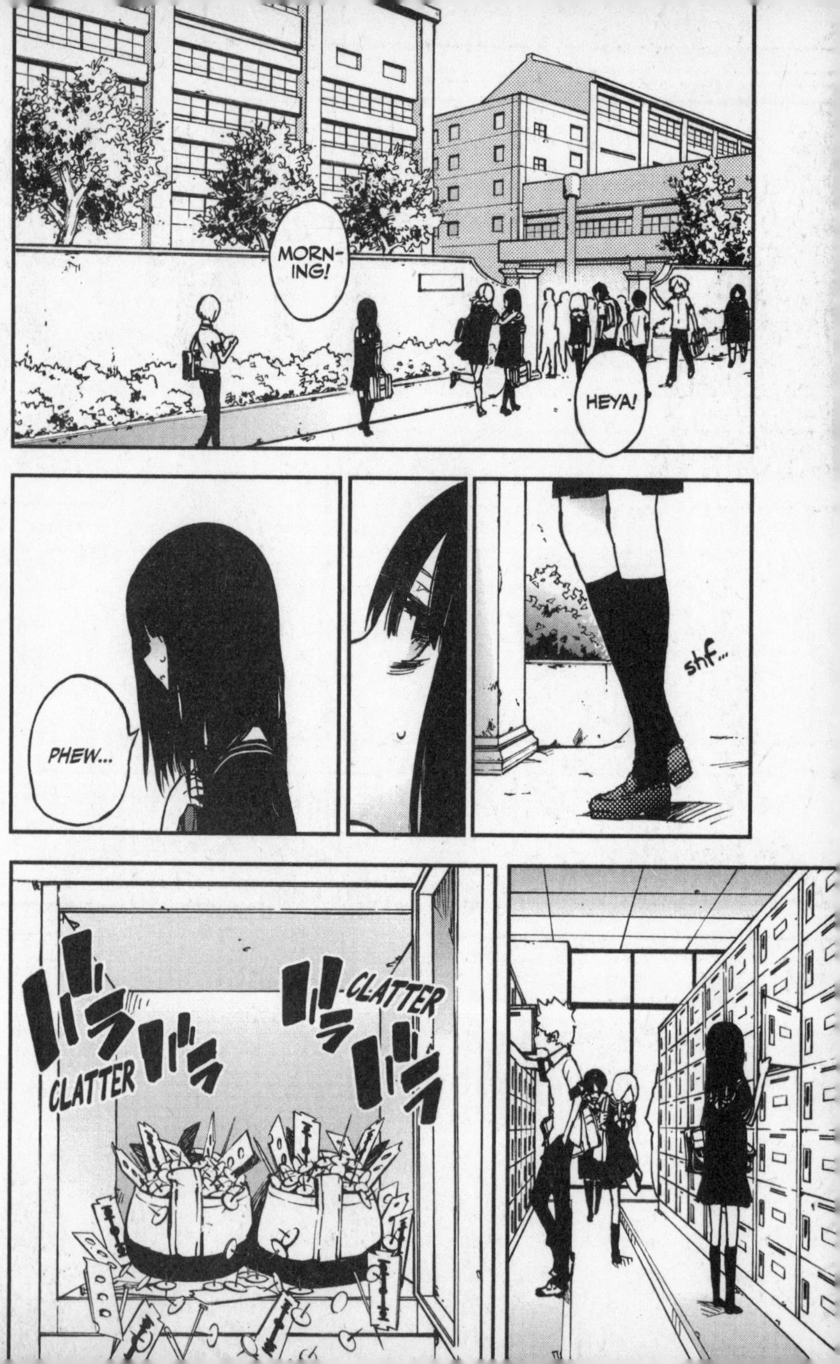
MORN-ING!
HEYA!
shf...
PHEW...
-CLATTER
CLATTER

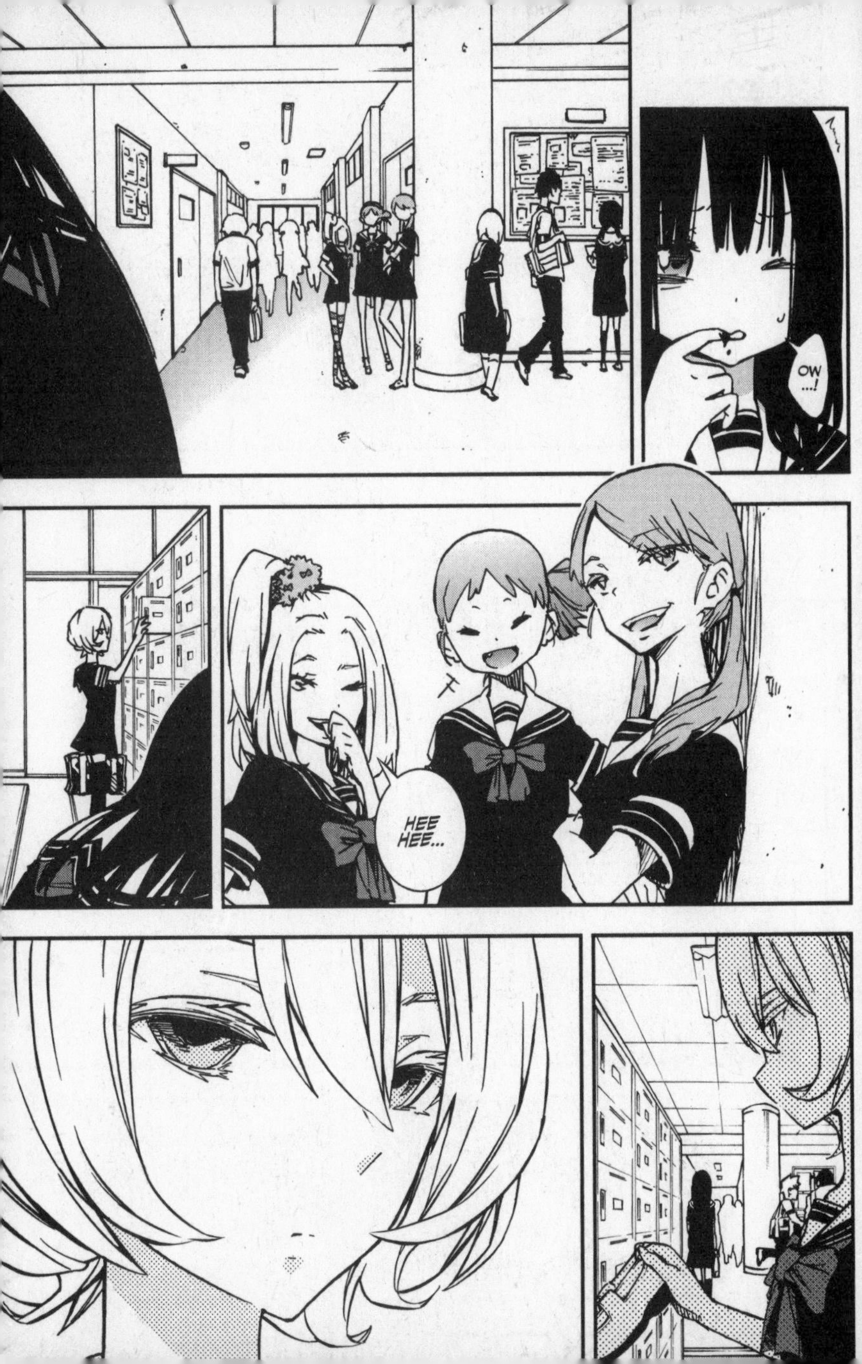
OW ...!
HEE HEE...

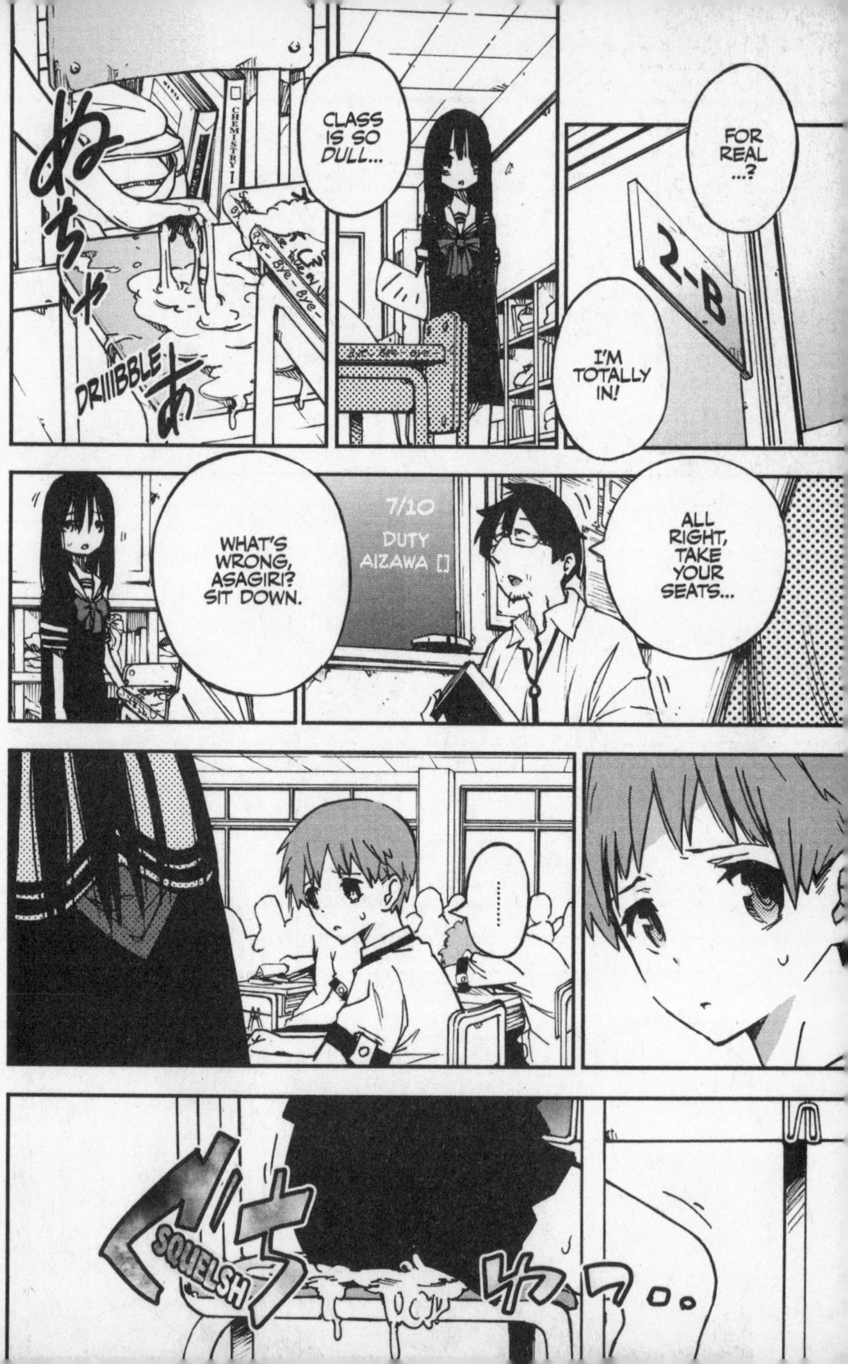
FOR REAL ...?
2-B
I'M TOTALLY IN!
CLASS IS SO DULL...
CHEMISTRY I
ぬちゃ
DRIIIBBLE
あ
ALL RIGHT, TAKE YOUR SEATS...
7/10
DUTY
AIZAWA []
WHAT'S WRONG, ASAGIRI? SIT DOWN.
……
ぐちゅっ。。
SQUELSH

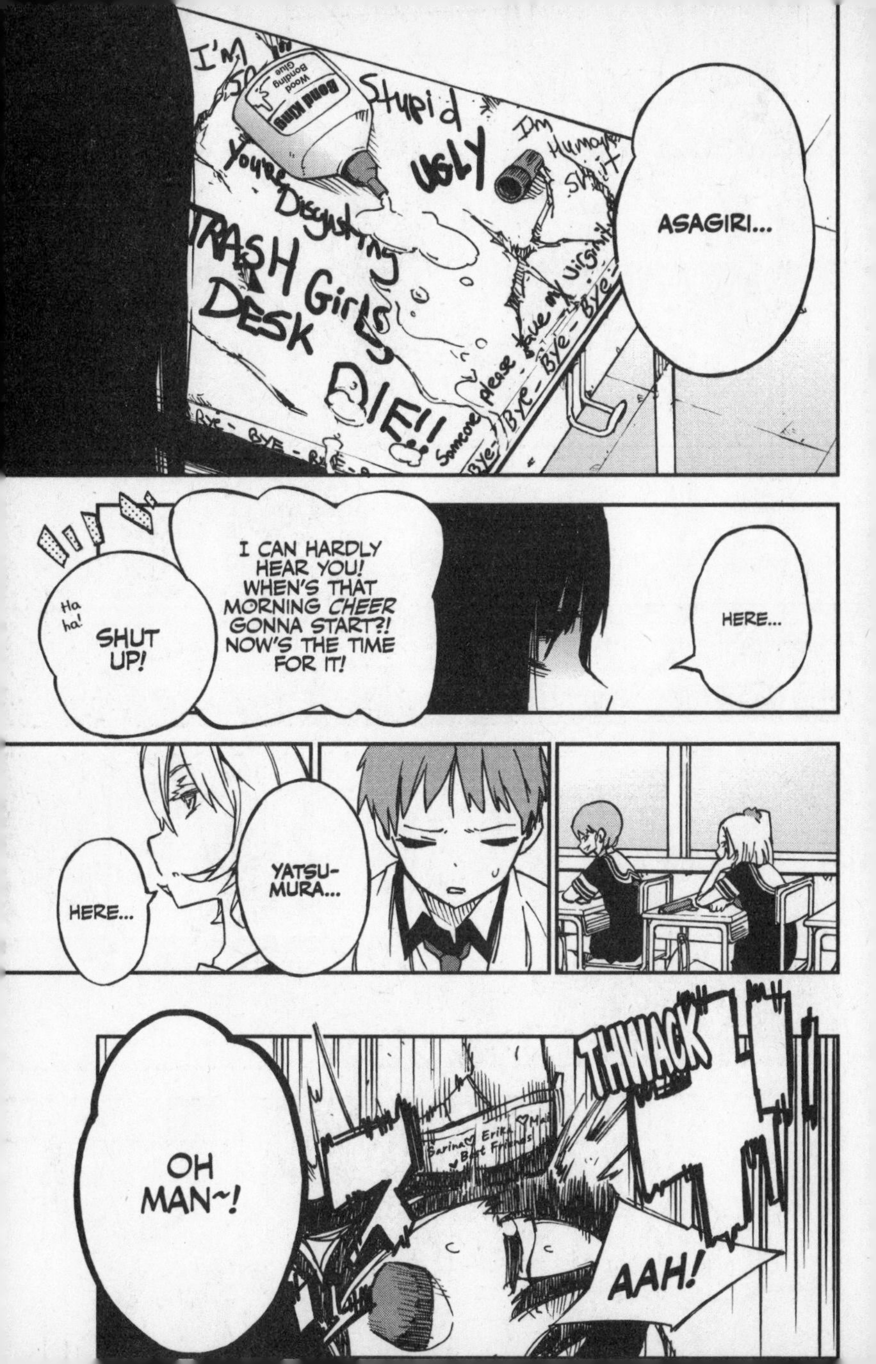

ASAGIRI...
Bond King
Wood Bonding Glue
Stupid
UGLY
You're Disgusting
TRASH Girl's DESK
DIE!!
Someone please save me
Bye-Bye-Bye
HERE...
I CAN HARDLY HEAR YOU! WHEN'S THAT MORNING *CHEER* GONNA START?! NOW'S THE TIME FOR IT!
Ha ha!
SHUT UP!
YATSU-MURA...
HERE...
THWACK
AAH!
Sarina♡ Erika♡ Mai
Best Friends
OH MAN~!

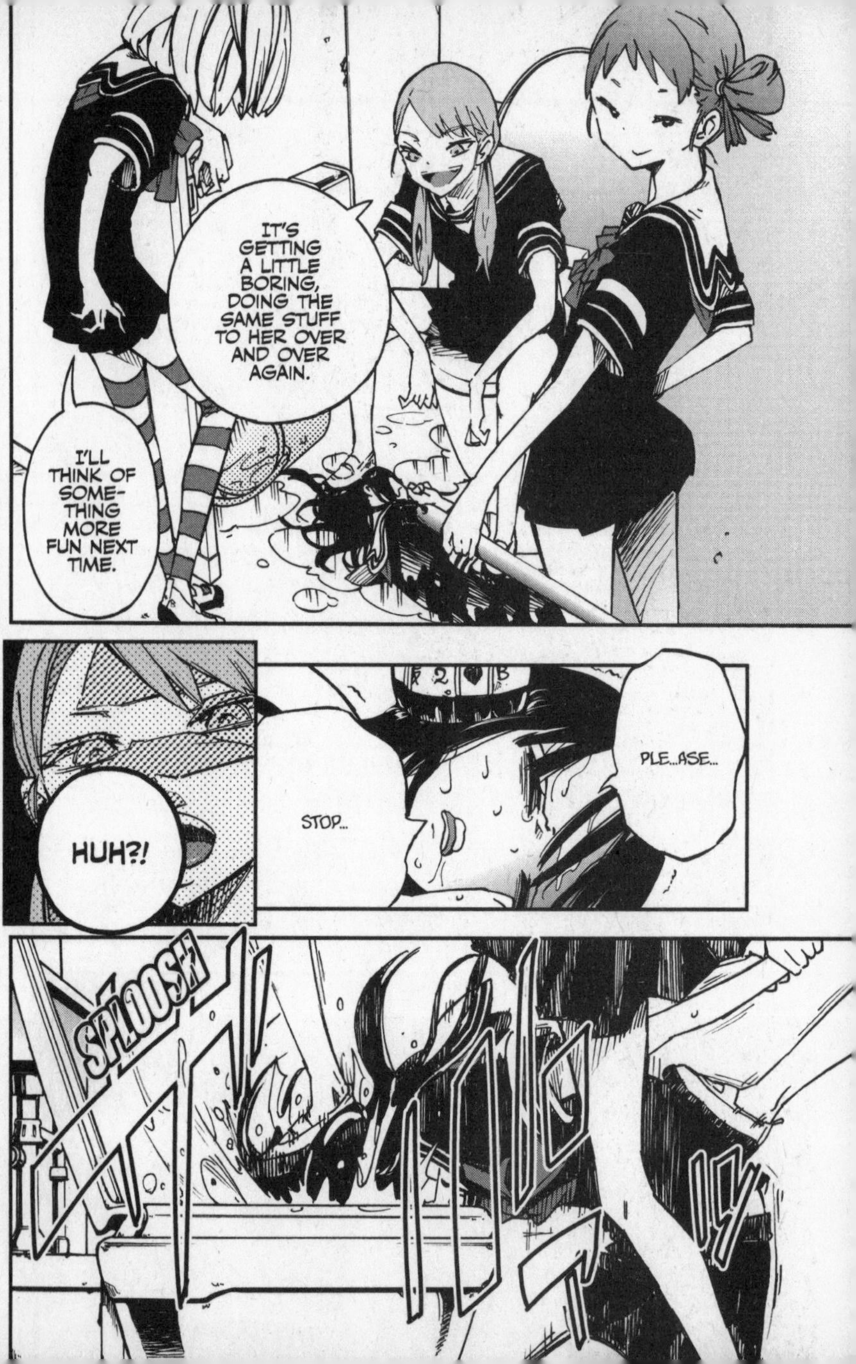
IT'S GETTING A LITTLE BORING, DOING THE SAME STUFF TO HER OVER AND OVER AGAIN.
I'LL THINK OF SOME-THING MORE FUN NEXT TIME.
PLE...ASE...
STOP...
HUH?!
SPLOOSH

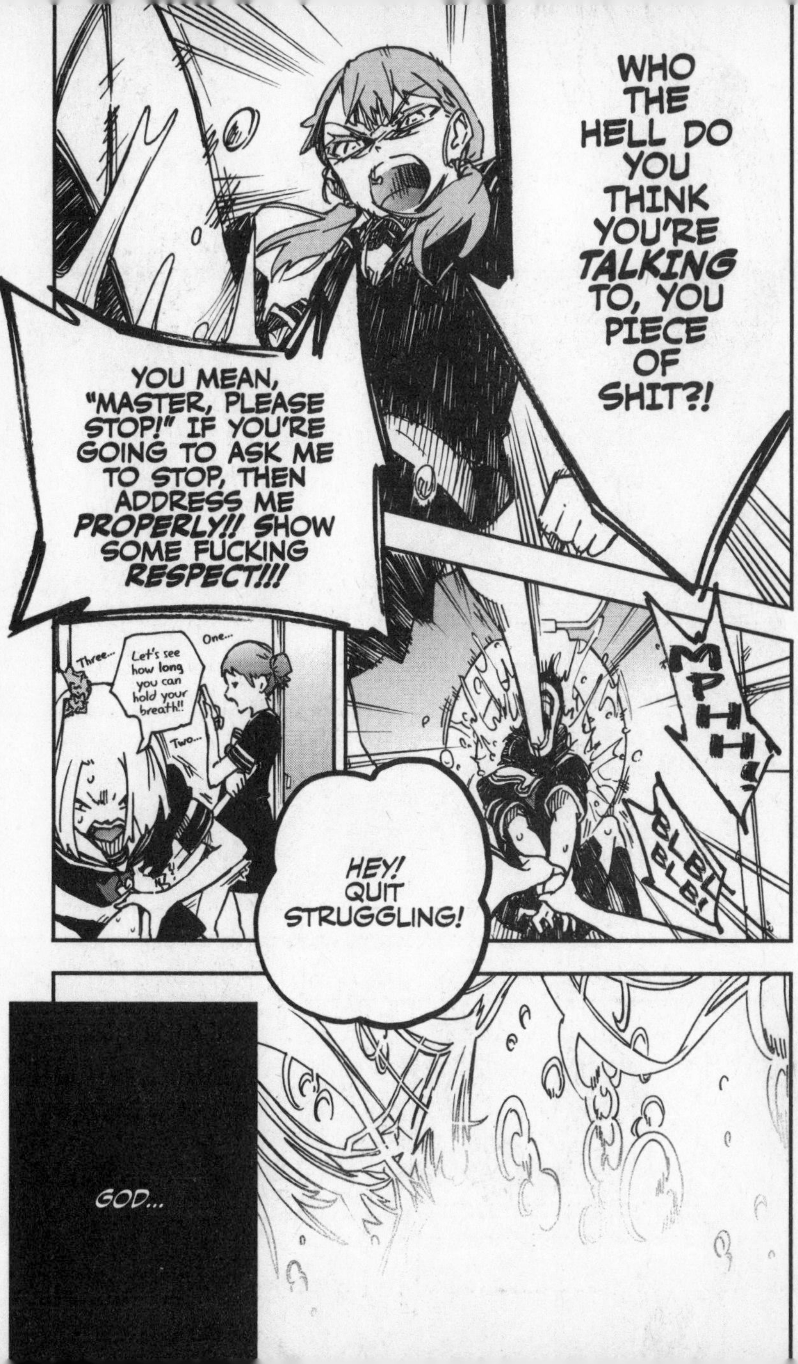
WHO THE HELL DO YOU THINK YOU'RE *TALKING* TO, YOU PIECE OF SHIT?!
YOU MEAN, "MASTER, PLEASE STOP!" IF YOU'RE GOING TO ASK ME TO STOP, THEN ADDRESS ME *PROPERLY!!* SHOW SOME FUCKING *RESPECT!!!*
MPHH!
BLBL BLB!
HEY! QUIT STRUGGLING!
One...
Let's see how long you can hold your breath!!
Three...
Two...
GOD...

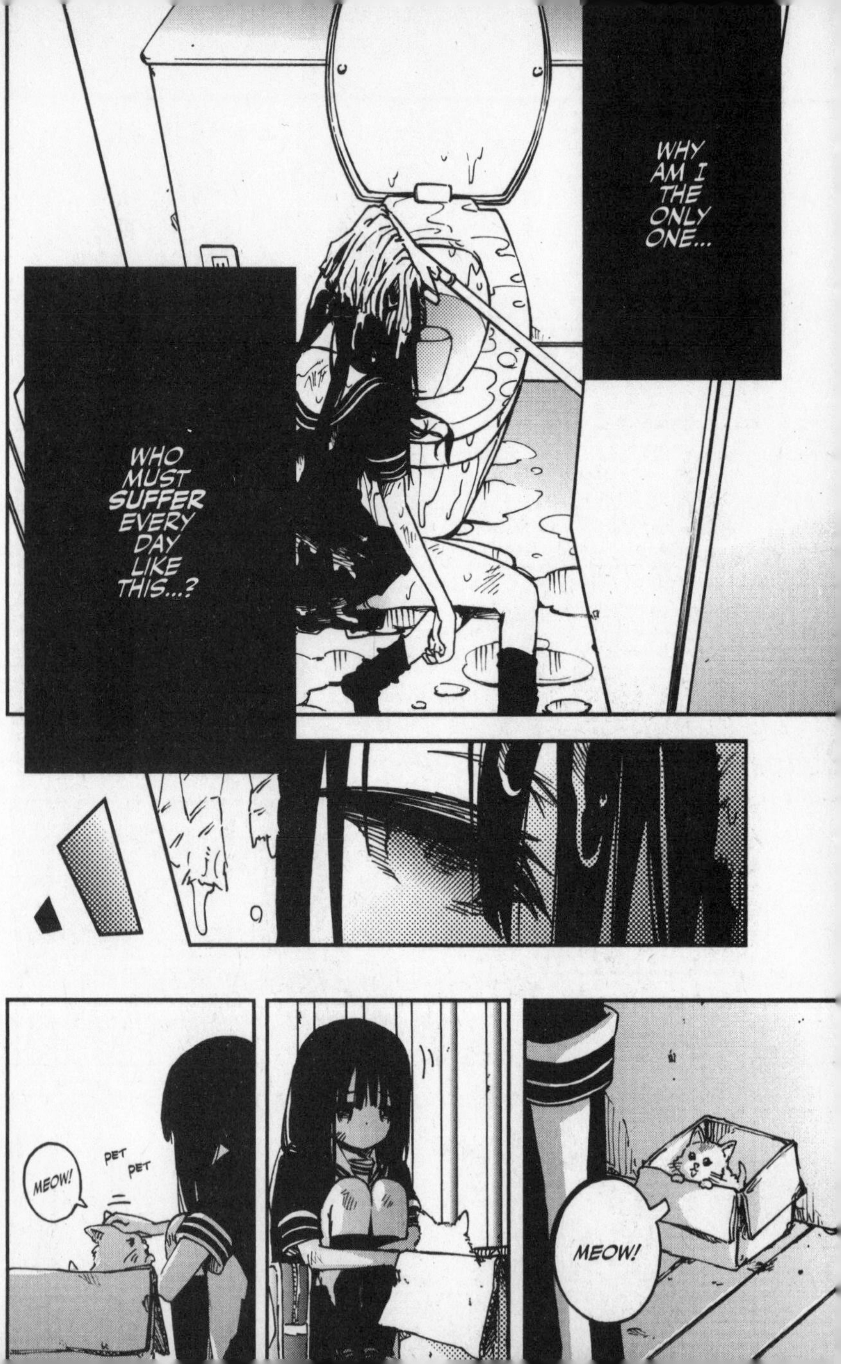
WHY AM I THE ONLY ONE...
WHO MUST SUFFER EVERY DAY LIKE THIS...?
MEOW!
MEOW!
PET PET

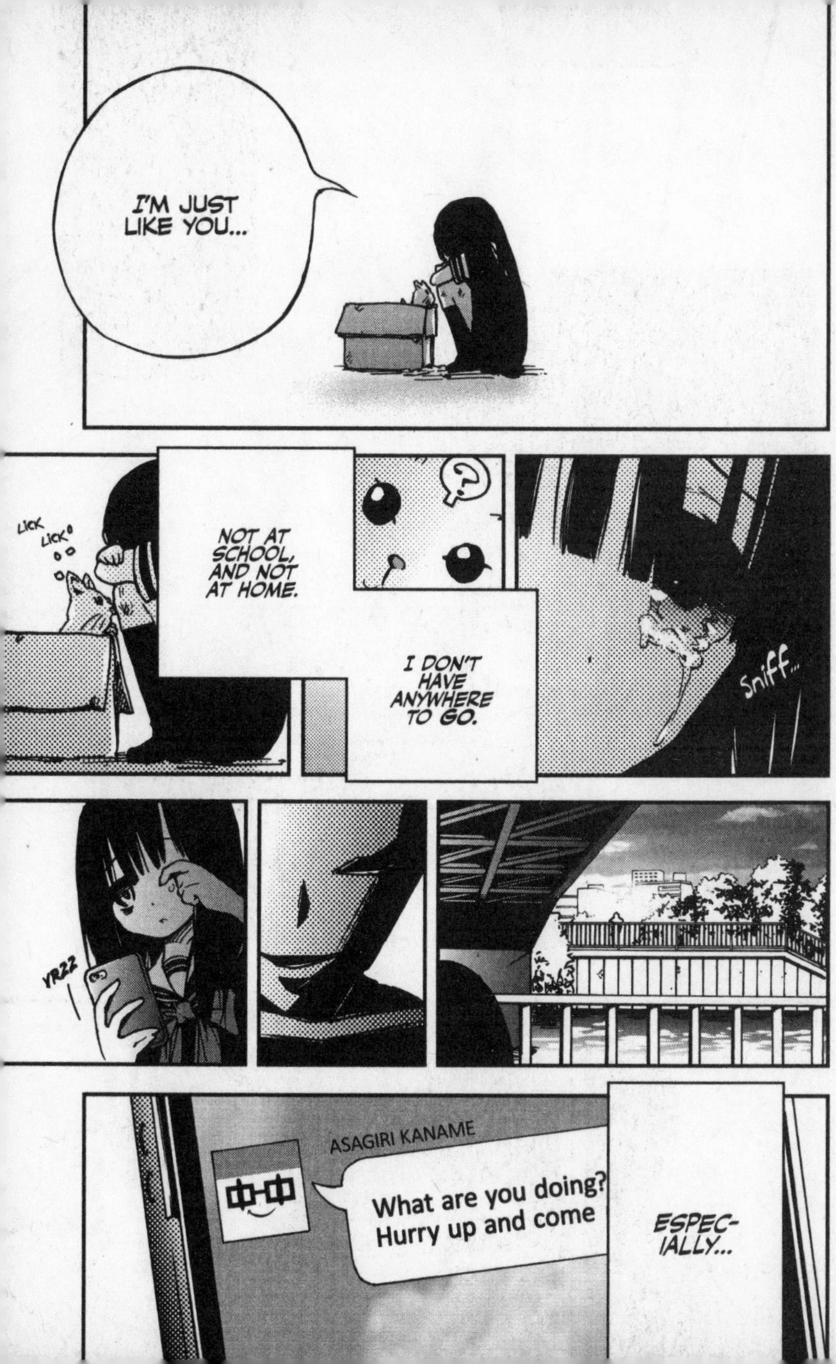
I'M JUST LIKE YOU...
Sniff...
NOT AT SCHOOL, AND NOT AT HOME.
I DON'T HAVE ANYWHERE TO GO.
LICK LICK
VRZZ
ESPEC-IALLY...
ASAGIRI KANAME
What are you doing? Hurry up and come

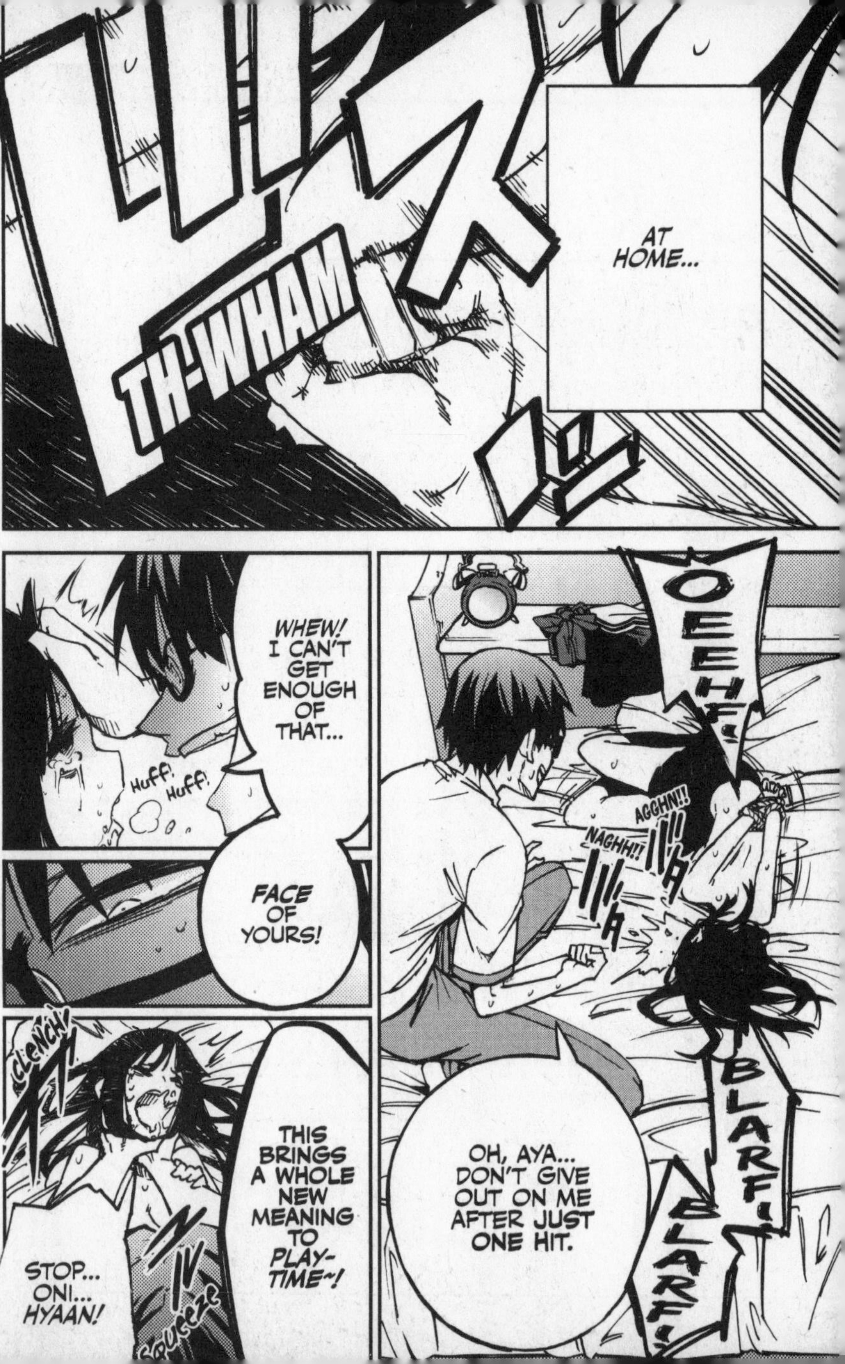
AT HOME...
TH-WHAM
OEEHF!
AGGHN!!
NAGHH!!
OH, AYA... DON'T GIVE OUT ON ME AFTER JUST ONE HIT.
BLARF!
BLARF!
WHEW! I CAN'T GET ENOUGH OF THAT...
Huff! Huff!
FACE OF YOURS!
THIS BRINGS A WHOLE NEW MEANING TO PLAY-TIME~!
CLENCH!
STOP... ONI... HYAAN!
SQUEEZE

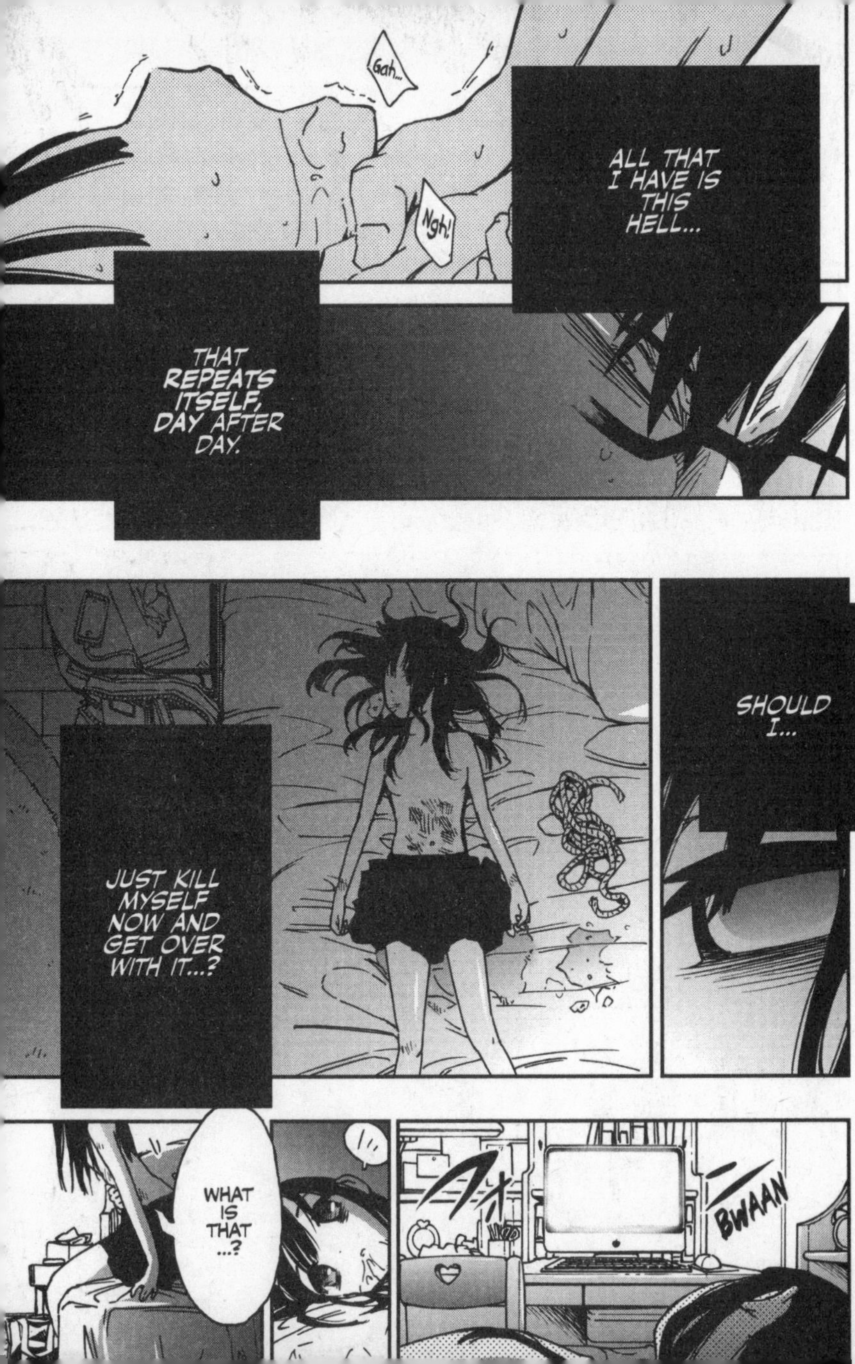
ALL THAT I HAVE IS THIS HELL...
Gah...
Ngh!
THAT REPEATS ITSELF, DAY AFTER DAY.
SHOULD I...
JUST KILL MYSELF NOW AND GET OVER WITH IT...?
BWAAN
WHAT IS THAT...?

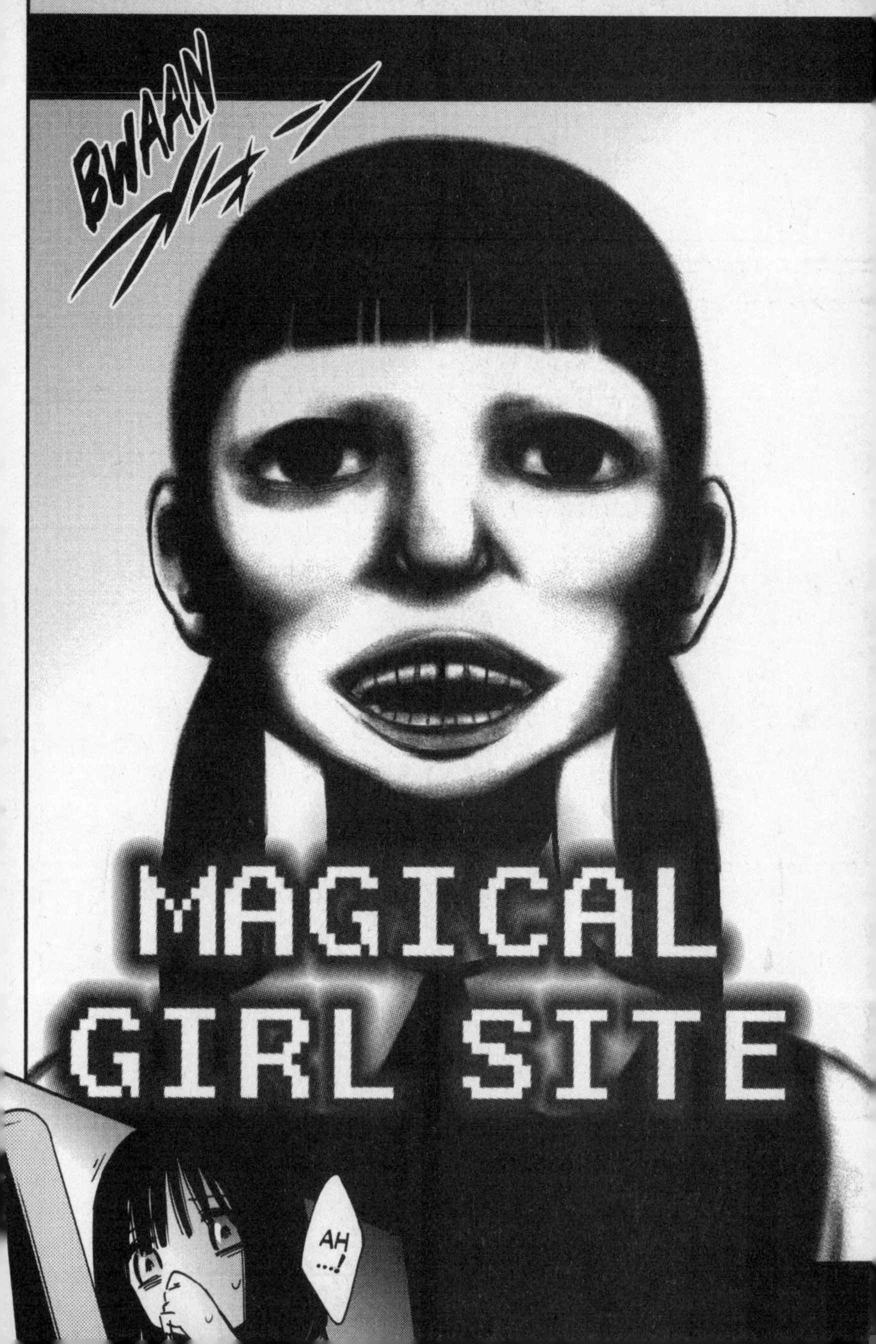
BWAAN
MAGICAL GIRL SITE
AH ...!

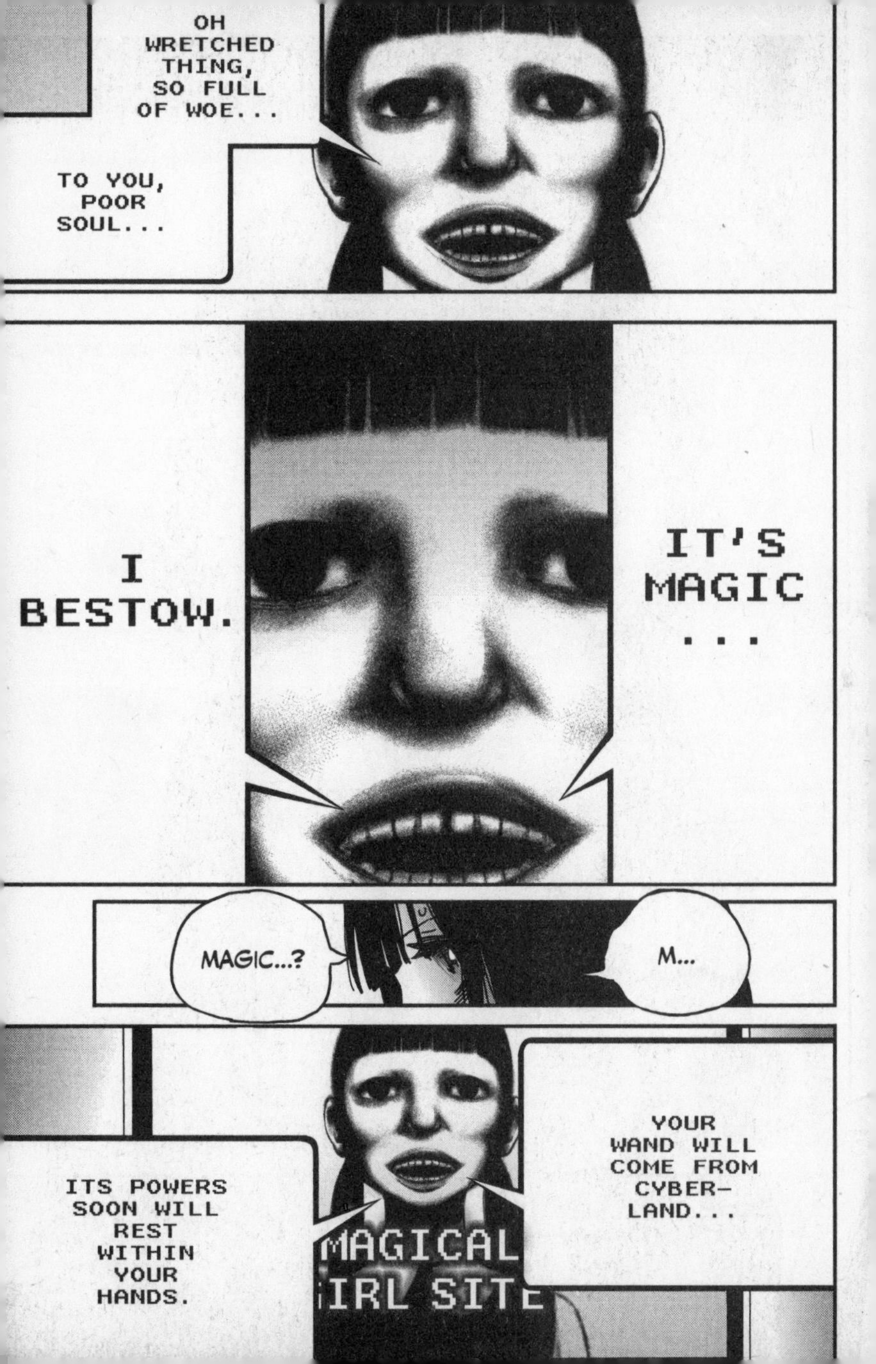
OH WRETCHED THING, SO FULL OF WOE...
TO YOU, POOR SOUL...
IT'S MAGIC...
I BESTOW.
M...
MAGIC...?
YOUR WAND WILL COME FROM CYBER-LAND...
ITS POWERS SOON WILL REST WITHIN YOUR HANDS.
MAGICAL
IRL SITE

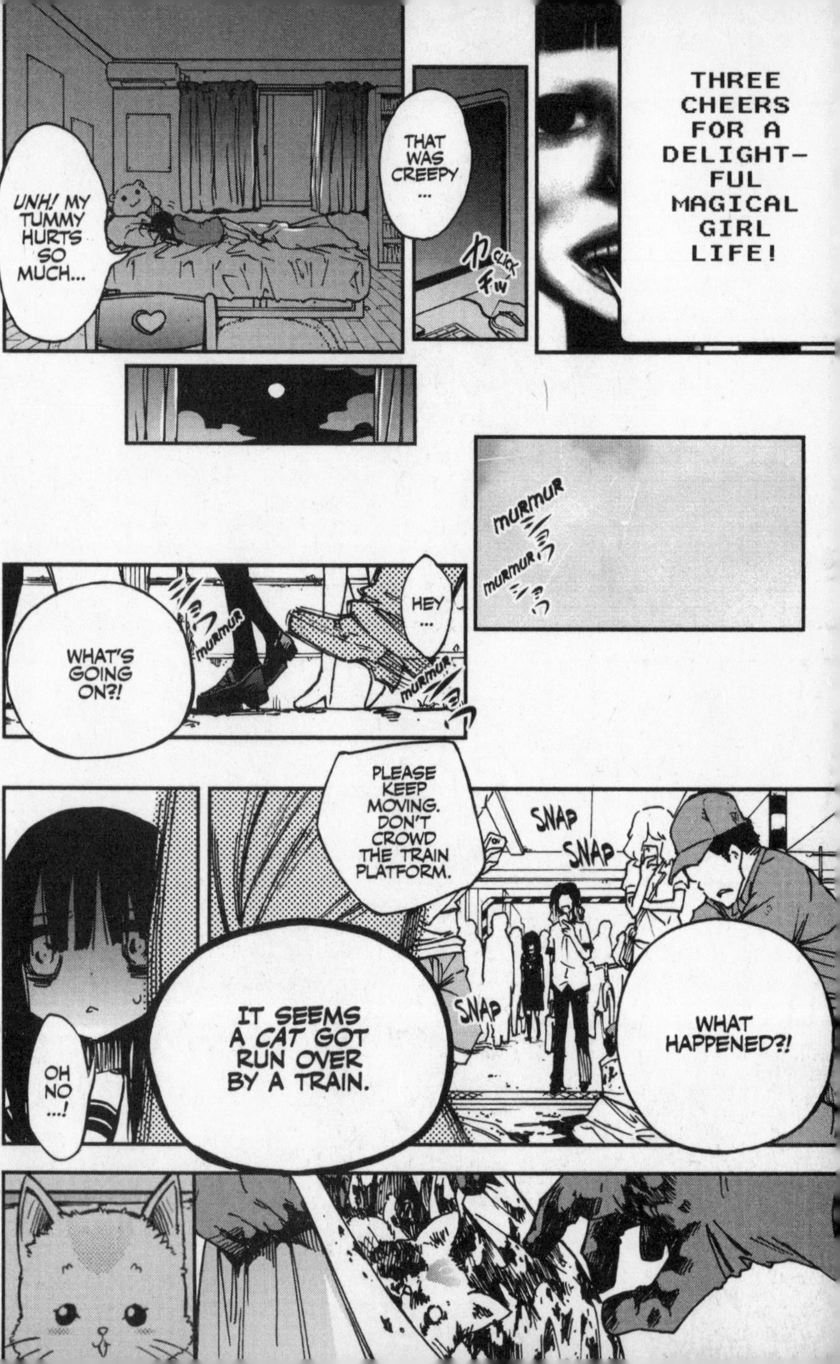
THREE CHEERS FOR A DELIGHTFUL MAGICAL GIRL LIFE!
THAT WAS CREEPY ...
CLICK
UNH! MY TUMMY HURTS SO MUCH...
murmur
murmur
HEY ...
murmur
murmur
WHAT'S GOING ON?!
PLEASE KEEP MOVING. DON'T CROWD THE TRAIN PLATFORM.
SNAP
SNAP
WHAT HAPPENED?!
SNAP
IT SEEMS A CAT GOT RUN OVER BY A TRAIN.
OH NO ...!

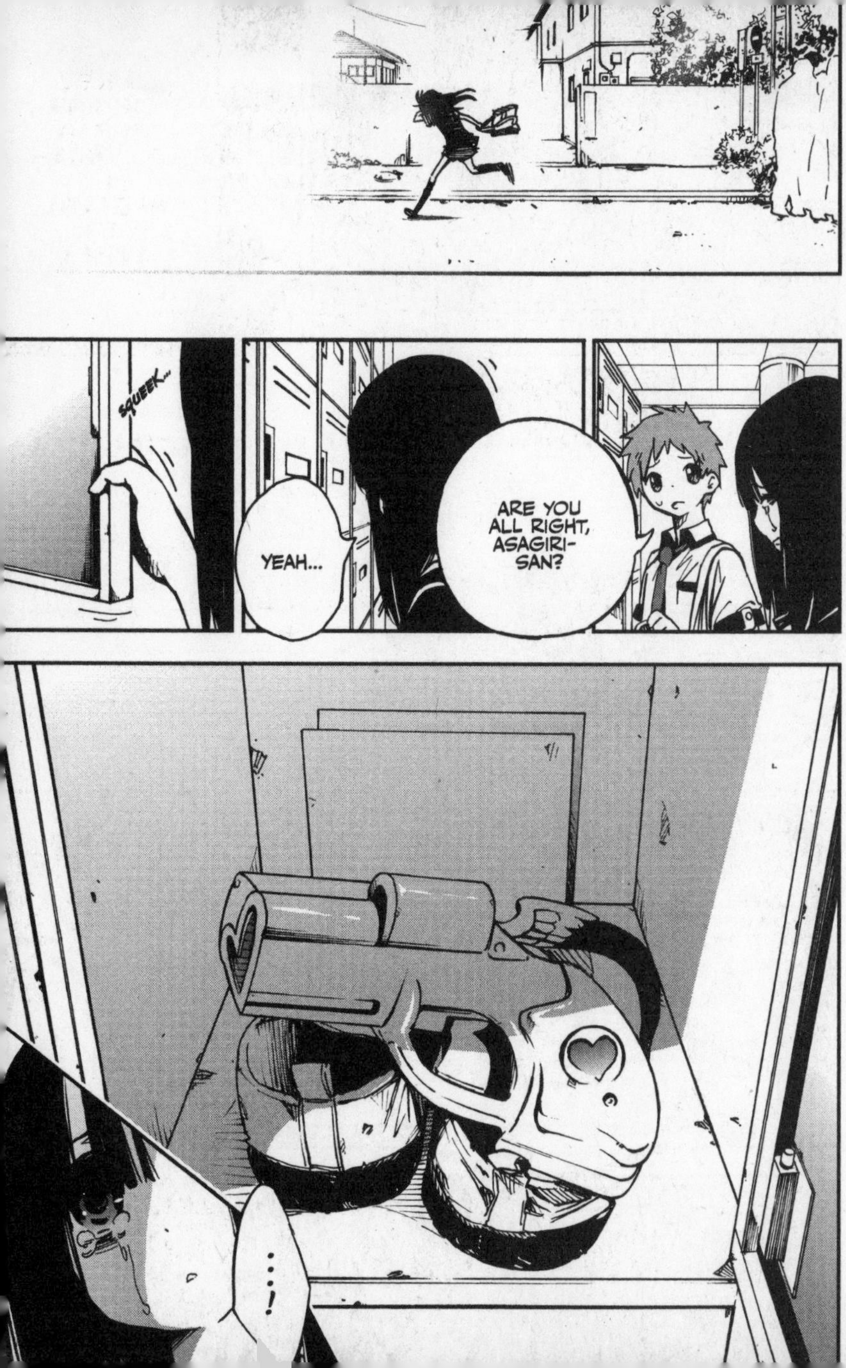
ARE YOU ALL RIGHT, ASAGIRI-SAN?
YEAH...
SQUEEK...
...!

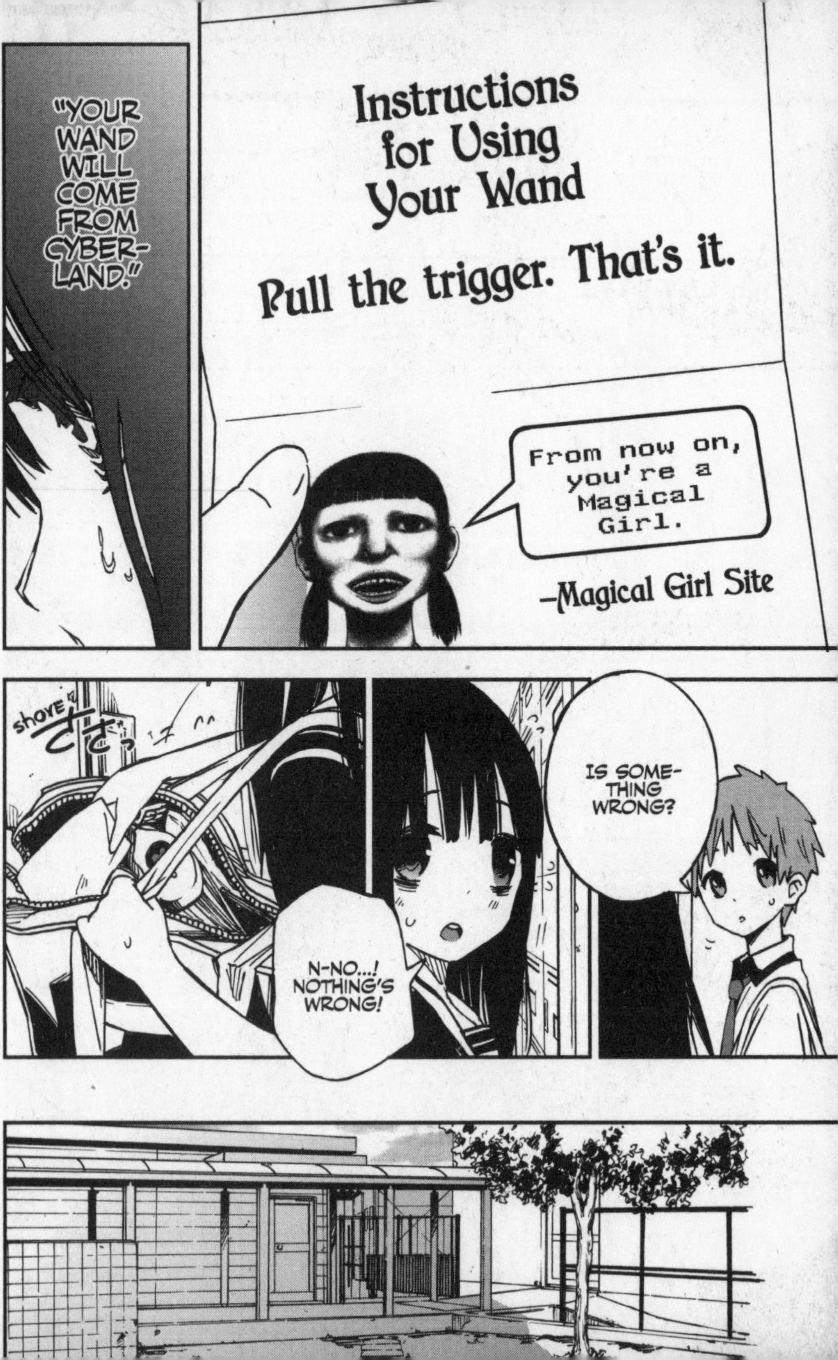
Instructions for Using Your Wand
Pull the trigger. That's it.
From now on, you're a Magical Girl.
–Magical Girl Site
"YOUR WAND WILL COME FROM CYBER-LAND."
IS SOME-THING WRONG?
N-NO...! NOTHING'S WRONG!
shove

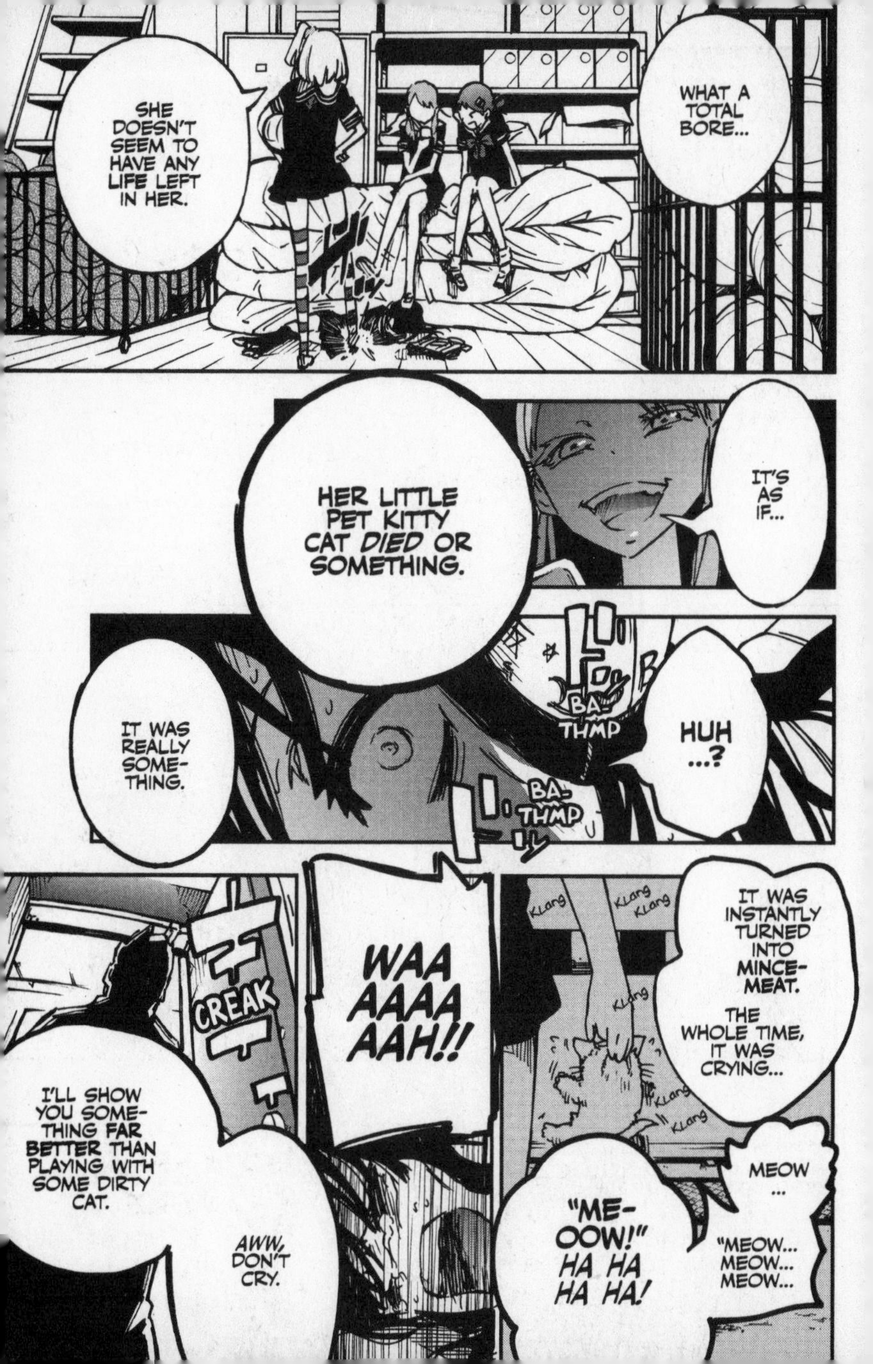
WHAT A TOTAL BORE...
SHE DOESN'T SEEM TO HAVE ANY LIFE LEFT IN HER.
IT'S AS IF...
HER LITTLE PET KITTY CAT *DIED* OR SOMETHING.
HUH ...?
BA-THMP
BA-THMP
IT WAS REALLY SOME-THING.
IT WAS INSTANTLY TURNED INTO MINCE-MEAT.
THE WHOLE TIME, IT WAS CRYING...
KLang KLang KLang
KLang
KLang
KLang
MEOW ...
"MEOW... MEOW... MEOW...
"ME-OOW!" HA HA HA HA!
WAA AAAA AAH!!
AWW, DON'T CRY.
CREAK
I'LL SHOW YOU SOME-THING FAR BETTER THAN PLAYING WITH SOME DIRTY CAT.

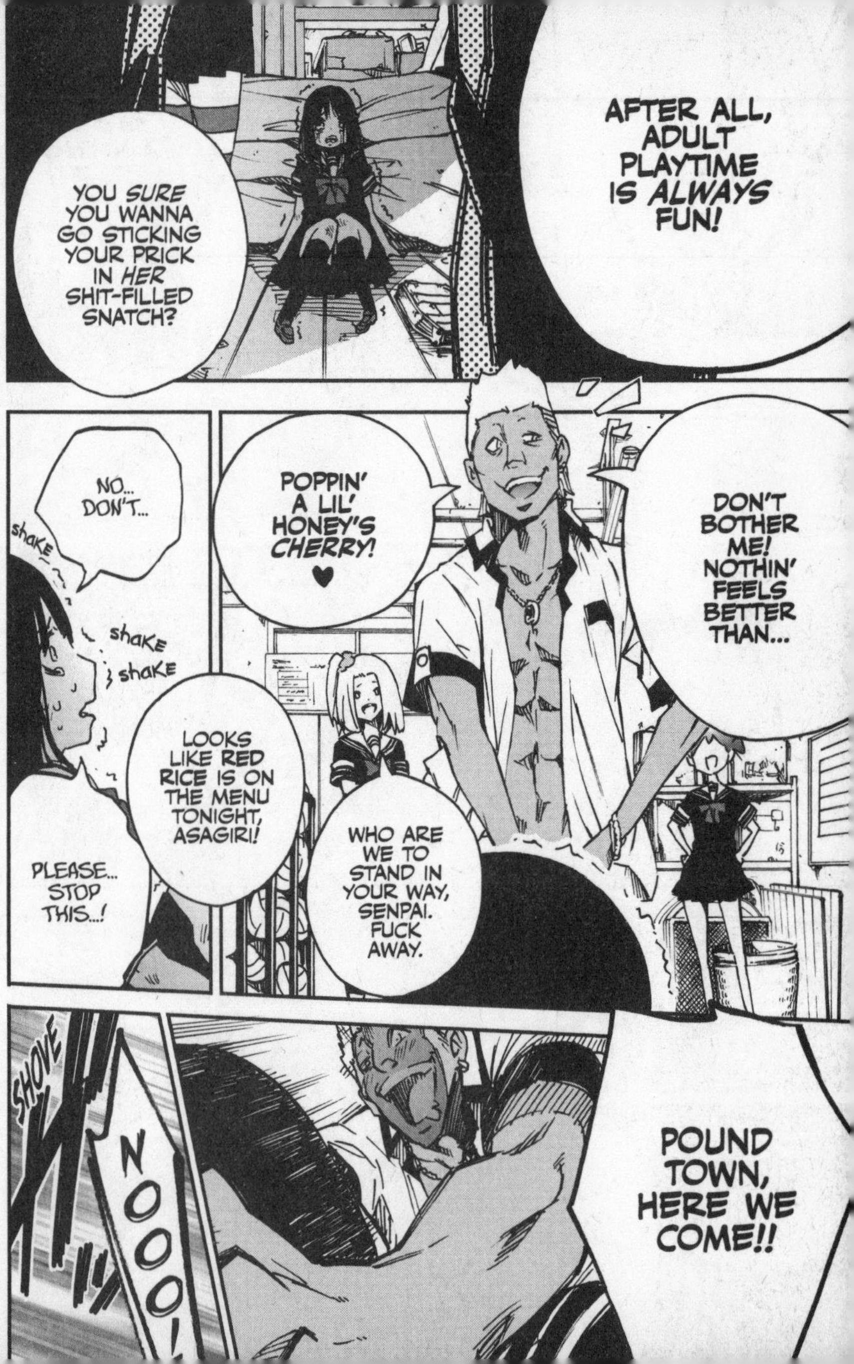
AFTER ALL, ADULT PLAYTIME IS *ALWAYS* FUN!
YOU *SURE* YOU WANNA GO STICKING YOUR PRICK IN *HER* SHIT-FILLED SNATCH?
DON'T BOTHER ME! NOTHIN' FEELS BETTER THAN...
POPPIN' A LIL' HONEY'S *CHERRY!* ♥
LOOKS LIKE RED RICE IS ON THE MENU TONIGHT, ASAGIRI!
WHO ARE WE TO STAND IN YOUR WAY, SENPAI. FUCK AWAY.
NO... DON'T...
shake
shake
shake
PLEASE... STOP THIS...!
POUND TOWN, HERE WE COME!!
SHOVE
NOOOO!!

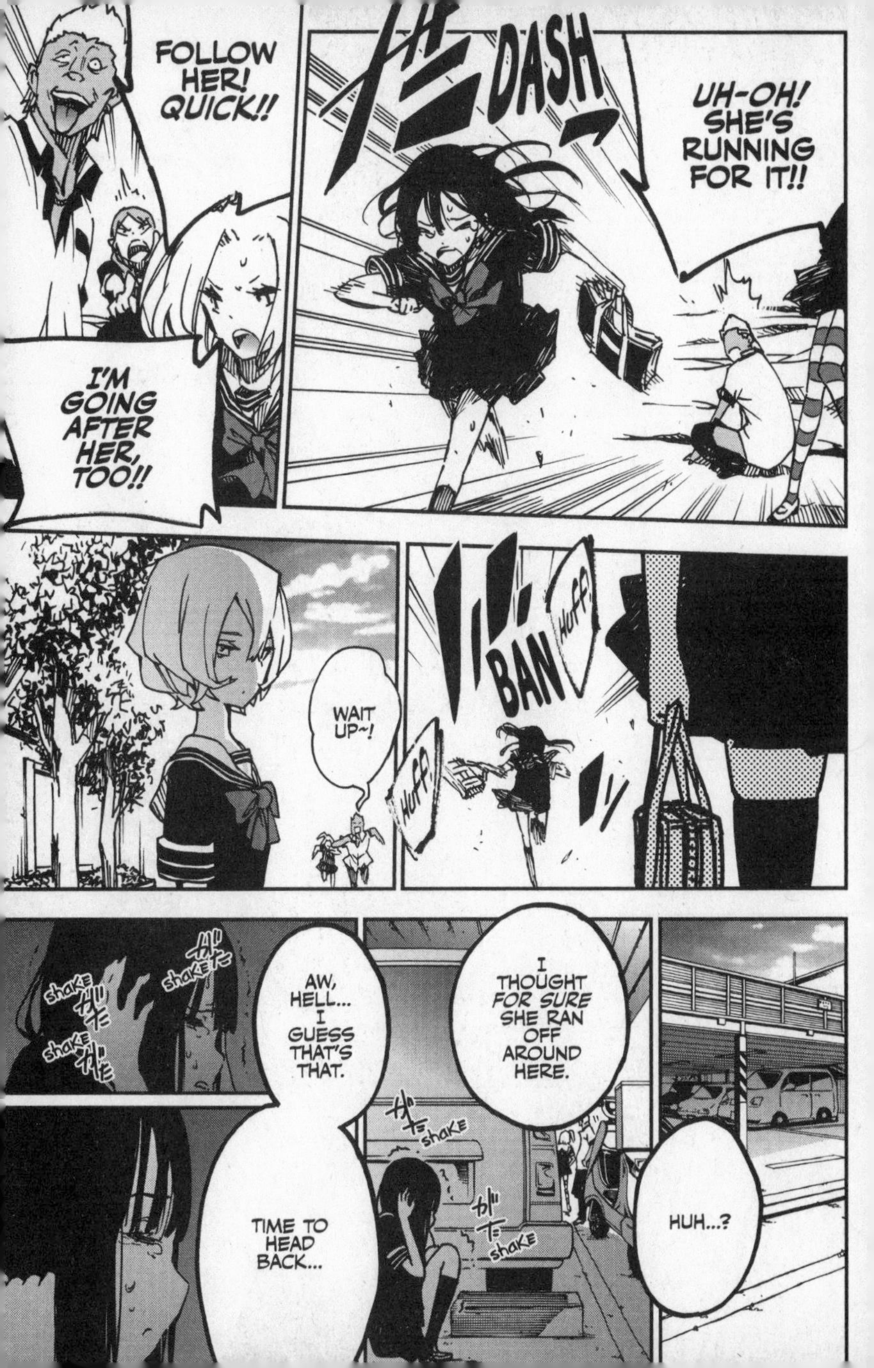
UH-OH! SHE'S RUNNING FOR IT!!
DASH
FOLLOW HER! QUICK!!
I'M GOING AFTER HER, TOO!!
HUFF!
BAN
HUFF!
WAIT UP~!
HUH...?
I THOUGHT FOR SURE SHE RAN OFF AROUND HERE.
AW, HELL... I GUESS THAT'S THAT.
shake
shake
TIME TO HEAD BACK...
shake
shake
shake

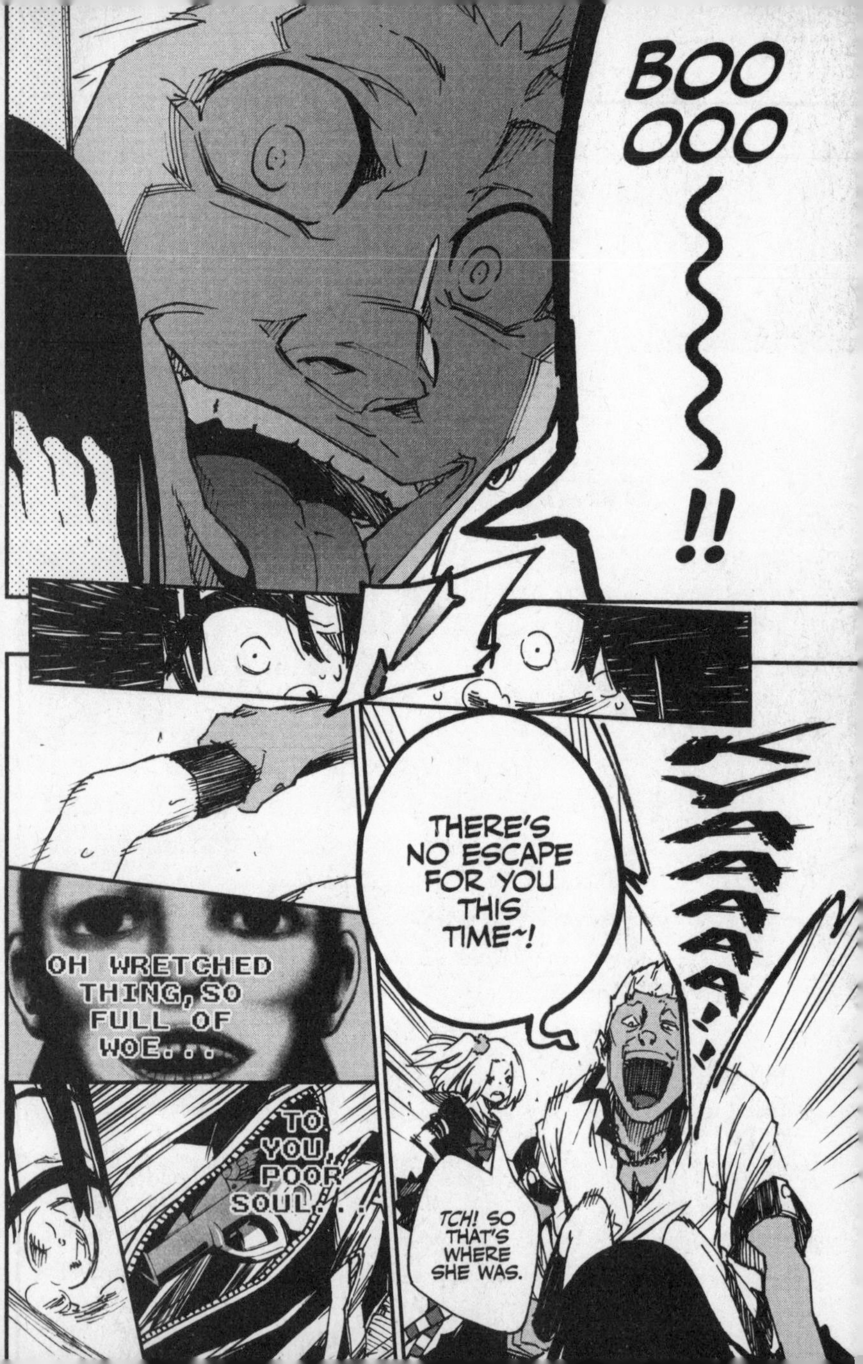
BOOOOO~!!
KYAAAAA!!
THERE'S NO ESCAPE FOR YOU THIS TIME~!
TCH! SO THAT'S WHERE SHE WAS.
OH WRETCHED THING, SO FULL OF WOE...
TO YOU, POOR SOUL...

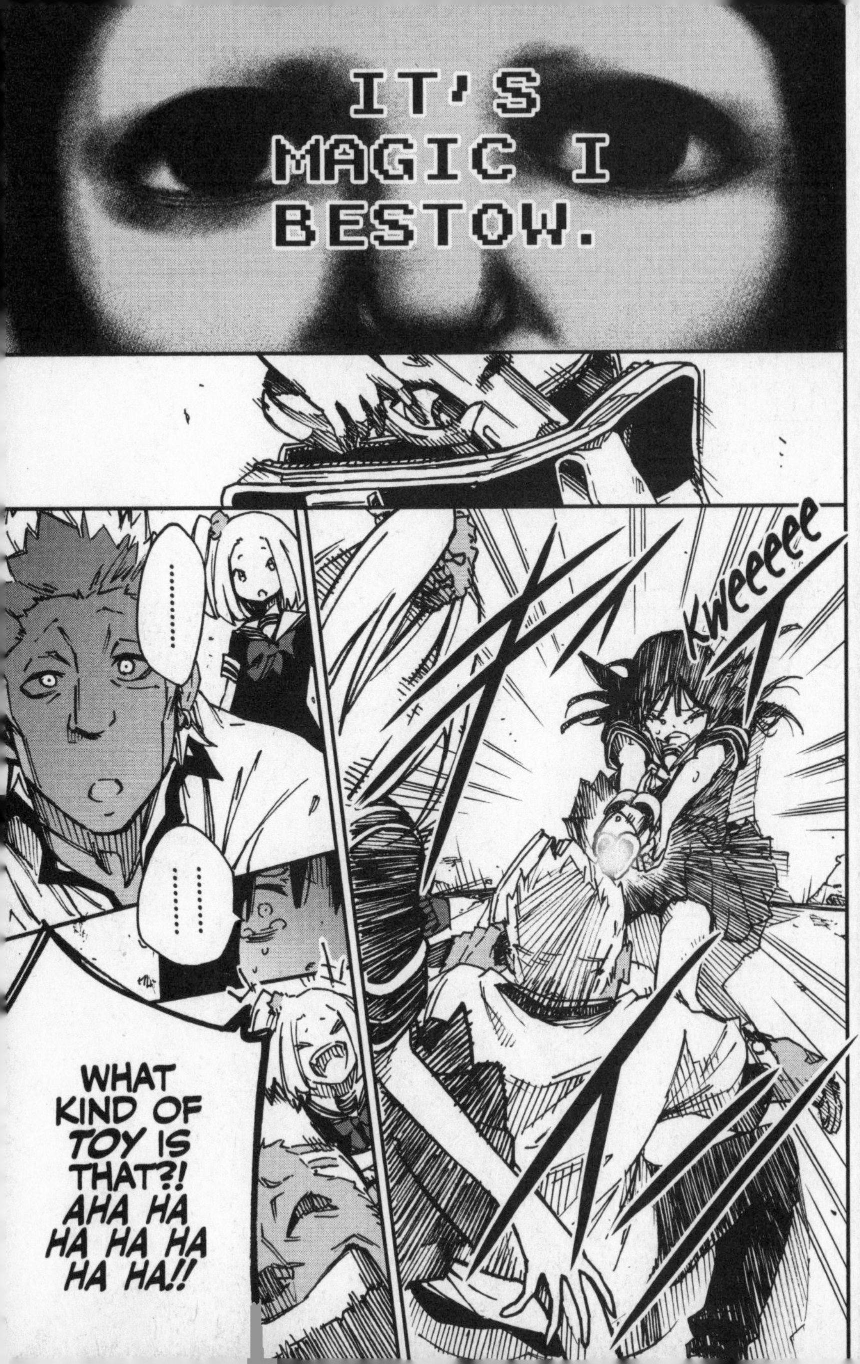
IT'S MAGIC I BESTOW.
Kweeeee
......
......!!
WHAT KIND OF TOY IS THAT?! AHA HA HA HA HA HA HA!!

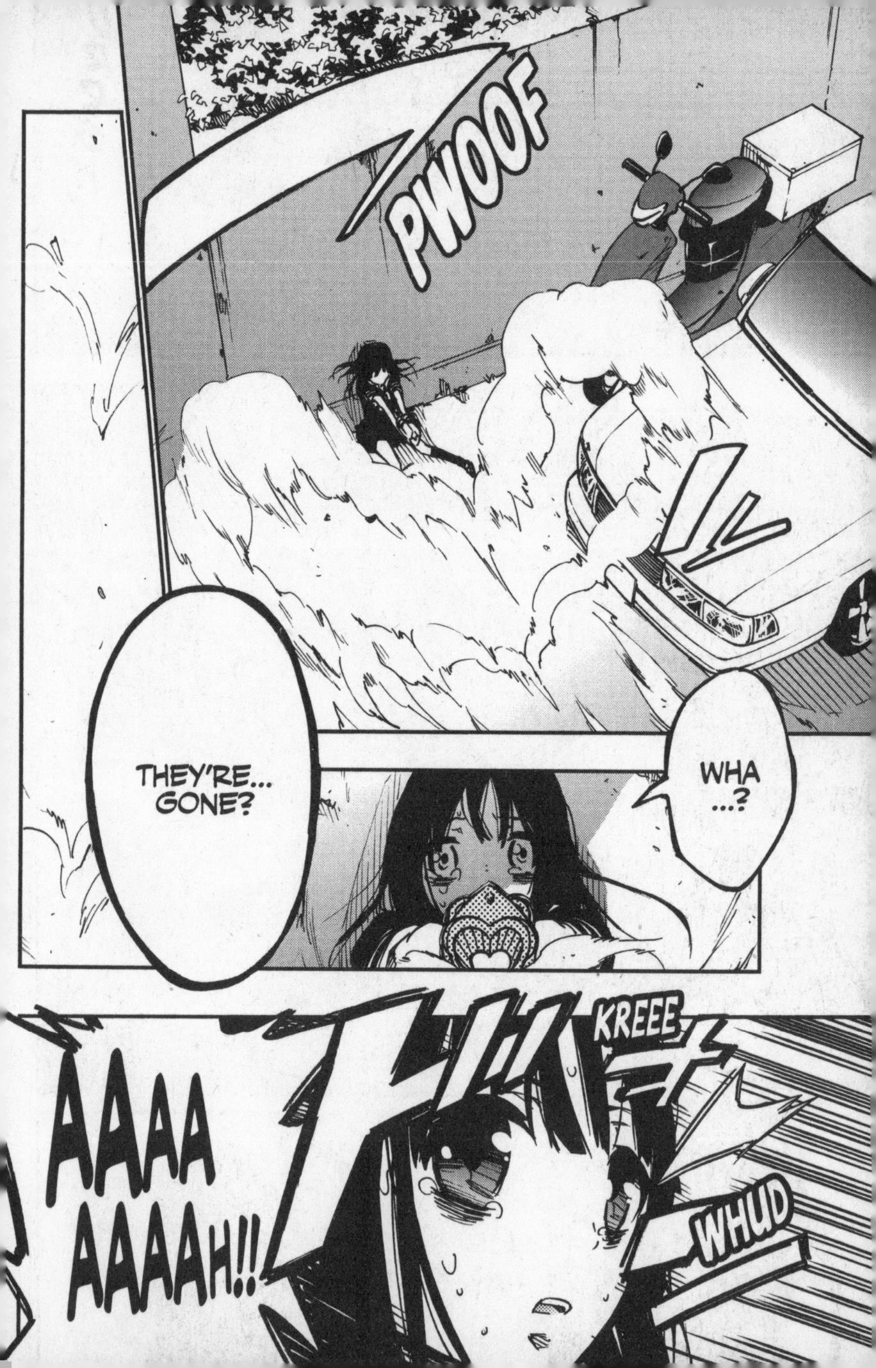
PWOOF
WHA ...?
THEY'RE... GONE?
KREEE
WHUD
AAAA AAAAH!!

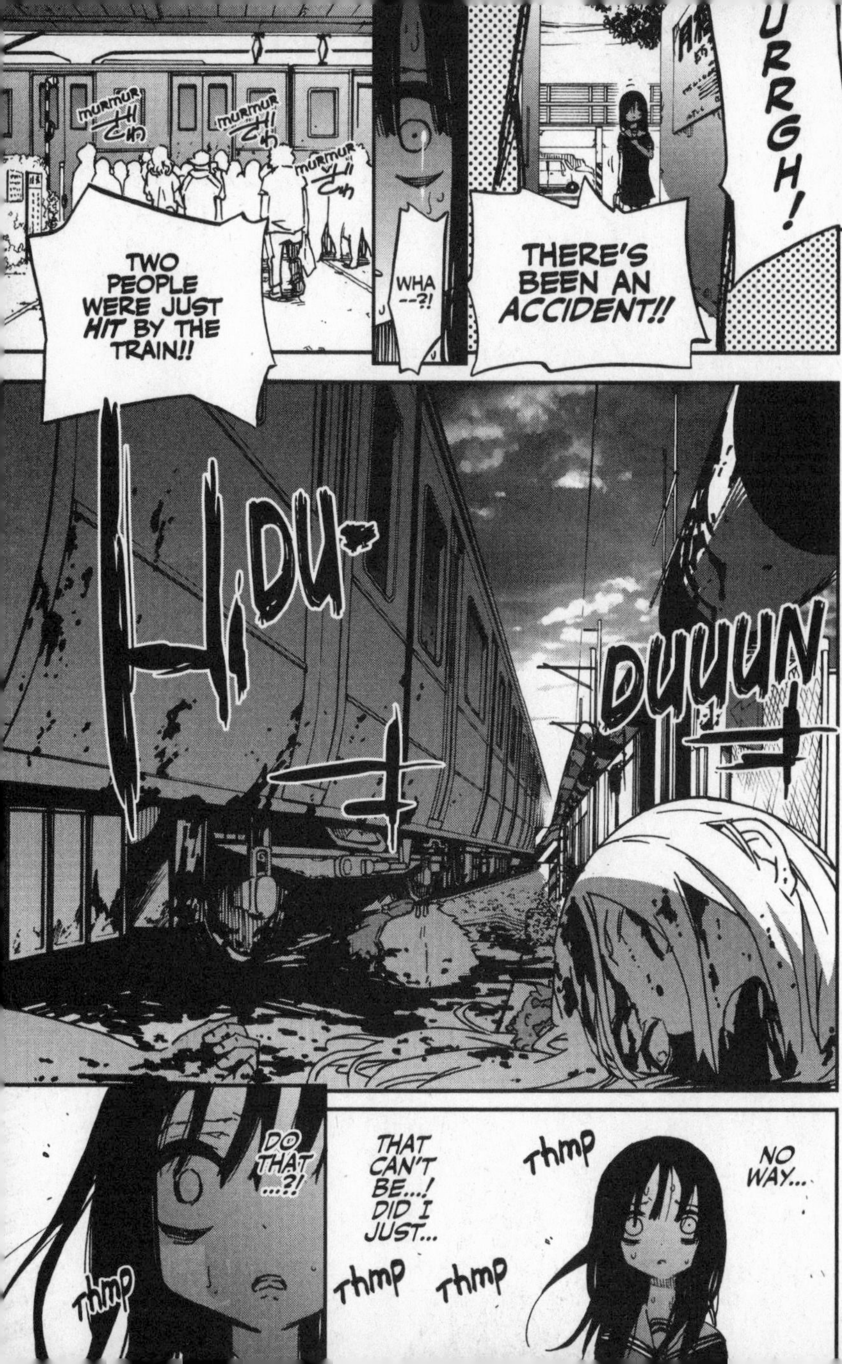
URRGH!
THERE'S BEEN AN ACCIDENT!!
WHA--?!
murmur
murmur
murmur
TWO PEOPLE WERE JUST HIT BY THE TRAIN!!
DU-
DUUUN
NO WAY...
thmp
thmp
thmp
THAT CAN'T BE...! DID I JUST...
DO THAT...?!
thmp

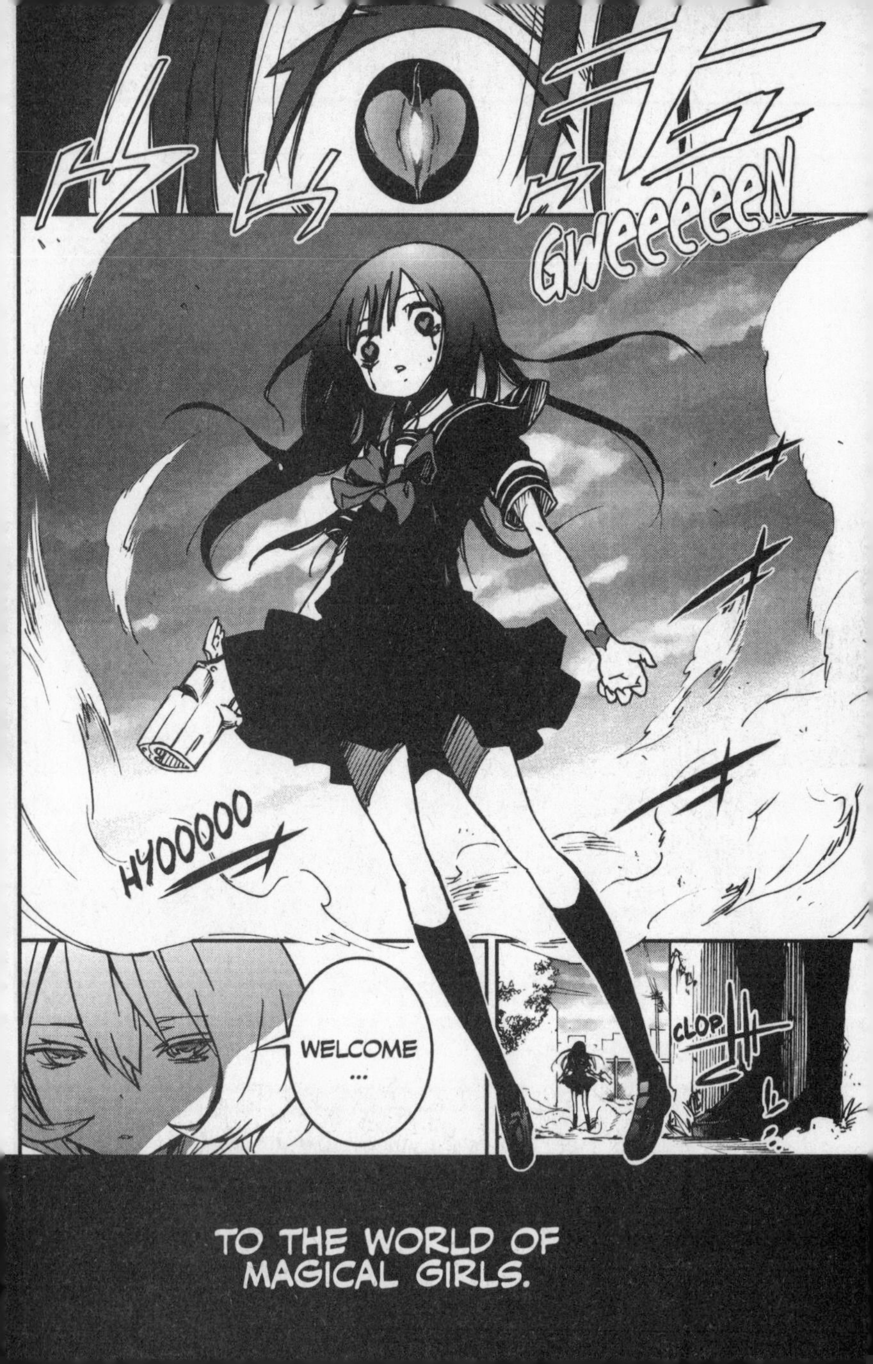
GWEEEEEN
HYOOOOO
CLOP
WELCOME ...
TO THE WORLD OF MAGICAL GIRLS.

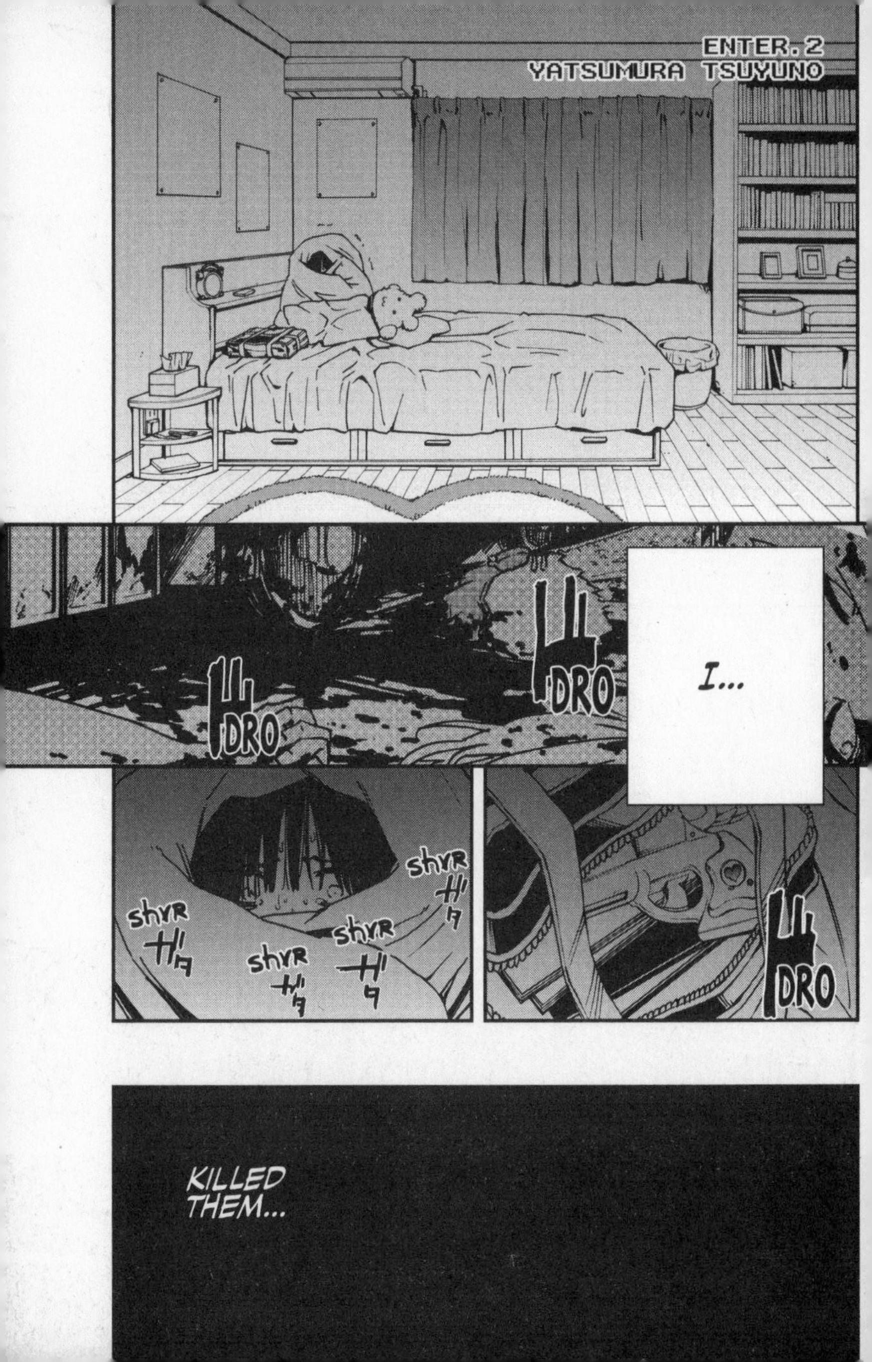
ENTER. 2
YATSUMURA TSUYUNO
I...
DRO
DRO
DRO
shvR
shvR
shvR
shvR
KILLED THEM...

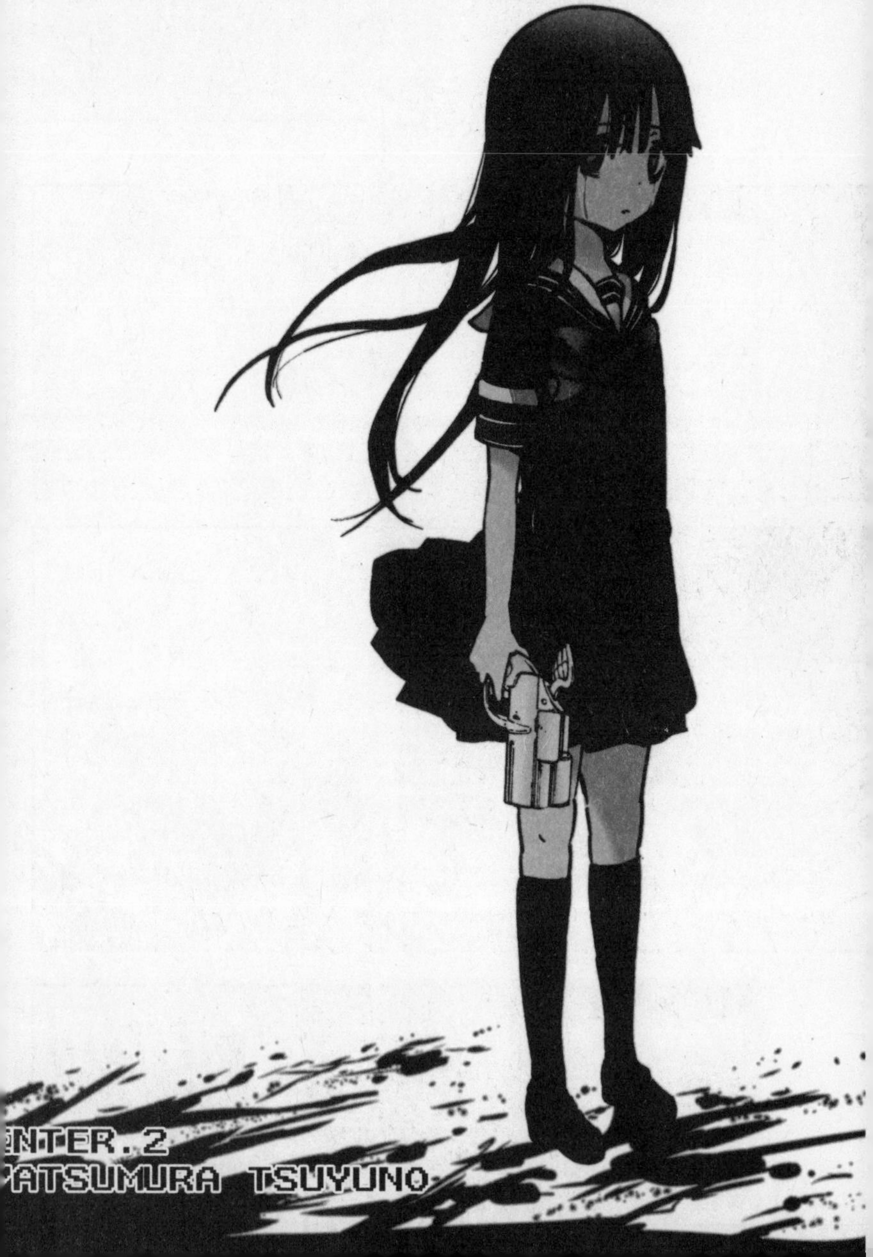
ENTER.2
ATSUMURA TSUYUNO

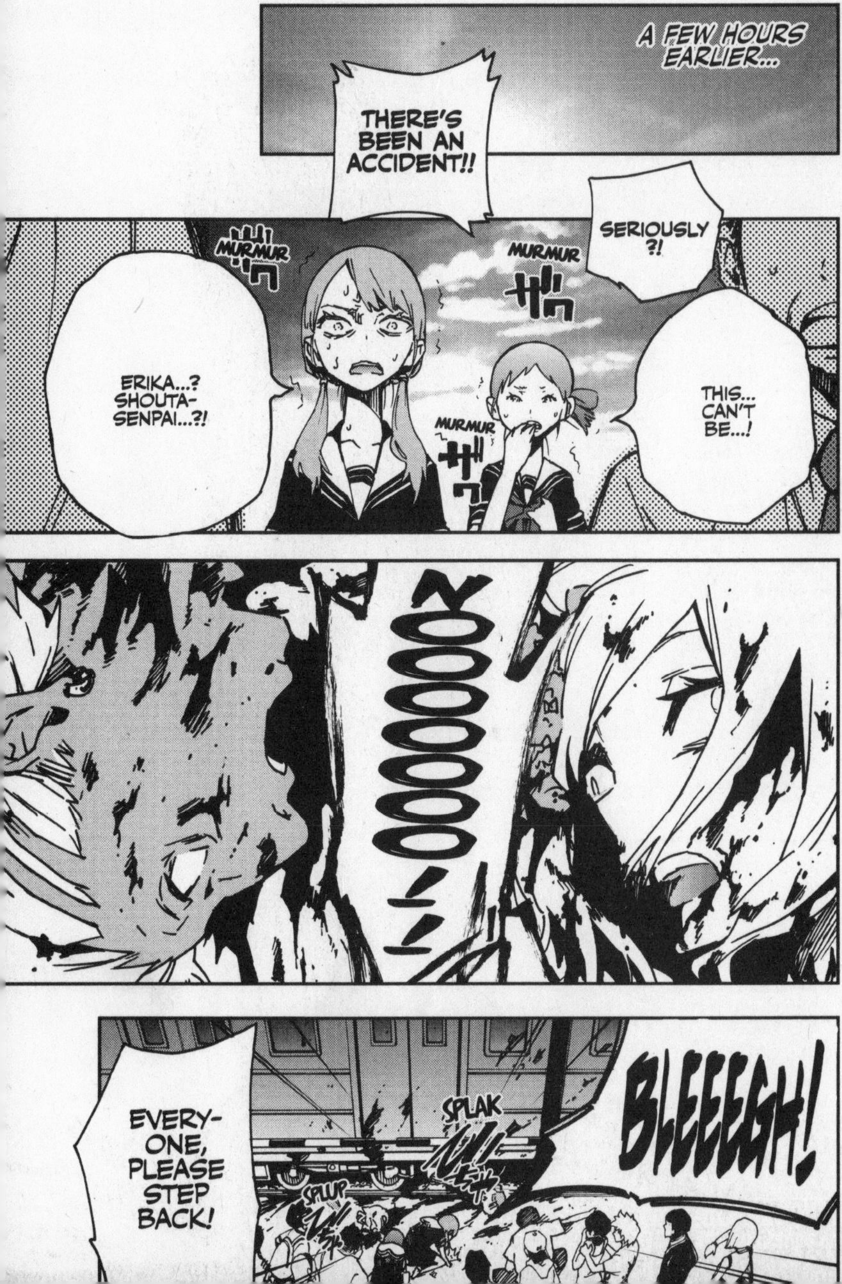
A FEW HOURS EARLIER...
THERE'S BEEN AN ACCIDENT!!
SERIOUSLY?!
MURMUR
THIS... CAN'T BE...!
MURMUR
ERIKA...? SHOUTA-SENPAI...?!
MURMUR
NOOOOOOO!!!
BLEEEGH!
SPLAK
SPLUP
EVERY-ONE, PLEASE STEP BACK!

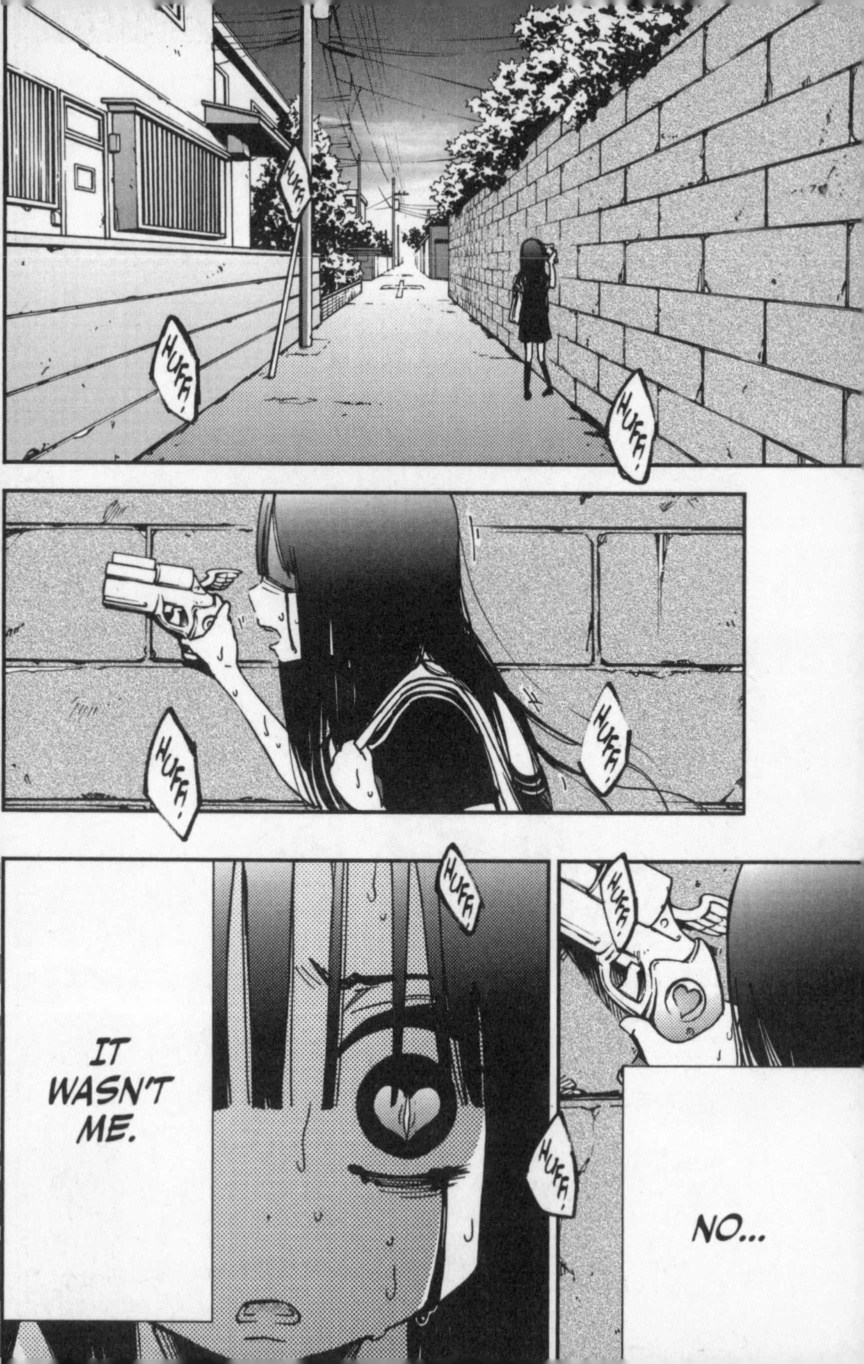
HUFF!
HUFF!
HUFF!
HUFF!
HUFF!
HUFF!
HUFF!
NO...
HUFF!
IT WASN'T ME.

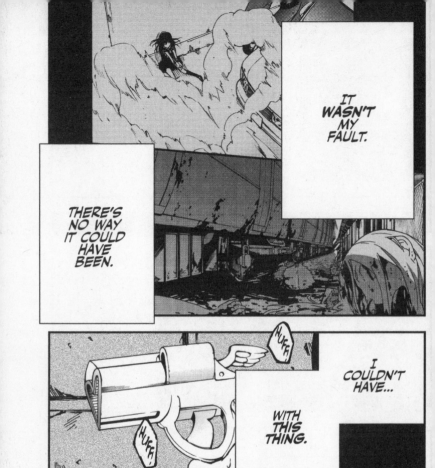

IT WASN'T MY FAULT.

THERE'S NO WAY IT COULD HAVE BEEN.

HUFF!

HUFF!

I COULDN'T HAVE...

WITH THIS THING.

MY HEAD...

IS KILLING ME...

WINCE

NNNGH!

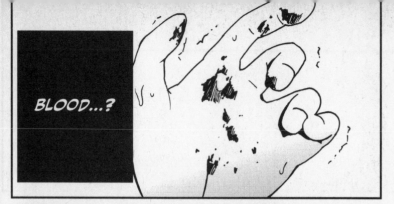

BLOOD...?

FROM MY EYES ...?!

HM? WHAT'S THIS...?

DOES MY HAIR SEEM LONGER ...?

AND WHY HAS IT BECOME SO RED...?!

AND WHY...

RSTL...

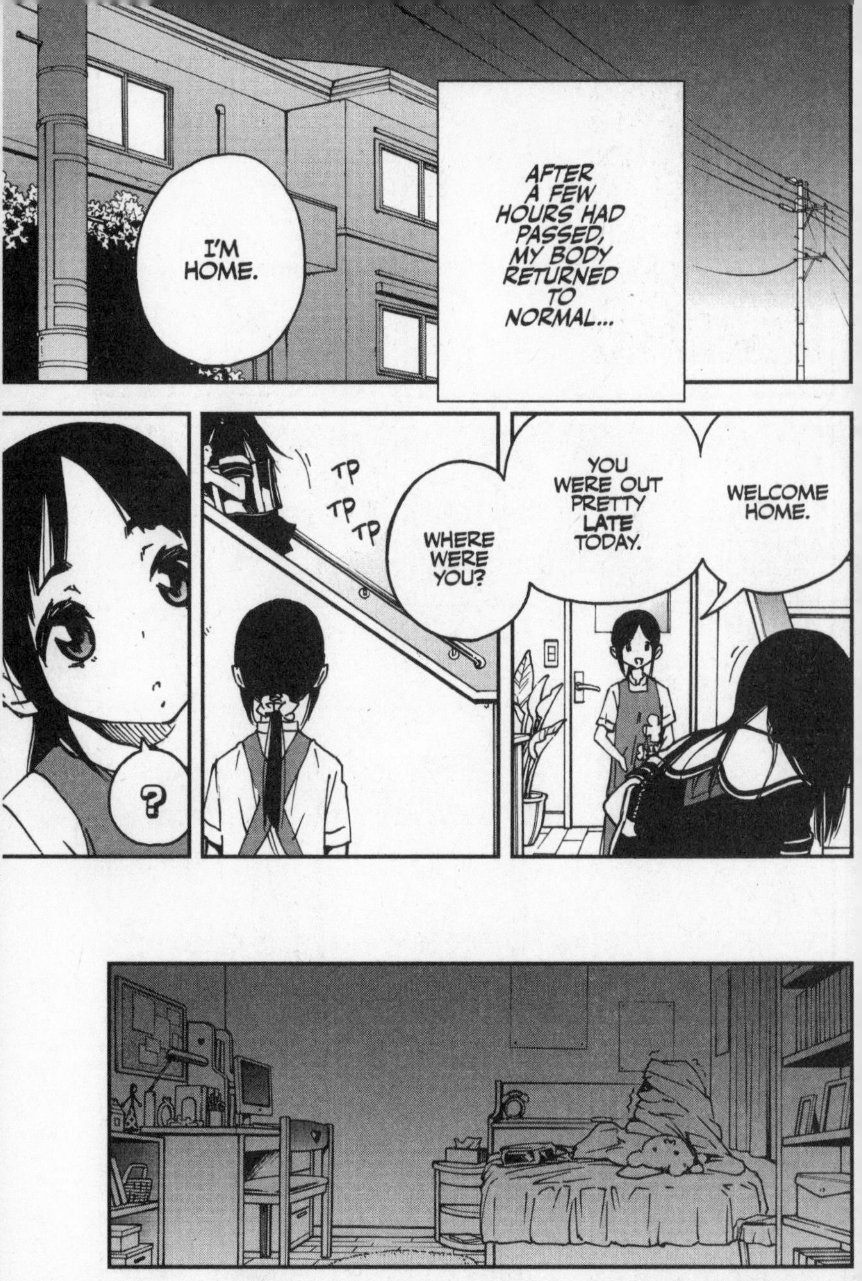
AFTER A FEW HOURS HAD PASSED, MY BODY RETURNED TO NORMAL...
I'M HOME.
WELCOME HOME.
YOU WERE OUT PRETTY LATE TODAY.
WHERE WERE YOU?
TP TP TP
?

MOM'S WORRIED ABOUT YOU...

HEEEY! AYA!

I'M WORRIED ABOUT YOU, TOO.

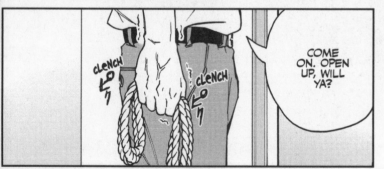

CLENCH

CLENCH

COME ON. OPEN UP, WILL YA?

DID I...

REALLY KILL THEM...?

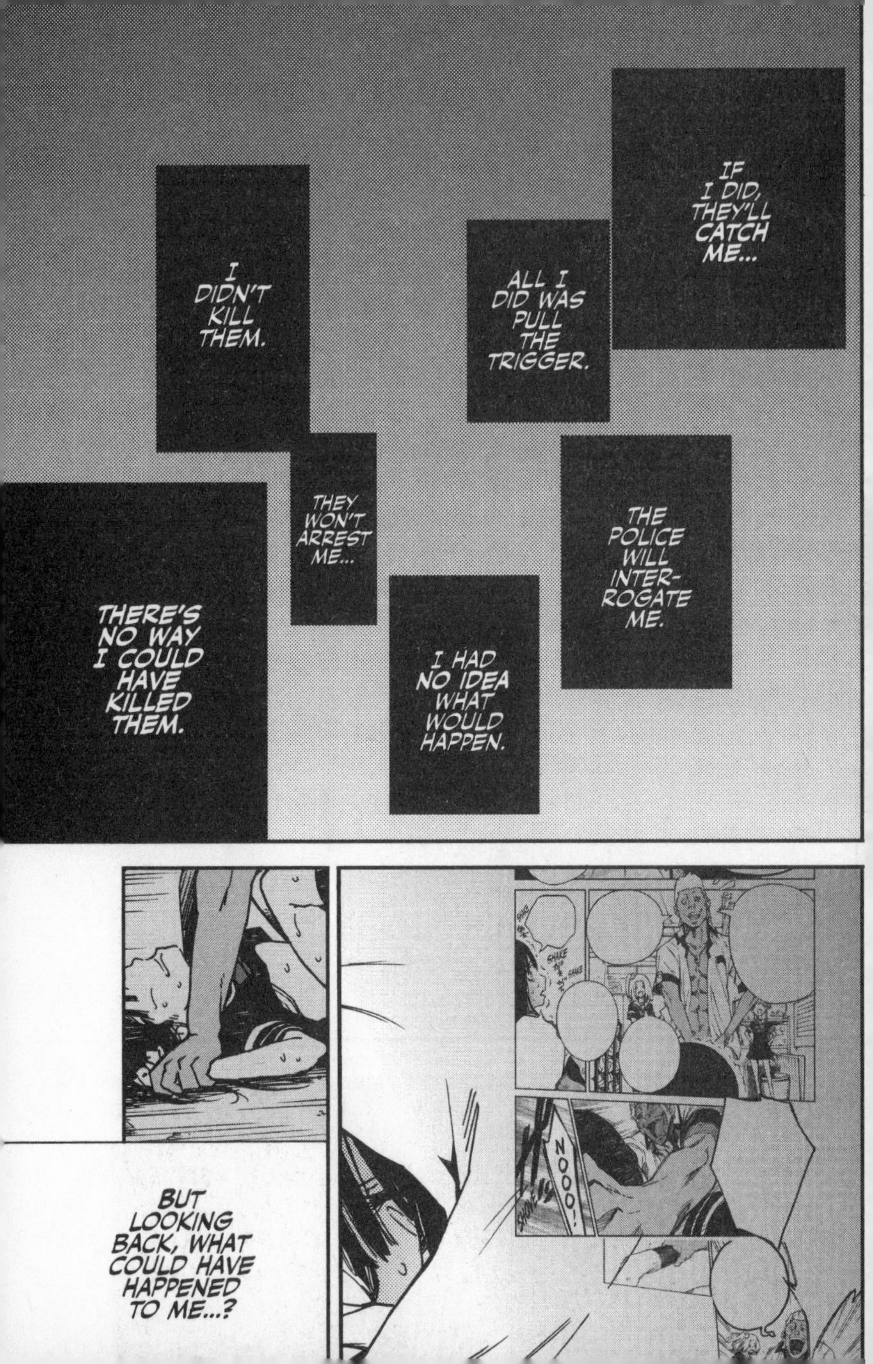
IF I DID, THEY'LL CATCH ME...
ALL I DID WAS PULL THE TRIGGER.
I DIDN'T KILL THEM.
THE POLICE WILL INTER-ROGATE ME.
THEY WON'T ARREST ME...
I HAD NO IDEA WHAT WOULD HAPPEN.
THERE'S NO WAY I COULD HAVE KILLED THEM.
NOOO!
BUT LOOKING BACK, WHAT COULD HAVE HAPPENED TO ME...?

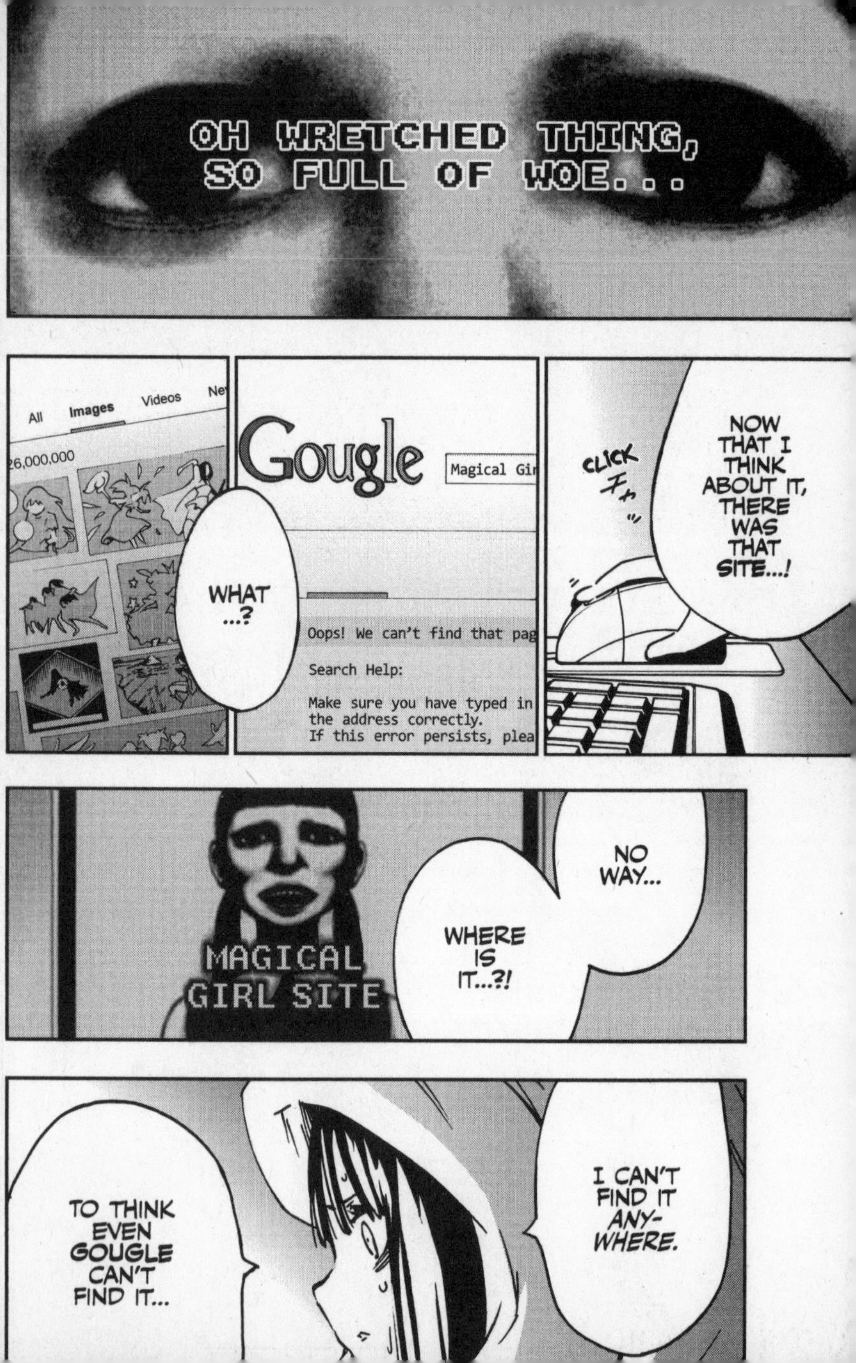
OH WRETCHED THING, SO FULL OF WOE...
CLICK
NOW THAT I THINK ABOUT IT, THERE WAS THAT SITE...!
Gougle
Magical Gir
Oops! We can't find that pag
Search Help:
Make sure you have typed in the address correctly.
If this error persists, plea
All
Images
Videos
26,000,000
WHAT...?
NO WAY...
WHERE IS IT...?!
MAGICAL GIRL SITE
I CAN'T FIND IT ANYWHERE.
TO THINK EVEN GOUGLE CAN'T FIND IT...

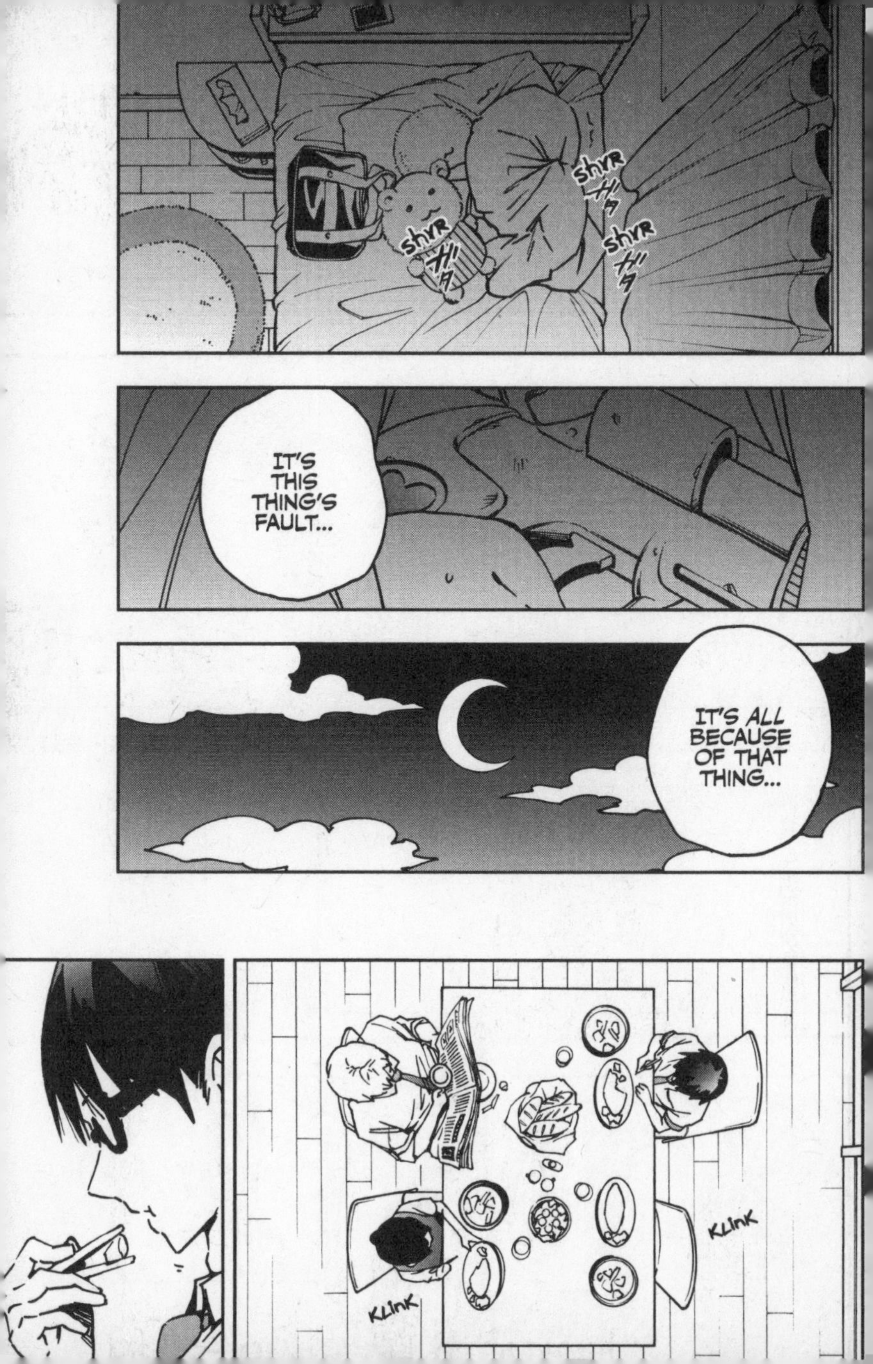
shYR
shYR
shYR
IT'S THIS THING'S FAULT...
IT'S ALL BECAUSE OF THAT THING...
KLink
KLink

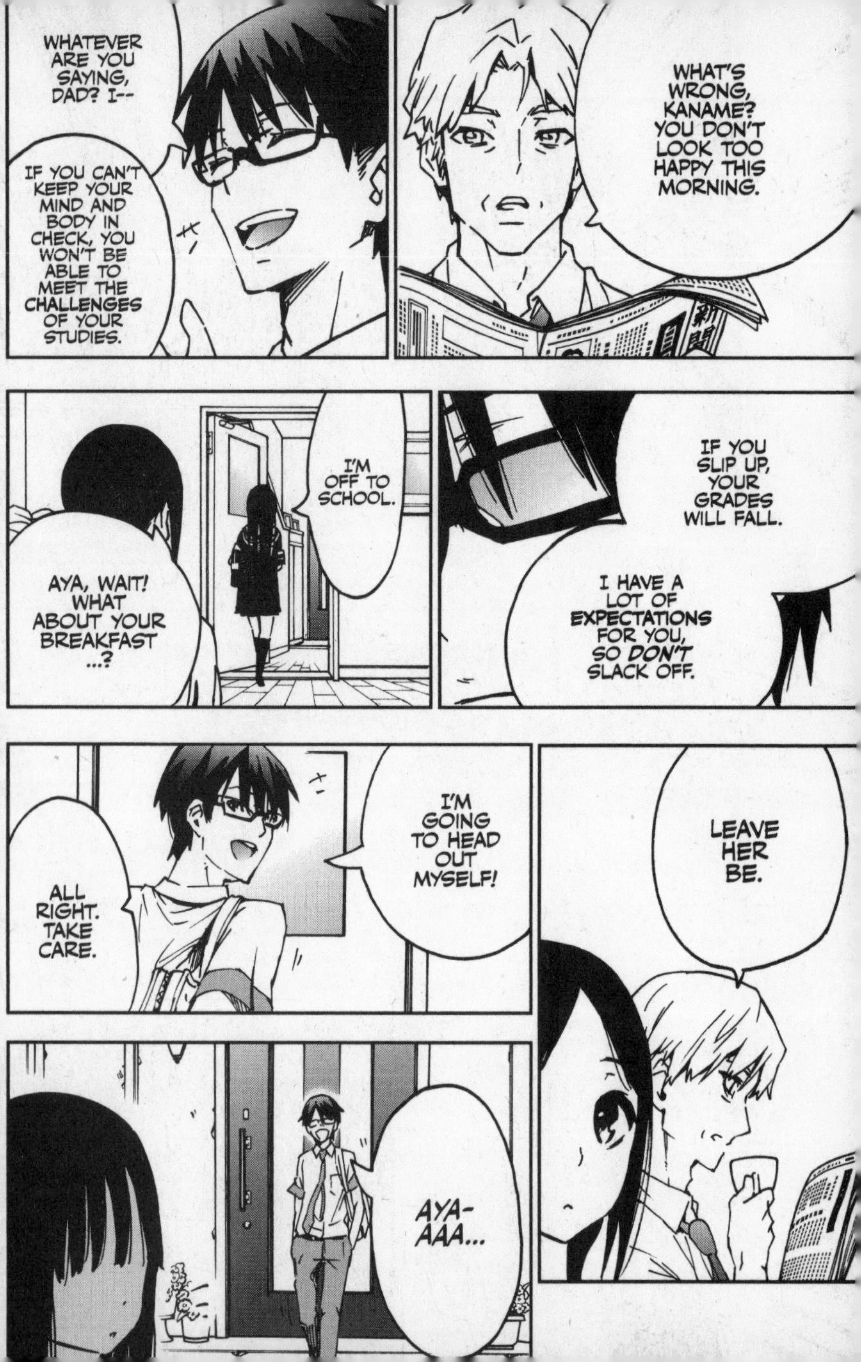
WHAT'S WRONG, KANAME? YOU DON'T LOOK TOO HAPPY THIS MORNING.
WHATEVER ARE YOU SAYING, DAD? I--
IF YOU CAN'T KEEP YOUR MIND AND BODY IN CHECK, YOU WON'T BE ABLE TO MEET THE CHALLENGES OF YOUR STUDIES.
IF YOU SLIP UP, YOUR GRADES WILL FALL.
I HAVE A LOT OF EXPECTATIONS FOR YOU, SO DON'T SLACK OFF.
I'M OFF TO SCHOOL.
AYA, WAIT! WHAT ABOUT YOUR BREAKFAST ...?
LEAVE HER BE.
I'M GOING TO HEAD OUT MYSELF!
ALL RIGHT. TAKE CARE.
AYA-AAA...

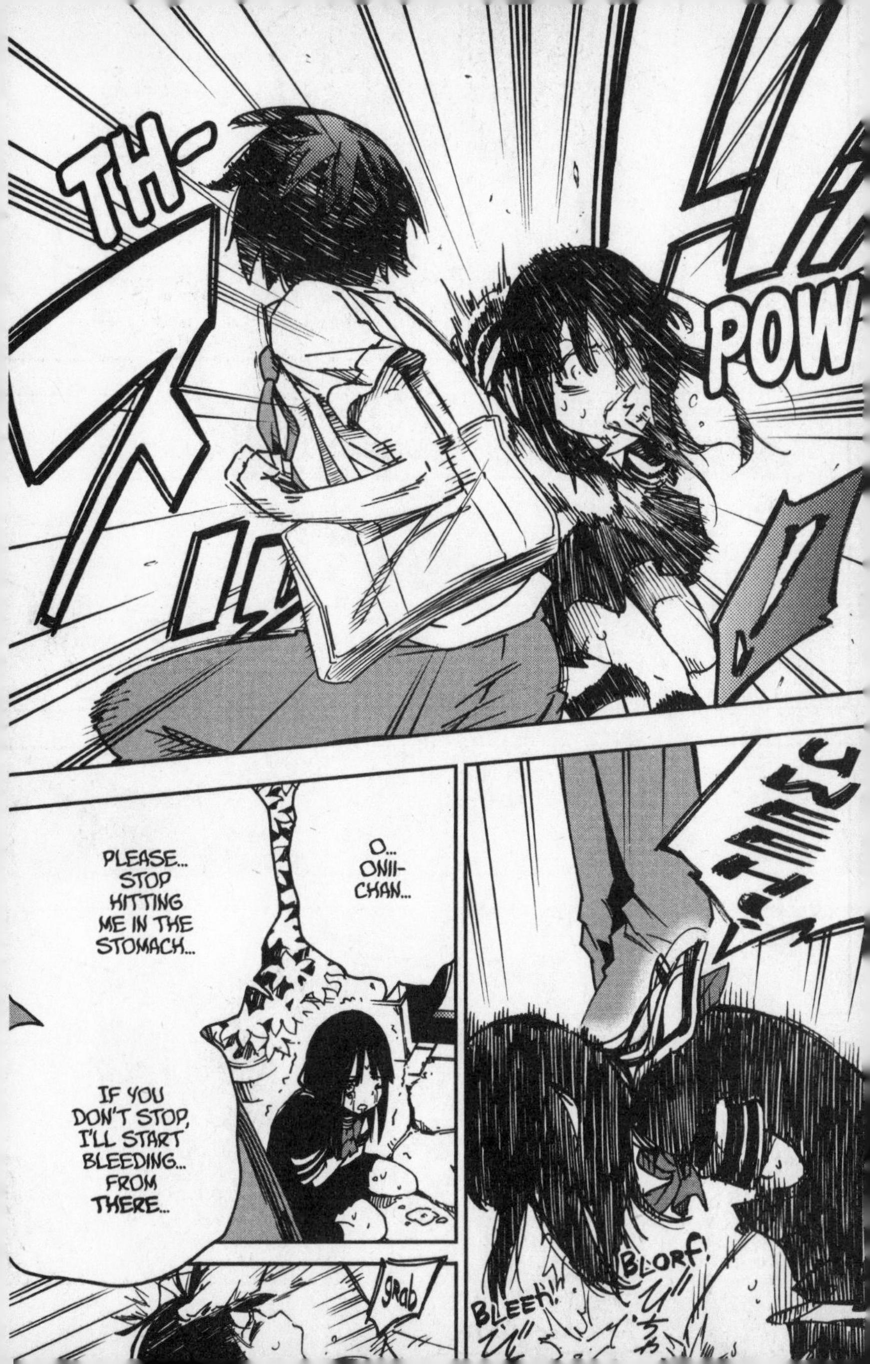
POW
TH-
BLORF!
BLEEH!
O... ONII-CHAN...
PLEASE... STOP HITTING ME IN THE STOMACH...
IF YOU DON'T STOP, I'LL START BLEEDING... FROM THERE...
grab

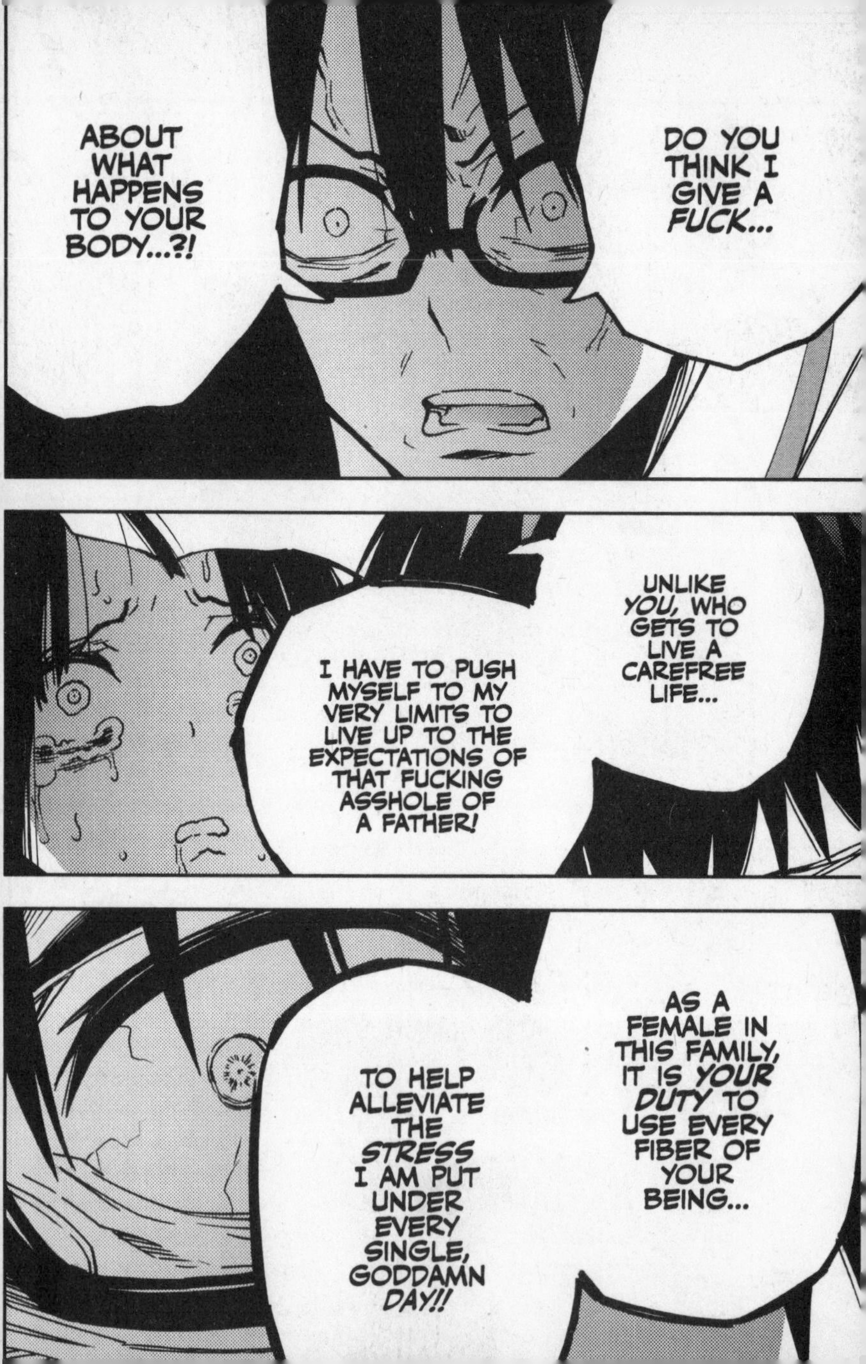
DO YOU THINK I GIVE A *FUCK*...
ABOUT WHAT HAPPENS TO YOUR BODY...?!
UNLIKE *YOU,* WHO GETS TO LIVE A CAREFREE LIFE...
I HAVE TO PUSH MYSELF TO MY VERY LIMITS TO LIVE UP TO THE EXPECTATIONS OF THAT FUCKING ASSHOLE OF A FATHER!
AS A FEMALE IN THIS FAMILY, IT IS *YOUR DUTY* TO USE EVERY FIBER OF YOUR BEING...
TO HELP ALLEVIATE THE *STRESS* I AM PUT UNDER EVERY SINGLE, GODDAMN *DAY!!*

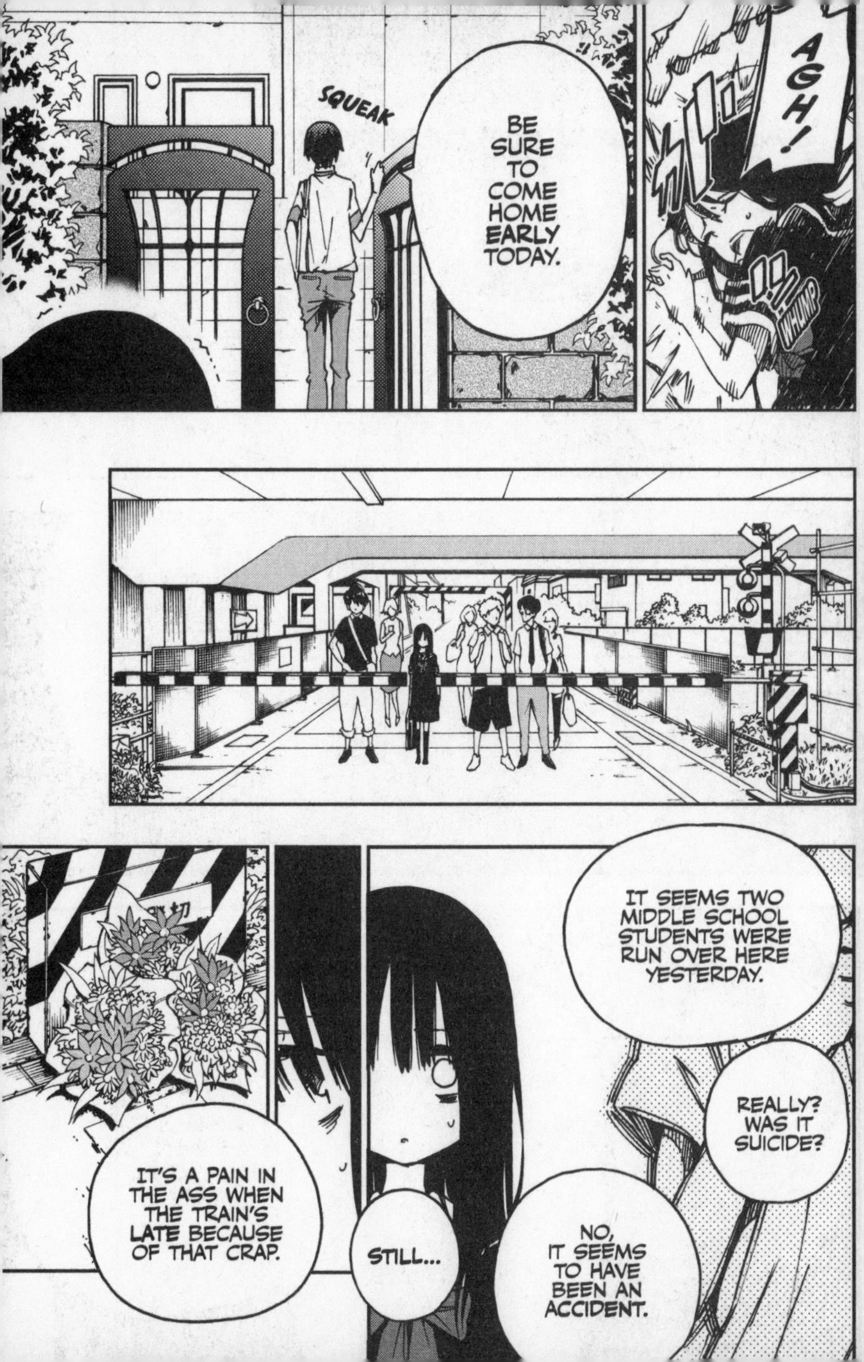
AGH!
WHUMP
SQUEAK
BE SURE TO COME HOME EARLY TODAY.
IT SEEMS TWO MIDDLE SCHOOL STUDENTS WERE RUN OVER HERE YESTERDAY.
REALLY? WAS IT SUICIDE?
NO, IT SEEMS TO HAVE BEEN AN ACCIDENT.
STILL...
IT'S A PAIN IN THE ASS WHEN THE TRAIN'S LATE BECAUSE OF THAT CRAP.

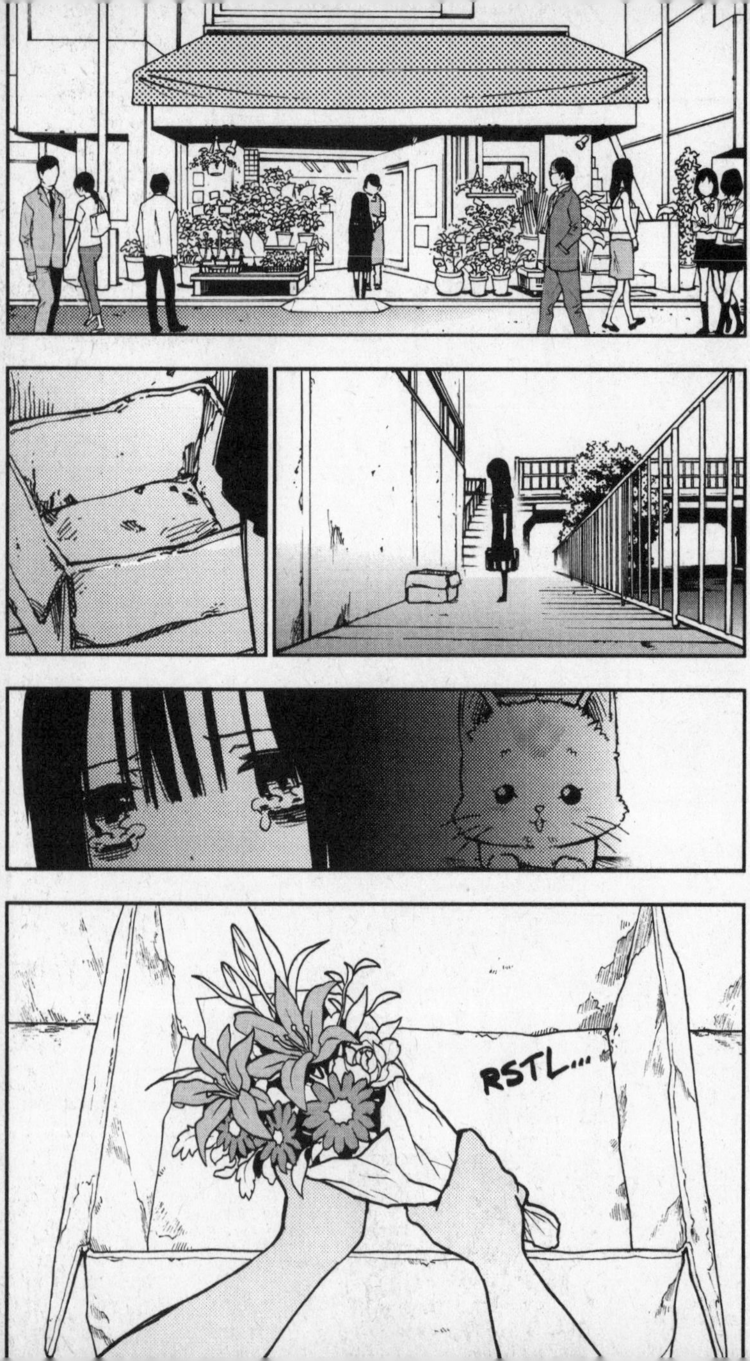
RSTL...

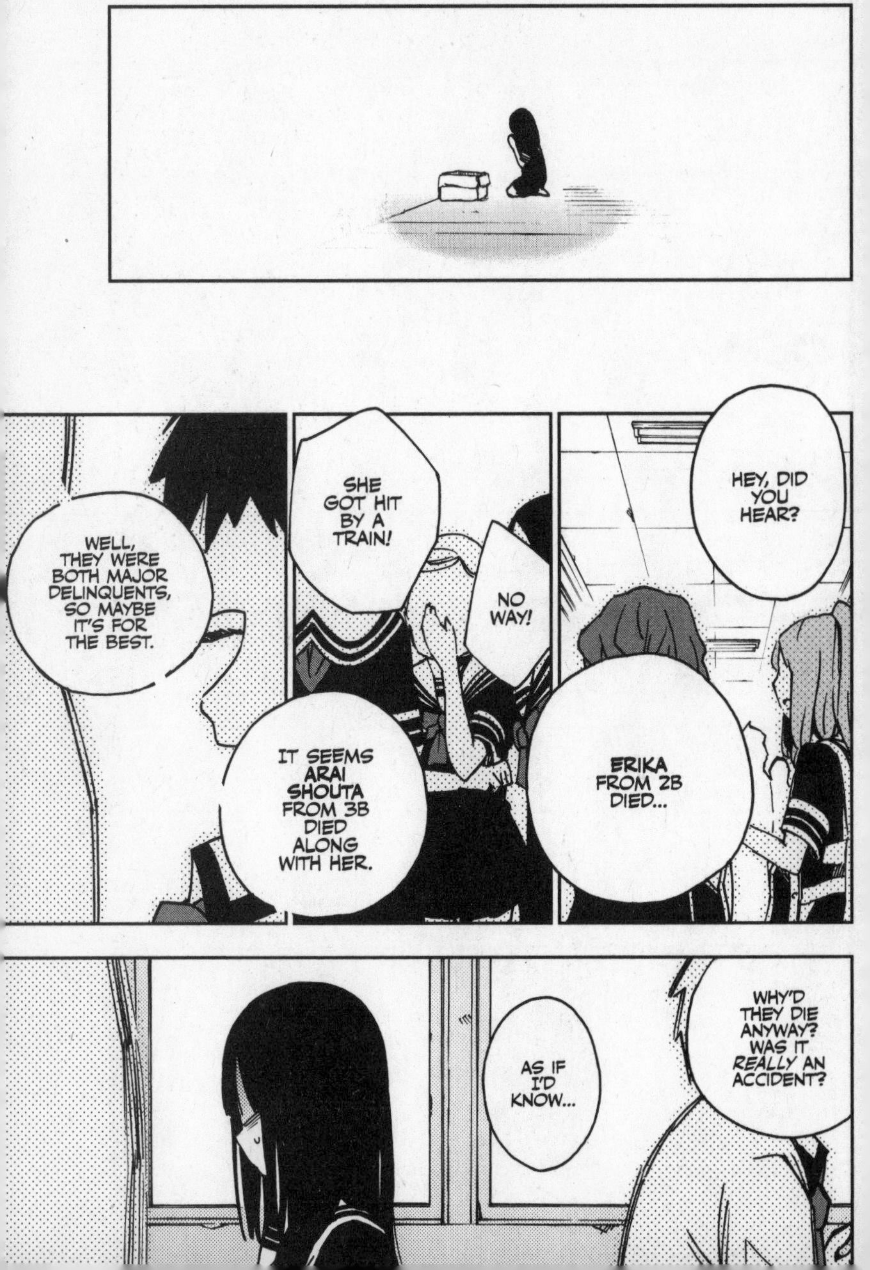
HEY, DID YOU HEAR?
ERIKA FROM 2B DIED...
SHE GOT HIT BY A TRAIN!
NO WAY!
IT SEEMS ARAI SHOUTA FROM 3B DIED ALONG WITH HER.
WELL, THEY WERE BOTH MAJOR DELINQUENTS, SO MAYBE IT'S FOR THE BEST.
WHY'D THEY DIE ANYWAY? WAS IT *REALLY* AN ACCIDENT?
AS IF I'D KNOW...

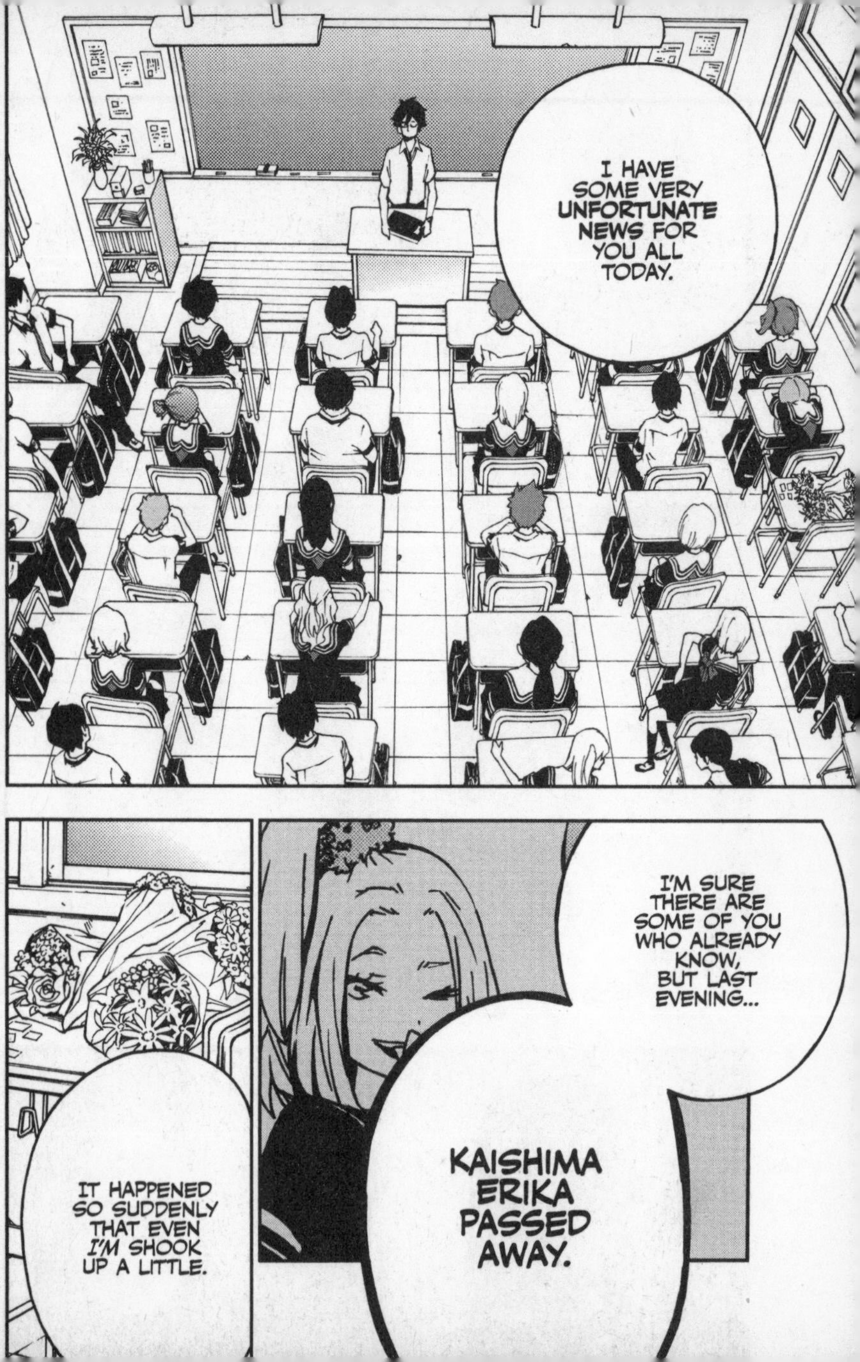
I HAVE SOME VERY UNFORTUNATE NEWS FOR YOU ALL TODAY.
I'M SURE THERE ARE SOME OF YOU WHO ALREADY KNOW, BUT LAST EVENING...
KAISHIMA ERIKA PASSED AWAY.
IT HAPPENED SO SUDDENLY THAT EVEN *I'M* SHOOK UP A LITTLE.

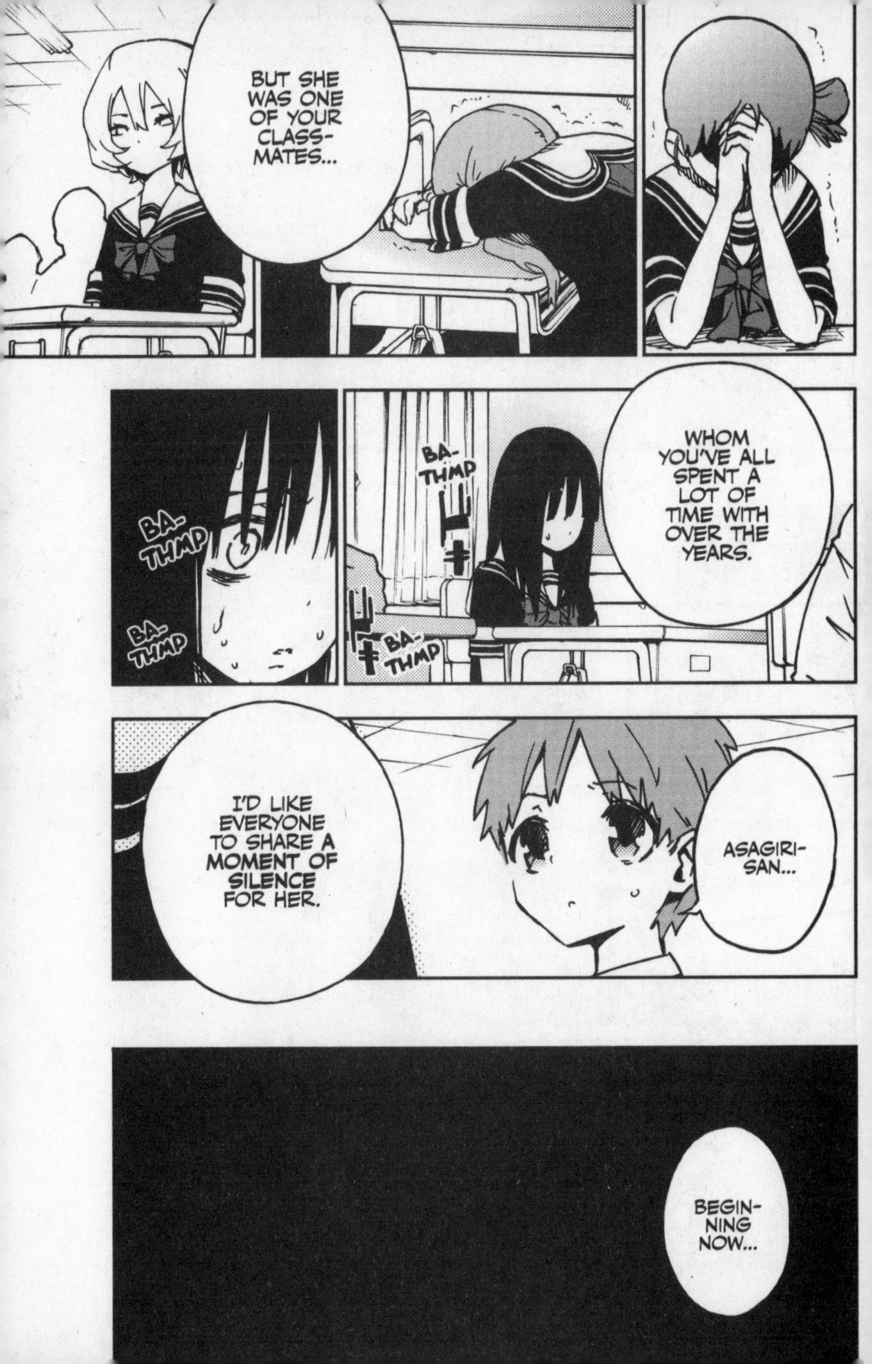
BUT SHE WAS ONE OF YOUR CLASS-MATES...
WHOM YOU'VE ALL SPENT A LOT OF TIME WITH OVER THE YEARS.
BA-THMP
BA-THMP
BA-THMP
BA-THMP
ASAGIRI-SAN...
I'D LIKE EVERYONE TO SHARE A MOMENT OF SILENCE FOR HER.
BEGIN-NING NOW...

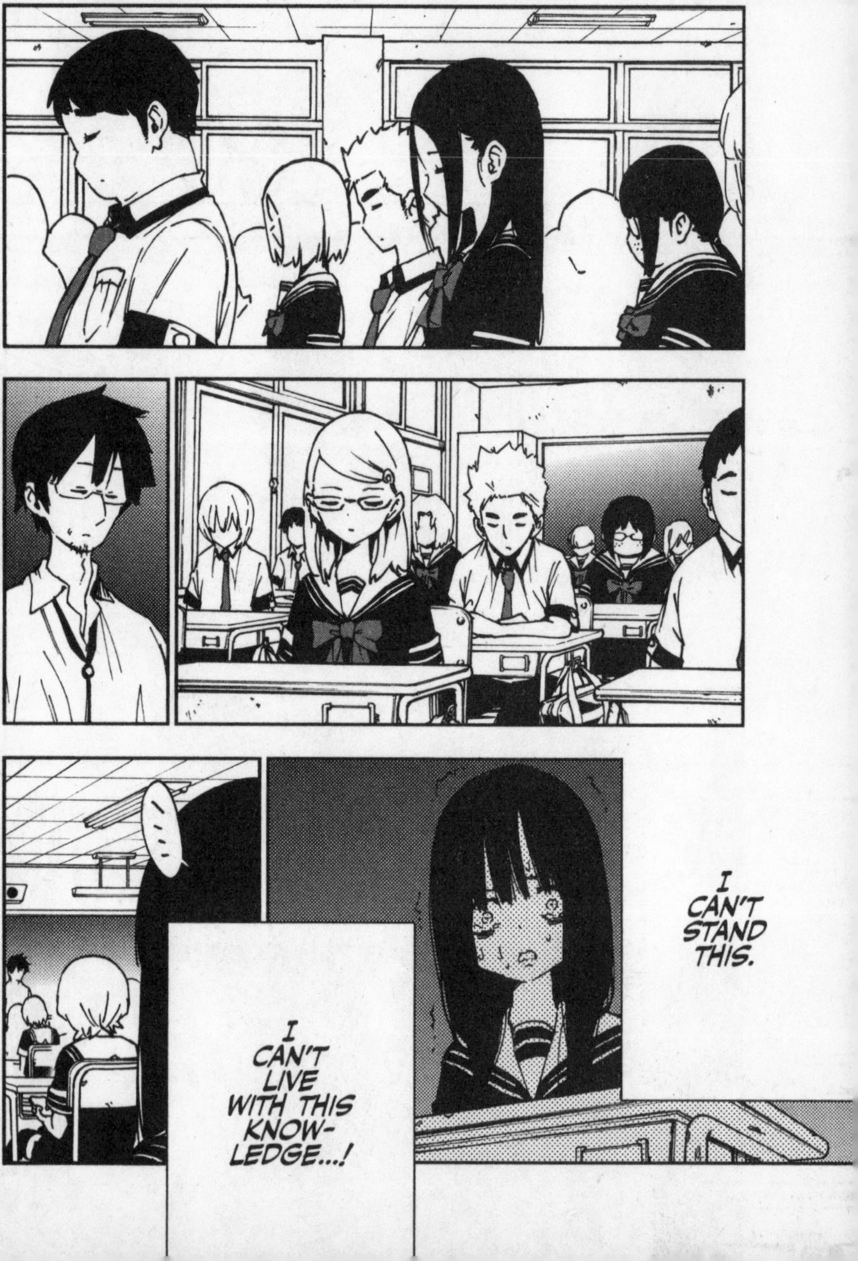
...
I CAN'T STAND THIS.
I CAN'T LIVE WITH THIS KNOW-LEDGE...!

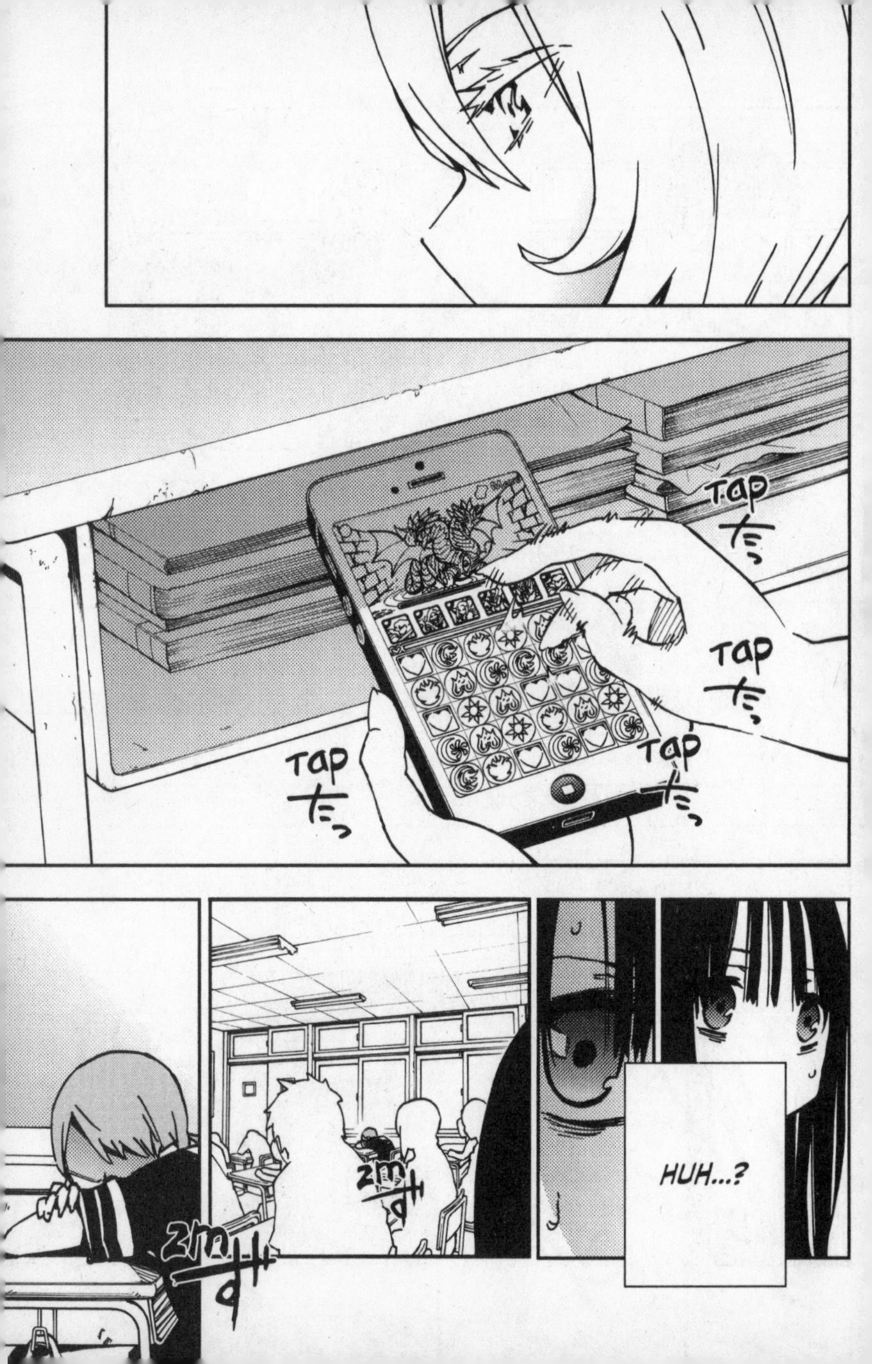
Tap
たっ
Tap
たっ
Tap
たっ
Tap
たっ
HUH...?

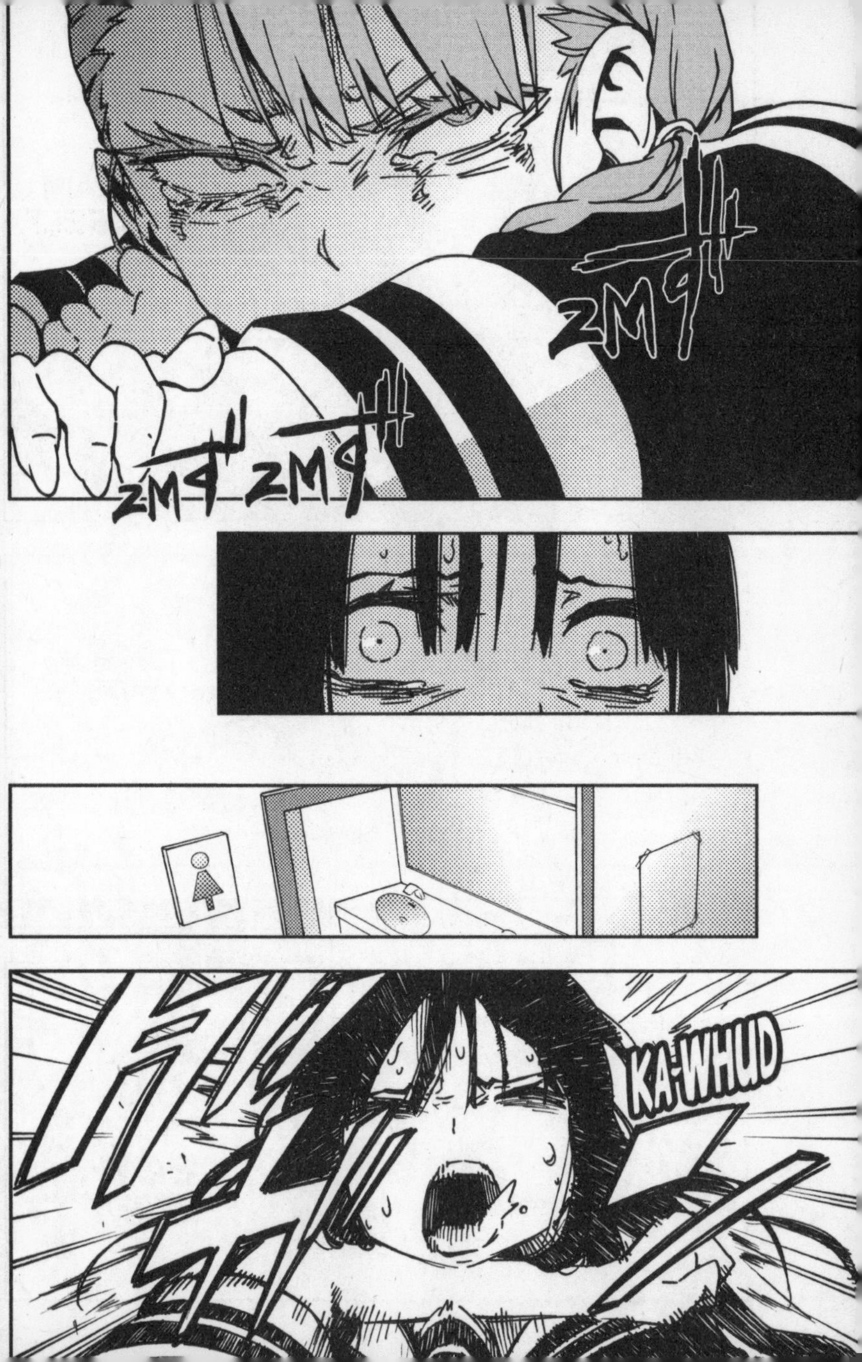
KA-WHUD

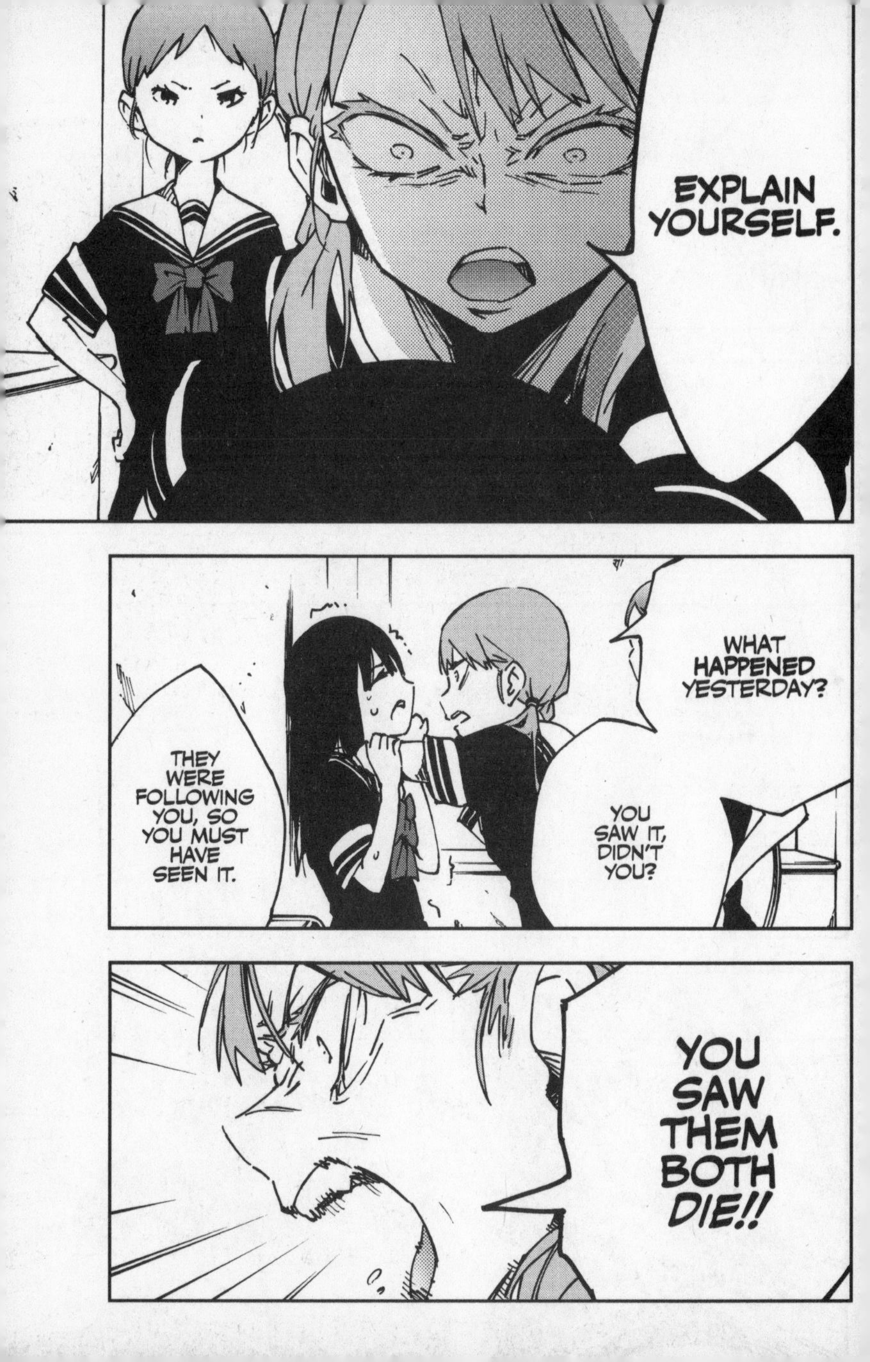
EXPLAIN YOURSELF.
WHAT HAPPENED YESTERDAY?
YOU SAW IT, DIDN'T YOU?
THEY WERE FOLLOWING YOU, SO YOU MUST HAVE SEEN IT.
YOU SAW THEM BOTH DIE!!

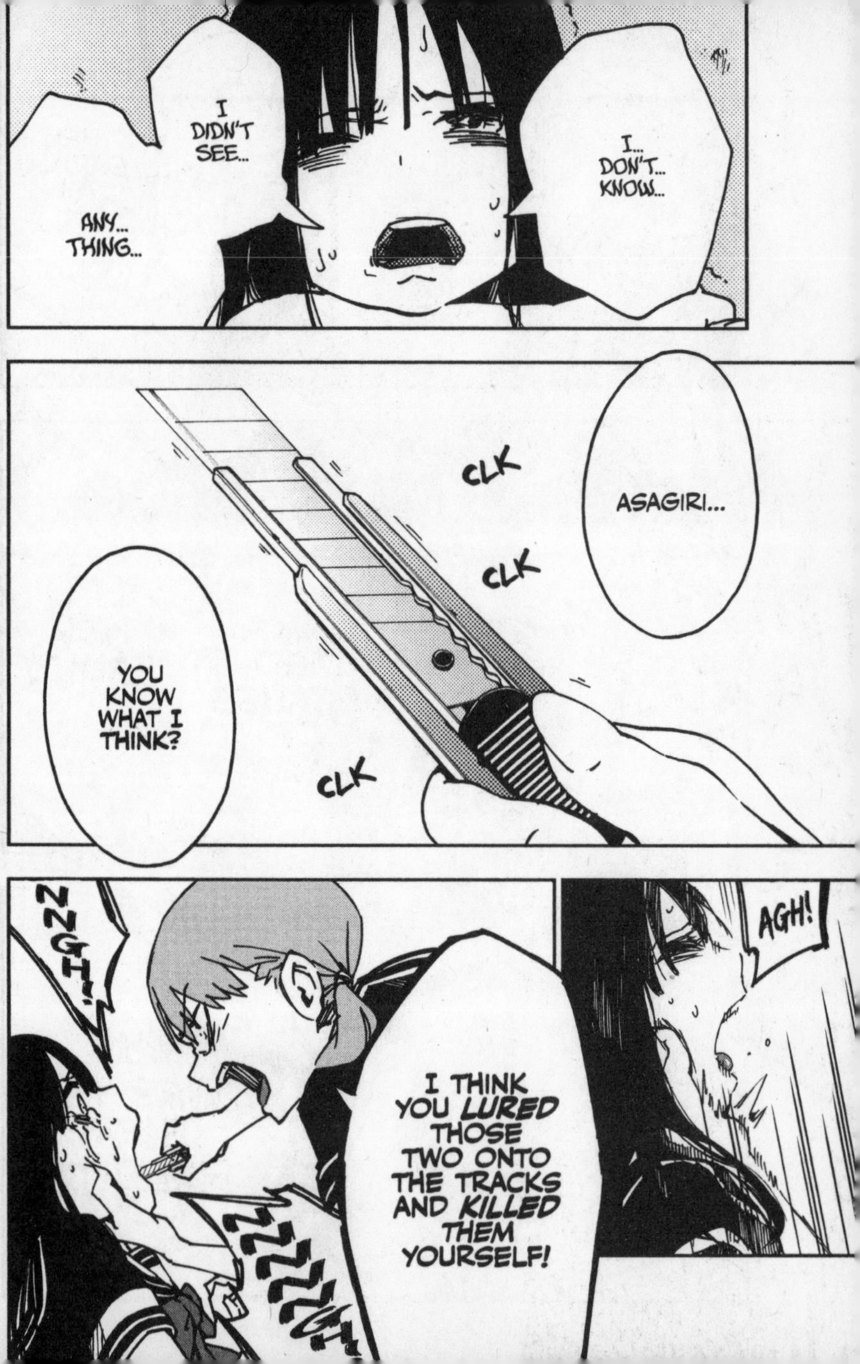
I... DON'T... KNOW...
I DIDN'T SEE...
ANY... THING...
ASAGIRI...
CLK
CLK
CLK
YOU KNOW WHAT I THINK?
AGH!
I THINK YOU *LURED* THOSE TWO ONTO THE TRACKS AND *KILLED* THEM YOURSELF!
NNGH!

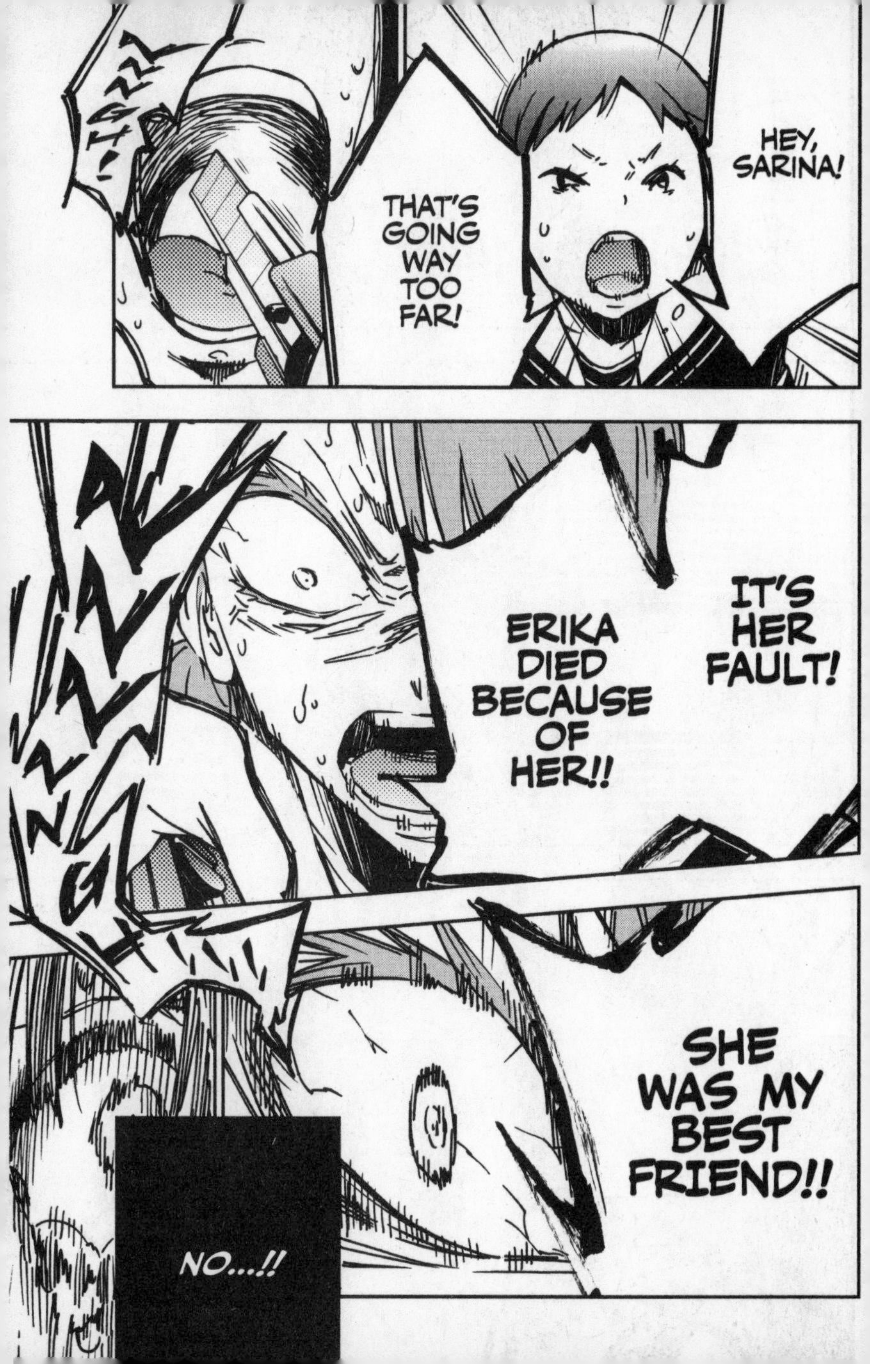
HEY, SARINA!
THAT'S GOING WAY TOO FAR!
IT'S HER FAULT!
ERIKA DIED BECAUSE OF HER!!
SHE WAS MY BEST FRIEND!!
NO...!!

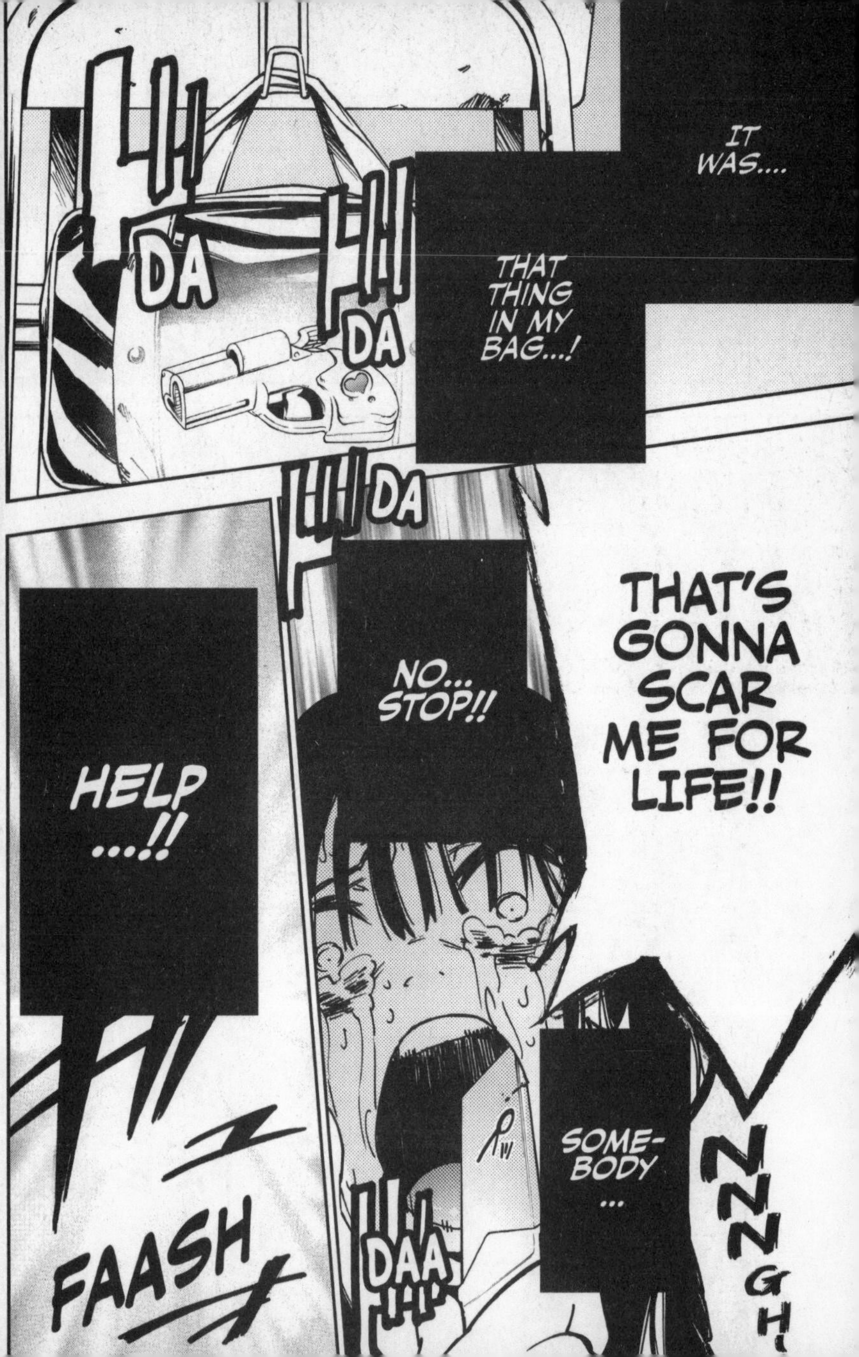
IT WAS....
THAT THING IN MY BAG...!
DA
DA
DA
THAT'S GONNA SCAR ME FOR LIFE!!
NO... STOP!!
HELP ....!!
SOMEBODY ...
NNNGH!
DAA
FAASH

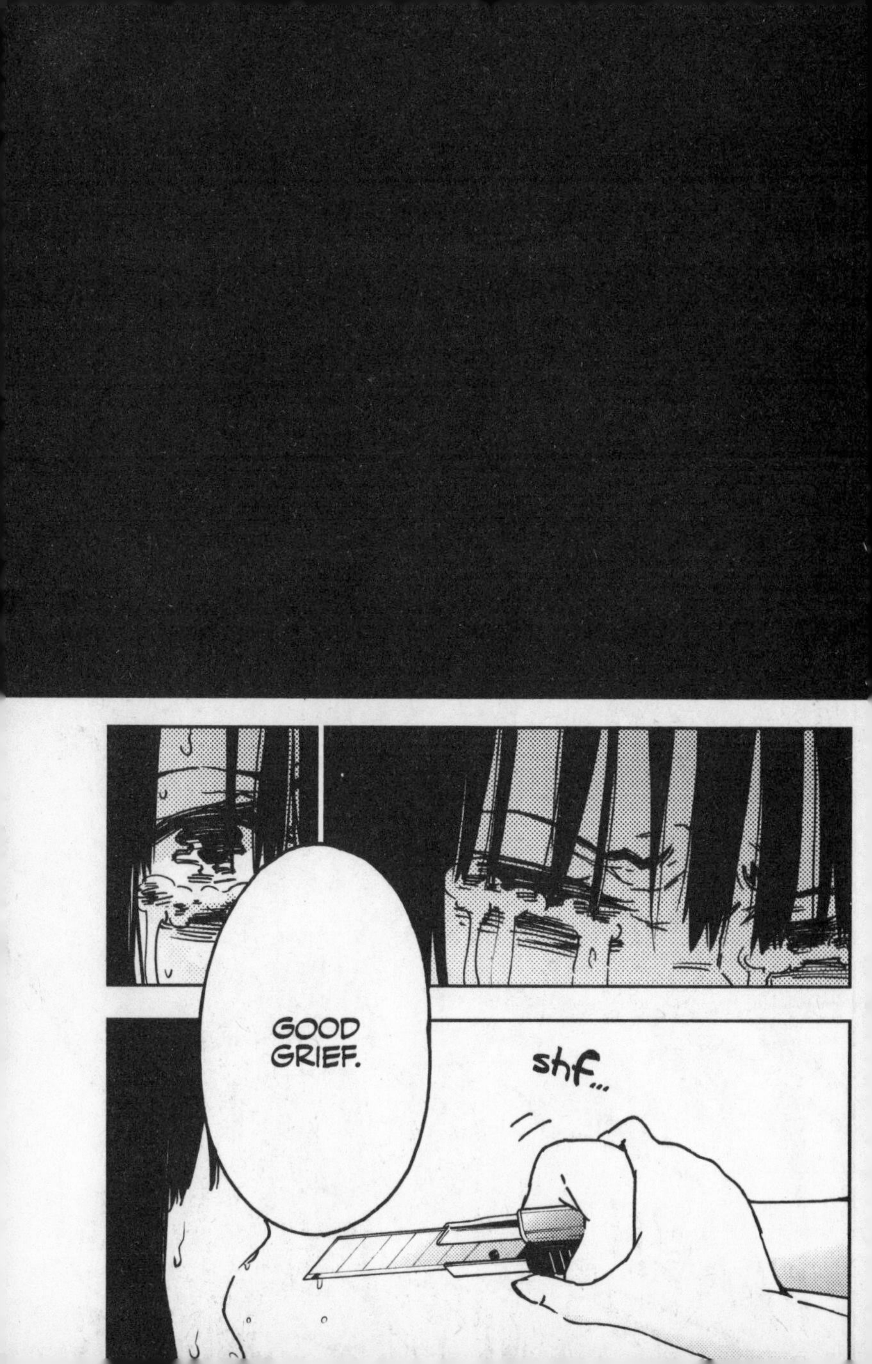
GOOD GRIEF.
shf...

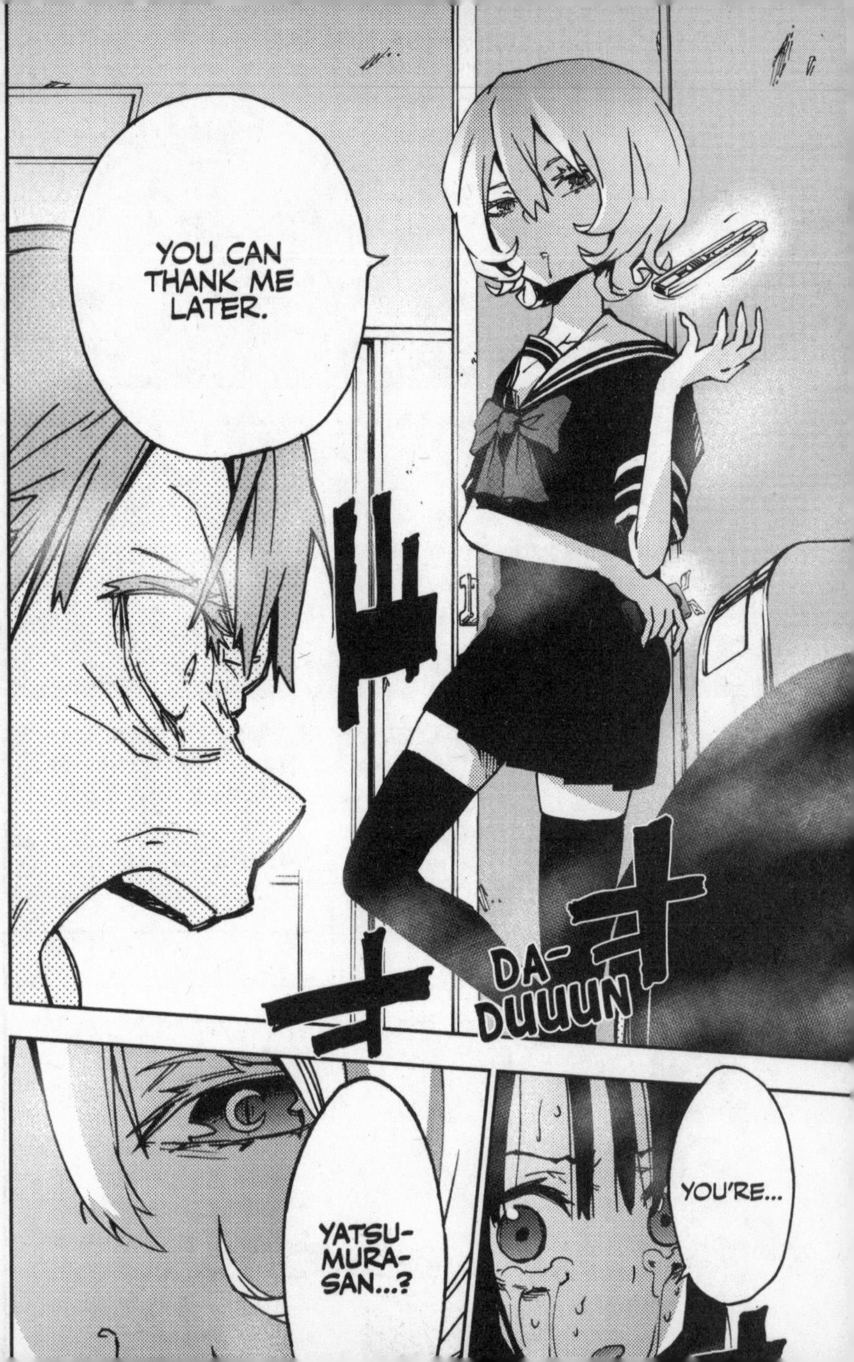
YOU CAN THANK ME LATER.
DA-DUUUN
YOU'RE...
YATSU-MURA-SAN...?

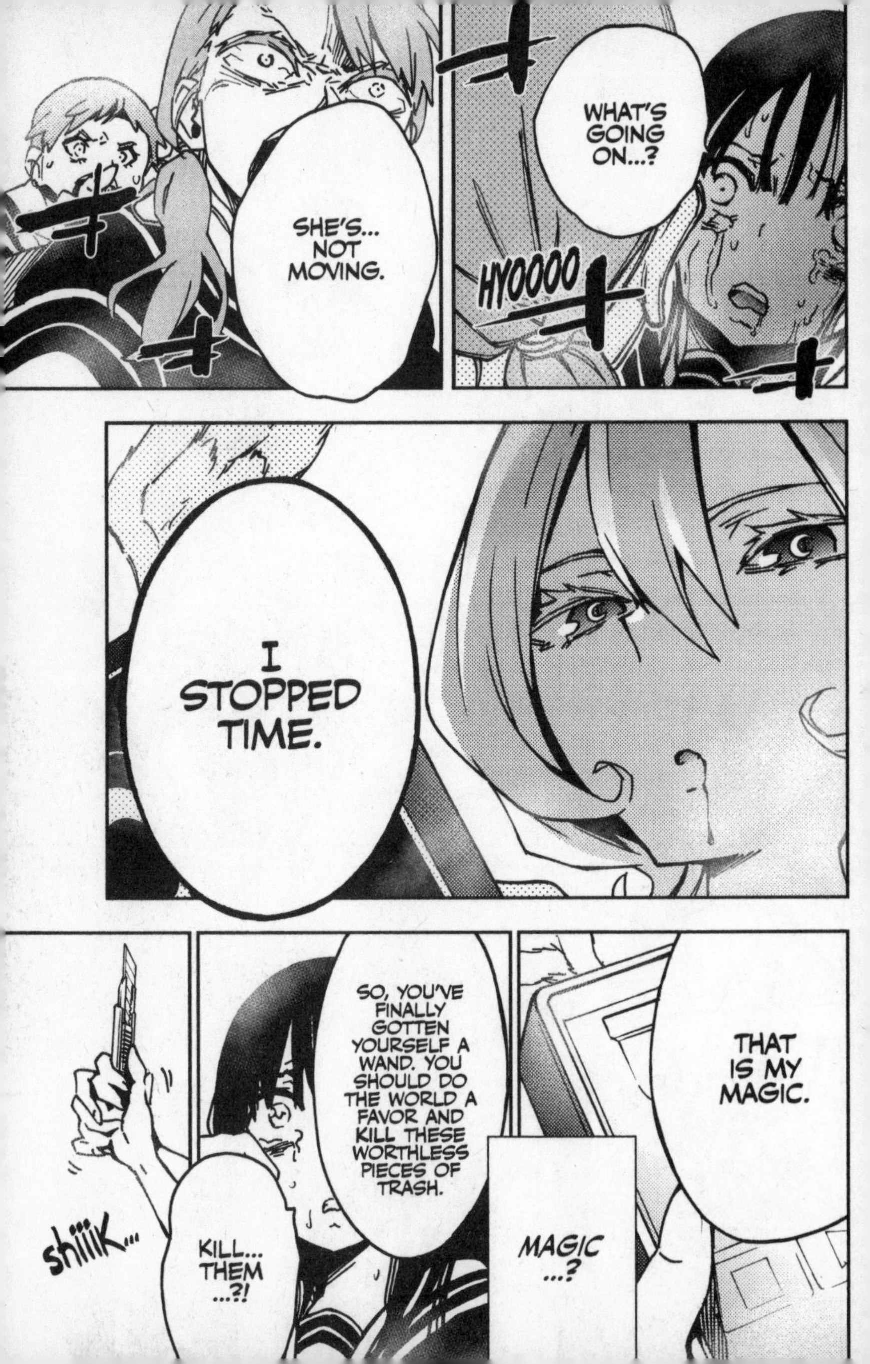
WHAT'S GOING ON...?
HYOOOO
SHE'S... NOT MOVING.
I STOPPED TIME.
THAT IS MY MAGIC.
MAGIC ...?
SO, YOU'VE FINALLY GOTTEN YOURSELF A WAND. YOU SHOULD DO THE WORLD A FAVOR AND KILL THESE WORTHLESS PIECES OF TRASH.
KILL... THEM ...?!
shiiik...

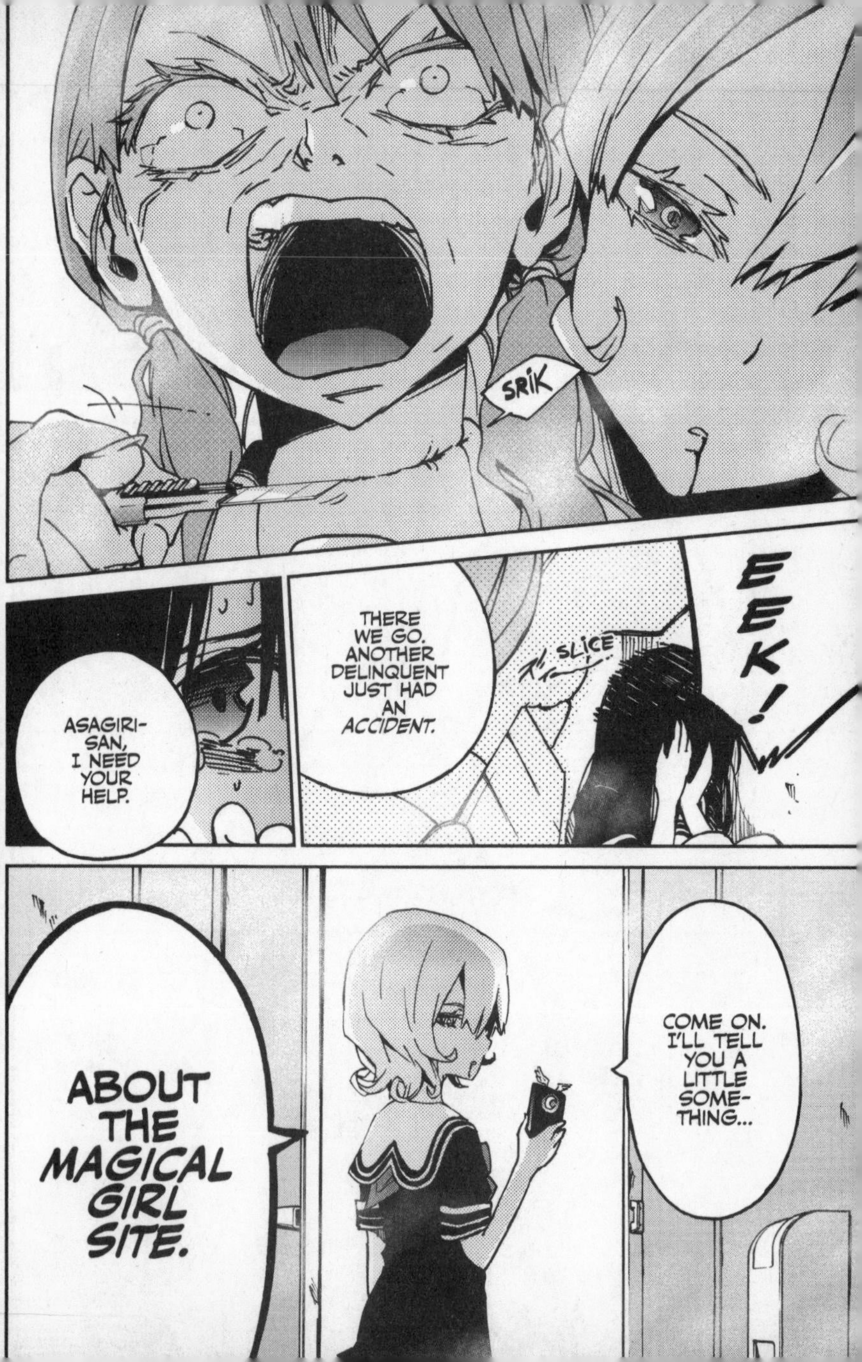
SRIK
EEK!
SLICE
THERE WE GO. ANOTHER DELINQUENT JUST HAD AN *ACCIDENT*.
ASAGIRI-SAN, I NEED YOUR HELP.
COME ON. I'LL TELL YOU A LITTLE SOME-THING...
ABOUT THE *MAGICAL GIRL SITE*.

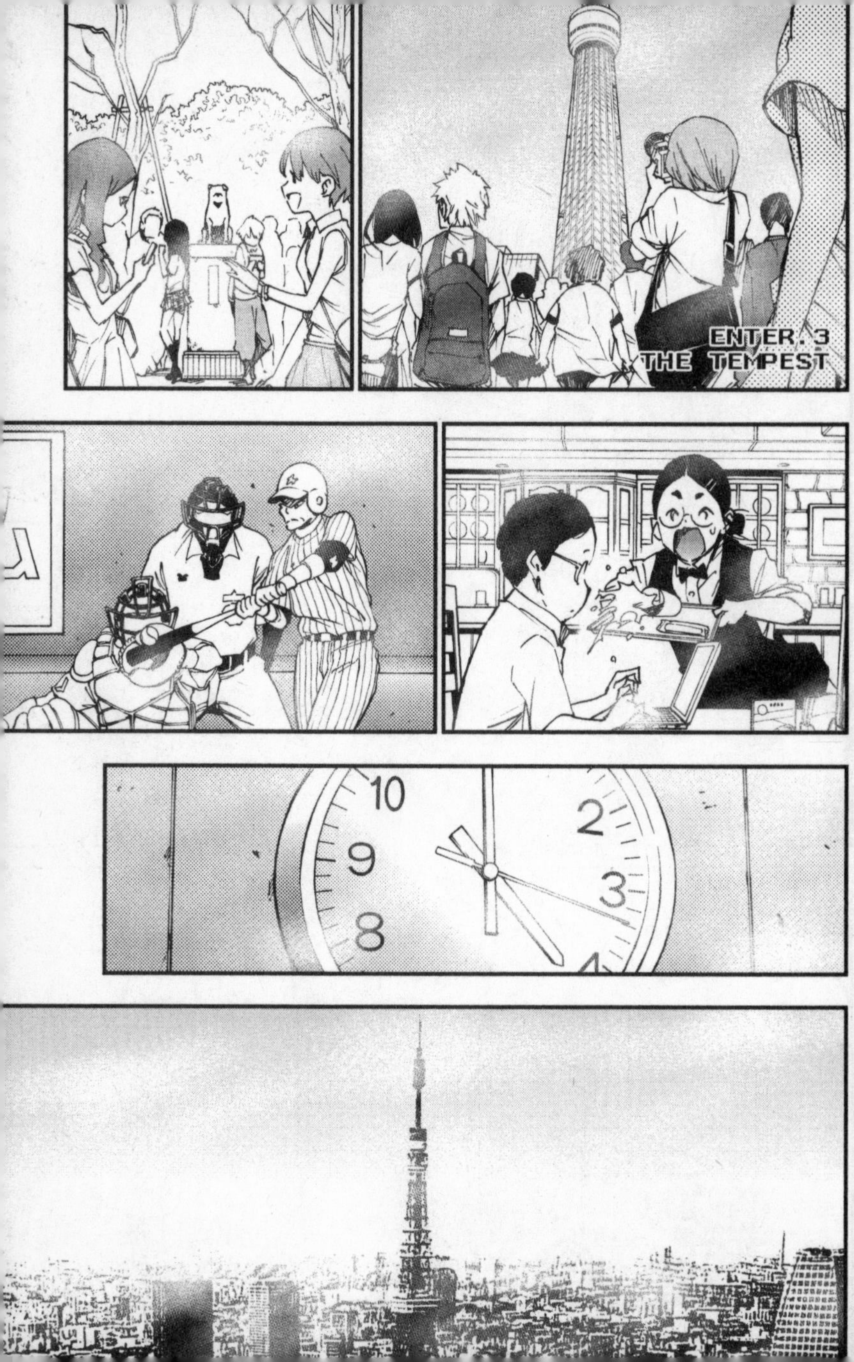
ENTER. 3
THE TEMPEST

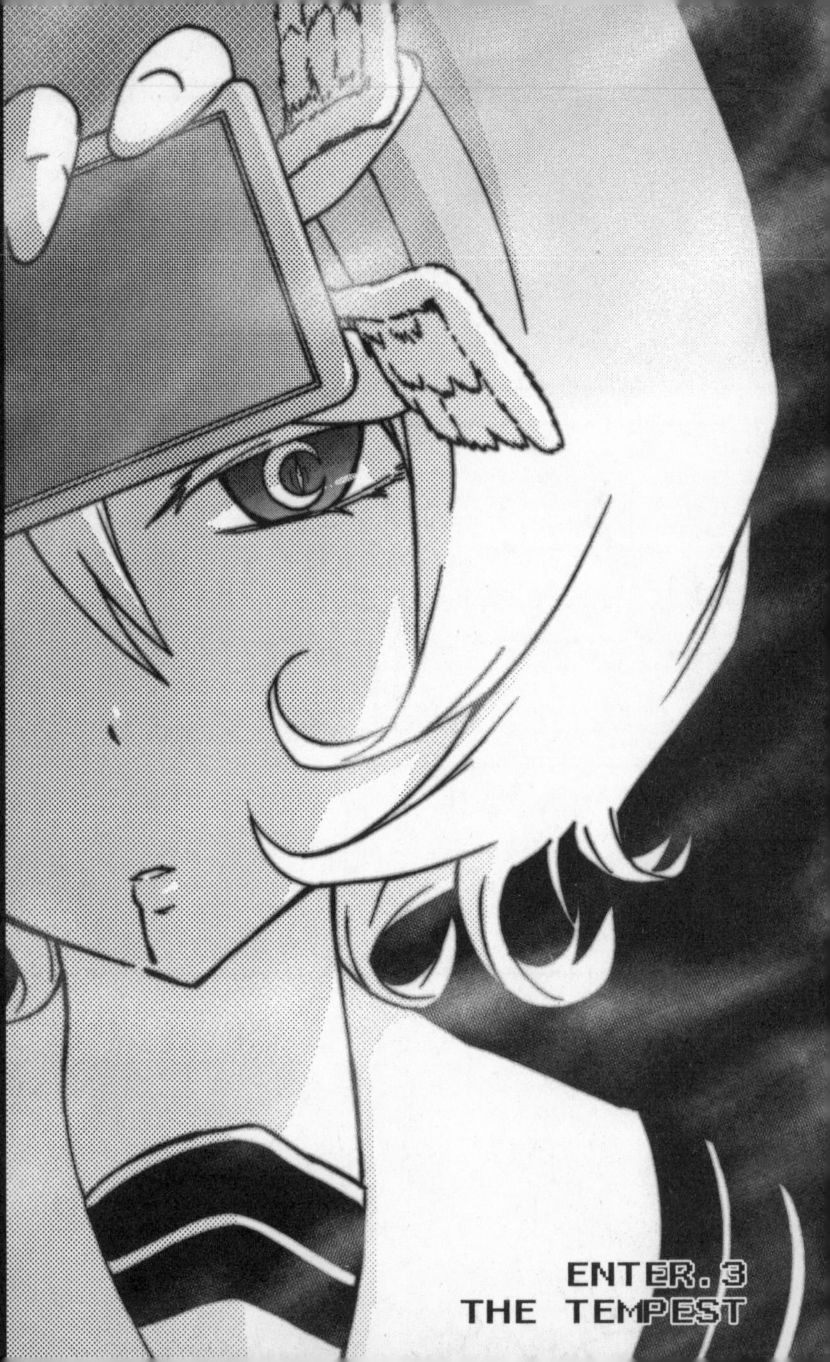
ENTER. 3
THE TEMPEST

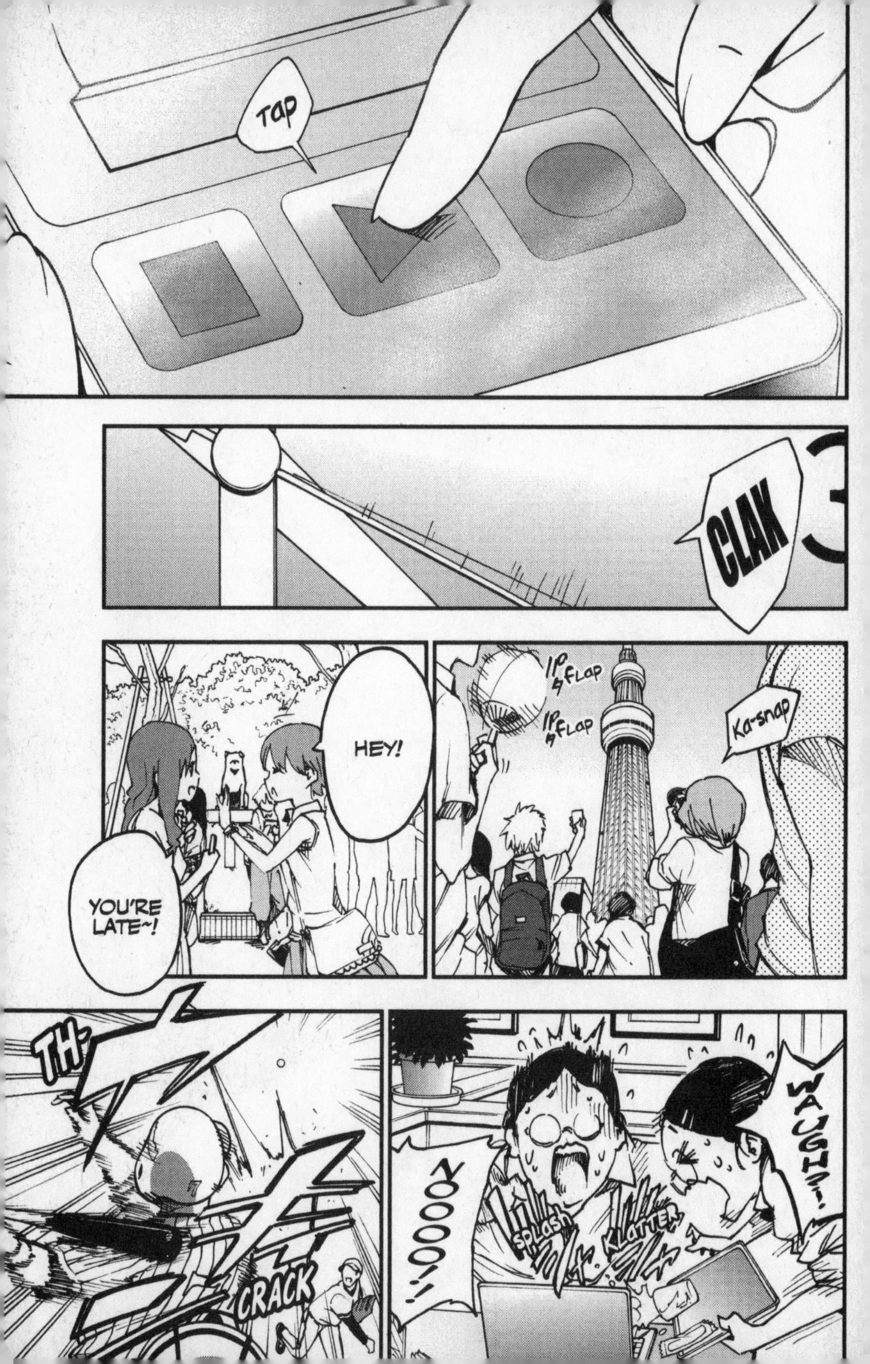
Tap
CLAK
Flap
Flap
Ka-snap
HEY!
YOU'RE LATE~!
WAUGH!!
NOOOOO!!
splash
KLATTER
TH-
CRACK

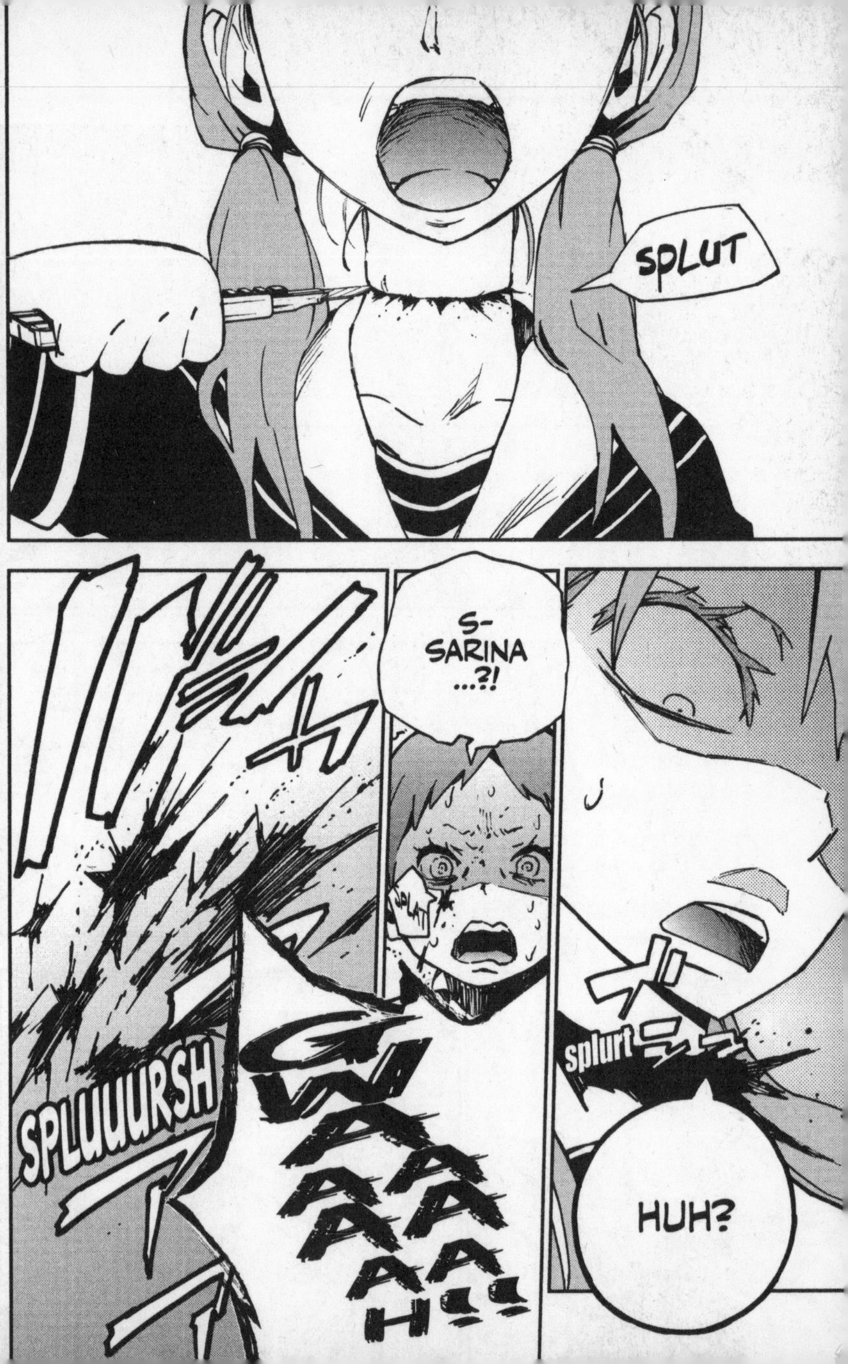
SPLUT
splurt
HUH?
S-SARINA...?!
SPLAT
SPLUUURSH
GWAAAAAAAH!!

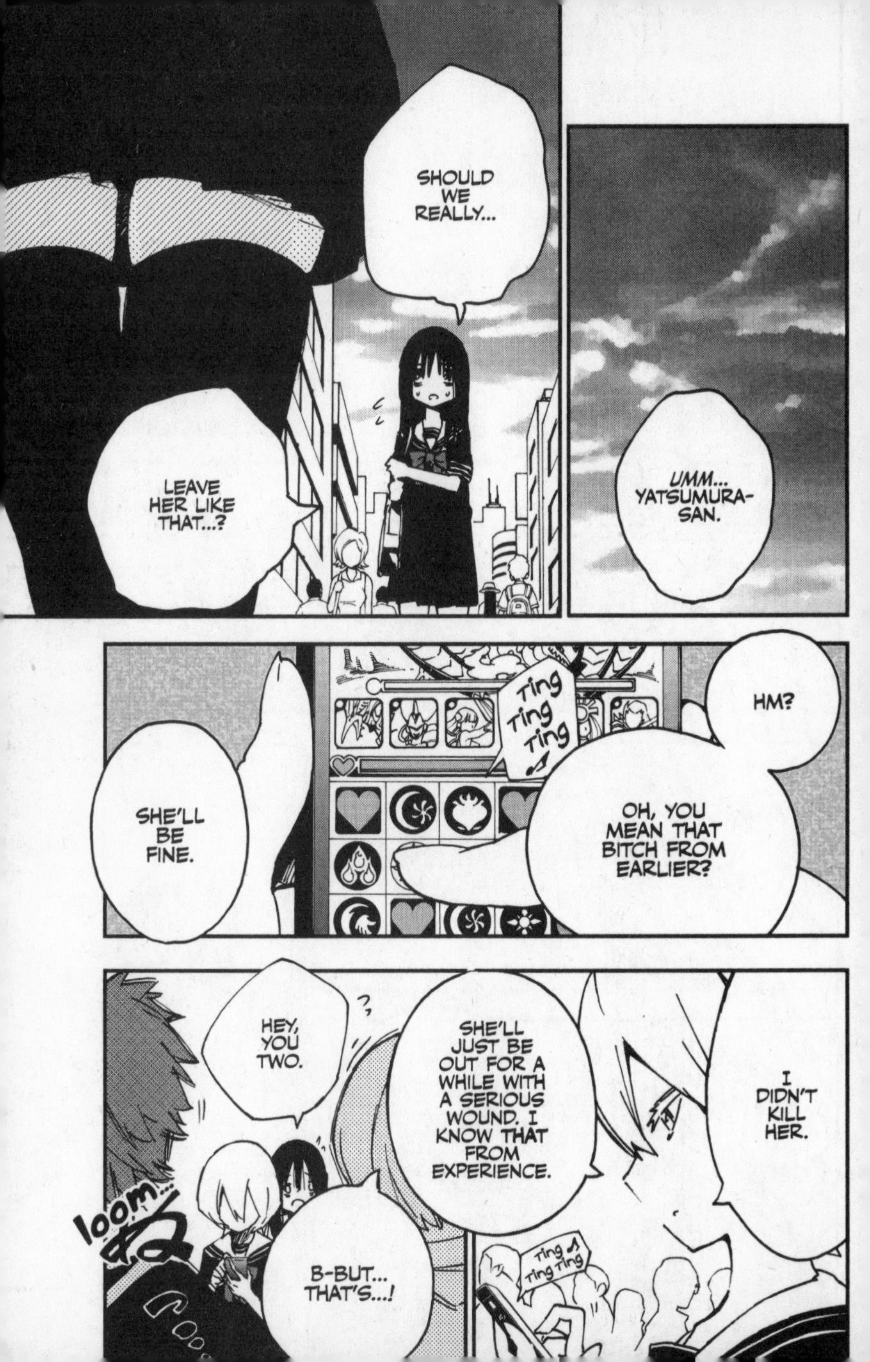
UMM... YATSUMURA-SAN.
SHOULD WE REALLY...
LEAVE HER LIKE THAT...?
HM?
Ting Ting Ting
OH, YOU MEAN THAT BITCH FROM EARLIER?
SHE'LL BE FINE.
I DIDN'T KILL HER.
SHE'LL JUST BE OUT FOR A WHILE WITH A SERIOUS WOUND. I KNOW THAT FROM EXPERIENCE.
HEY, YOU TWO.
Ting Ting Ting
B-BUT... THAT'S...!
loom...

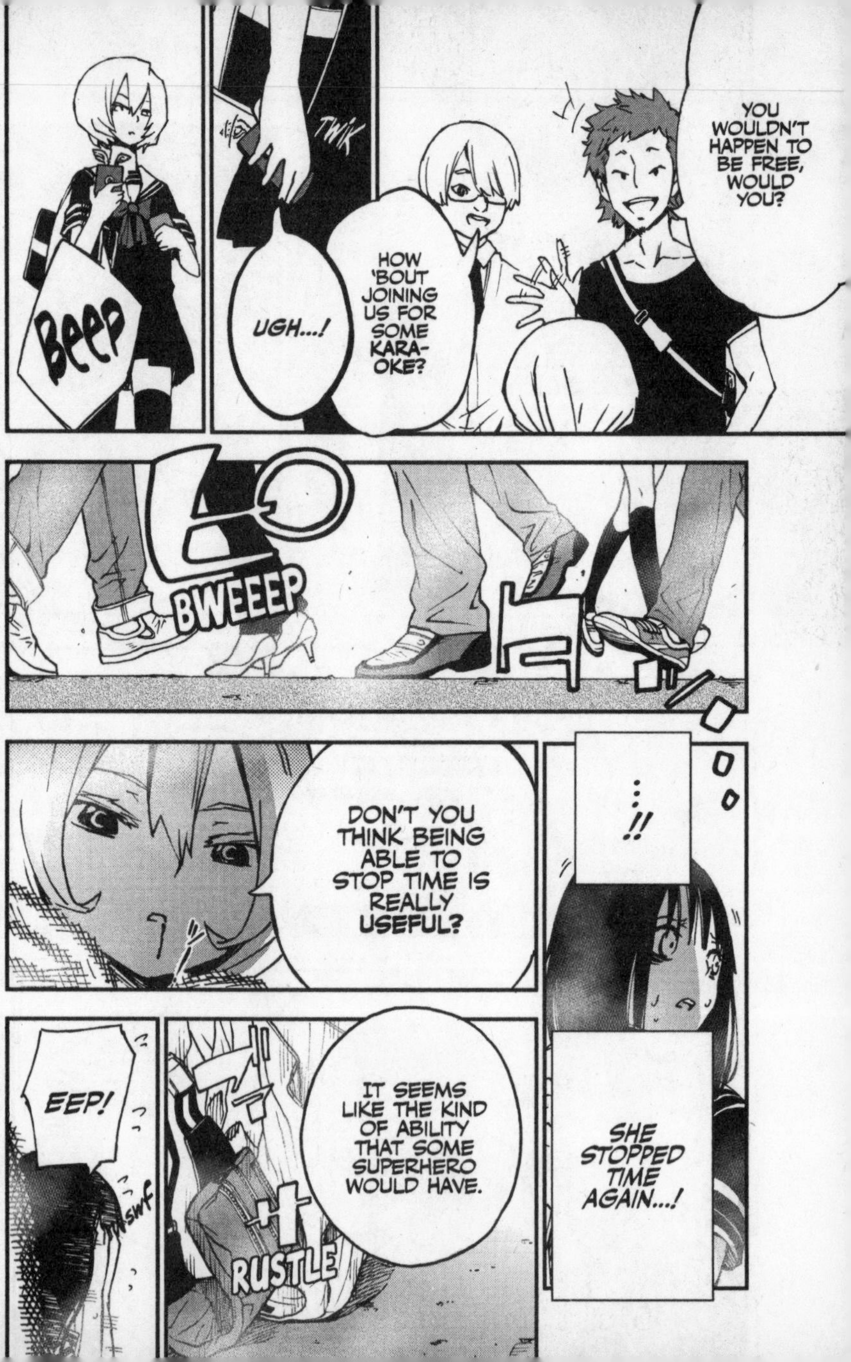
YOU WOULDN'T HAPPEN TO BE FREE, WOULD YOU?
HOW 'BOUT JOINING US FOR SOME KARAOKE?
TWIK
UGH...!
Beep
BWEEEP
...!!
SHE STOPPED TIME AGAIN...!
DON'T YOU THINK BEING ABLE TO STOP TIME IS REALLY USEFUL?
IT SEEMS LIKE THE KIND OF ABILITY THAT SOME SUPERHERO WOULD HAVE.
RUSTLE
EEP!
swf

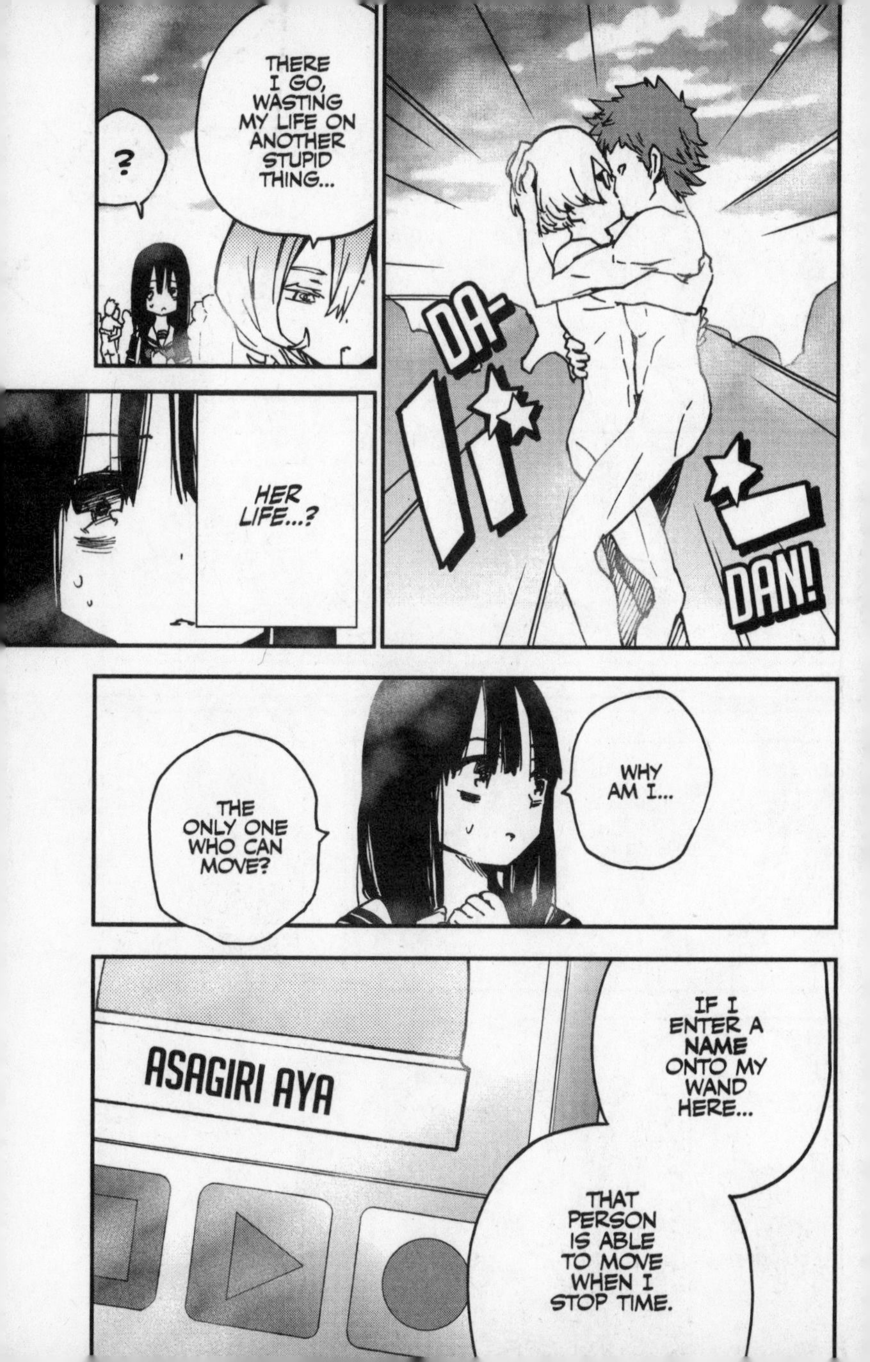
DA-
DAN!
THERE I GO, WASTING MY LIFE ON ANOTHER STUPID THING...
?
HER LIFE...?
WHY AM I...
THE ONLY ONE WHO CAN MOVE?
IF I ENTER A NAME ONTO MY WAND HERE...
ASAGIRI AYA
THAT PERSON IS ABLE TO MOVE WHEN I STOP TIME.

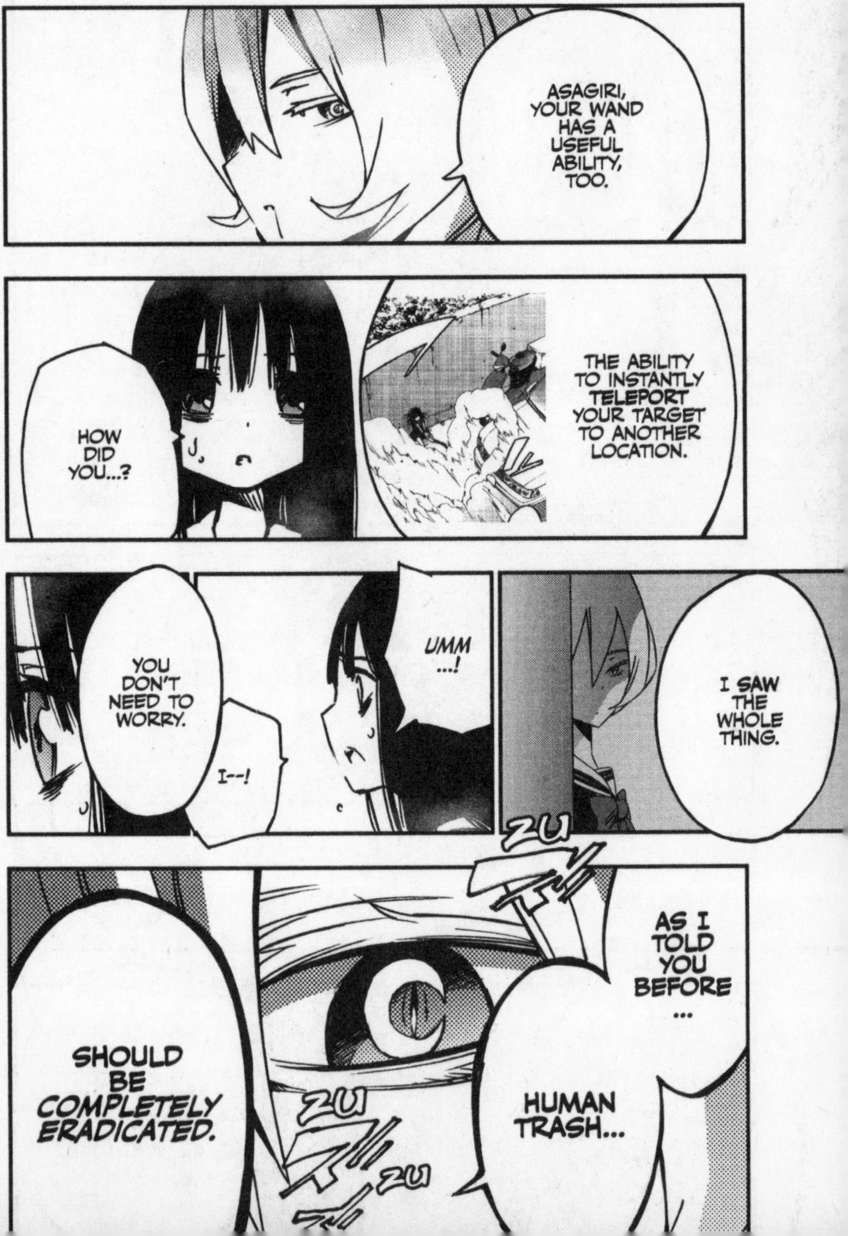
ASAGIRI, YOUR WAND HAS A USEFUL ABILITY, TOO.
THE ABILITY TO INSTANTLY TELEPORT YOUR TARGET TO ANOTHER LOCATION.
HOW DID YOU...?
I SAW THE WHOLE THING.
UMM ...!
I--!
YOU DON'T NEED TO WORRY.
ZU
AS I TOLD YOU BEFORE ...
HUMAN TRASH...
SHOULD BE COMPLETELY ERADICATED.
ZU
ZU

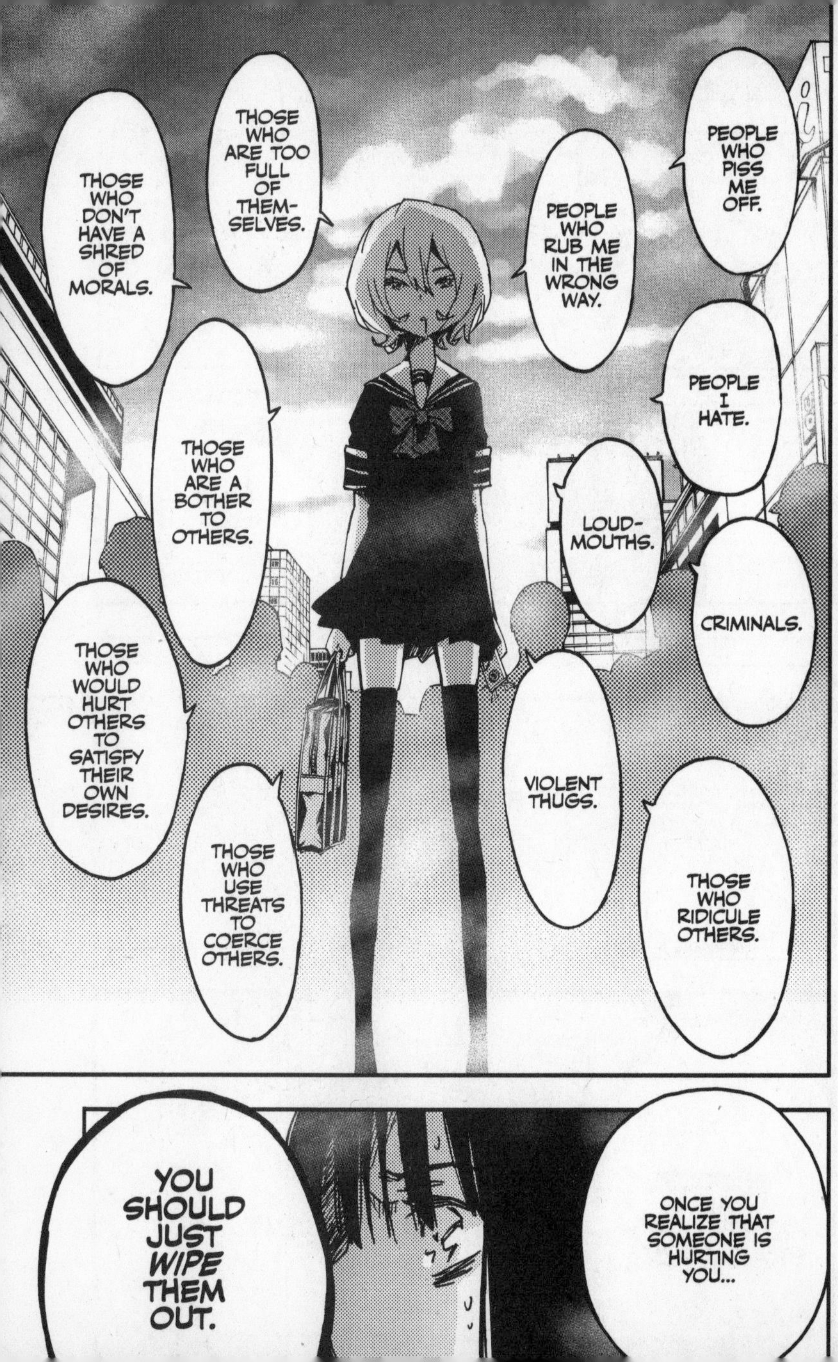
PEOPLE WHO PISS ME OFF.
PEOPLE WHO RUB ME IN THE WRONG WAY.
THOSE WHO ARE TOO FULL OF THEM-SELVES.
THOSE WHO DON'T HAVE A SHRED OF MORALS.
PEOPLE I HATE.
LOUD-MOUTHS.
THOSE WHO ARE A BOTHER TO OTHERS.
CRIMINALS.
VIOLENT THUGS.
THOSE WHO WOULD HURT OTHERS TO SATISFY THEIR OWN DESIRES.
THOSE WHO RIDICULE OTHERS.
THOSE WHO USE THREATS TO COERCE OTHERS.
ONCE YOU REALIZE THAT SOMEONE IS HURTING YOU...
YOU SHOULD JUST *WIPE* THEM OUT.

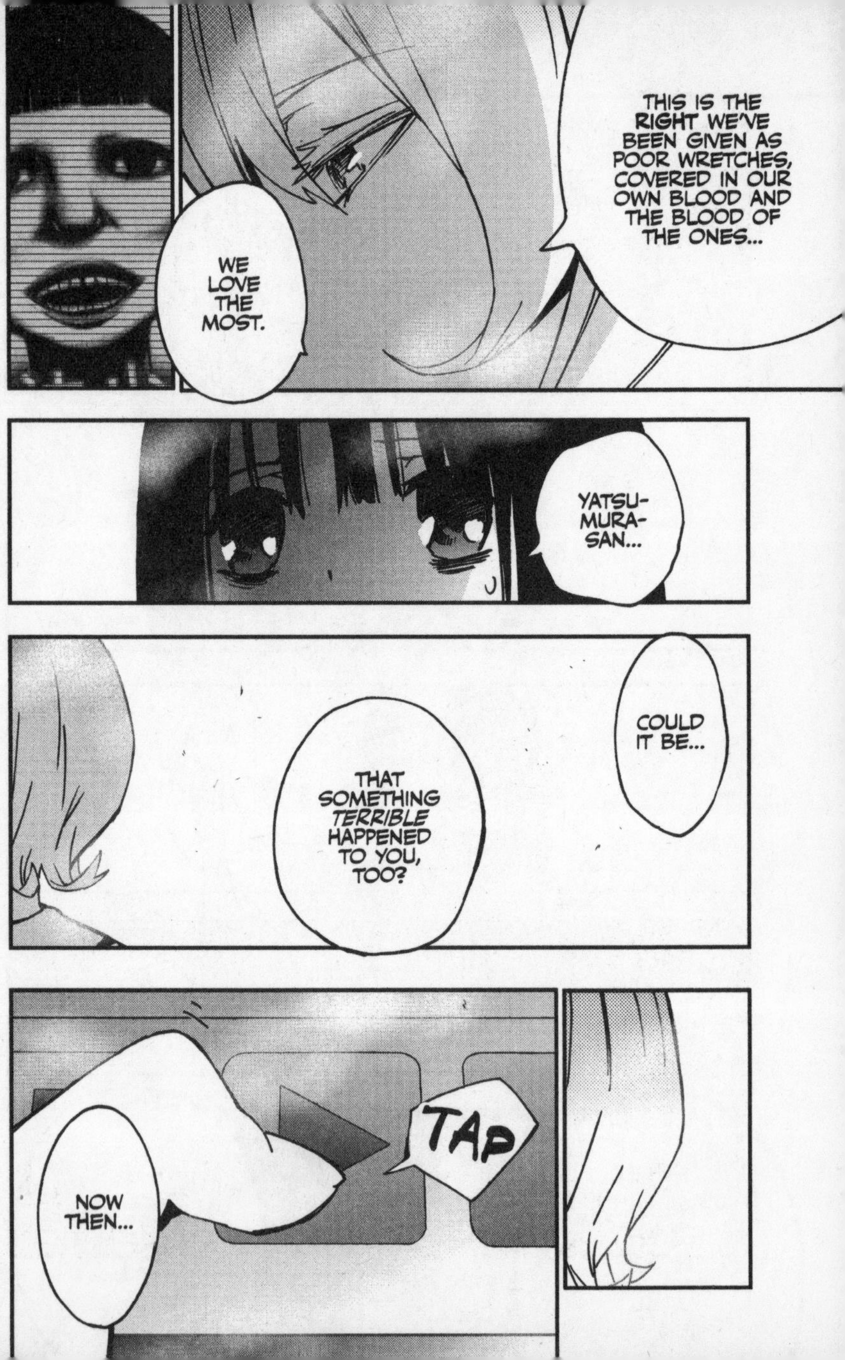
THIS IS THE RIGHT WE'VE BEEN GIVEN AS POOR WRETCHES, COVERED IN OUR OWN BLOOD AND THE BLOOD OF THE ONES...
WE LOVE THE MOST.
YATSU-MURA-SAN...
COULD IT BE...
THAT SOMETHING *TERRIBLE* HAPPENED TO YOU, TOO?
TAP
NOW THEN...

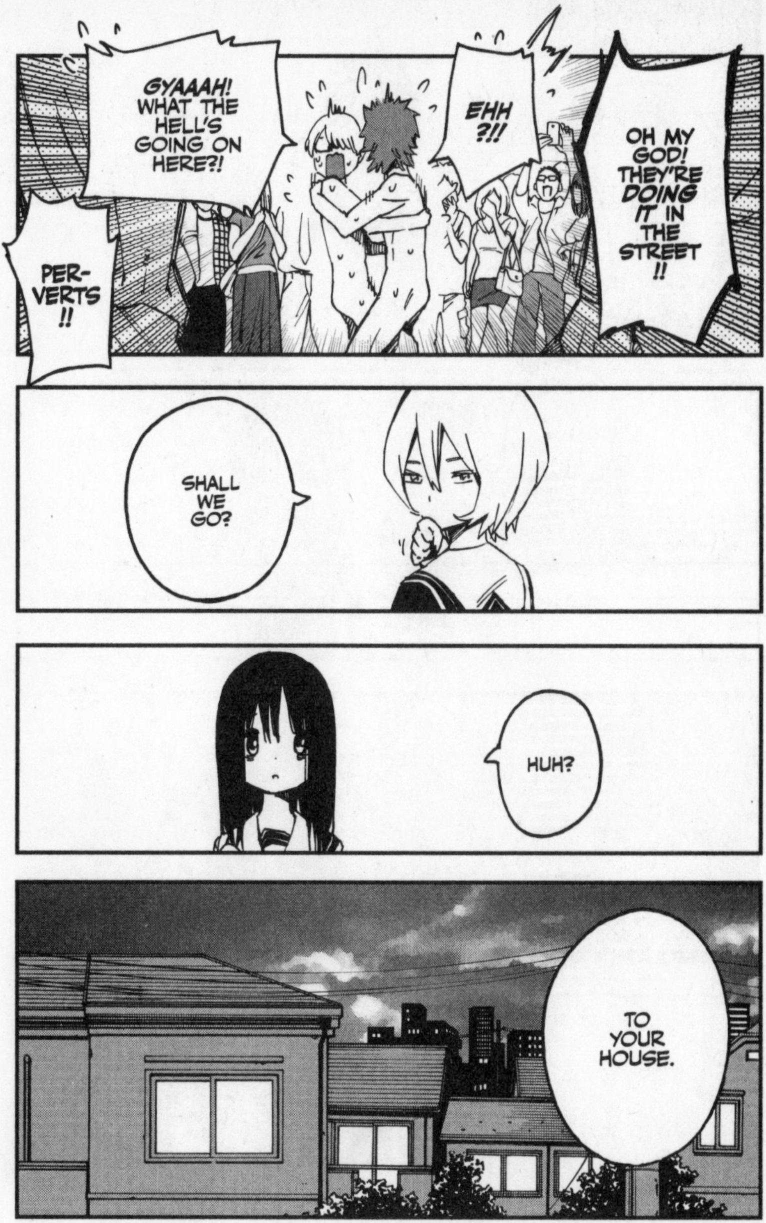
OH MY GOD! THEY'RE DOING IT IN THE STREET!!
EHH?!!
GYAAAH! WHAT THE HELL'S GOING ON HERE?!
PER-VERTS!!
SHALL WE GO?
HUH?
TO YOUR HOUSE.

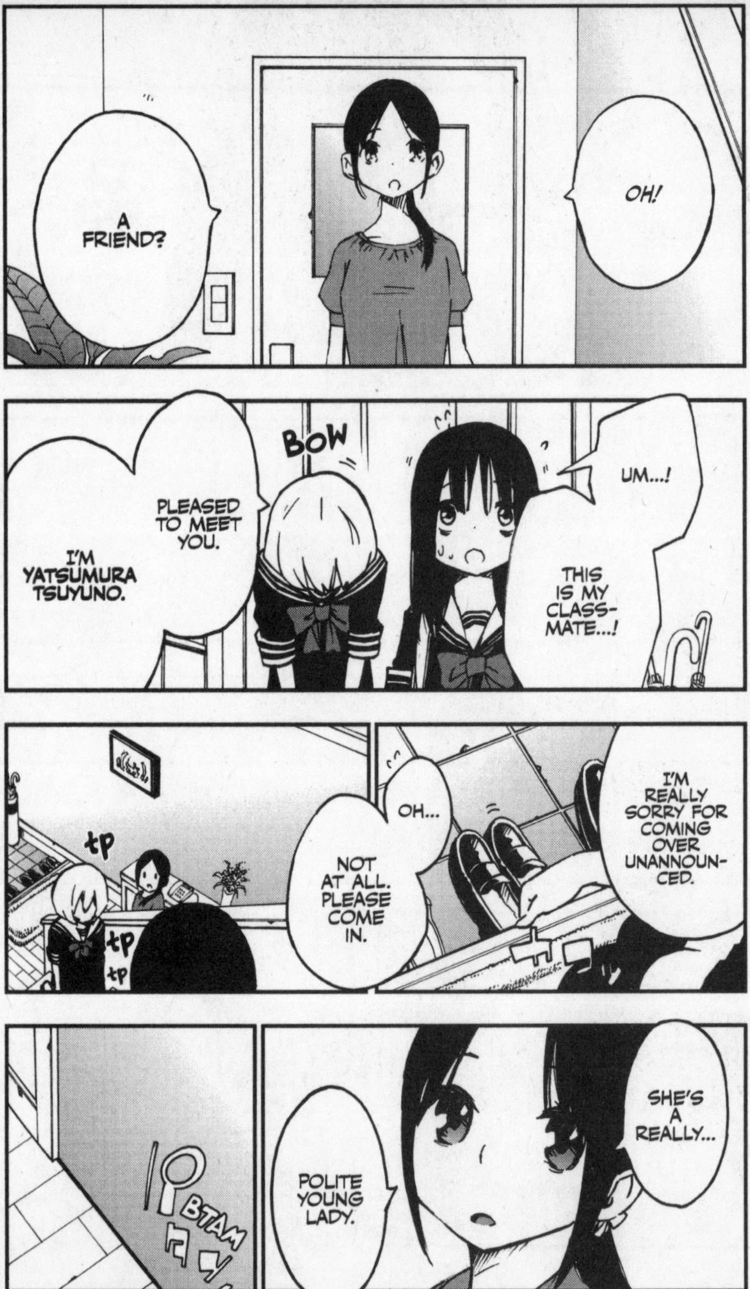
OH!
A FRIEND?
UM...!
THIS IS MY CLASS-MATE...!
BOW
PLEASED TO MEET YOU.
I'M YATSUMURA TSUYUNO.
I'M REALLY SORRY FOR COMING OVER UNANNOUN-CED.
OH...
NOT AT ALL. PLEASE COME IN.
tp
tp
tp
SHE'S A REALLY...
POLITE YOUNG LADY.
BTAM

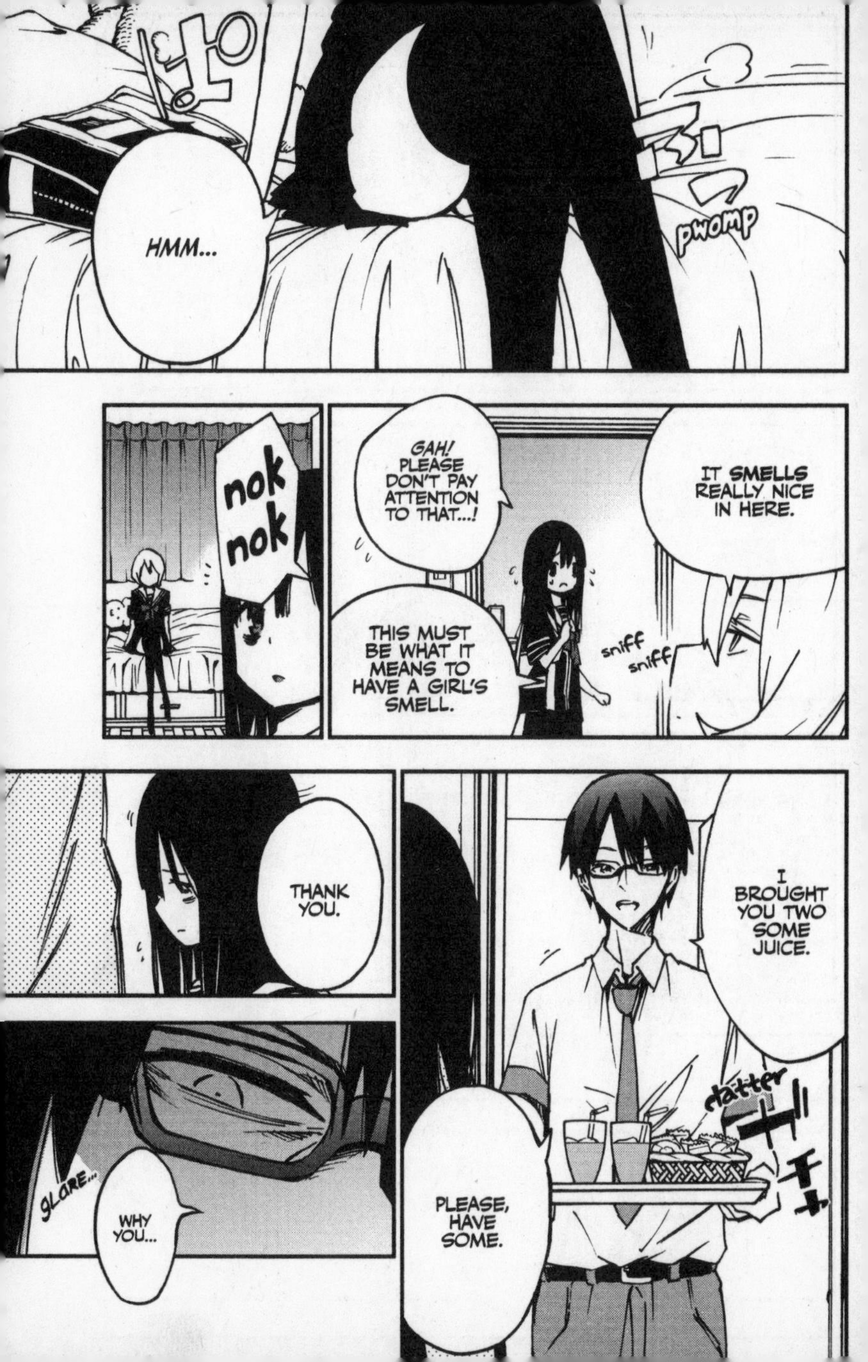
pwomp
HMM...
IT SMELLS REALLY NICE IN HERE.
GAH! PLEASE DON'T PAY ATTENTION TO THAT...!
sniff sniff
THIS MUST BE WHAT IT MEANS TO HAVE A GIRL'S SMELL.
nok nok
I BROUGHT YOU TWO SOME JUICE.
clatter
PLEASE, HAVE SOME.
THANK YOU.
GLARE...
WHY YOU...

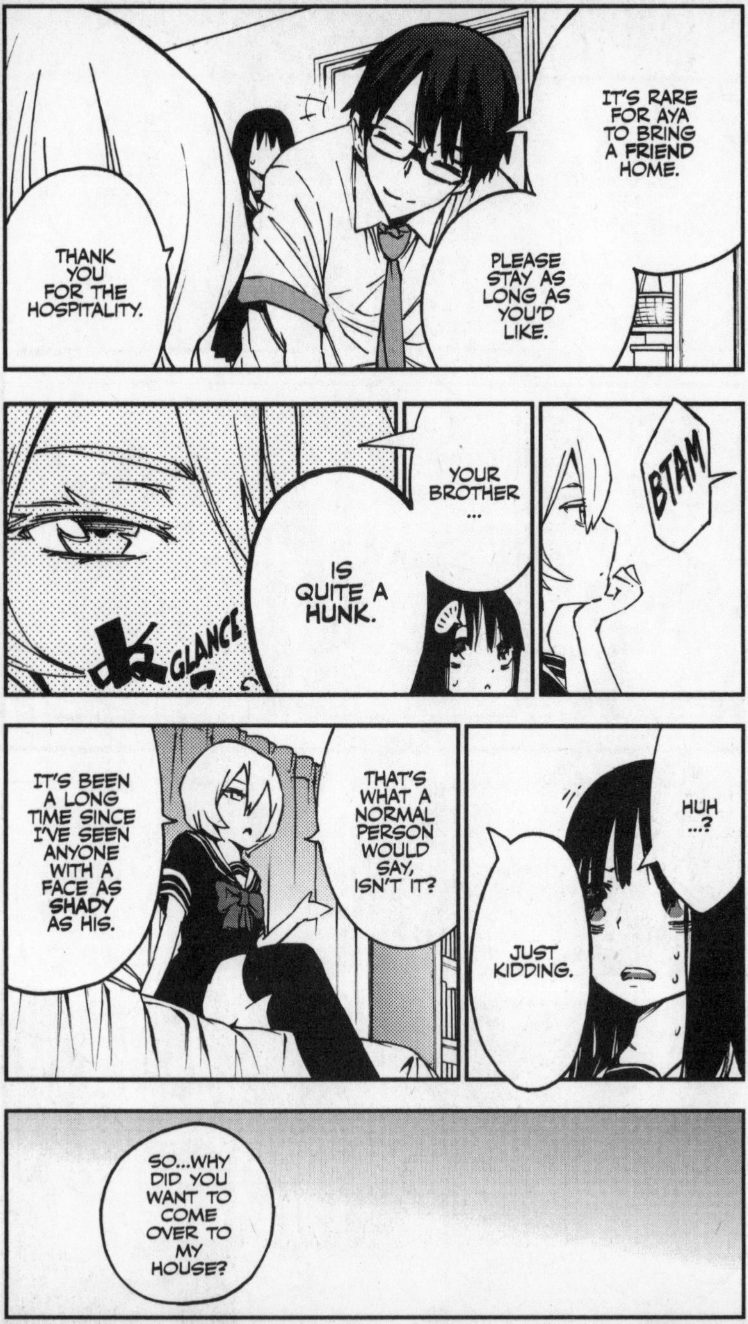
IT'S RARE FOR AYA TO BRING A FRIEND HOME.
PLEASE STAY AS LONG AS YOU'D LIKE.
THANK YOU FOR THE HOSPITALITY.
BTAM
YOUR BROTHER ...
IS QUITE A HUNK.
GLANCE
HUH ...?
JUST KIDDING.
THAT'S WHAT A NORMAL PERSON WOULD SAY, ISN'T IT?
IT'S BEEN A LONG TIME SINCE I'VE SEEN ANYONE WITH A FACE AS SHADY AS HIS.
SO...WHY DID YOU WANT TO COME OVER TO MY HOUSE?

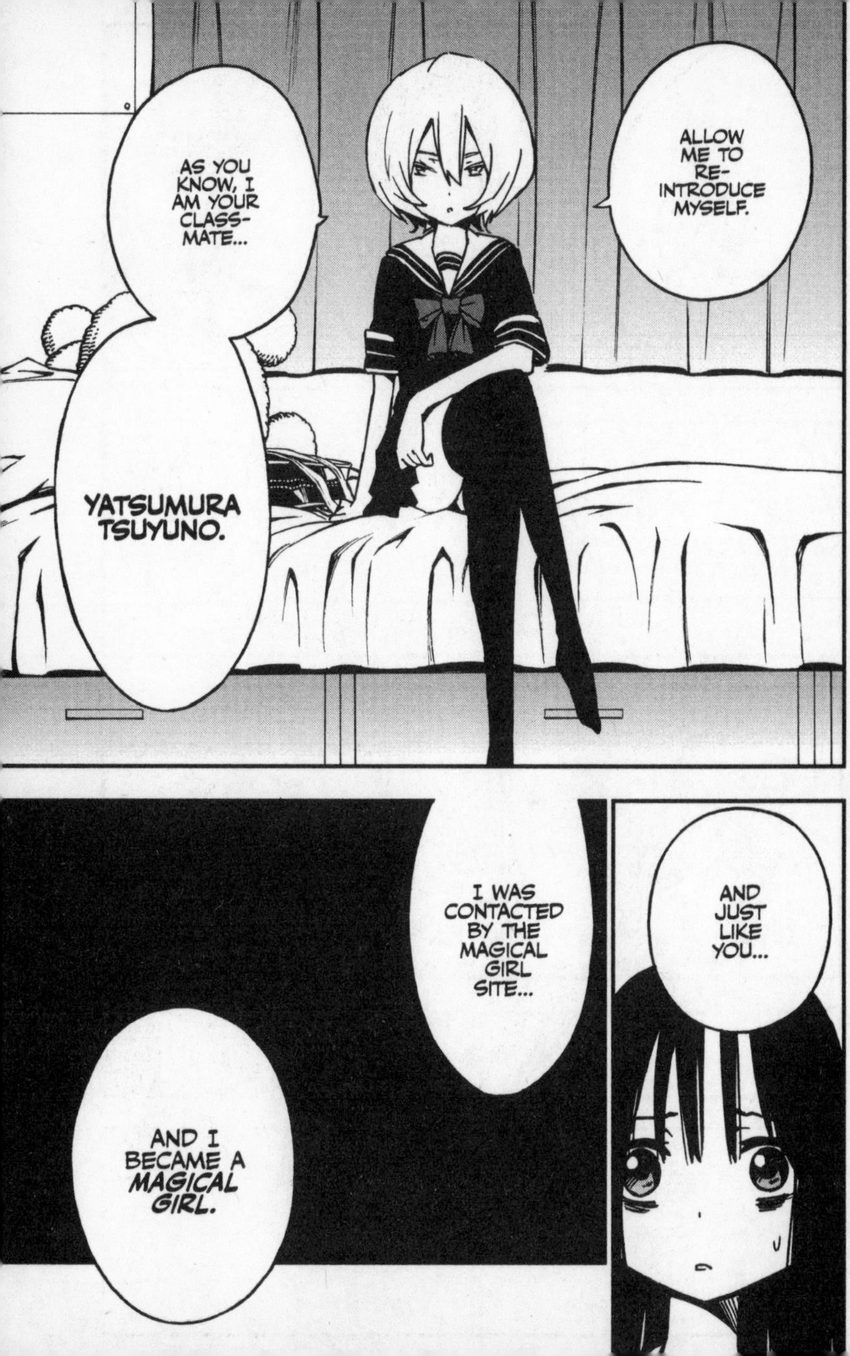
ALLOW ME TO RE-INTRODUCE MYSELF.
AS YOU KNOW, I AM YOUR CLASS-MATE...
YATSUMURA TSUYUNO.
AND JUST LIKE YOU...
I WAS CONTACTED BY THE MAGICAL GIRL SITE...
AND I BECAME A *MAGICAL GIRL*.

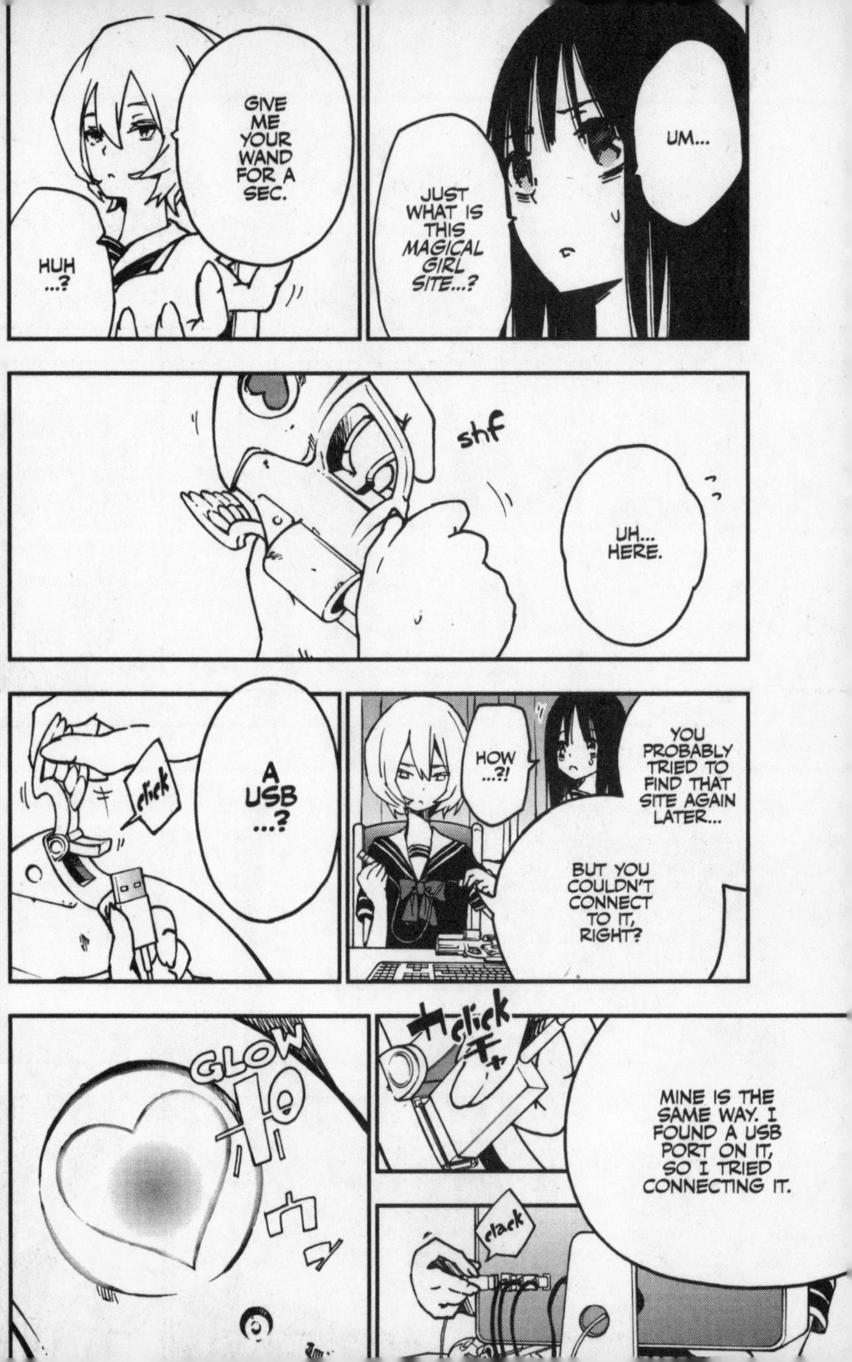
UM...
JUST WHAT IS THIS MAGICAL GIRL SITE...?
GIVE ME YOUR WAND FOR A SEC.
HUH ...?
shf
UH... HERE.
YOU PROBABLY TRIED TO FIND THAT SITE AGAIN LATER...
BUT YOU COULDN'T CONNECT TO IT, RIGHT?
HOW ...?!
A USB ...?
click
click
MINE IS THE SAME WAY. I FOUND A USB PORT ON IT, SO I TRIED CONNECTING IT.
clack
GLOW

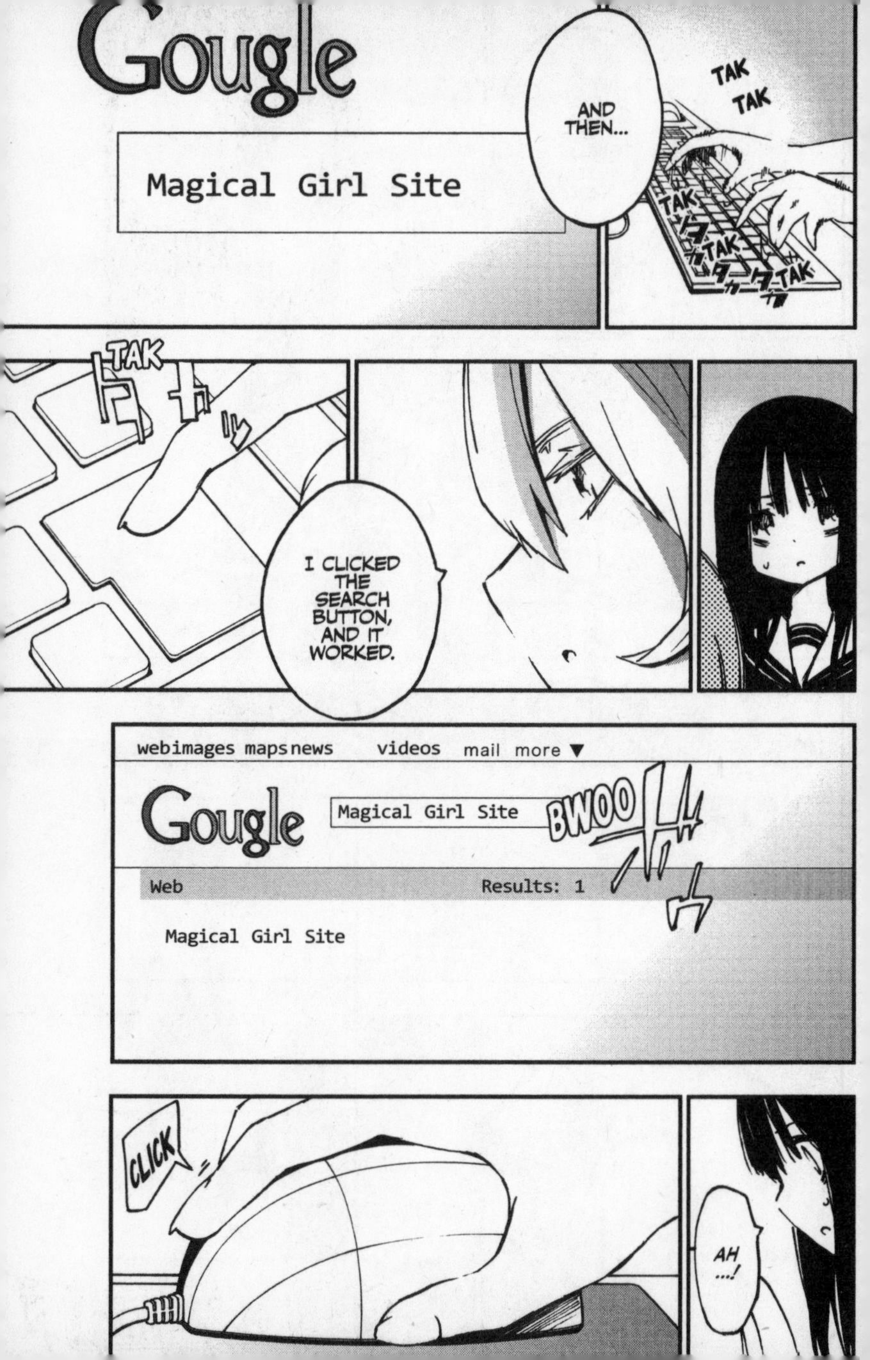
AND THEN...
TAK TAK
TAK TAK TAK
Gougle
Magical Girl Site
I CLICKED THE SEARCH BUTTON, AND IT WORKED.
TAK
webimages mapsnews videos mail more ▼
Gougle
Magical Girl Site
BWOOSH
Web
Results: 1
Magical Girl Site
AH ...!
CLICK

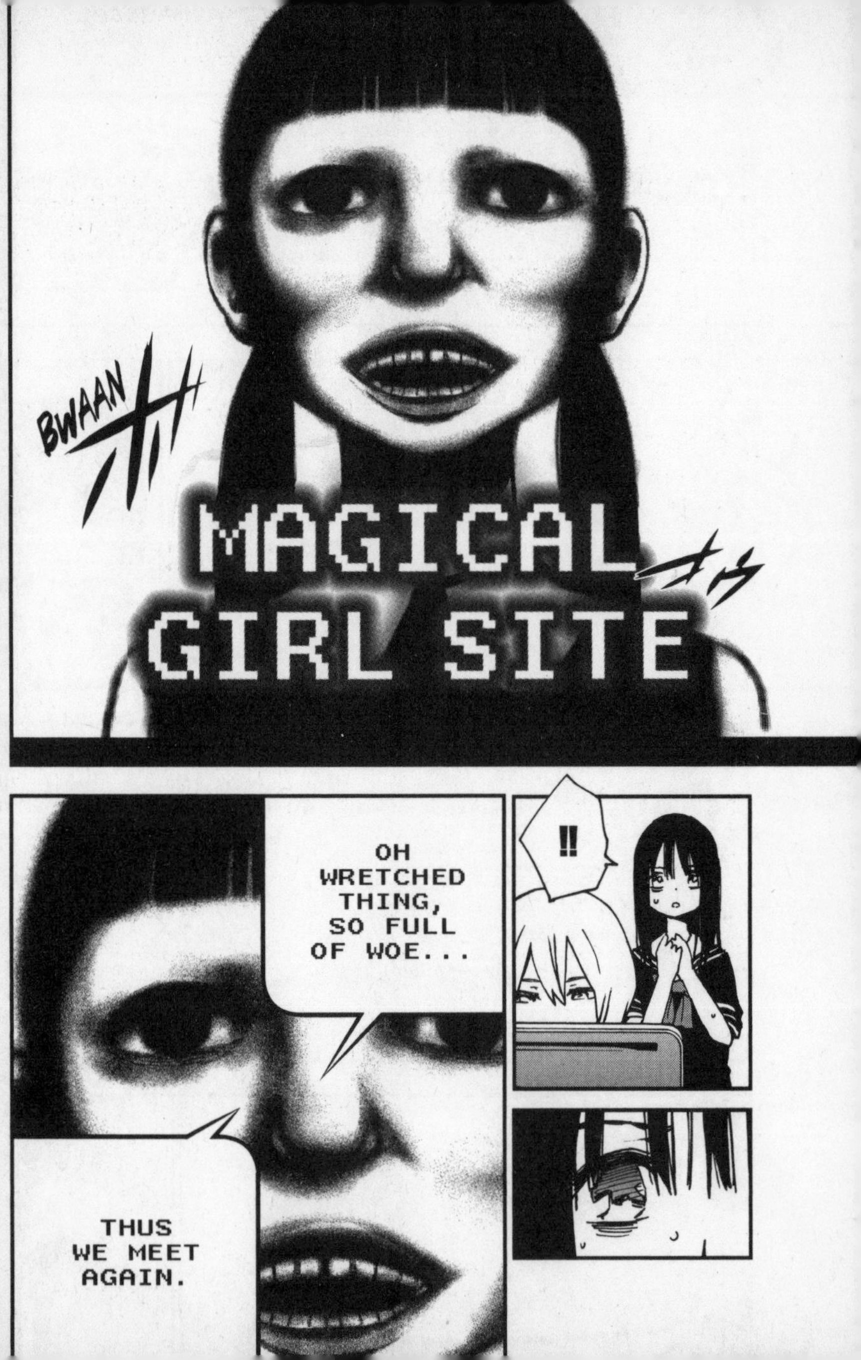
BWAAN
MAGICAL GIRL SITE
!!
OH WRETCHED THING, SO FULL OF WOE...
THUS WE MEET AGAIN.

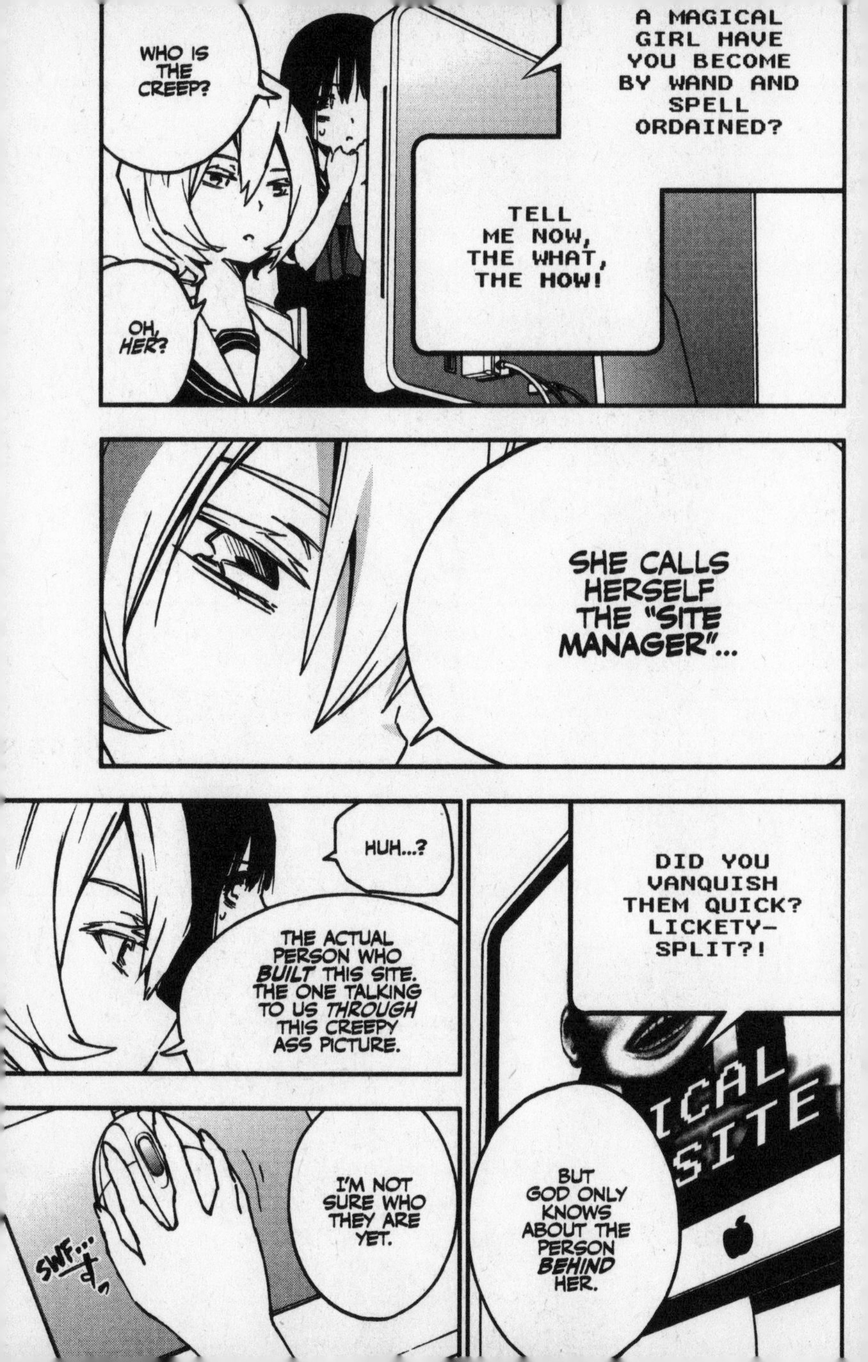
A MAGICAL GIRL HAVE YOU BECOME BY WAND AND SPELL ORDAINED?
TELL ME NOW, THE WHAT, THE HOW!
WHO IS THE CREEP?
OH, HER?
SHE CALLS HERSELF THE "SITE MANAGER"...
DID YOU VANQUISH THEM QUICK? LICKETY-SPLIT?!
ICAL SITE
BUT GOD ONLY KNOWS ABOUT THE PERSON *BEHIND* HER.
HUH...?
THE ACTUAL PERSON WHO *BUILT* THIS SITE. THE ONE TALKING TO US *THROUGH* THIS CREEPY ASS PICTURE.
I'M NOT SURE WHO THEY ARE YET.
SWF... す

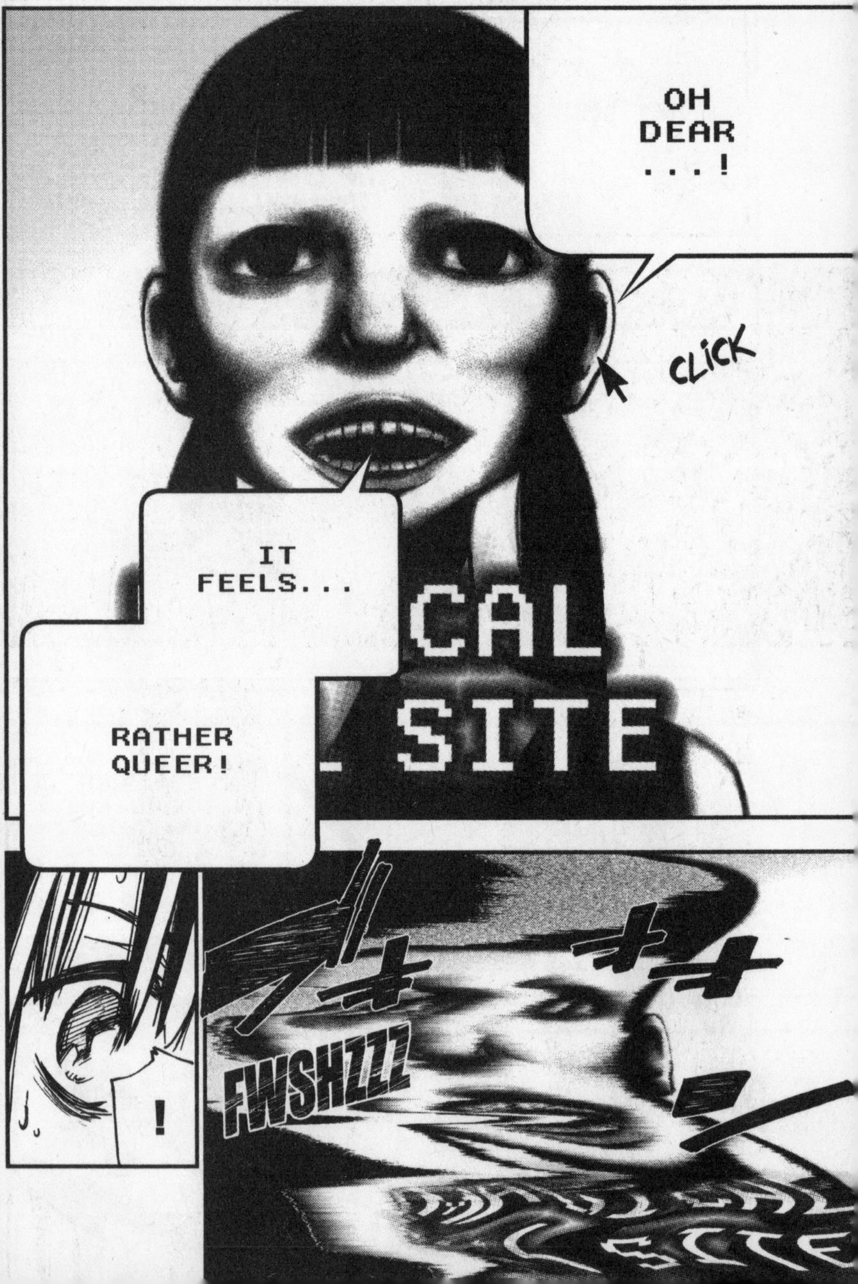
OH DEAR ...!
CLICK
IT FEELS...
RATHER QUEER!
CAL
SITE
FWSHZZZ
!

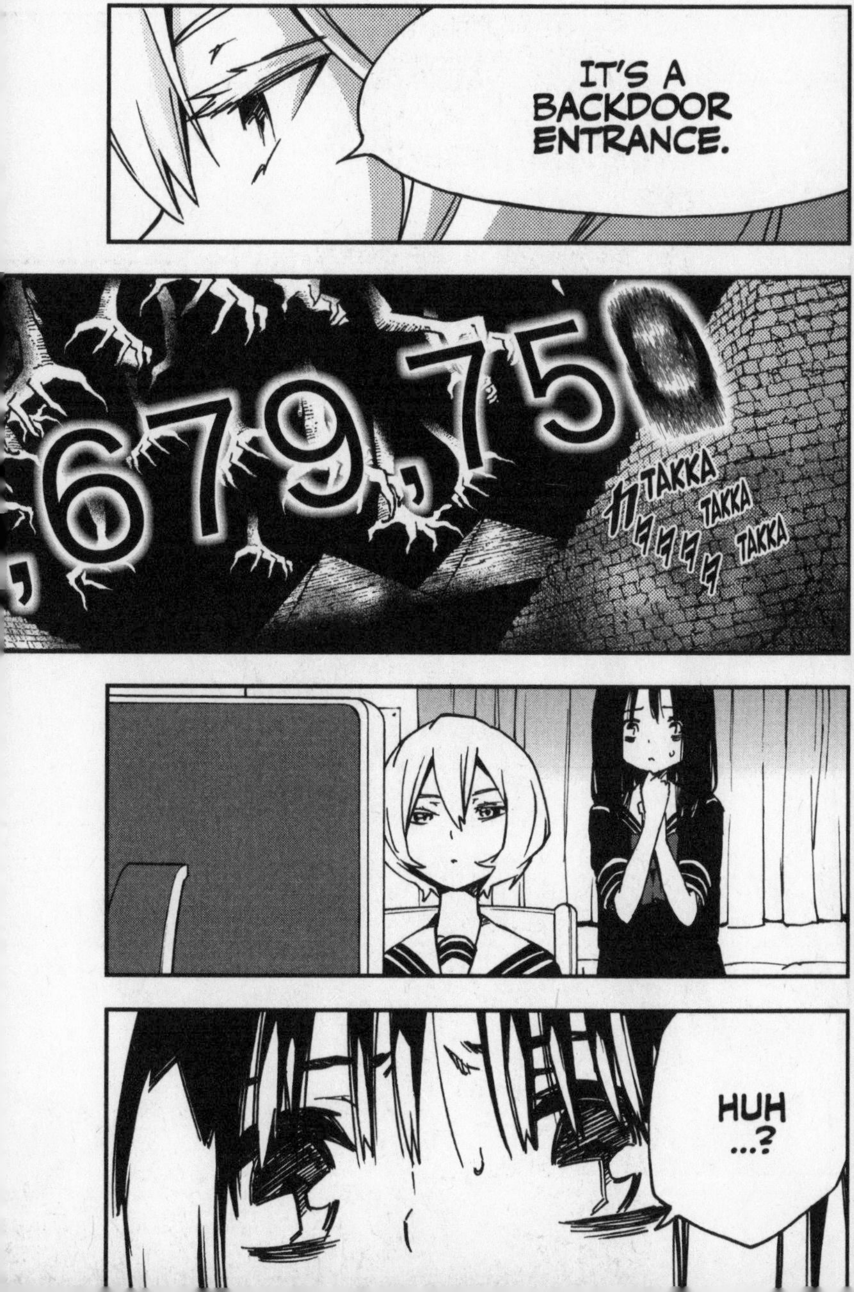
IT'S A BACKDOOR ENTRANCE.
,679,750
TAKKA
TAKKA
TAKKA
HUH ...?

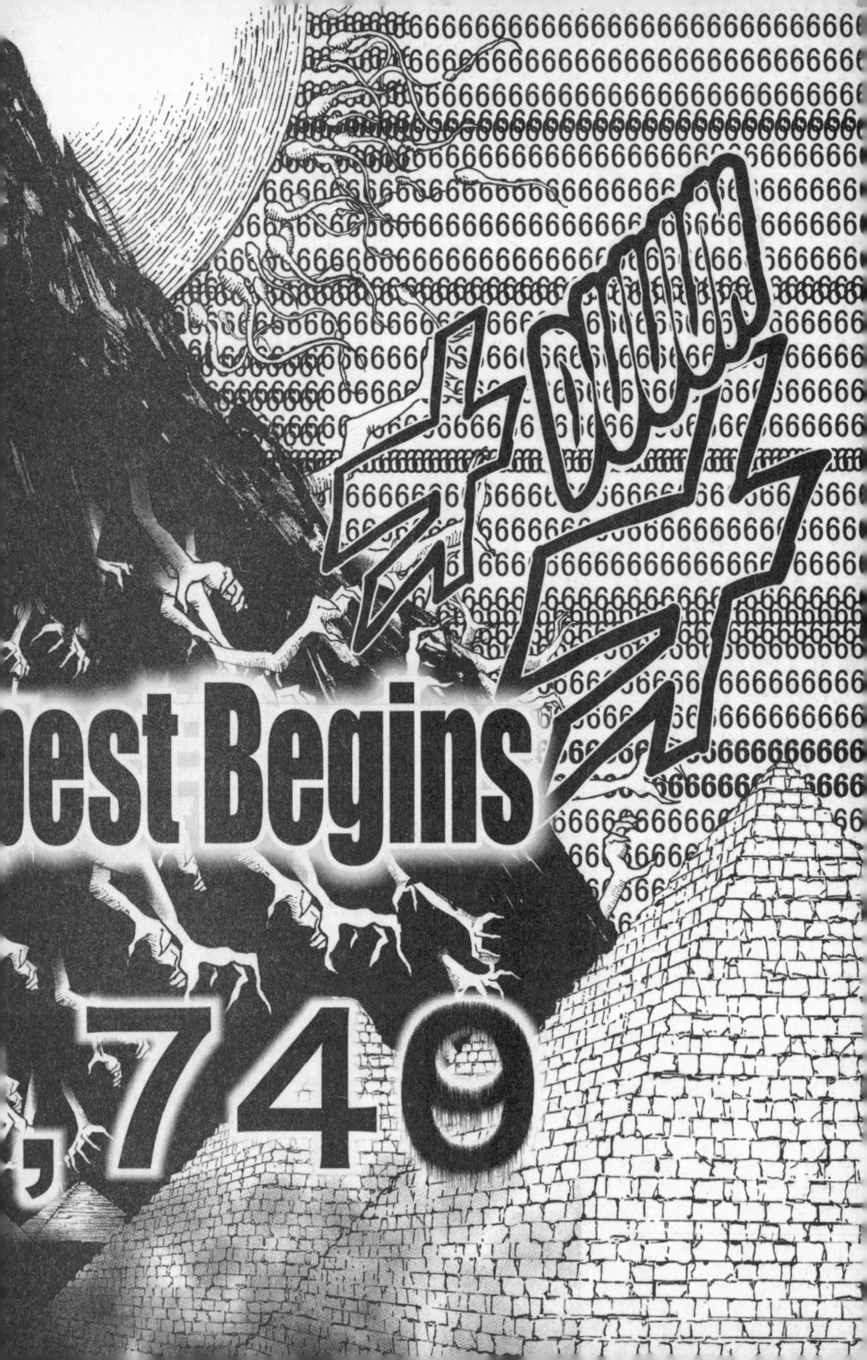
est Begins
,749

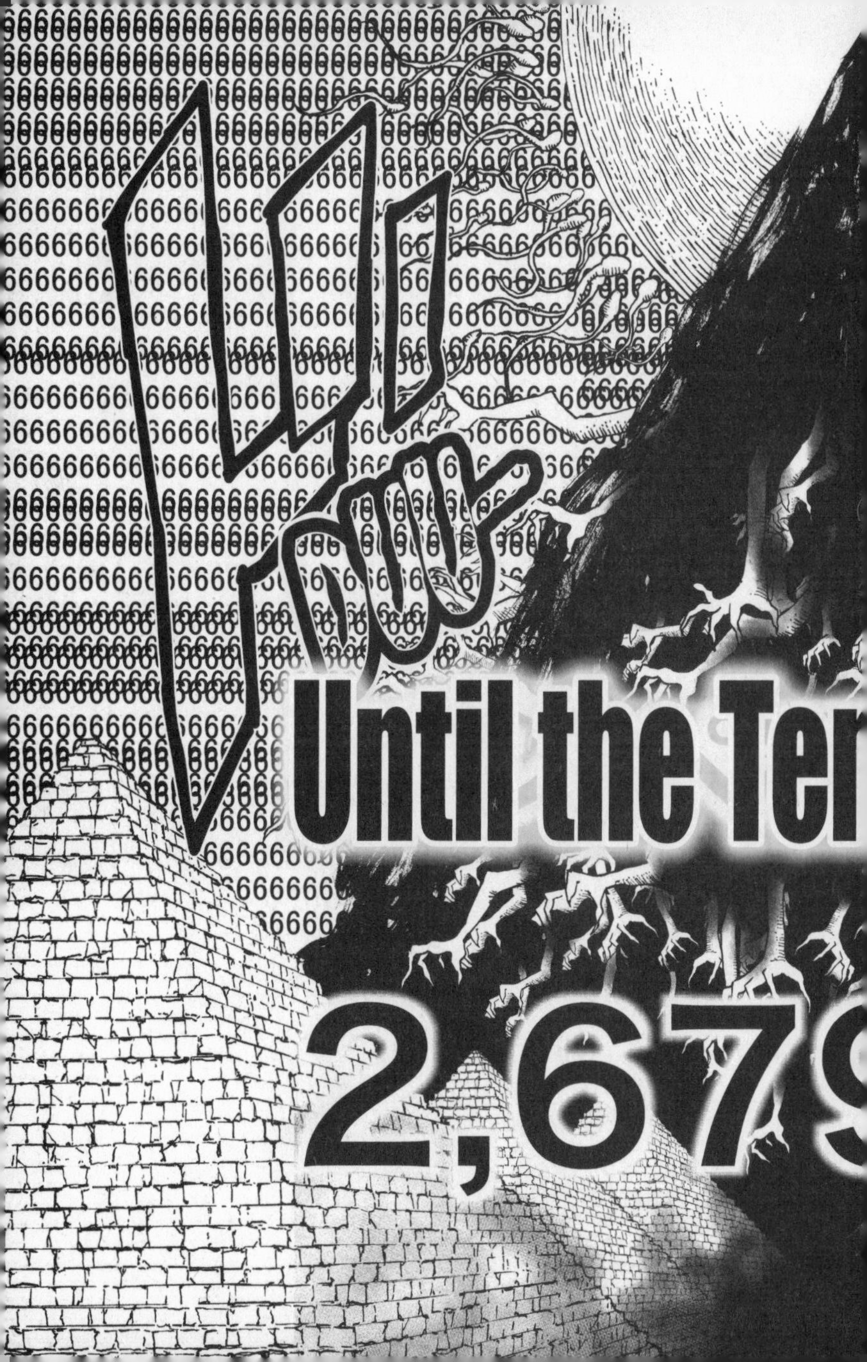
Until the Ter
2,679

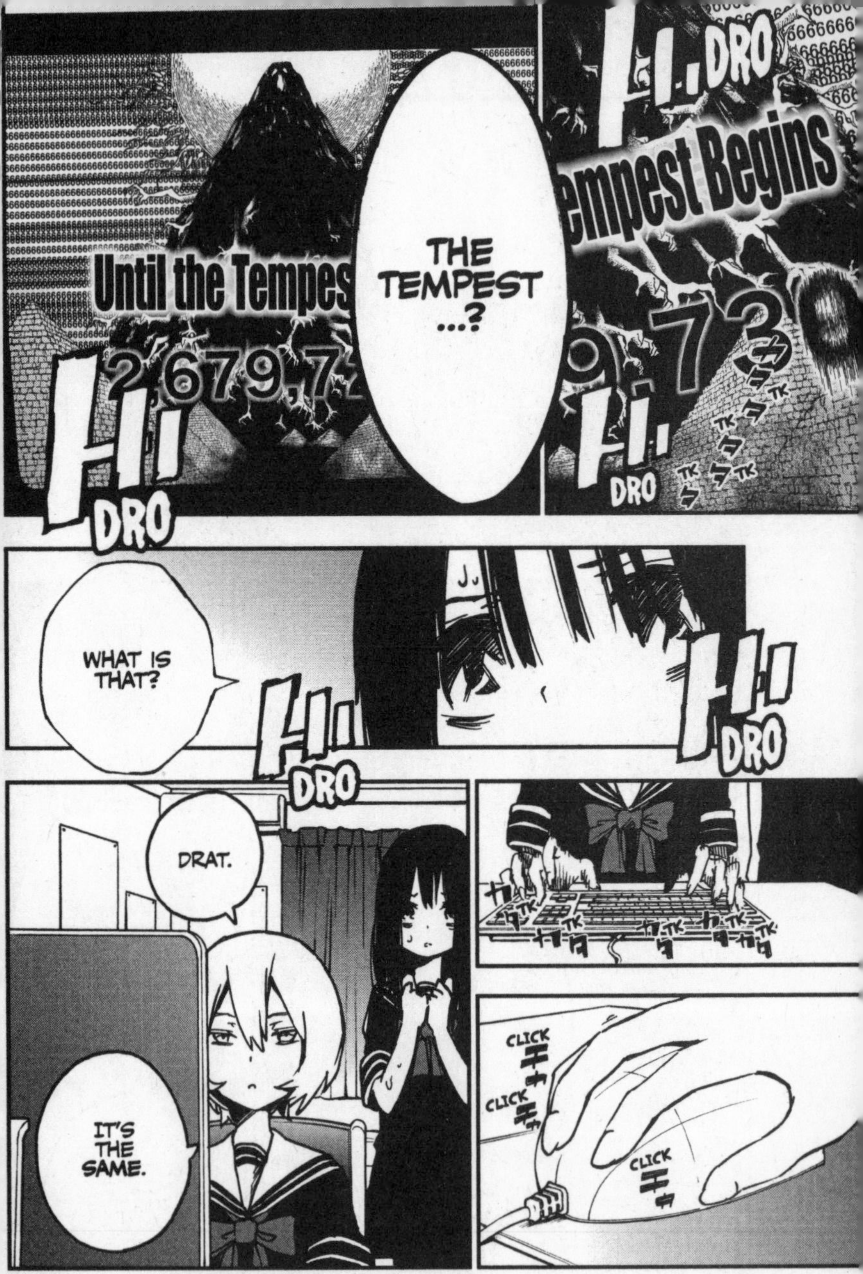
DRO
empest Begins
73
DRO
TK TK TK TK TK
THE TEMPEST ...?
Until the Tempes
2,679,72
DRO
DRO
WHAT IS THAT?
DRO
TK TK TK TK
CLICK
CLICK
CLICK
DRAT.
IT'S THE SAME.

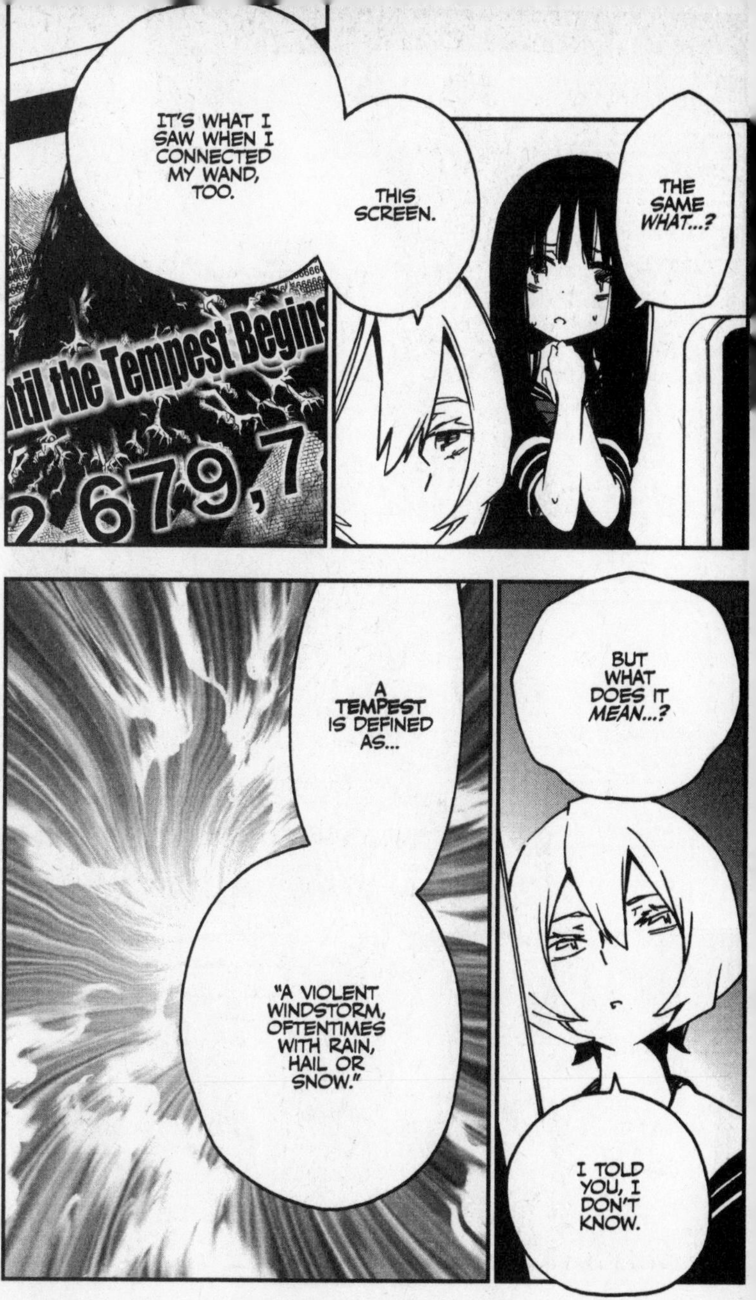
THE SAME *WHAT...?*
THIS SCREEN.
IT'S WHAT I SAW WHEN I CONNECTED MY WAND, TOO.
ntil the Tempest Begins
2,679,7
BUT WHAT DOES IT *MEAN...?*
I TOLD YOU, I DON'T KNOW.
A TEMPEST IS DEFINED AS...
"A VIOLENT WINDSTORM, OFTENTIMES WITH RAIN, HAIL OR SNOW."

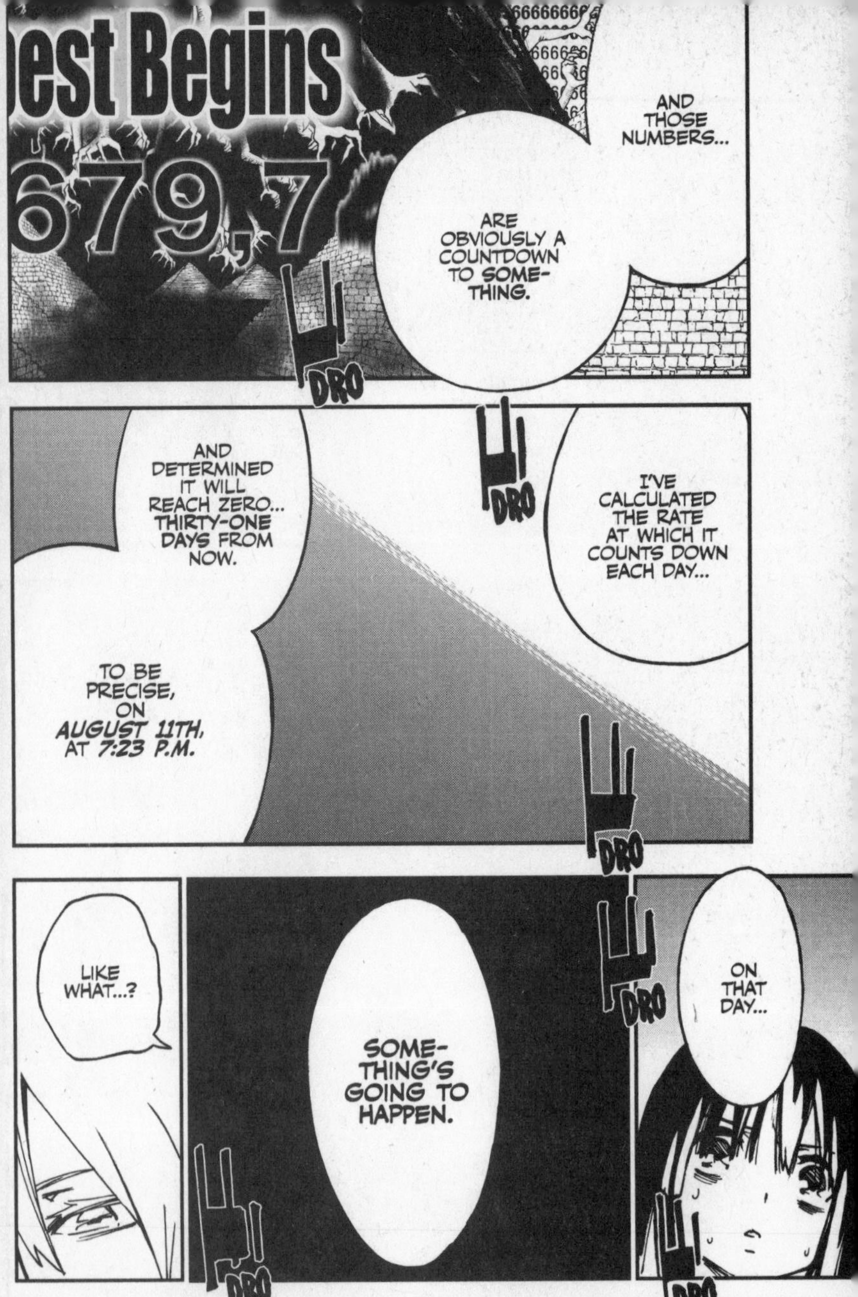

est Begins
679,7
AND THOSE NUMBERS...
ARE OBVIOUSLY A COUNTDOWN TO SOME-THING.
DRO
DRO
I'VE CALCULATED THE RATE AT WHICH IT COUNTS DOWN EACH DAY...
AND DETERMINED IT WILL REACH ZERO... THIRTY-ONE DAYS FROM NOW.
TO BE PRECISE, ON AUGUST 11TH, AT 7:23 P.M.
DRO
DRO
ON THAT DAY...
DRO
SOME-THING'S GOING TO HAPPEN.
DRO
LIKE WHAT...?

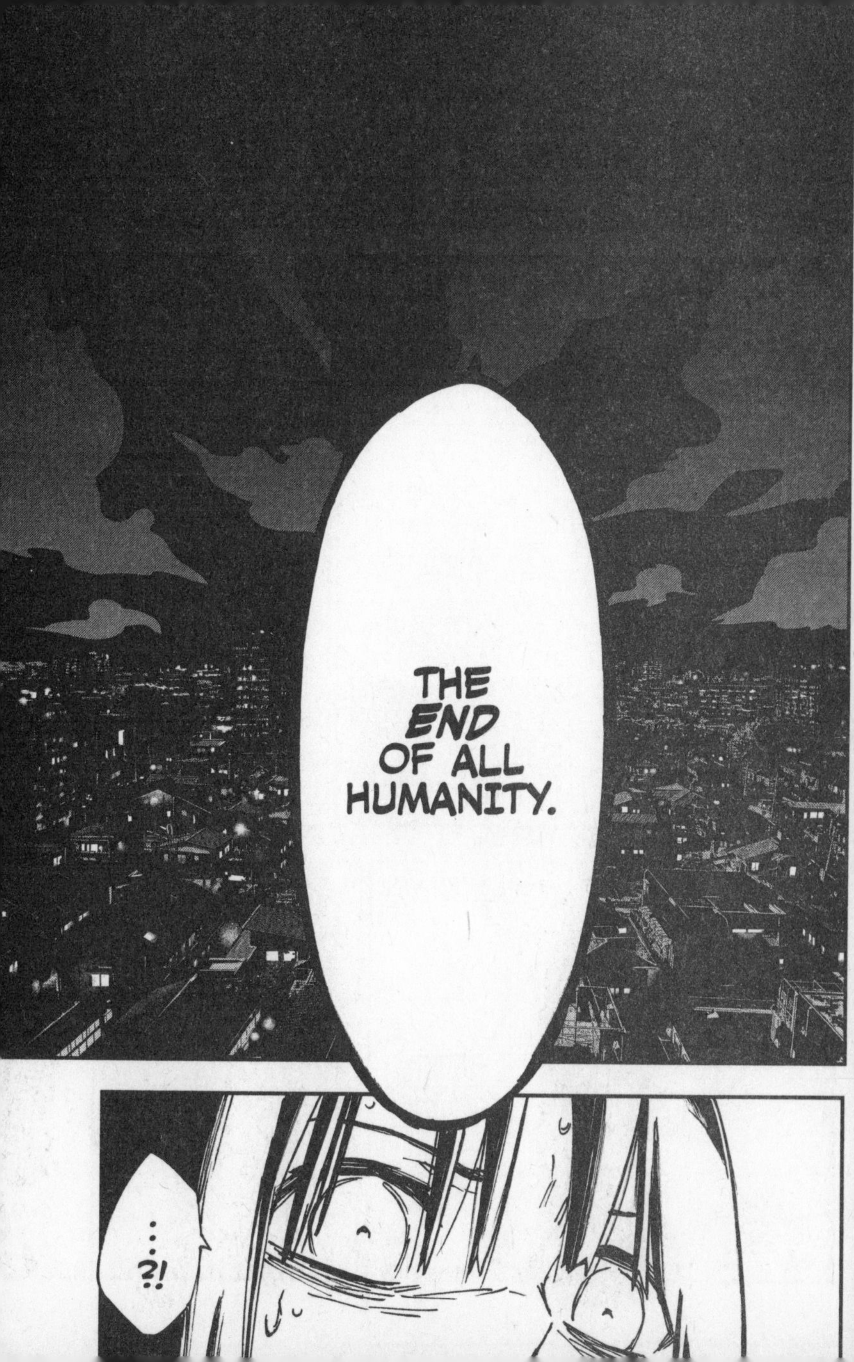
THE *END* OF ALL HUMANITY.
...?!

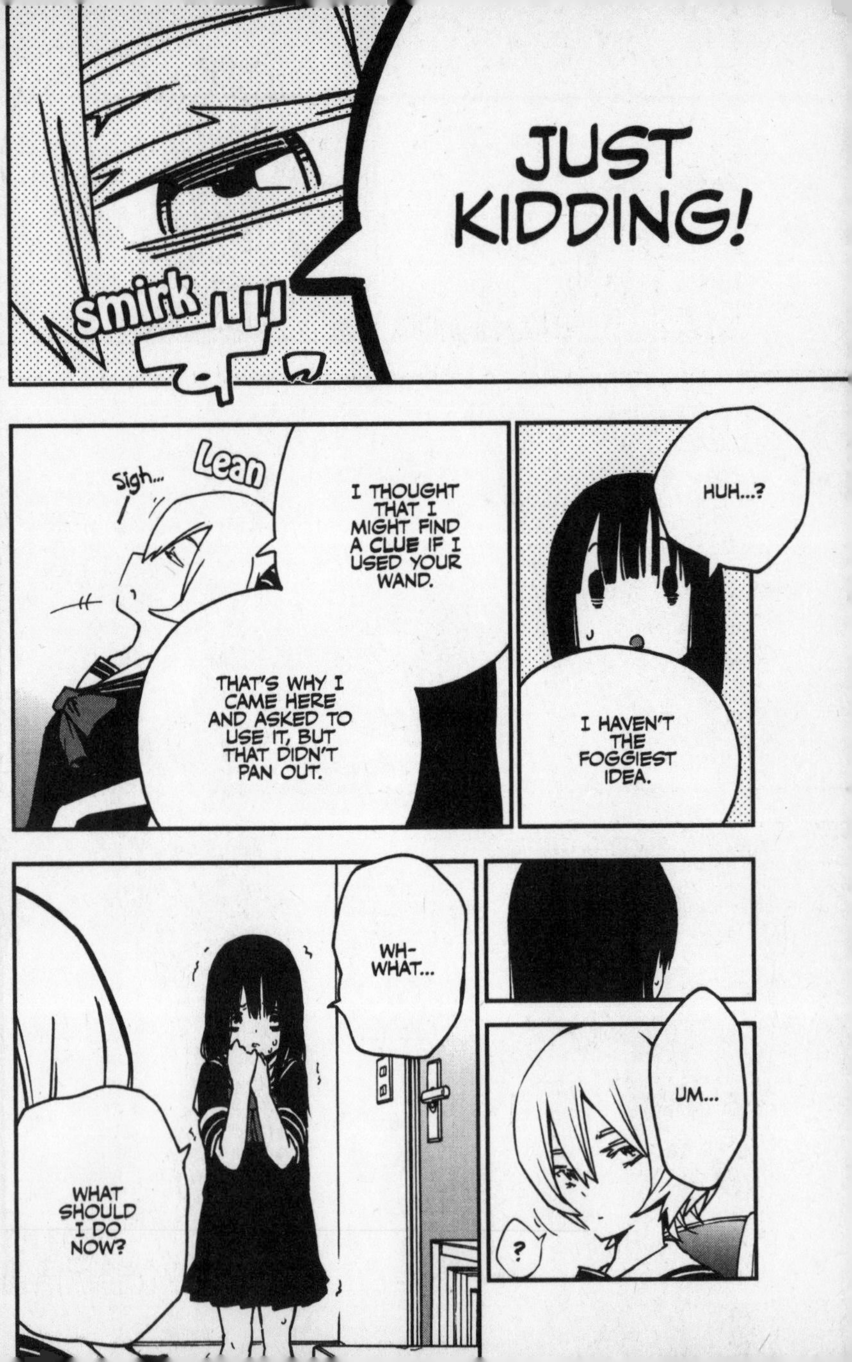
JUST KIDDING!
smirk
HUH...?
I HAVEN'T THE FOGGIEST IDEA.
I THOUGHT THAT I MIGHT FIND A CLUE IF I USED YOUR WAND.
Lean
Sigh...
THAT'S WHY I CAME HERE AND ASKED TO USE IT, BUT THAT DIDN'T PAN OUT.
UM...
?
WH-WHAT...
WHAT SHOULD I DO NOW?

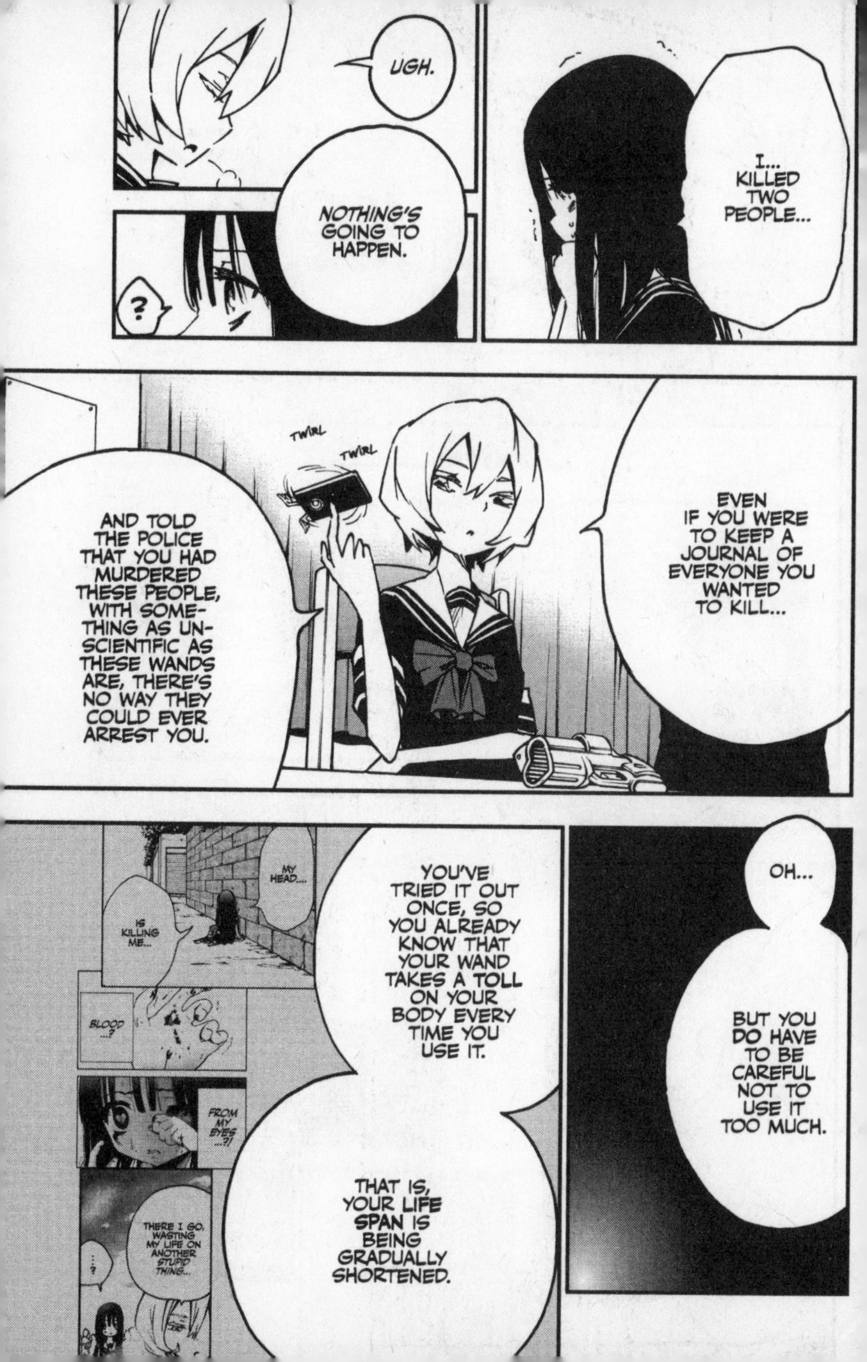
I... KILLED TWO PEOPLE...
UGH.
NOTHING'S GOING TO HAPPEN.
?
EVEN IF YOU WERE TO KEEP A JOURNAL OF EVERYONE YOU WANTED TO KILL...
TWIRL
TWIRL
AND TOLD THE POLICE THAT YOU HAD MURDERED THESE PEOPLE, WITH SOMETHING AS UNSCIENTIFIC AS THESE WANDS ARE, THERE'S NO WAY THEY COULD EVER ARREST YOU.
OH...
BUT YOU DO HAVE TO BE CAREFUL NOT TO USE IT TOO MUCH.
YOU'VE TRIED IT OUT ONCE, SO YOU ALREADY KNOW THAT YOUR WAND TAKES A TOLL ON YOUR BODY EVERY TIME YOU USE IT.
THAT IS, YOUR LIFE SPAN IS BEING GRADUALLY SHORTENED.
MY HEAD...
IS KILLING ME...
BLOOD ...?
FROM MY EYES ...?!
THERE I GO, WASTING MY LIFE ON ANOTHER STUPID THING...
...?

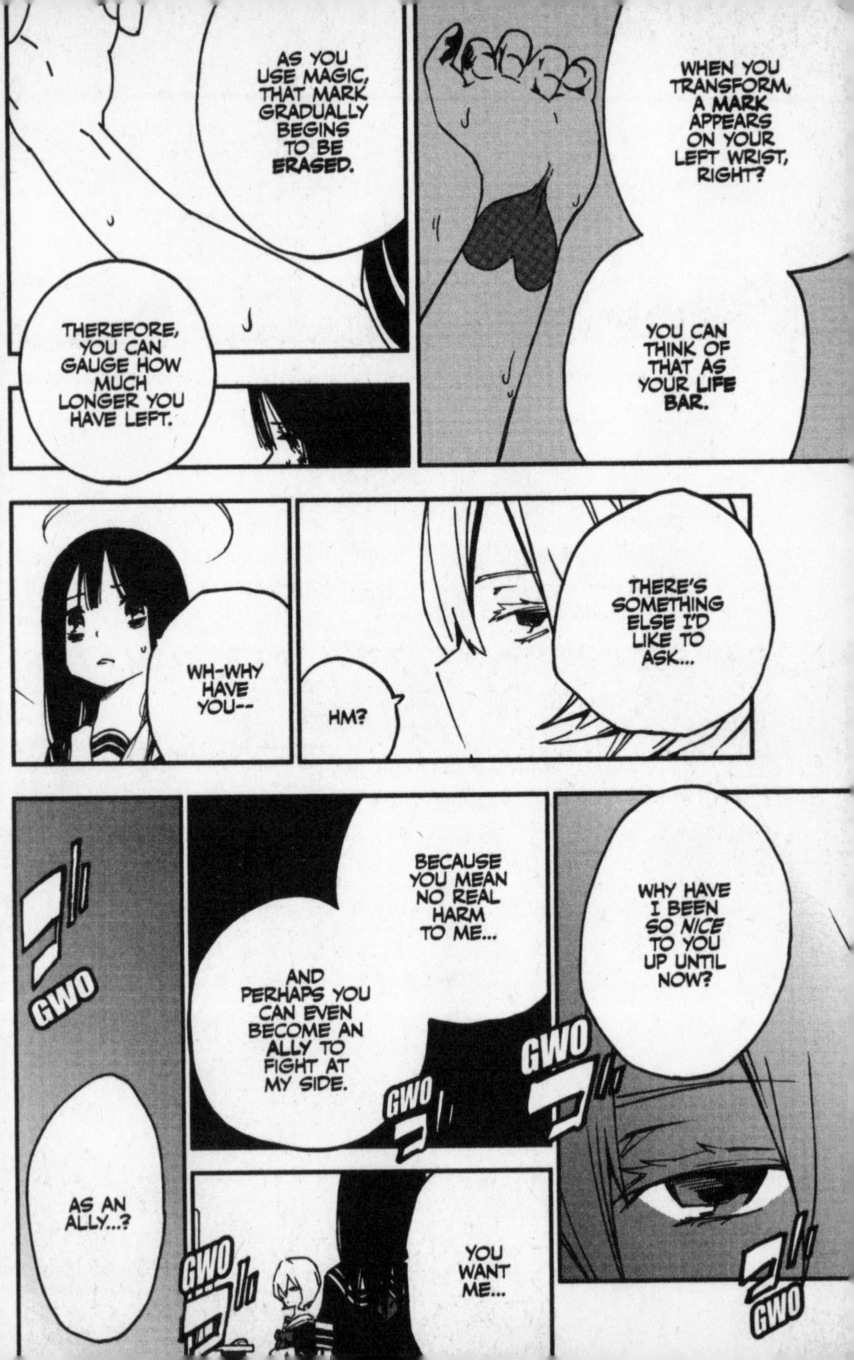
WHEN YOU TRANSFORM, A MARK APPEARS ON YOUR LEFT WRIST, RIGHT?
YOU CAN THINK OF THAT AS YOUR LIFE BAR.
AS YOU USE MAGIC, THAT MARK GRADUALLY BEGINS TO BE ERASED.
THEREFORE, YOU CAN GAUGE HOW MUCH LONGER YOU HAVE LEFT.
THERE'S SOMETHING ELSE I'D LIKE TO ASK...
HM?
WH-WHY HAVE YOU--
WHY HAVE I BEEN SO *NICE* TO YOU UP UNTIL NOW?
GWO
GWO
BECAUSE YOU MEAN NO REAL HARM TO ME...
AND PERHAPS YOU CAN EVEN BECOME AN ALLY TO FIGHT AT MY SIDE.
GWO
YOU WANT ME...
GWO
GWO
AS AN ALLY...?

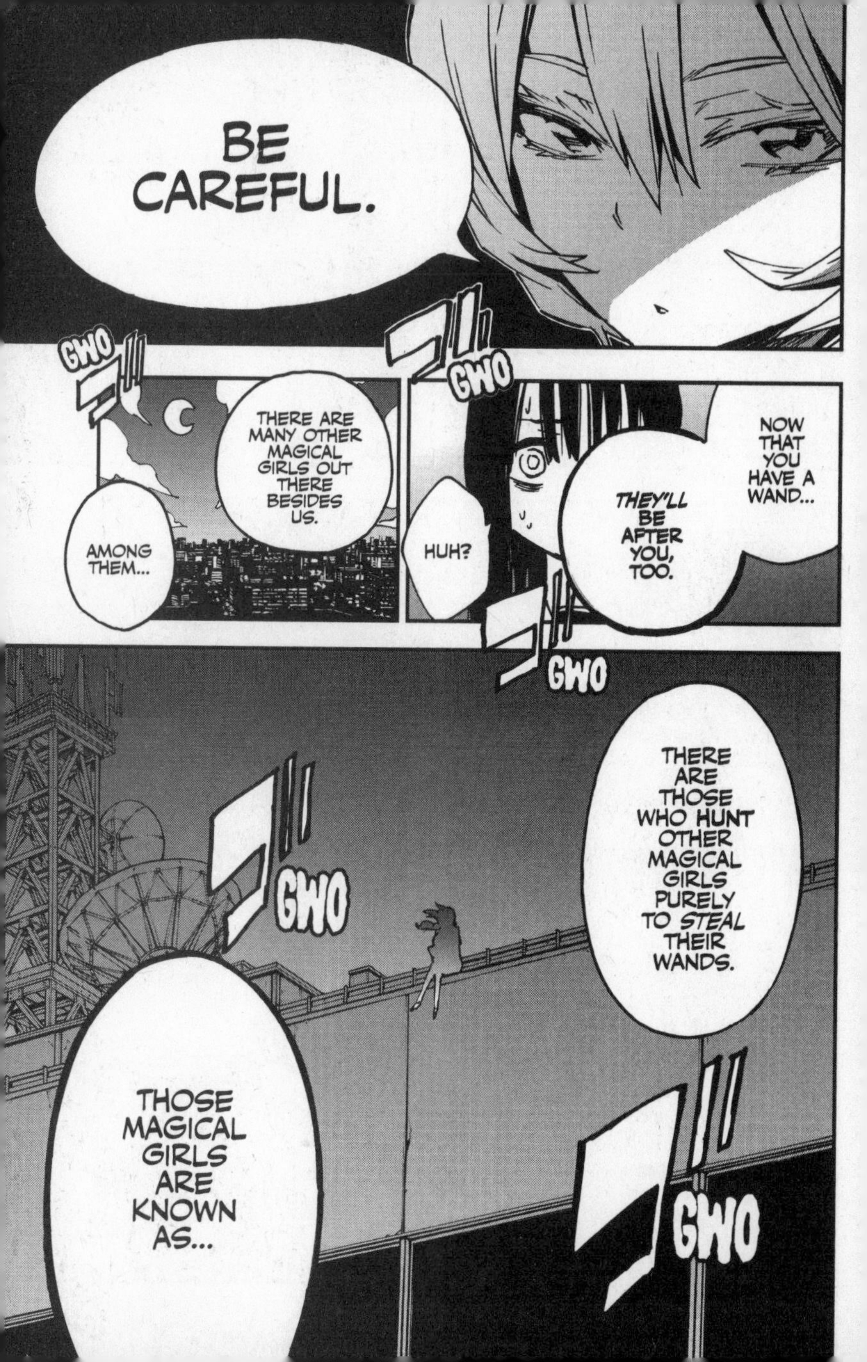
BE CAREFUL.
GWO
GWO
NOW THAT YOU HAVE A WAND...
THEY'LL BE AFTER YOU, TOO.
HUH?
GWO
THERE ARE MANY OTHER MAGICAL GIRLS OUT THERE BESIDES US.
AMONG THEM...
GWO
THERE ARE THOSE WHO HUNT OTHER MAGICAL GIRLS PURELY TO *STEAL* THEIR WANDS.
GWO
THOSE MAGICAL GIRLS ARE KNOWN AS...
GWO

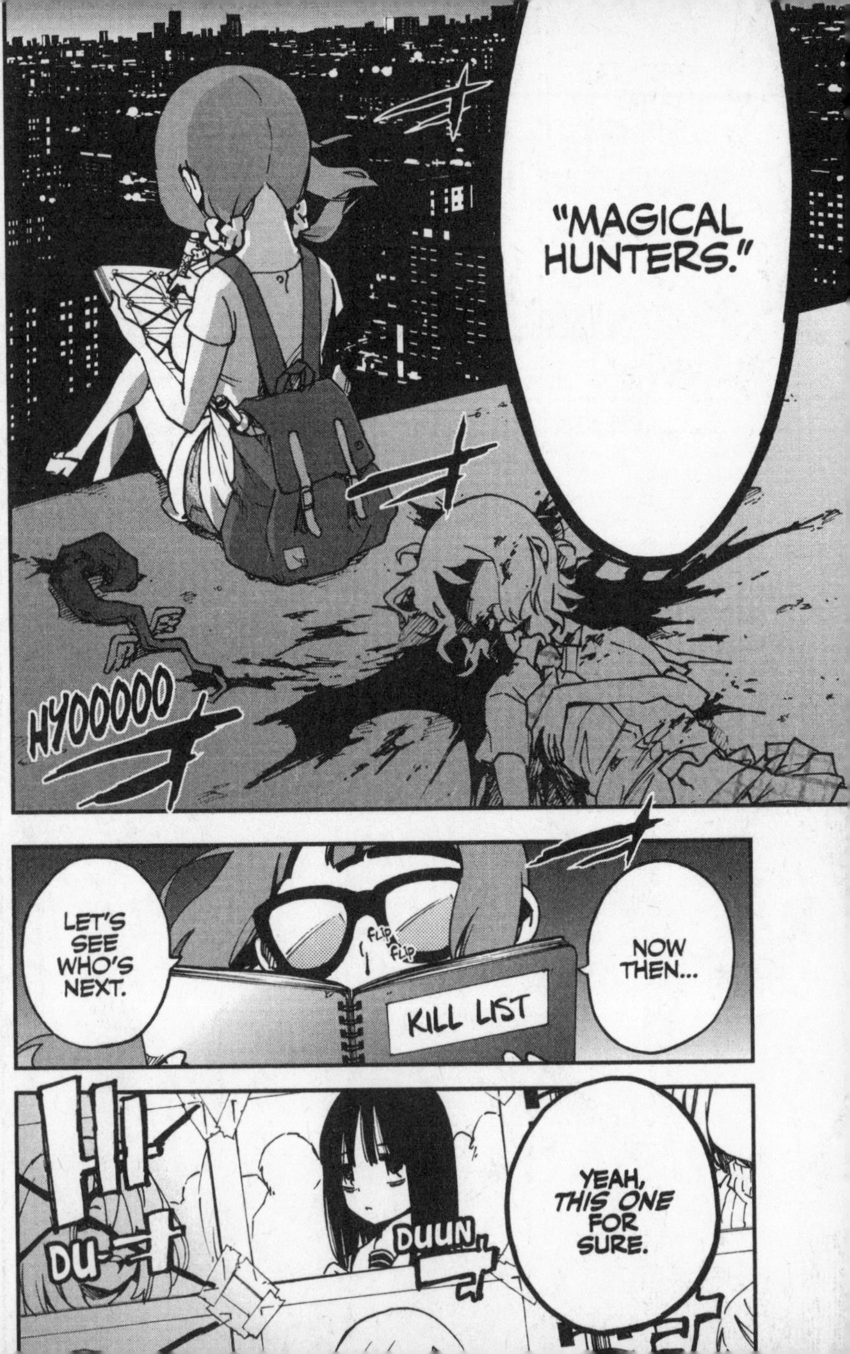
"MAGICAL HUNTERS."
HYOOOOO
NOW THEN...
LET'S SEE WHO'S NEXT.
FLIP FLIP
KILL LIST
YEAH, THIS ONE FOR SURE.
DUUN
DU

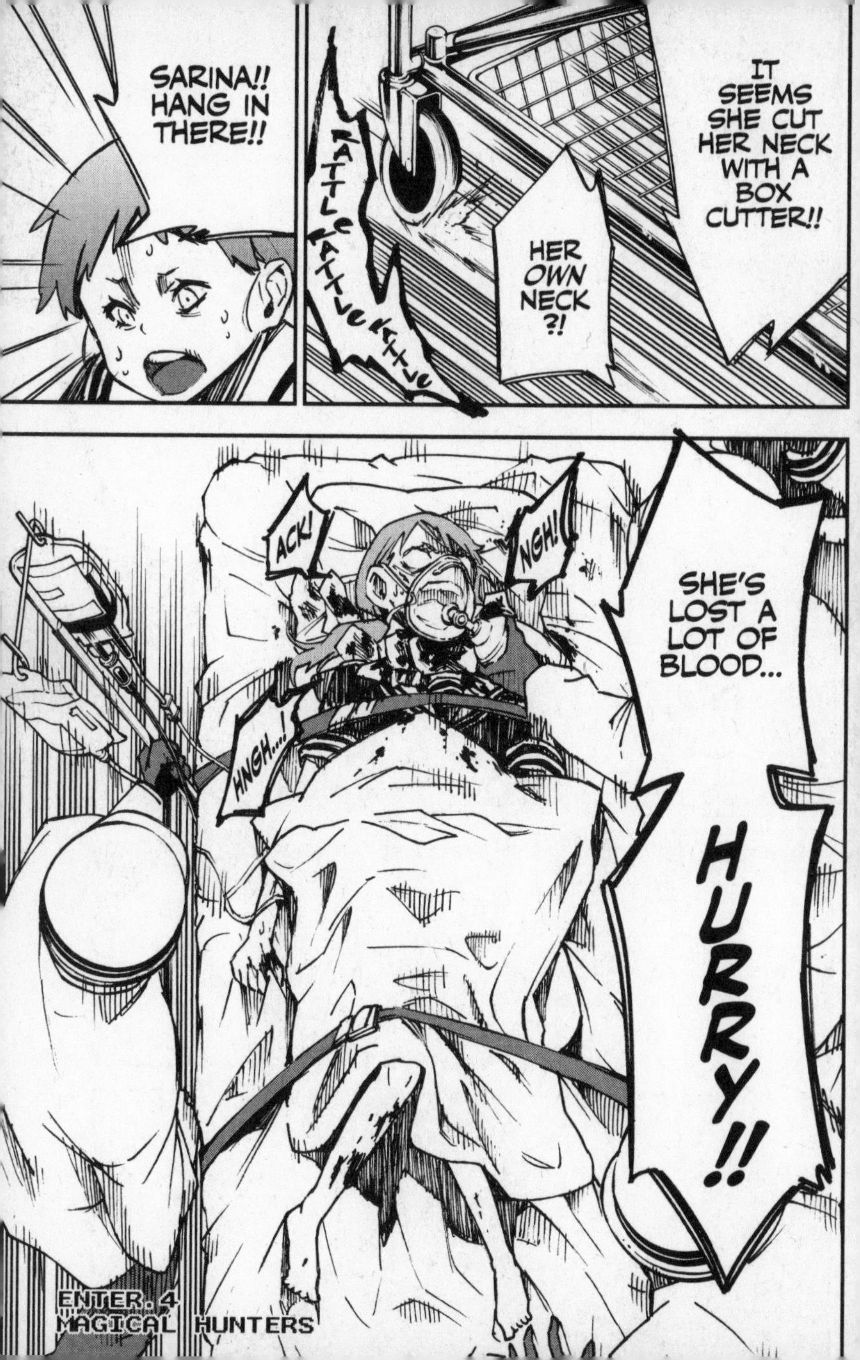
IT SEEMS SHE CUT HER NECK WITH A BOX CUTTER!!
HER OWN NECK?!
RATTLE RATTLE RATTLE RATTLE
SARINA!! HANG IN THERE!!
SHE'S LOST A LOT OF BLOOD...
HURRY!!
NGH!
ACK!
HNGH...!

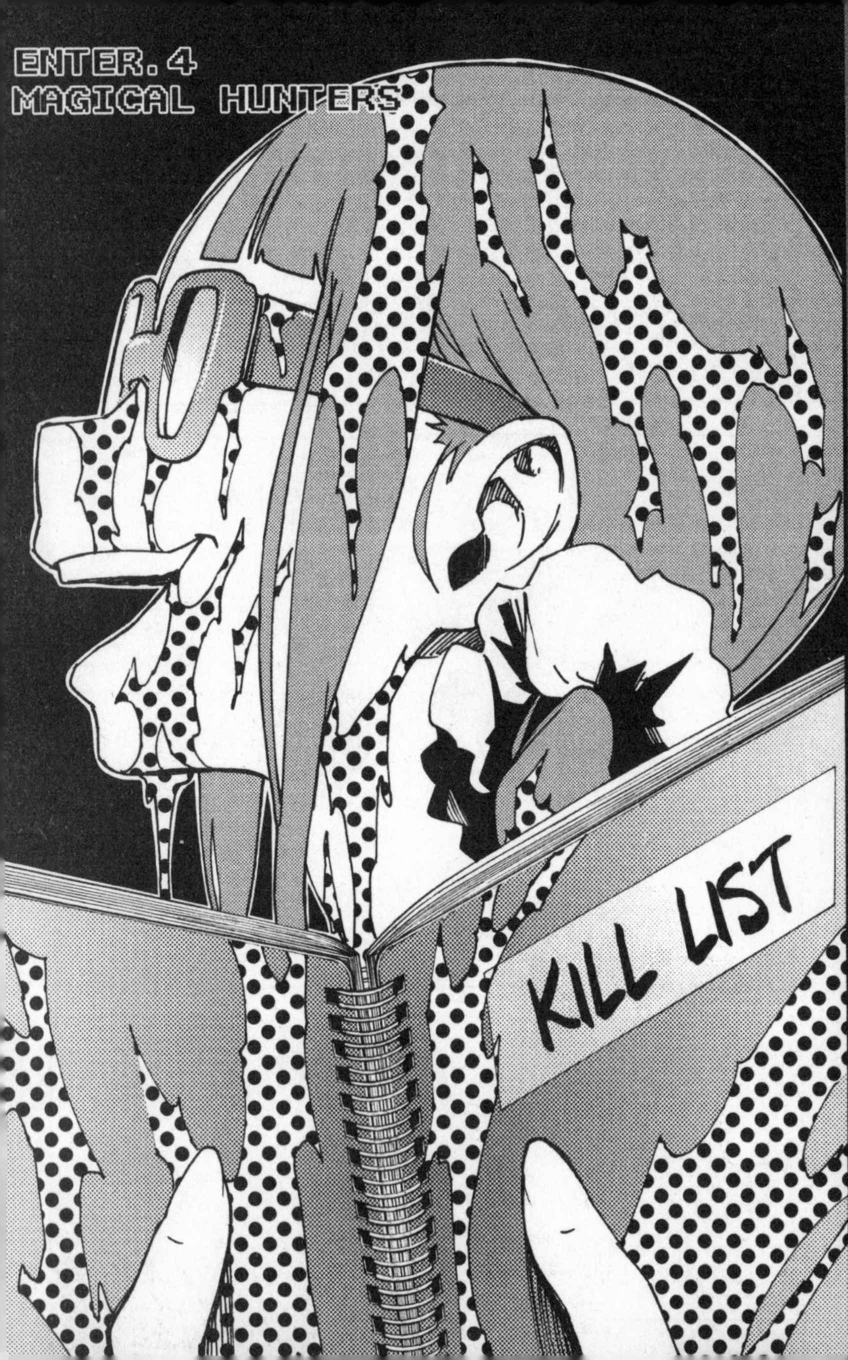
ENTER. 4
MAGICAL HUNTERS
KILL LIST

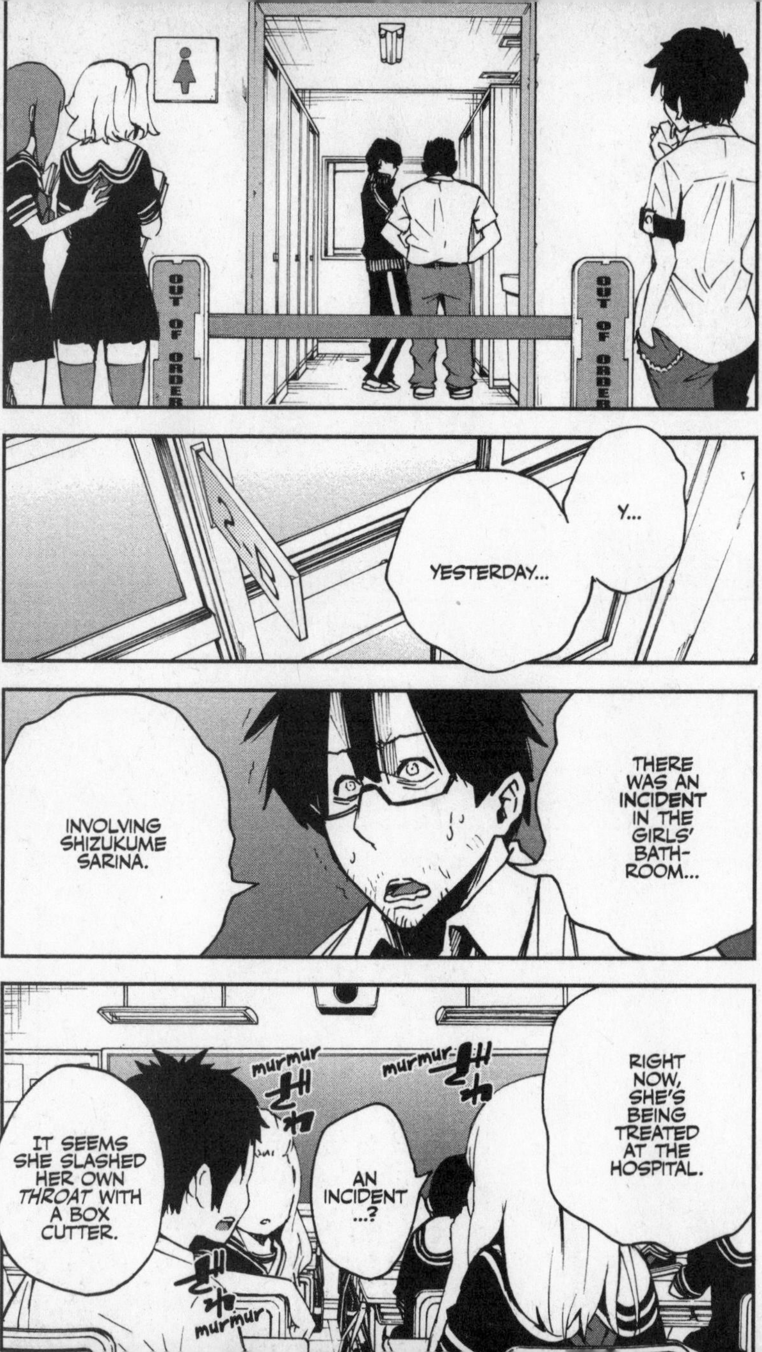
OUT OF ORDER
OUT OF ORDER
Y...
YESTERDAY...
THERE WAS AN INCIDENT IN THE GIRLS' BATHROOM...
INVOLVING SHIZUKUME SARINA.
RIGHT NOW, SHE'S BEING TREATED AT THE HOSPITAL.
murmur
murmur
AN INCIDENT ...?
IT SEEMS SHE SLASHED HER OWN *THROAT* WITH A BOX CUTTER.
murmur

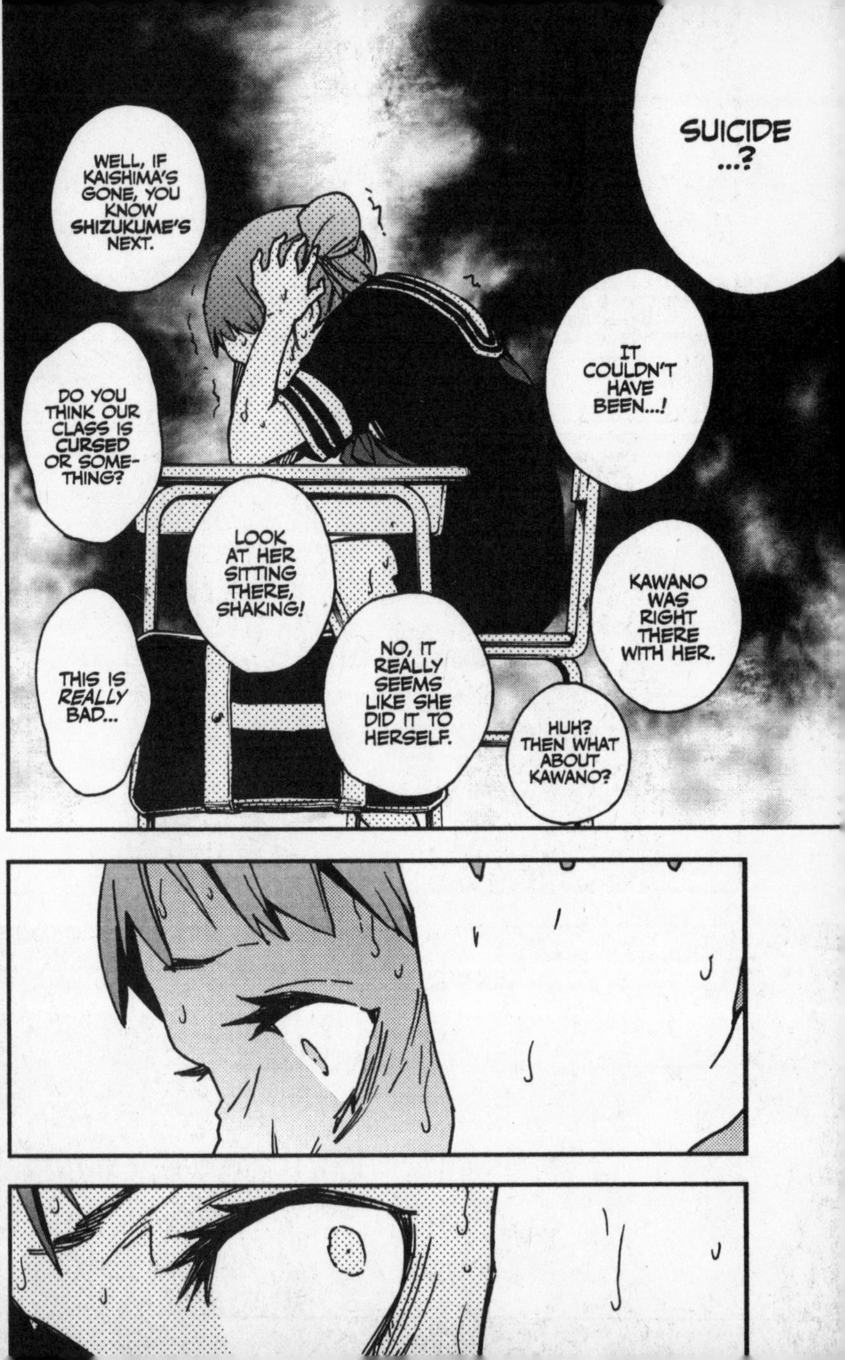
SUICIDE ...?
IT COULDN'T HAVE BEEN...!
KAWANO WAS RIGHT THERE WITH HER.
HUH? THEN WHAT ABOUT KAWANO?
WELL, IF KAISHIMA'S GONE, YOU KNOW SHIZUKUME'S NEXT.
NO, IT REALLY SEEMS LIKE SHE DID IT TO HERSELF.
LOOK AT HER SITTING THERE, SHAKING!
DO YOU THINK OUR CLASS IS CURSED OR SOME-THING?
THIS IS *REALLY* BAD...

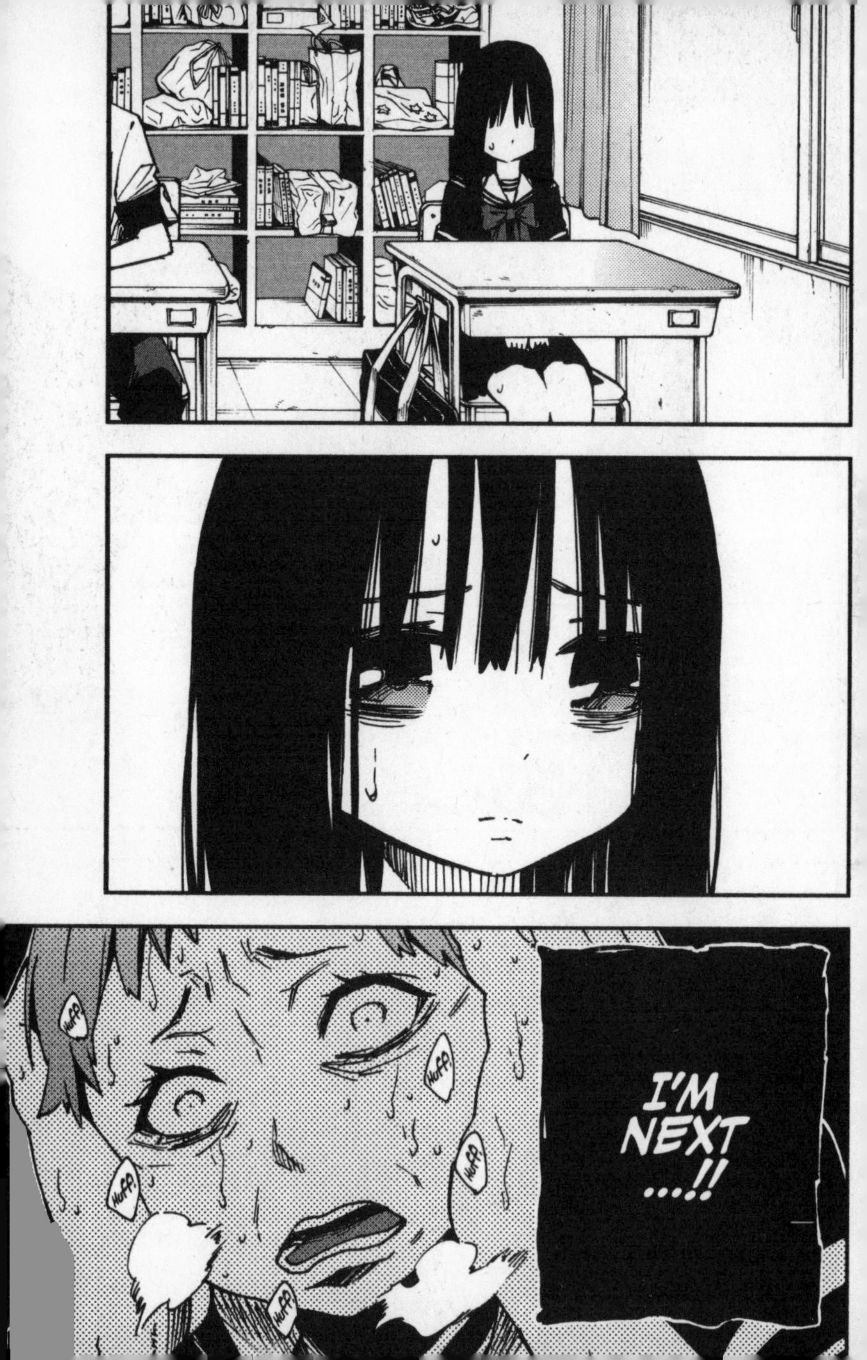
I'M NEXT ....!!
Huff
Huff
Huff
Huff
Huff
Huff

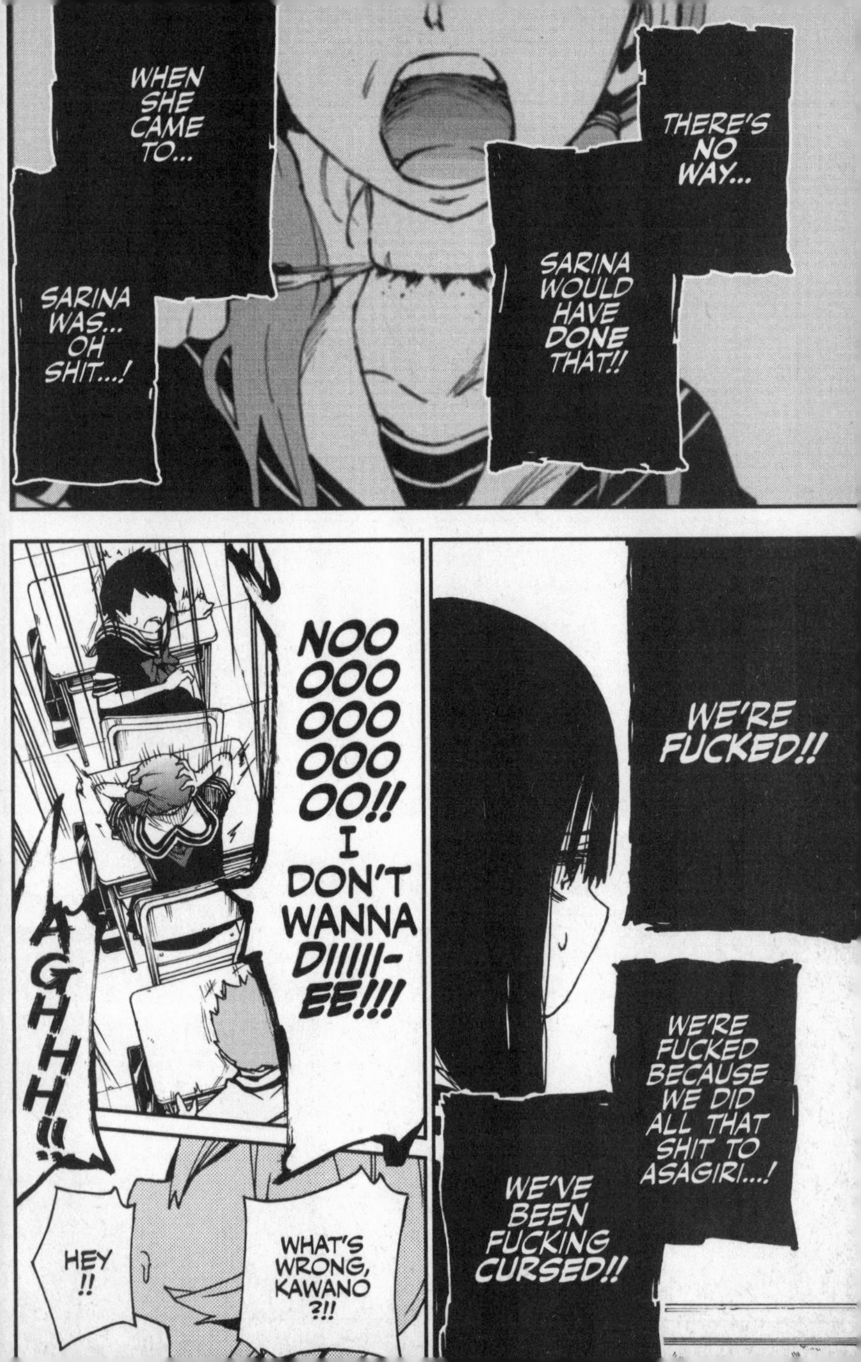
THERE'S NO WAY...
SARINA WOULD HAVE DONE THAT!!
WHEN SHE CAME TO...
SARINA WAS... OH SHIT...!
WE'RE FUCKED!!
WE'RE FUCKED BECAUSE WE DID ALL THAT SHIT TO ASAGIRI...!
WE'VE BEEN FUCKING CURSED!!
NOOOOOOOOOOOOOOOOOOOOOOOO!! I DON'T WANNA DIIIII-EE!!!
AGHHHH!!
WHAT'S WRONG, KAWANO?!!
HEY!!

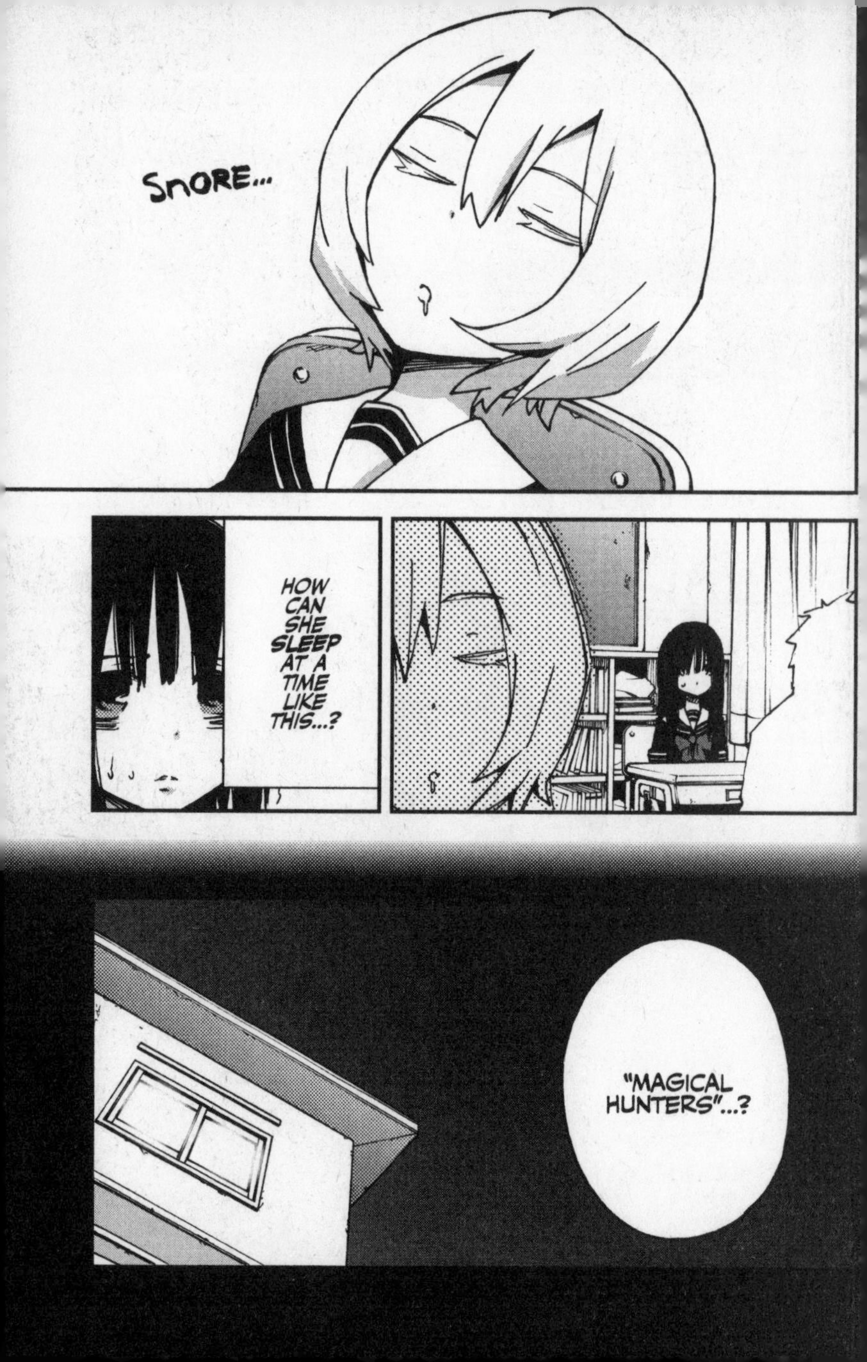
SNORE...
HOW CAN SHE SLEEP AT A TIME LIKE THIS...?
"MAGICAL HUNTERS"...?

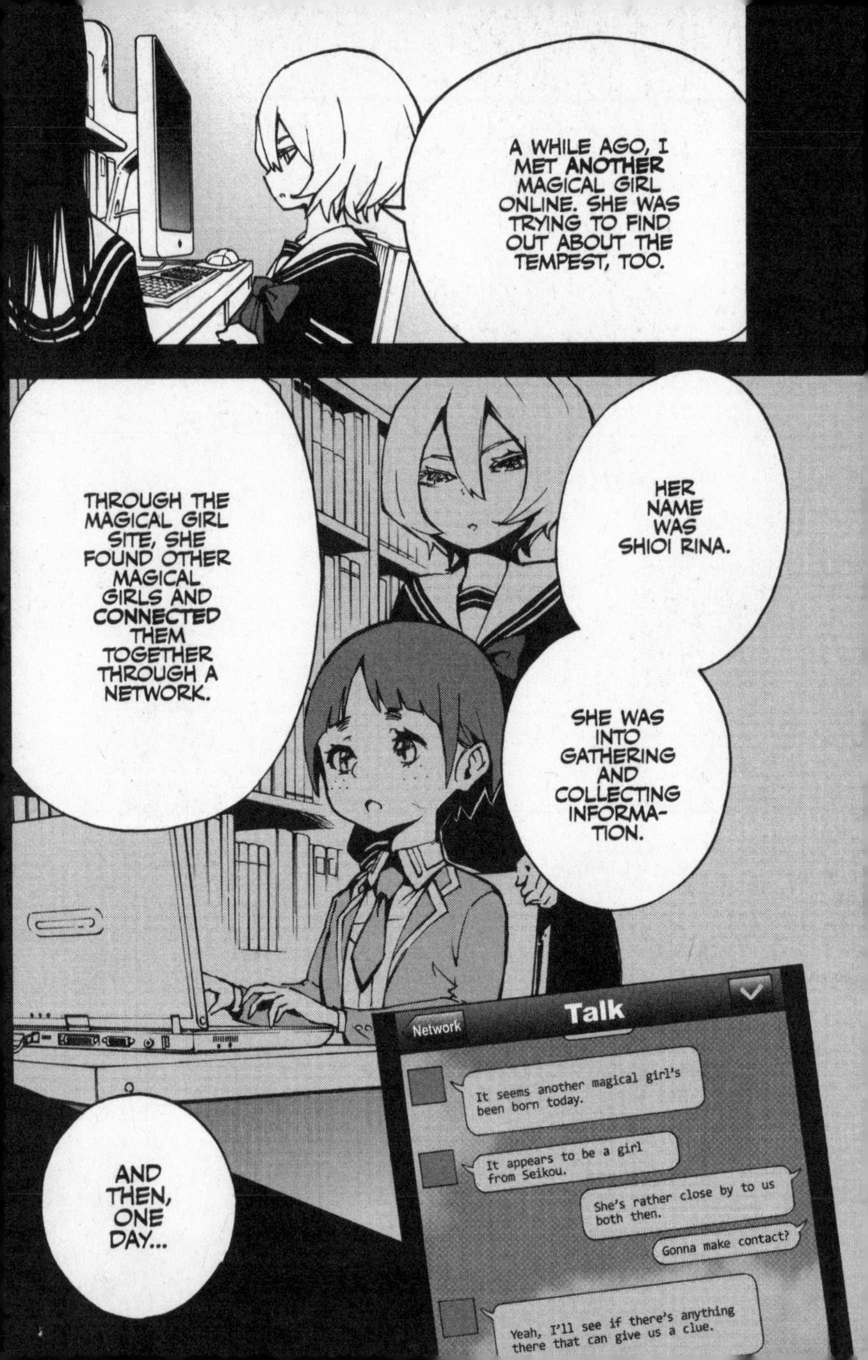

A WHILE AGO, I MET **ANOTHER** MAGICAL GIRL ONLINE. SHE WAS TRYING TO FIND OUT ABOUT THE TEMPEST, TOO.
HER NAME WAS SHIOI RINA.
SHE WAS INTO GATHERING AND COLLECTING INFORMA-TION.
THROUGH THE MAGICAL GIRL SITE, SHE FOUND OTHER MAGICAL GIRLS AND CONNECTED THEM TOGETHER THROUGH A NETWORK.
AND THEN, ONE DAY...
Network
Talk
It seems another magical girl's been born today.
It appears to be a girl from Seikou.
She's rather close by to us both then.
Gonna make contact?
Yeah, I'll see if there's anything there that can give us a clue.

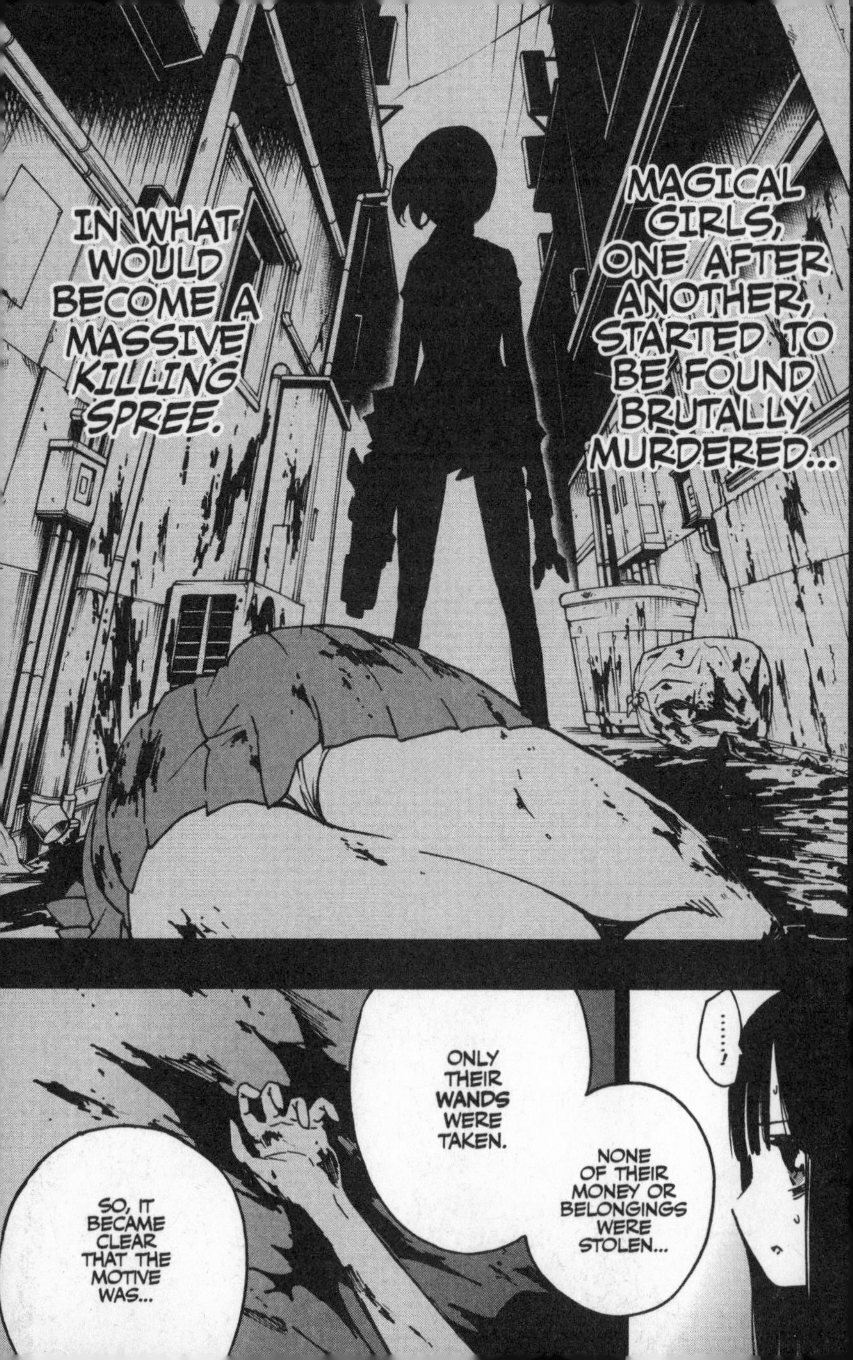
MAGICAL GIRLS, ONE AFTER ANOTHER, STARTED TO BE FOUND BRUTALLY MURDERED...
IN WHAT WOULD BECOME A MASSIVE KILLING SPREE.
......!
ONLY THEIR WANDS WERE TAKEN.
NONE OF THEIR MONEY OR BELONGINGS WERE STOLEN...
SO, IT BECAME CLEAR THAT THE MOTIVE WAS...

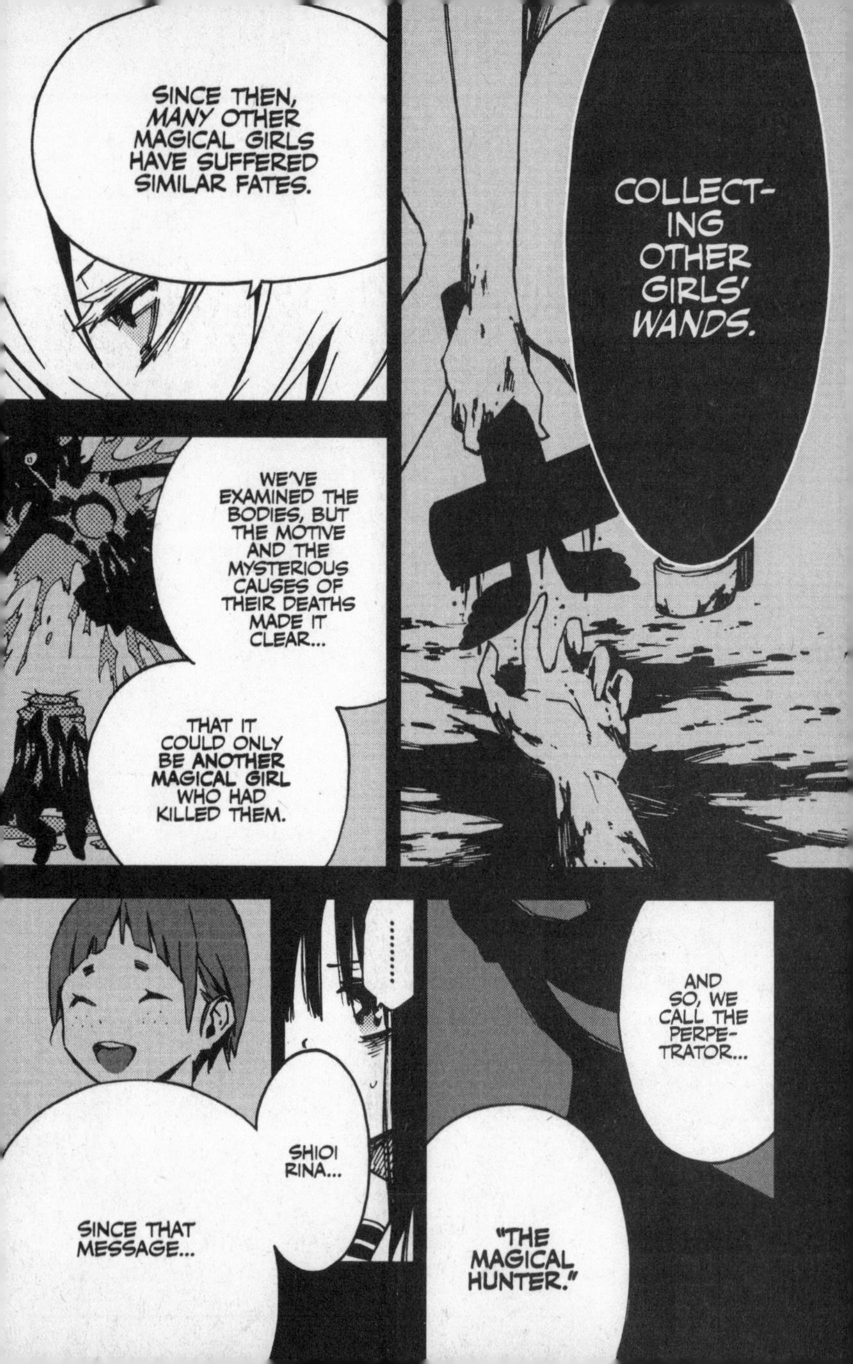
COLLECTING OTHER GIRLS' *WANDS.*
SINCE THEN, *MANY* OTHER MAGICAL GIRLS HAVE SUFFERED SIMILAR FATES.
WE'VE EXAMINED THE BODIES, BUT THE MOTIVE AND THE MYSTERIOUS CAUSES OF THEIR DEATHS MADE IT CLEAR...
THAT IT COULD ONLY BE ANOTHER MAGICAL GIRL WHO HAD KILLED THEM.
AND SO, WE CALL THE PERPETRATOR...
"THE MAGICAL HUNTER."
......
SHIOI RINA...
SINCE THAT MESSAGE...

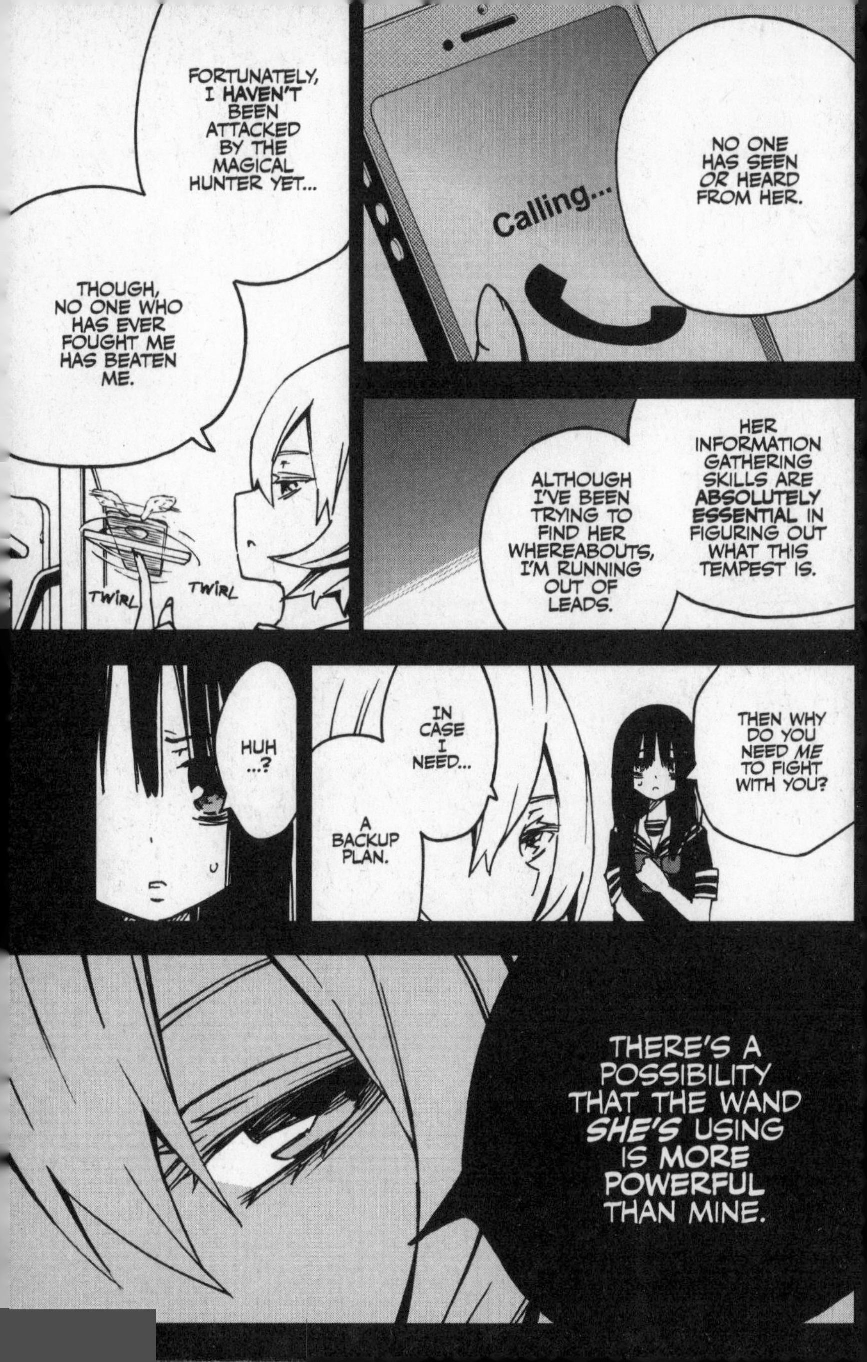
Calling...
NO ONE HAS SEEN OR HEARD FROM HER.
HER INFORMATION GATHERING SKILLS ARE ABSOLUTELY ESSENTIAL IN FIGURING OUT WHAT THIS TEMPEST IS.
ALTHOUGH I'VE BEEN TRYING TO FIND HER WHEREABOUTS, I'M RUNNING OUT OF LEADS.
FORTUNATELY, I HAVEN'T BEEN ATTACKED BY THE MAGICAL HUNTER YET...
THOUGH, NO ONE WHO HAS EVER FOUGHT ME HAS BEATEN ME.
TWIRL
TWIRL
THEN WHY DO YOU NEED ME TO FIGHT WITH YOU?
IN CASE I NEED...
A BACKUP PLAN.
HUH ...?
THERE'S A POSSIBILITY THAT THE WAND SHE'S USING IS MORE POWERFUL THAN MINE.

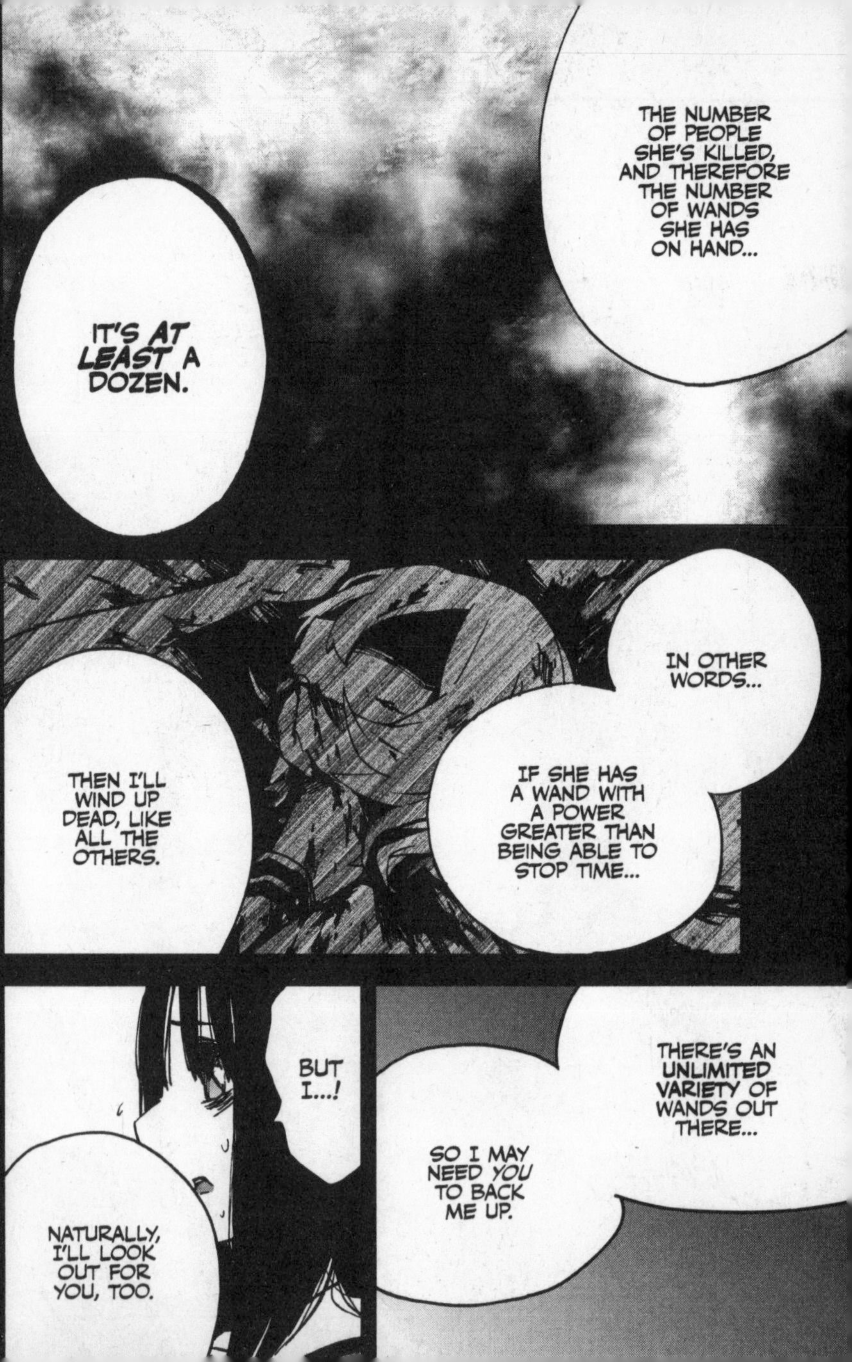
THE NUMBER OF PEOPLE SHE'S KILLED, AND THEREFORE THE NUMBER OF WANDS SHE HAS ON HAND...
IT'S *AT LEAST* A DOZEN.
IN OTHER WORDS...
IF SHE HAS A WAND WITH A POWER GREATER THAN BEING ABLE TO STOP TIME...
THEN I'LL WIND UP DEAD, LIKE ALL THE OTHERS.
THERE'S AN UNLIMITED VARIETY OF WANDS OUT THERE...
SO I MAY NEED *YOU* TO BACK ME UP.
BUT I...!
NATURALLY, I'LL LOOK OUT FOR YOU, TOO.

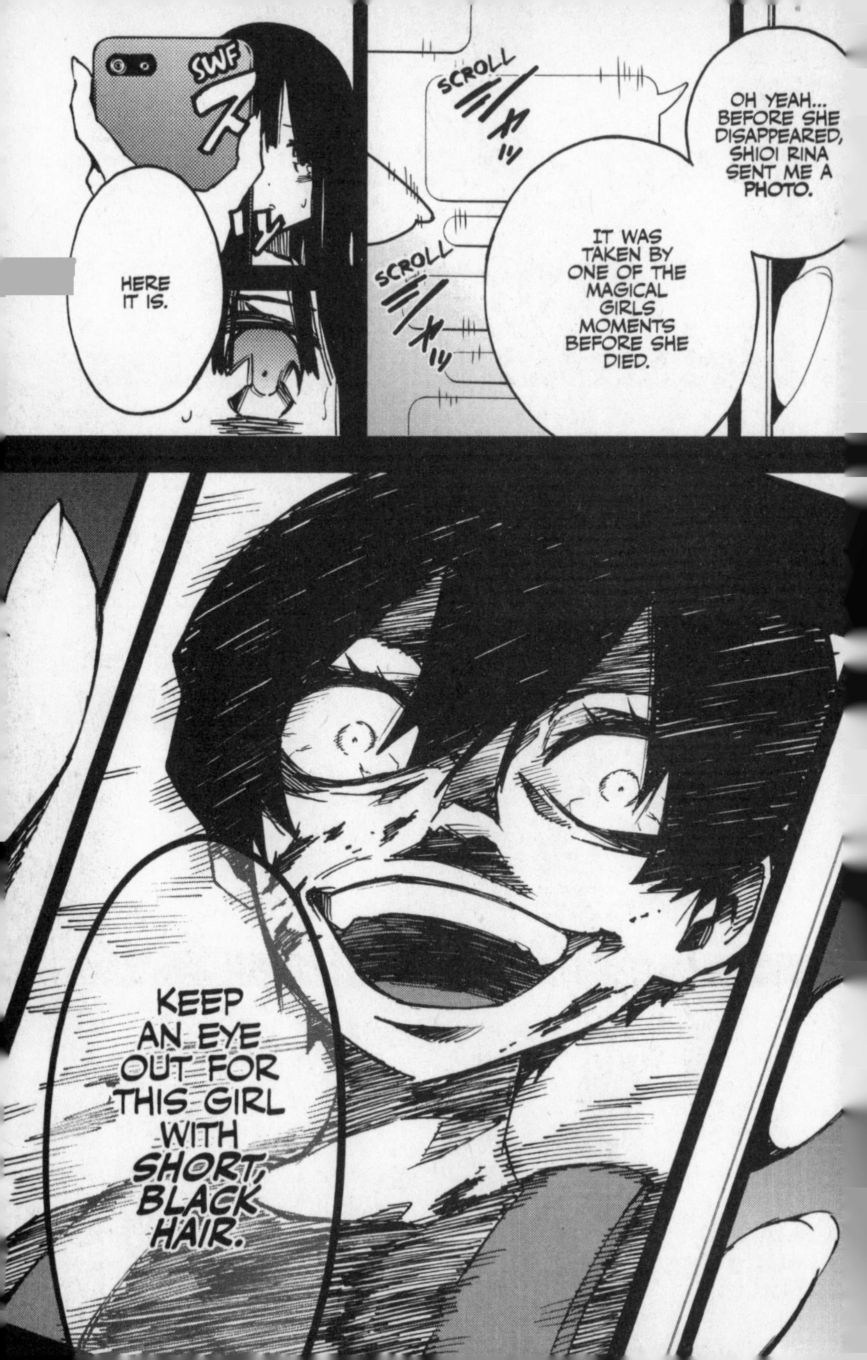
OH YEAH... BEFORE SHE DISAPPEARED, SHIOI RINA SENT ME A PHOTO.
IT WAS TAKEN BY ONE OF THE MAGICAL GIRLS MOMENTS BEFORE SHE DIED.
SCROLL
SCROLL
SWF
HERE IT IS.
KEEP AN EYE OUT FOR THIS GIRL WITH SHORT, BLACK HAIR.

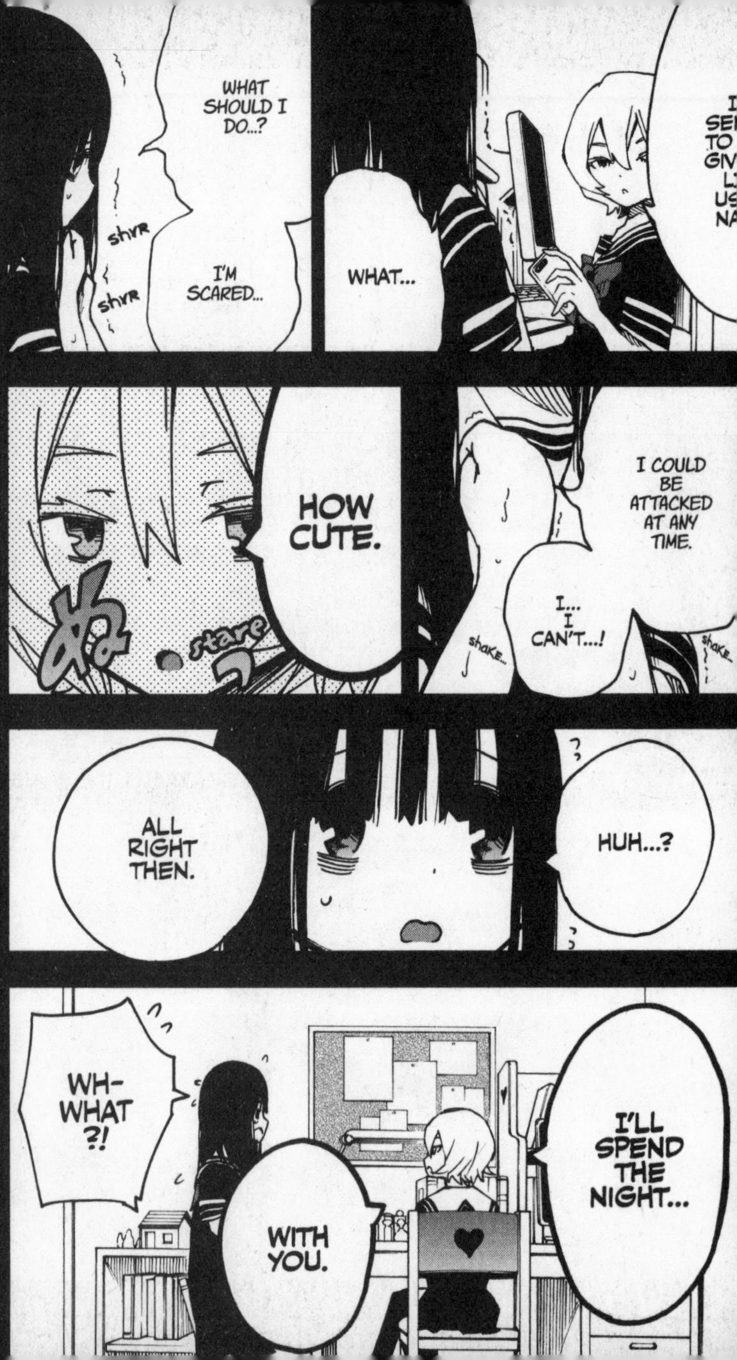
WHAT...
WHAT SHOULD I DO...?
shvr
shvr
I'M SCARED...
I COULD BE ATTACKED AT ANY TIME.
shake...
I... I CAN'T...!
shake...
HOW CUTE.
ぬっ
stare
HUH...?
ALL RIGHT THEN.
I'LL SPEND THE NIGHT...
WITH YOU.
WH-WHAT?!

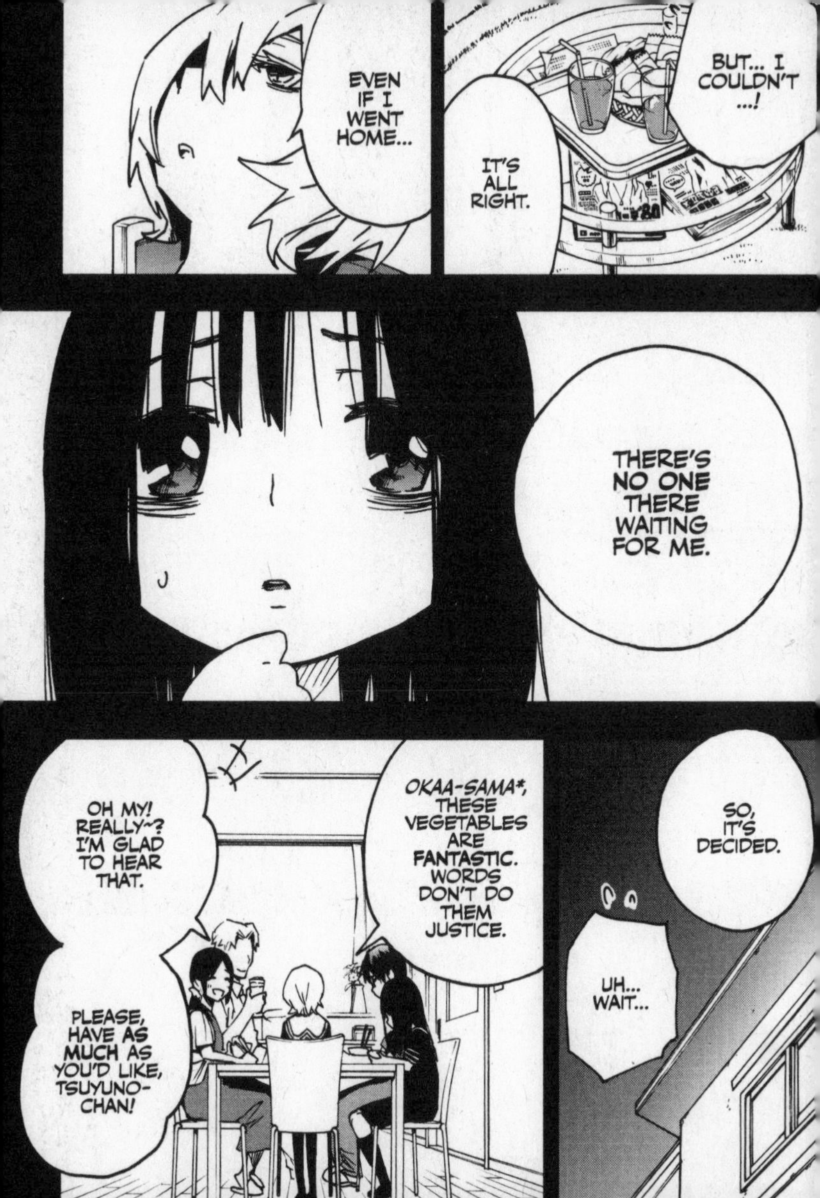
BUT... I COULDN'T ...!
IT'S ALL RIGHT.
EVEN IF I WENT HOME...
THERE'S NO ONE THERE WAITING FOR ME.
SO, IT'S DECIDED.
UH... WAIT...
OKAA-SAMA*, THESE VEGETABLES ARE FANTASTIC. WORDS DON'T DO THEM JUSTICE.
OH MY! REALLY~? I'M GLAD TO HEAR THAT.
PLEASE, HAVE AS MUCH AS YOU'D LIKE, TSUYUNO-CHAN!

*Okaa-sama is an extremely polite and formal honorific for "mother."

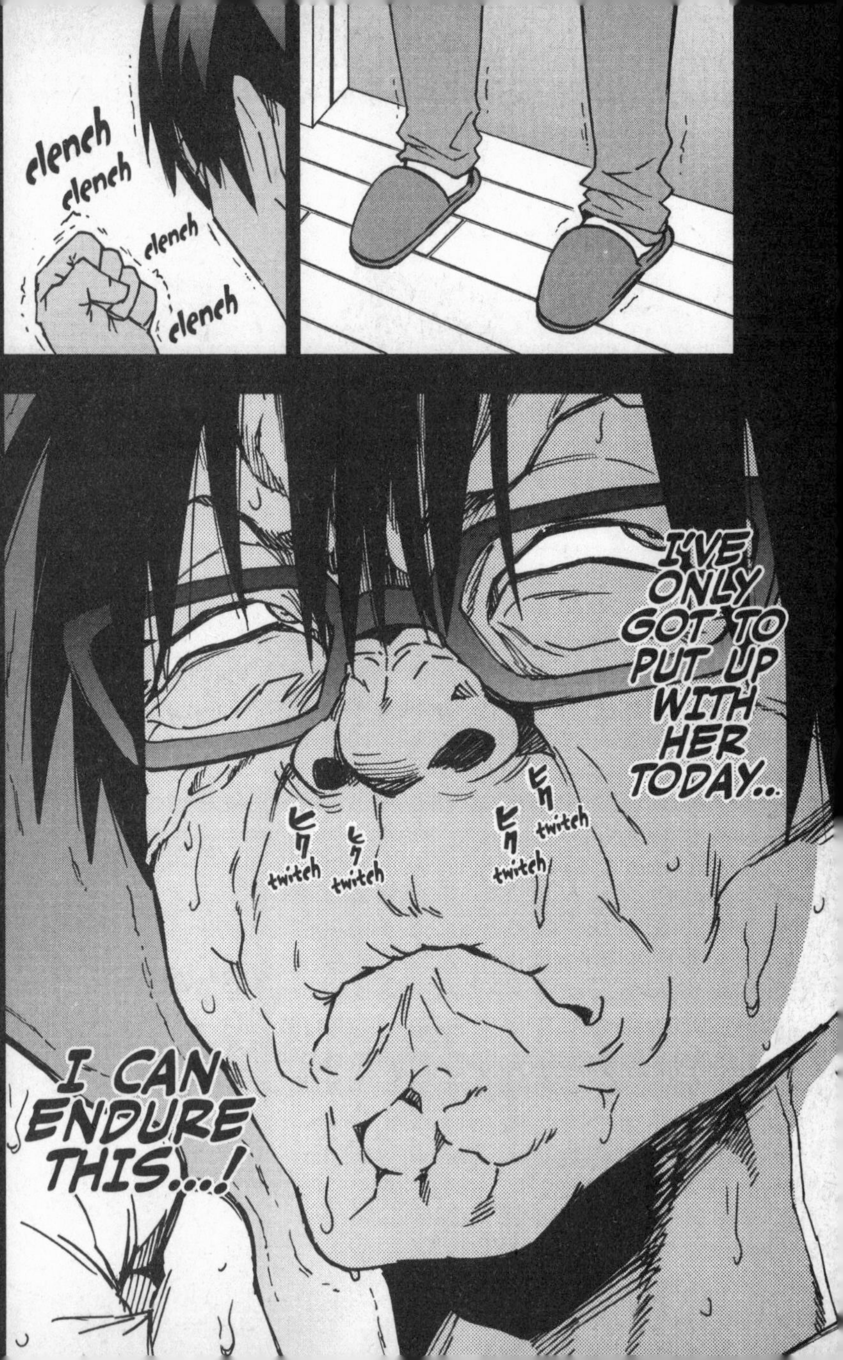
clench
clench
clench
clench
I'VE ONLY GOT TO PUT UP WITH HER TODAY...
ヒク twitch
ヒク twitch
ヒク twitch
ヒク twitch
I CAN ENDURE THIS...!

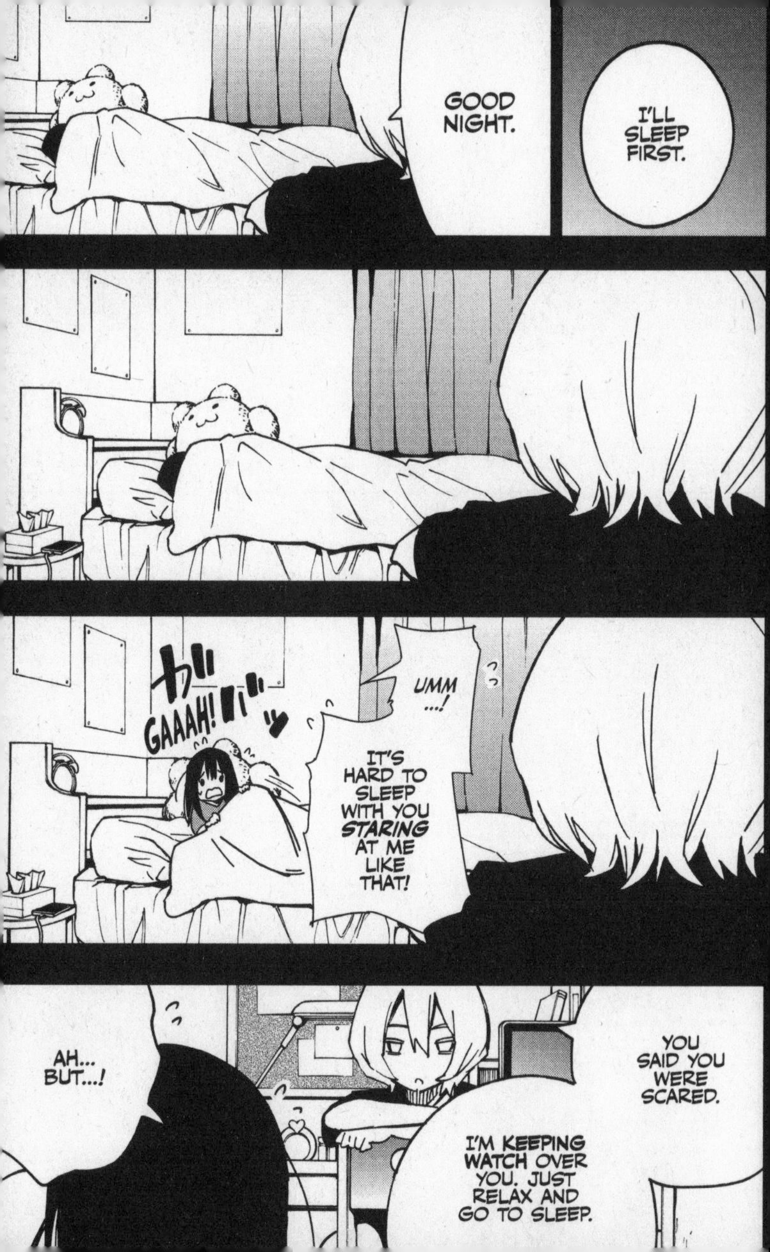
I'LL SLEEP FIRST.
GOOD NIGHT.
UMM ...!
IT'S HARD TO SLEEP WITH YOU STARING AT ME LIKE THAT!
GAAAH!
YOU SAID YOU WERE SCARED.
I'M KEEPING WATCH OVER YOU. JUST RELAX AND GO TO SLEEP.
AH... BUT...!

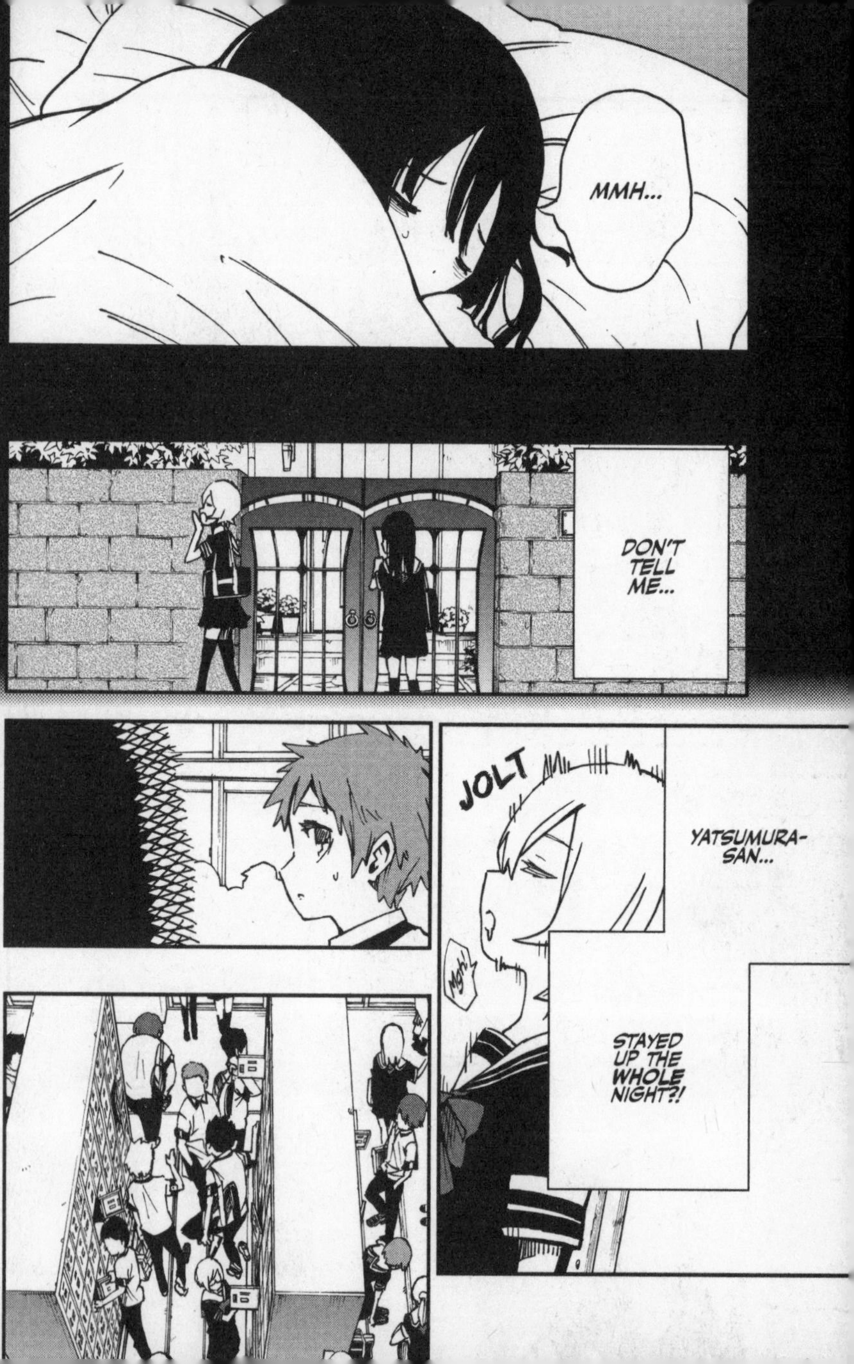
MMH...
DON'T TELL ME...
JOLT
YATSUMURA-SAN...
Mgh!
STAYED UP THE WHOLE NIGHT?!

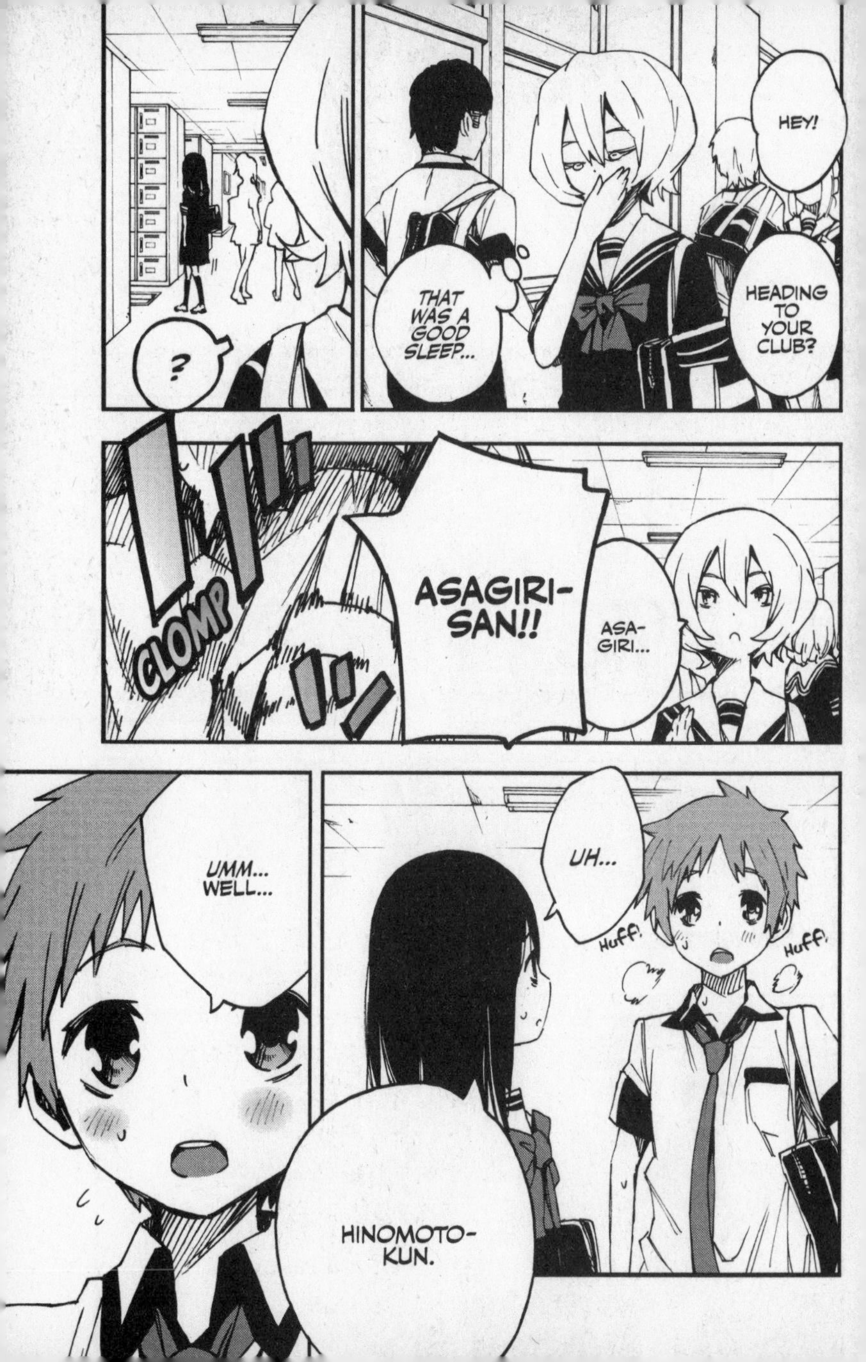
HEY!
HEADING TO YOUR CLUB?
THAT WAS A GOOD SLEEP...
?
ASA-GIRI...
ASAGIRI-SAN!!
CLOMP
UH...
Huff!
Huff!
UMM... WELL...
HINOMOTO-KUN.

MIND IF I WALK HOME WITH YOU?

HUH--?!

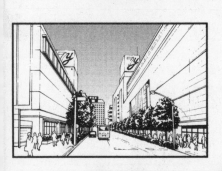

UH... S-SURE...!

WHAT'S THIS...?

I.... UH...

ER...

IT'S OKAY...

SORRY FOR ASKING YOU OUT OF THE BLUE...TO WALK HOME AND ALL...!

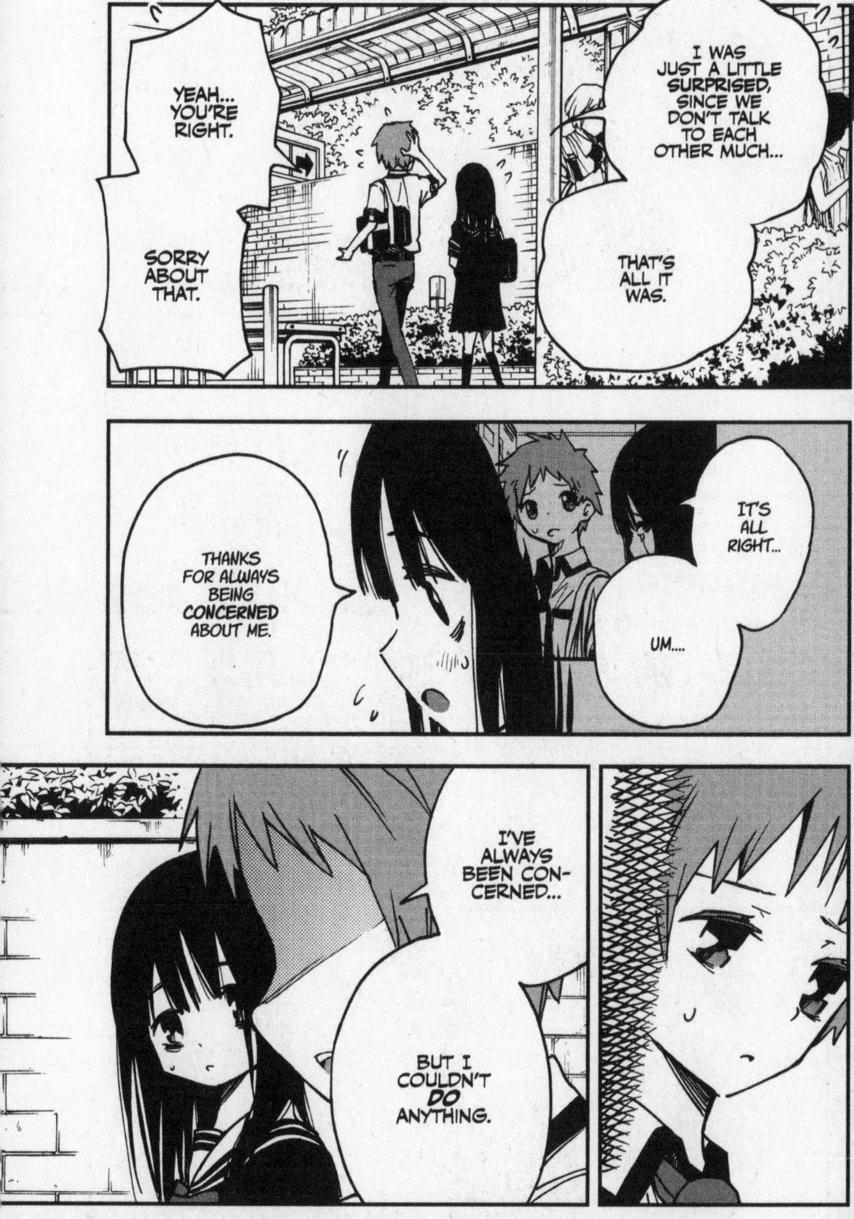
I WAS JUST A LITTLE SURPRISED, SINCE WE DON'T TALK TO EACH OTHER MUCH...
THAT'S ALL IT WAS.
YEAH... YOU'RE RIGHT.
SORRY ABOUT THAT.
IT'S ALL RIGHT...
UM....
THANKS FOR ALWAYS BEING CONCERNED ABOUT ME.
I'VE ALWAYS BEEN CON-CERNED...
BUT I COULDN'T *DO* ANYTHING.

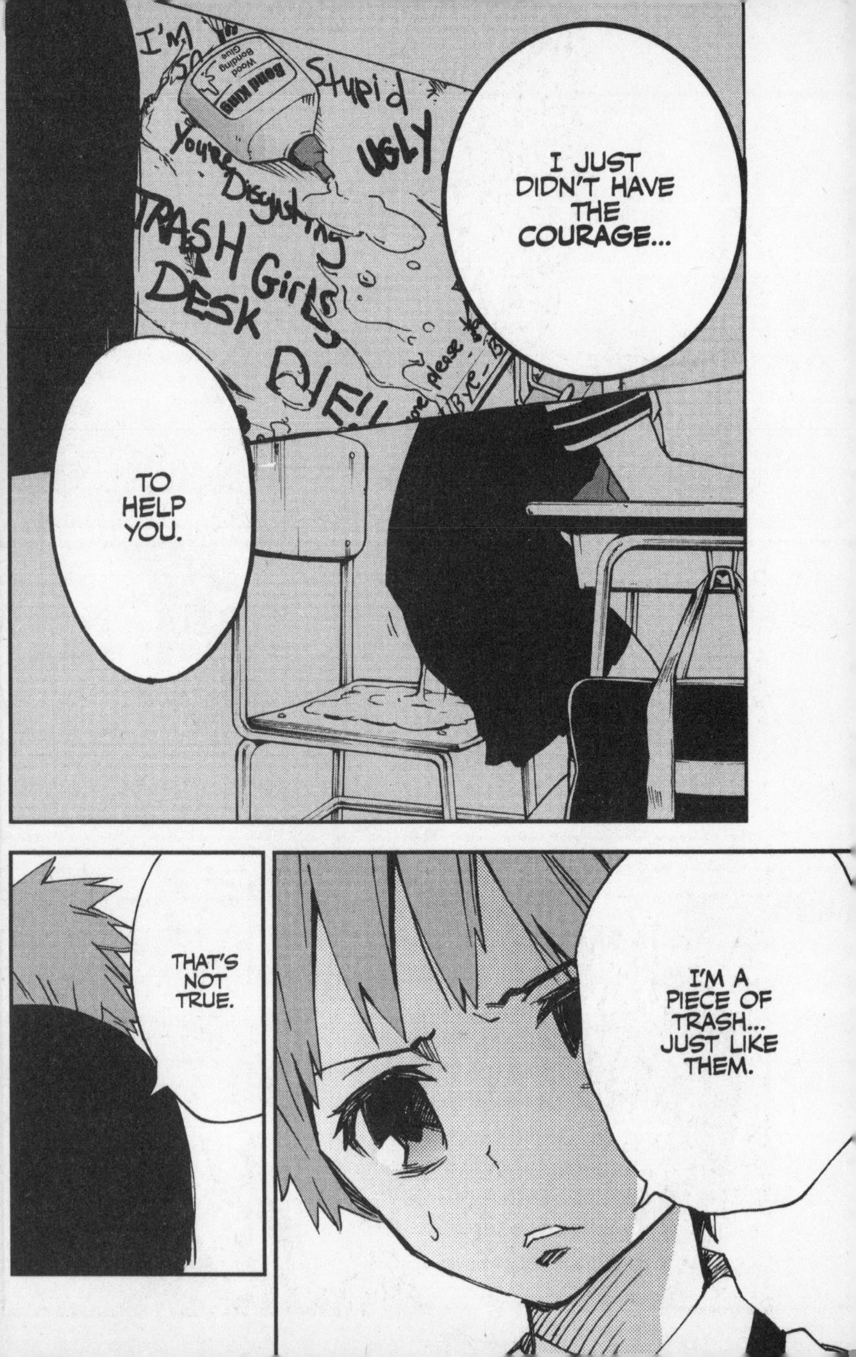
I JUST DIDN'T HAVE THE COURAGE...
TO HELP YOU.
Bond King
Wood Bonding Glue
Stupid
UGLY
You're Disgusting
TRASH Girls DESK
DIE!!
I'M A PIECE OF TRASH... JUST LIKE THEM.
THAT'S NOT TRUE.

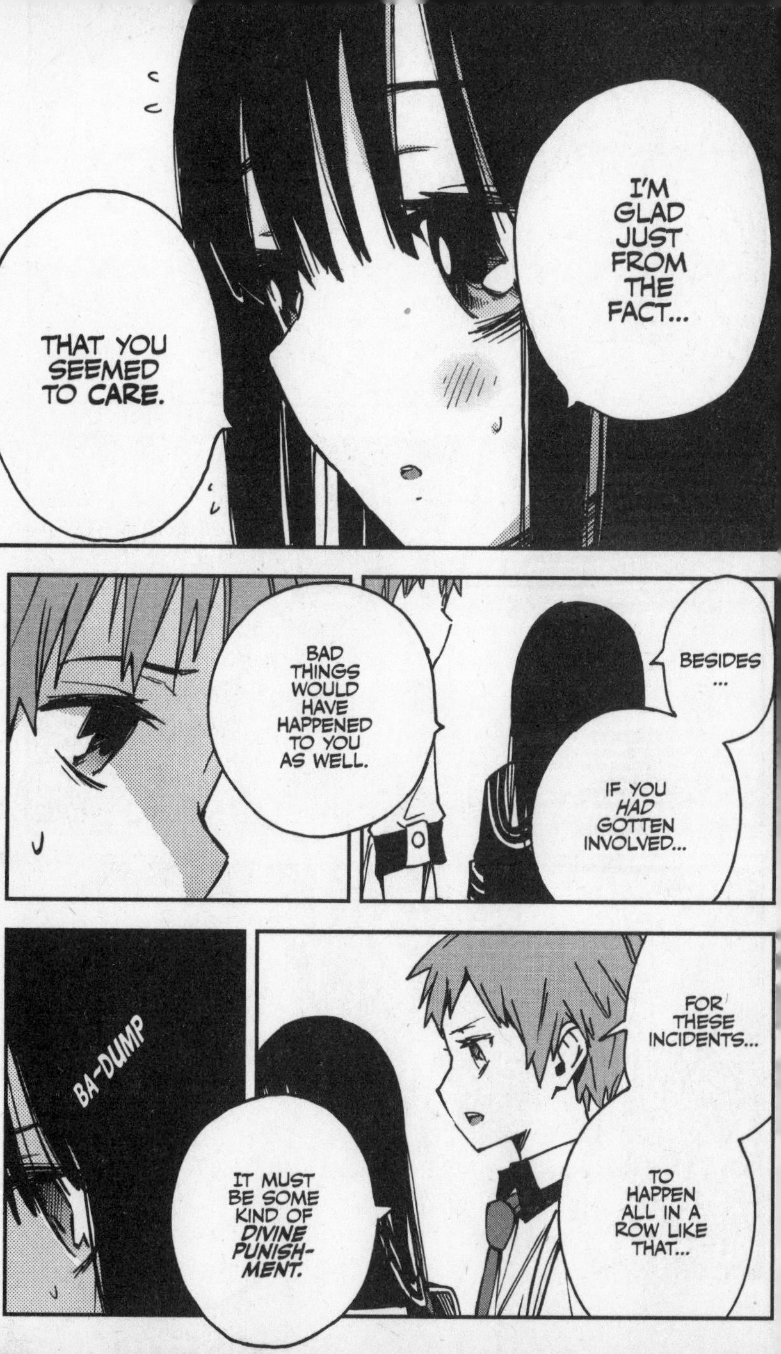
I'M GLAD JUST FROM THE FACT...
THAT YOU SEEMED TO CARE.
BESIDES ...
IF YOU *HAD* GOTTEN INVOLVED...
BAD THINGS WOULD HAVE HAPPENED TO YOU AS WELL.
FOR THESE INCIDENTS...
TO HAPPEN ALL IN A ROW LIKE THAT...
IT MUST BE SOME KIND OF *DIVINE PUNISHMENT.*
BA-DUMP

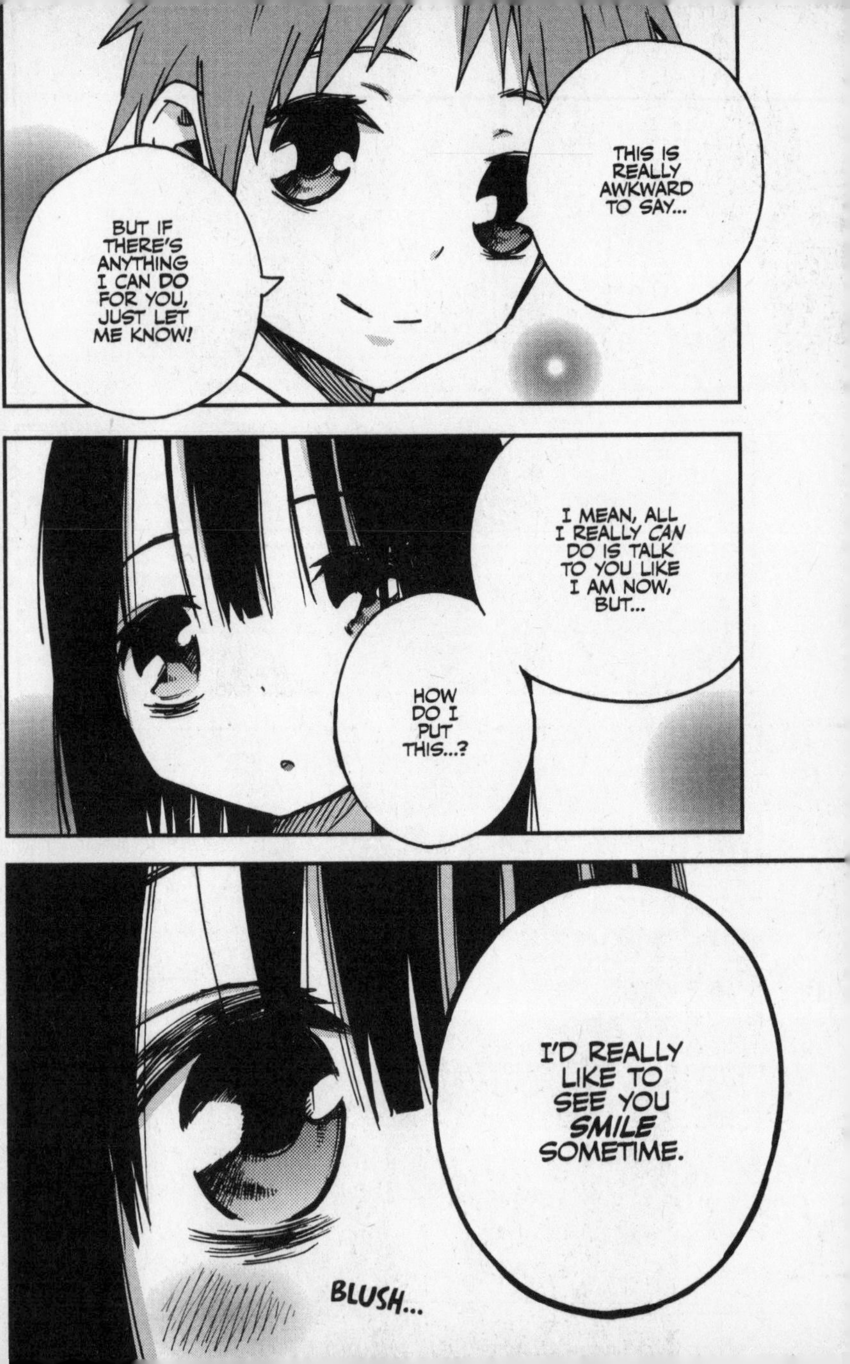
THIS IS REALLY AWKWARD TO SAY...
BUT IF THERE'S ANYTHING I CAN DO FOR YOU, JUST LET ME KNOW!
I MEAN, ALL I REALLY *CAN* DO IS TALK TO YOU LIKE I AM NOW, BUT...
HOW DO I PUT THIS...?
I'D REALLY LIKE TO SEE YOU ***SMILE*** SOMETIME.
BLUSH...

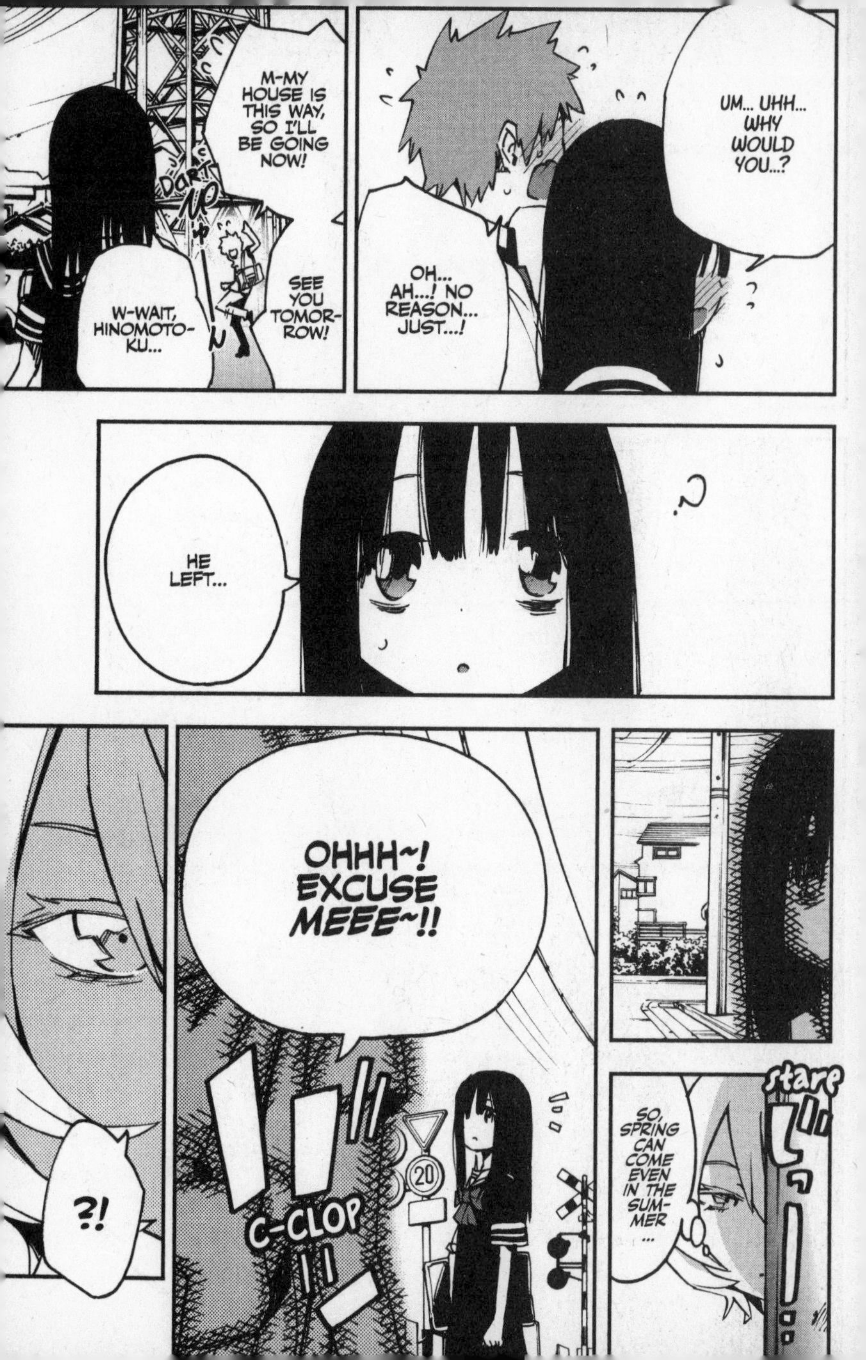
UM... UHH... WHY WOULD YOU...?
OH... AH...! NO REASON... JUST...!
M-MY HOUSE IS THIS WAY, SO I'LL BE GOING NOW!
DART
SEE YOU TOMOR-ROW!
W-WAIT, HINOMOTO-KU...
HE LEFT...
stare
SO, SPRING CAN COME EVEN IN THE SUM-MER...
OHHH~! EXCUSE MEEE~!!
20
C-CLOP
?!

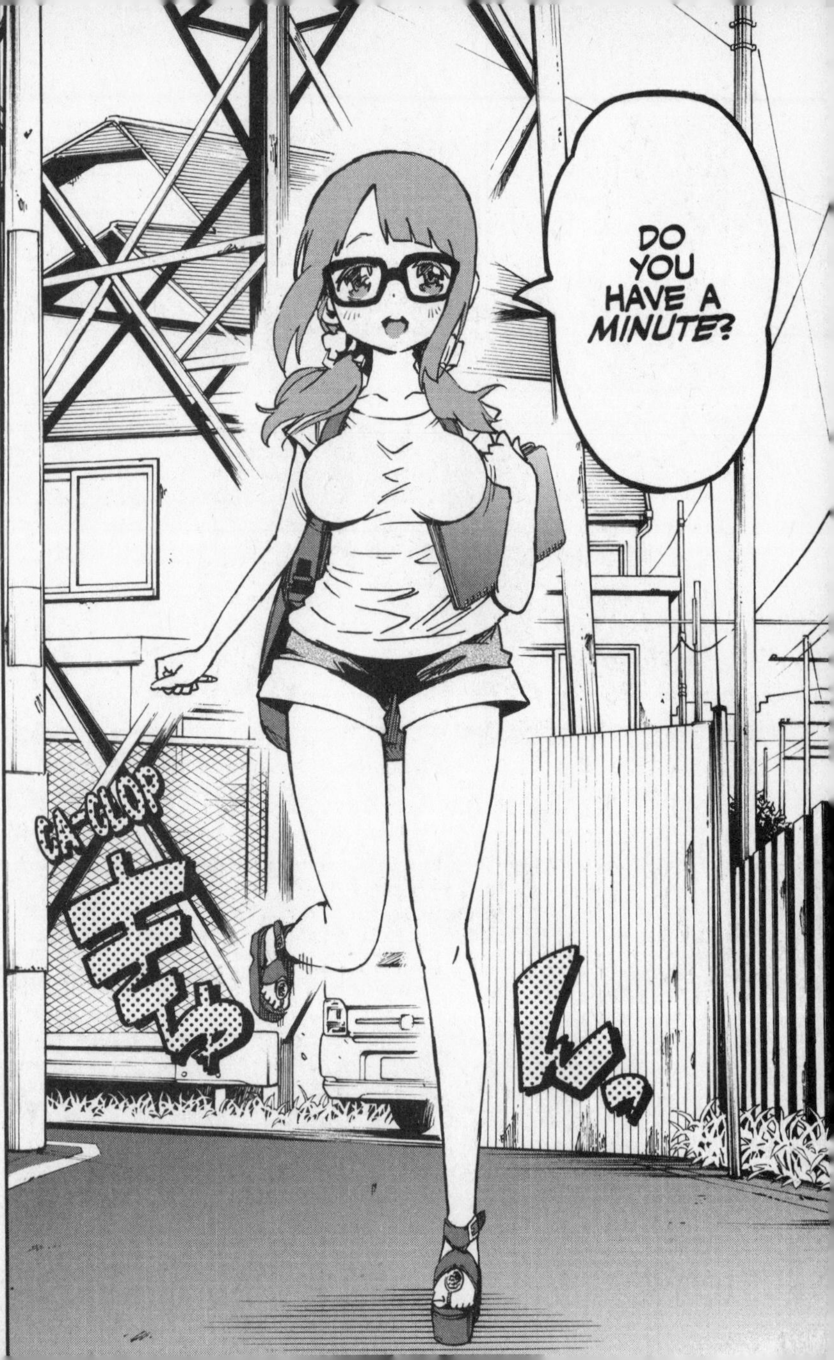
DO YOU HAVE A MINUTE?
CA-CLOP

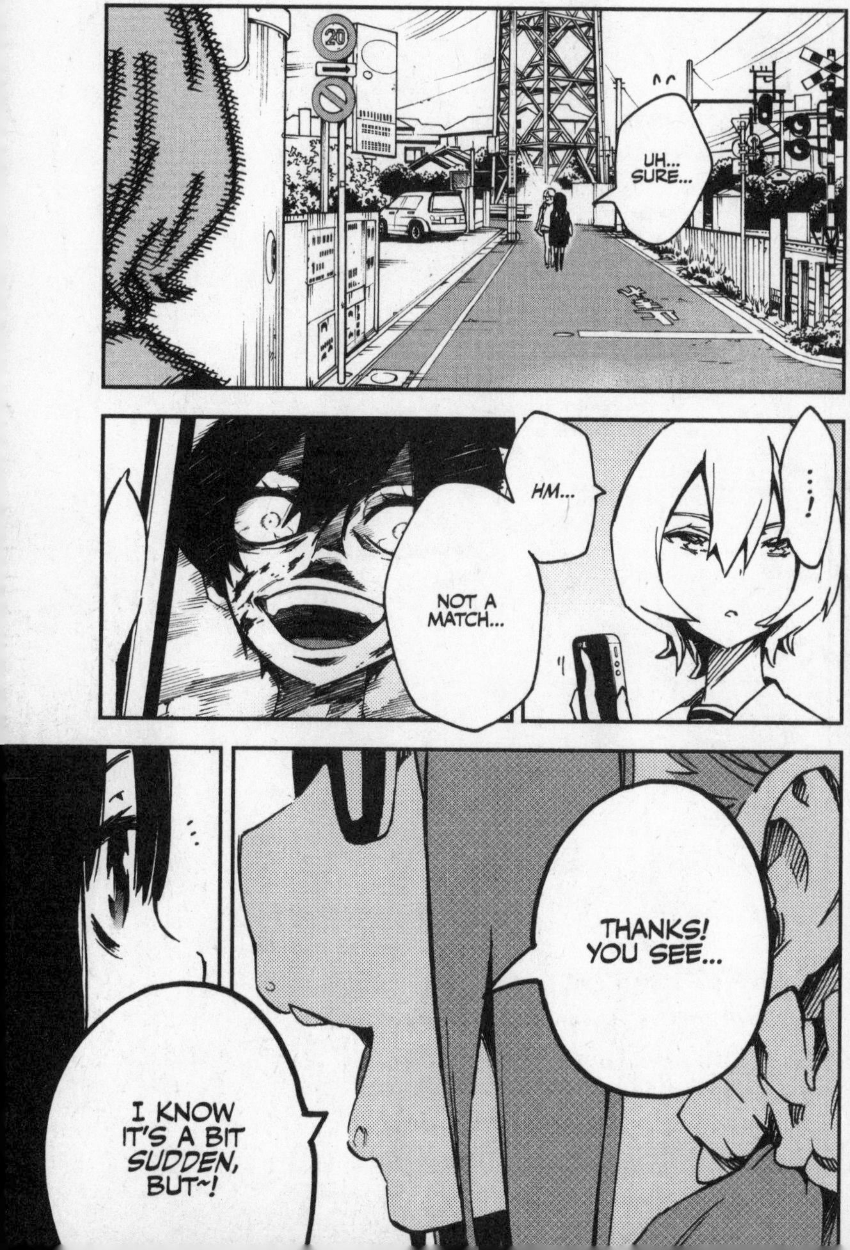

UH... SURE...
...!
HM...
NOT A MATCH...
THANKS! YOU SEE...
I KNOW IT'S A BIT *SUDDEN,* BUT~!
...

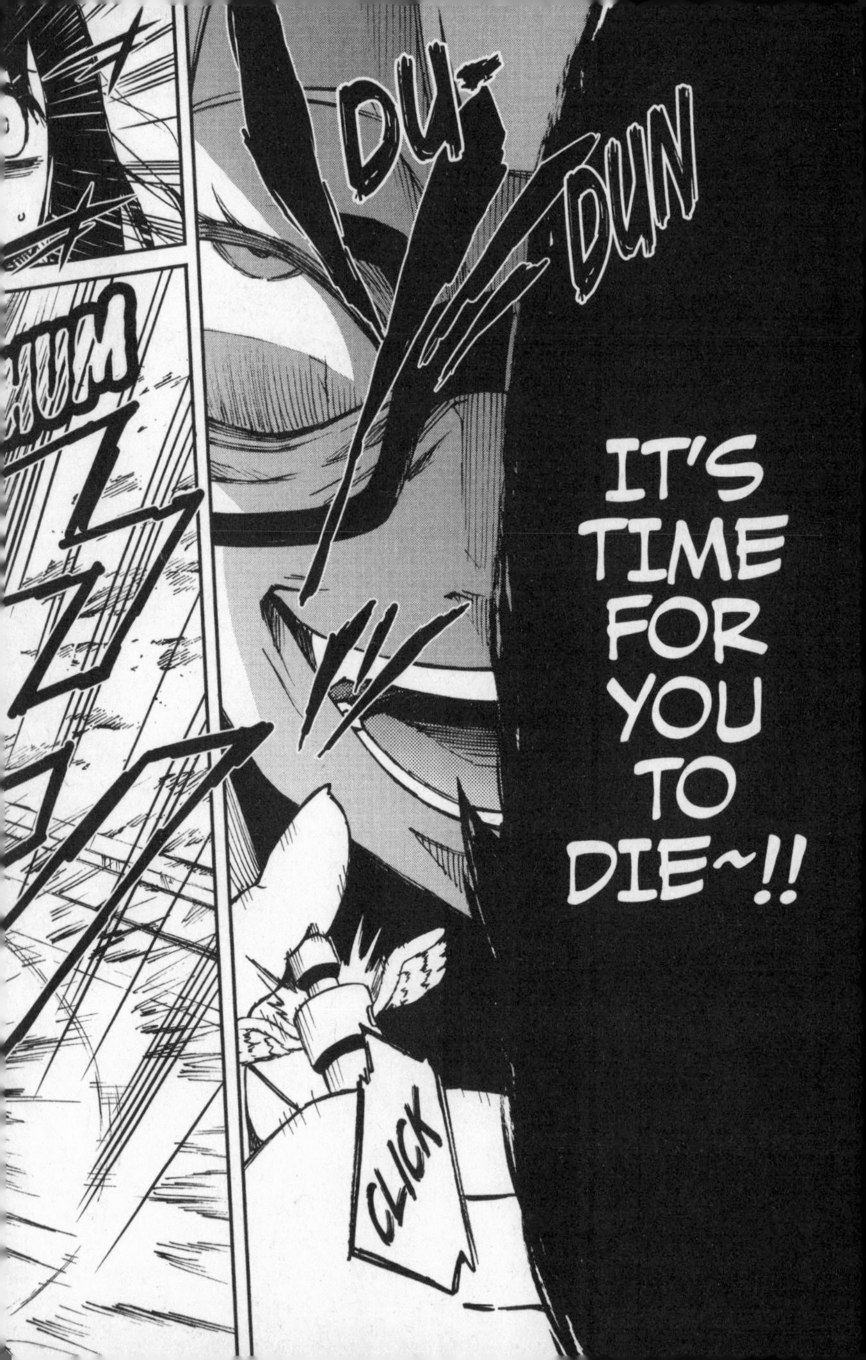
DU-
DUN
IT'S TIME FOR YOU TO DIE~!!
CLICK
HUM

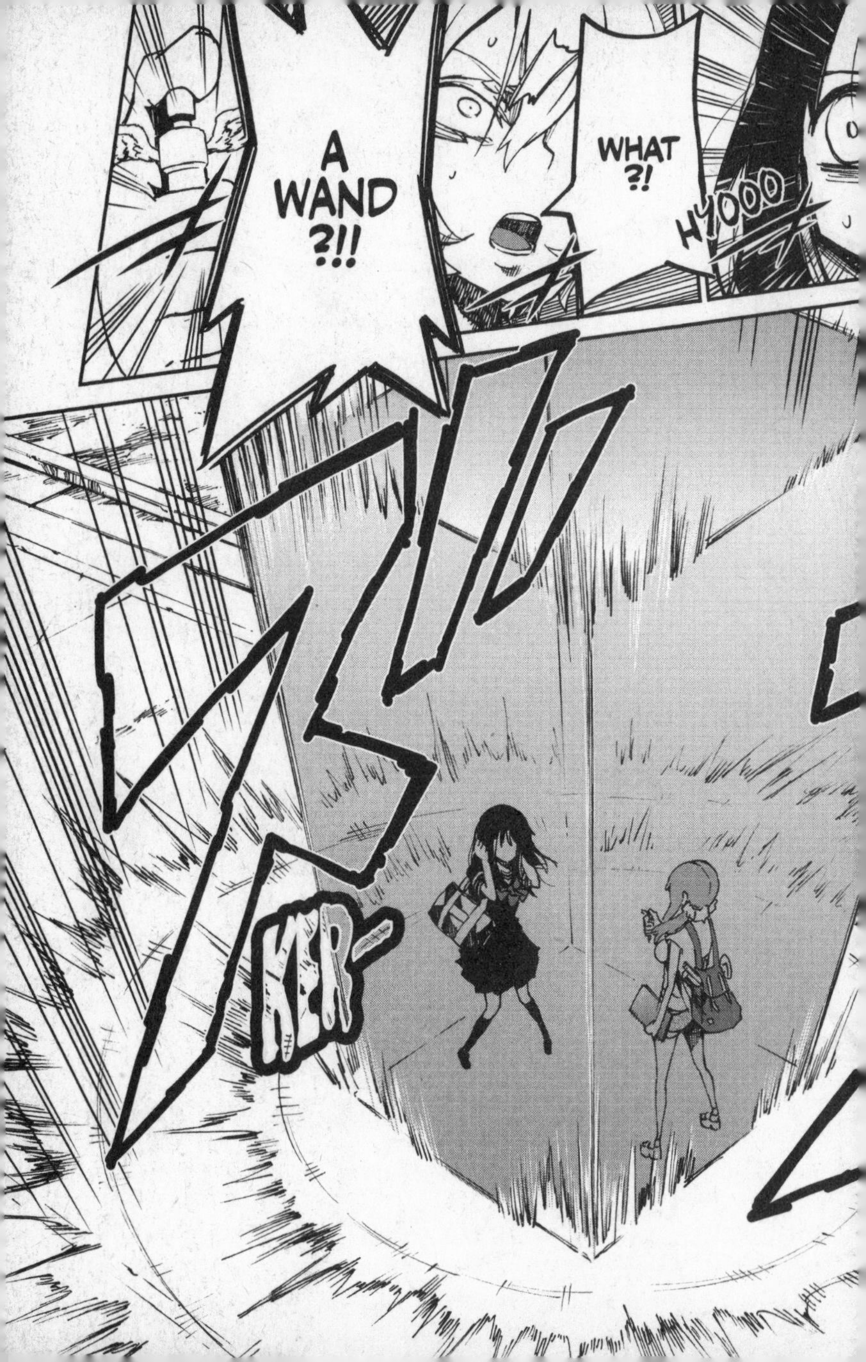
WHAT ?!
HYOOO
A WAND ?!!
KRR-

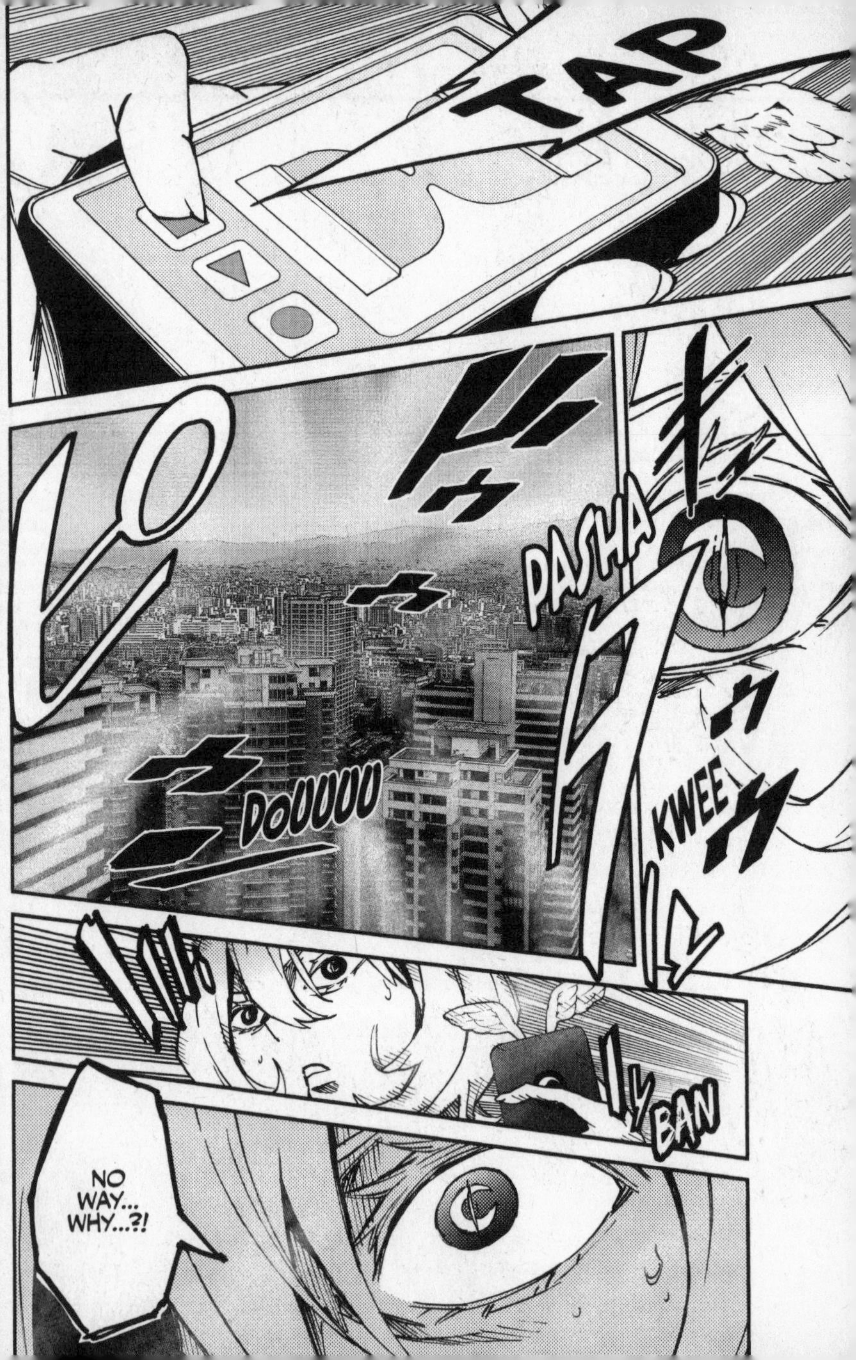
TAP
PASHA
KWEE
DOUUUU
BAN
NO WAY... WHY...?!

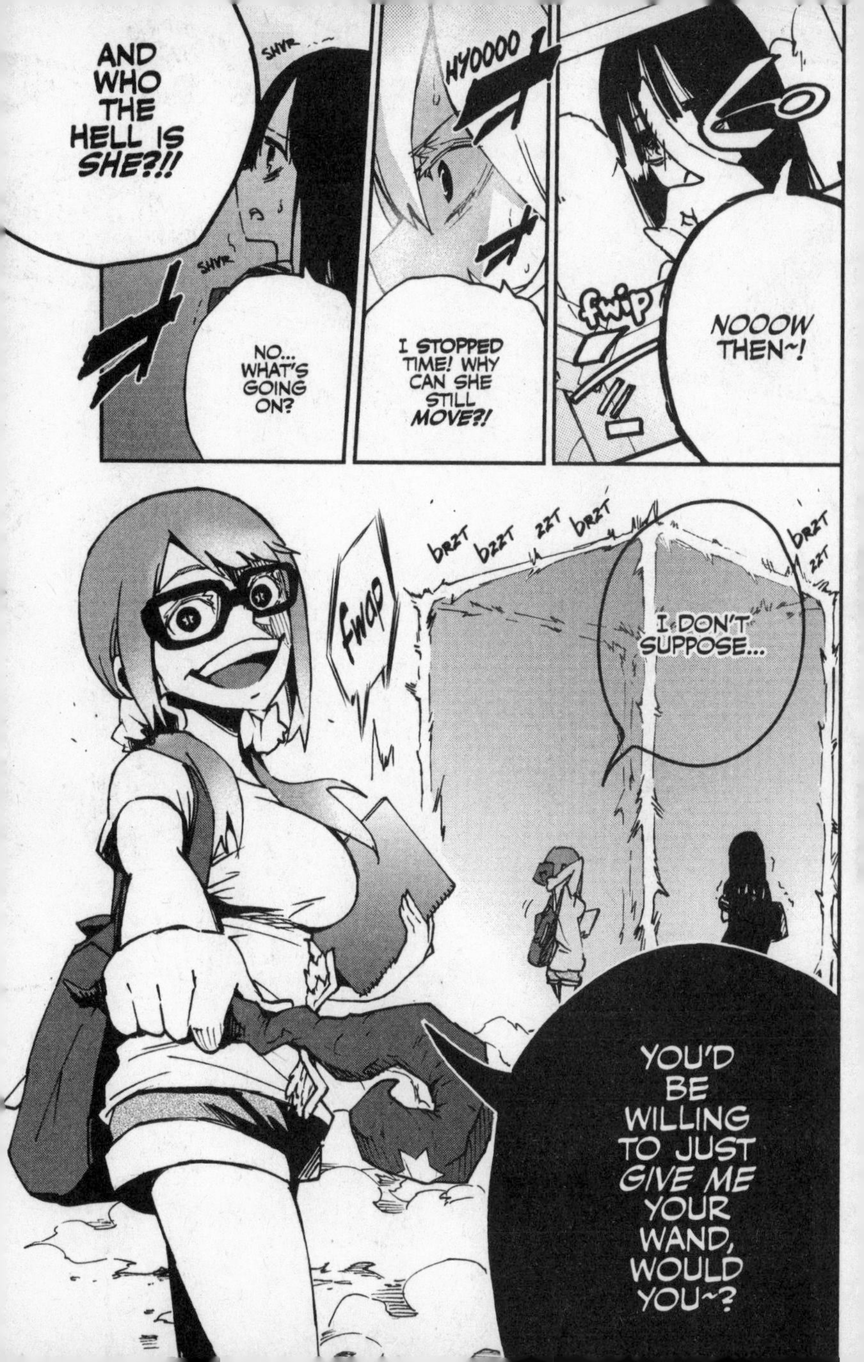
fwip
NOOOW THEN~!
HYOOOO
I STOPPED TIME! WHY CAN SHE STILL MOVE?!
SHVR
AND WHO THE HELL IS SHE?!!
SHVR
NO... WHAT'S GOING ON?
brzt
zzt
brzt
zzt
bzzt
brzt
I DON'T SUPPOSE...
fwap
YOU'D BE WILLING TO JUST GIVE ME YOUR WAND, WOULD YOU~?

MAGICAL GIRL
SITE

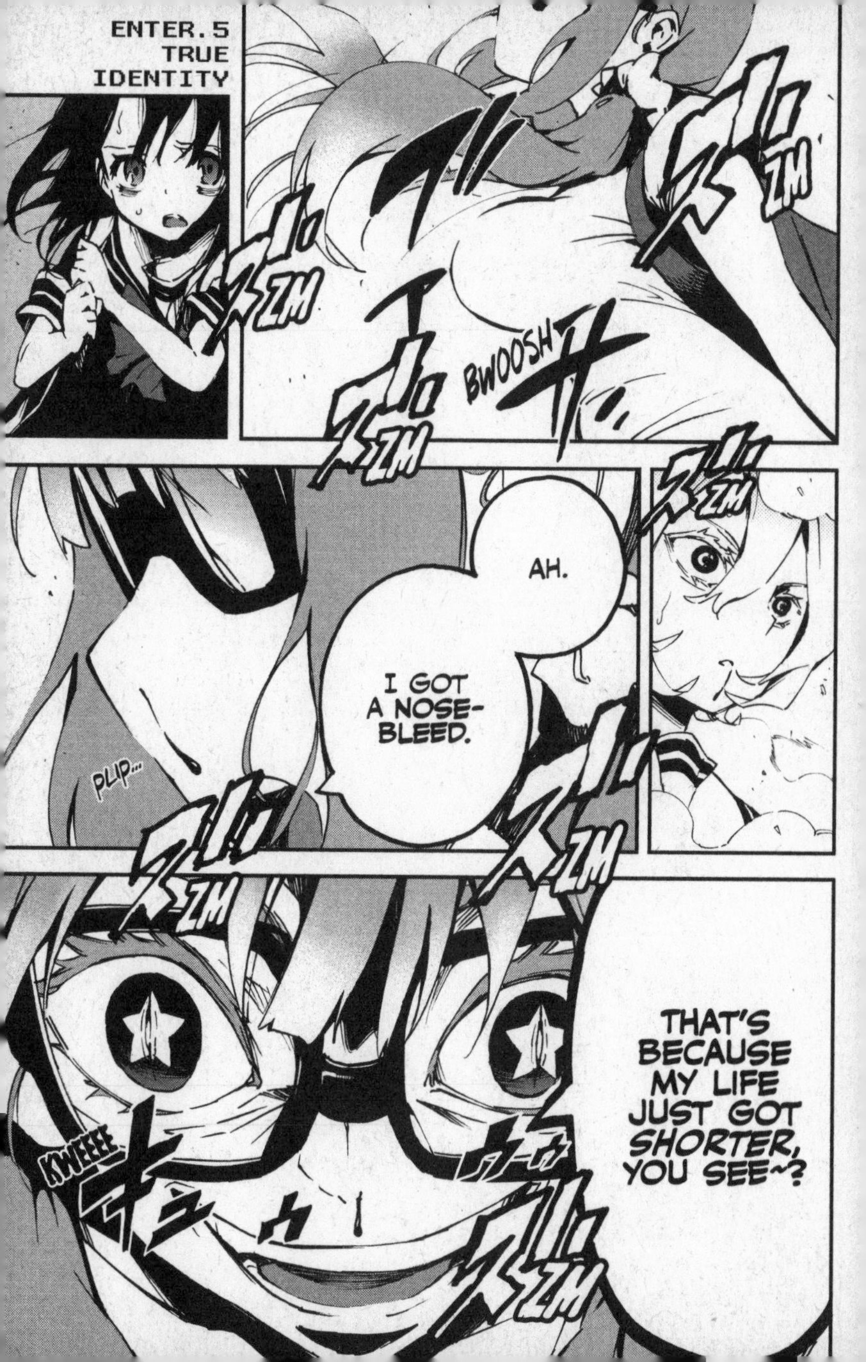
ENTER. 5
TRUE
IDENTITY
ZM
BWOOSH
ZM
ZM
ZM
AH.
I GOT A NOSE-BLEED.
PLIP...
ZM
ZM
THAT'S BECAUSE MY LIFE JUST GOT SHORTER, YOU SEE~?
KWEEEE
ZM

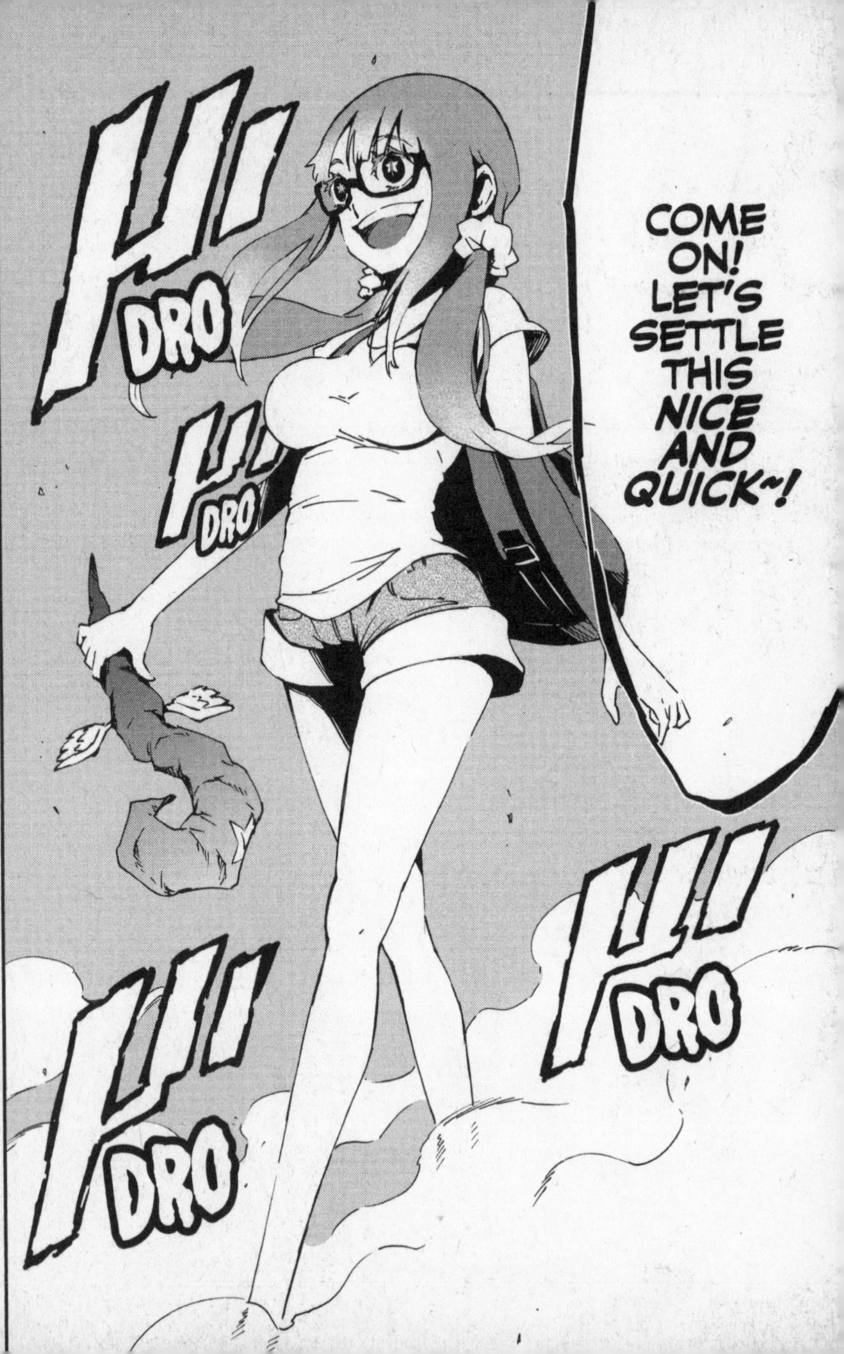
COME ON! LET'S SETTLE THIS NICE AND QUICK~!
DRO
DRO
DRO
DRO

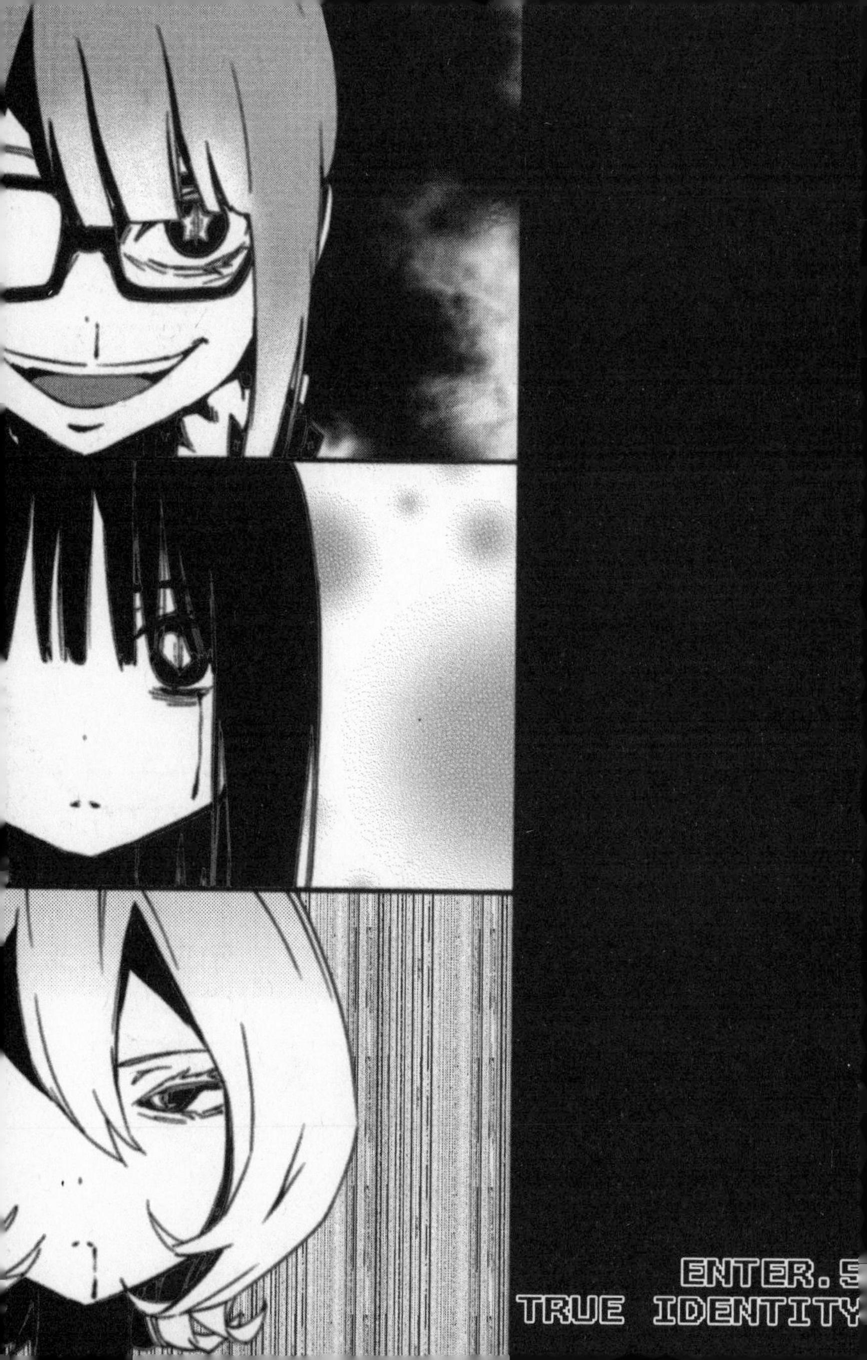
ENTER.5
TRUE IDENTITY

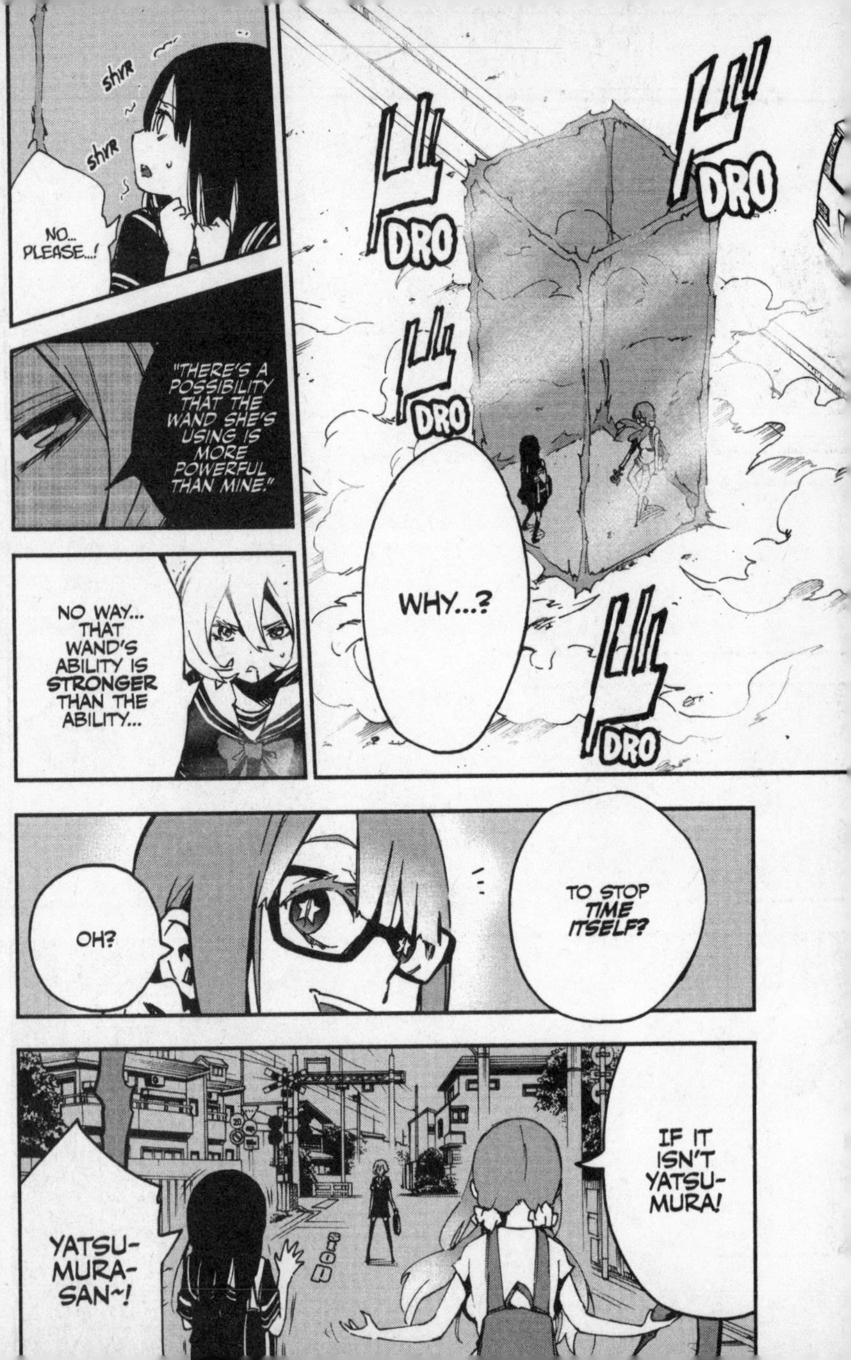
DRO
DRO
DRO
WHY...?
DRO
shvr
shvr
NO... PLEASE...!
"THERE'S A POSSIBILITY THAT THE WAND SHE'S USING IS MORE POWERFUL THAN MINE."
NO WAY... THAT WAND'S ABILITY IS STRONGER THAN THE ABILITY...
TO STOP TIME ITSELF?
OH?
IF IT ISN'T YATSU-MURA!
stop
YATSU-MURA-SAN~!

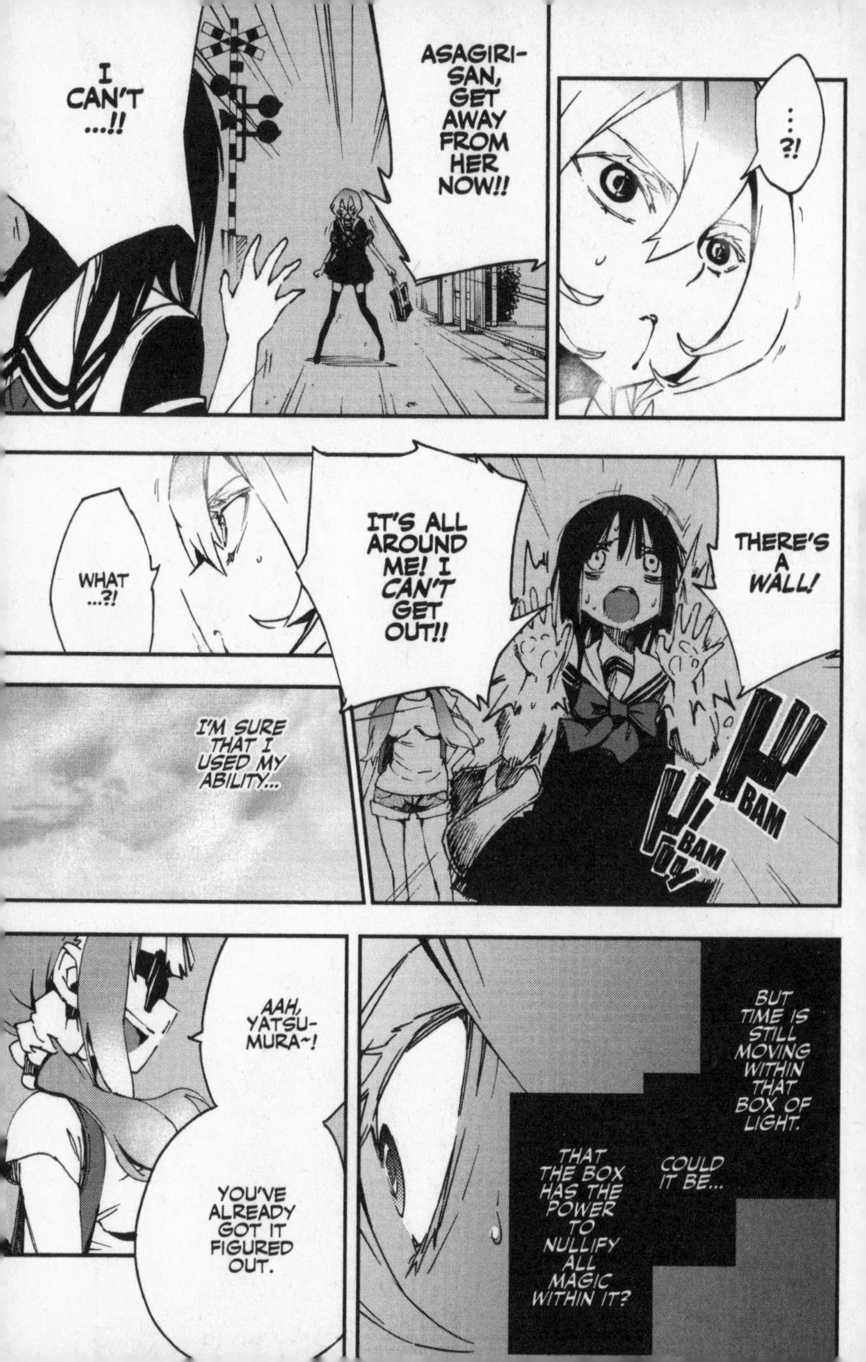
...?!
ASAGIRI-SAN, GET AWAY FROM HER NOW!!
I CAN'T ...!!
THERE'S A WALL!
IT'S ALL AROUND ME! I CAN'T GET OUT!!
BAM
BAM
WHAT ...?!
I'M SURE THAT I USED MY ABILITY...
BUT TIME IS STILL MOVING WITHIN THAT BOX OF LIGHT.
COULD IT BE...
THAT THE BOX HAS THE POWER TO NULLIFY ALL MAGIC WITHIN IT?
AAH, YATSUMURA~!
YOU'VE ALREADY GOT IT FIGURED OUT.

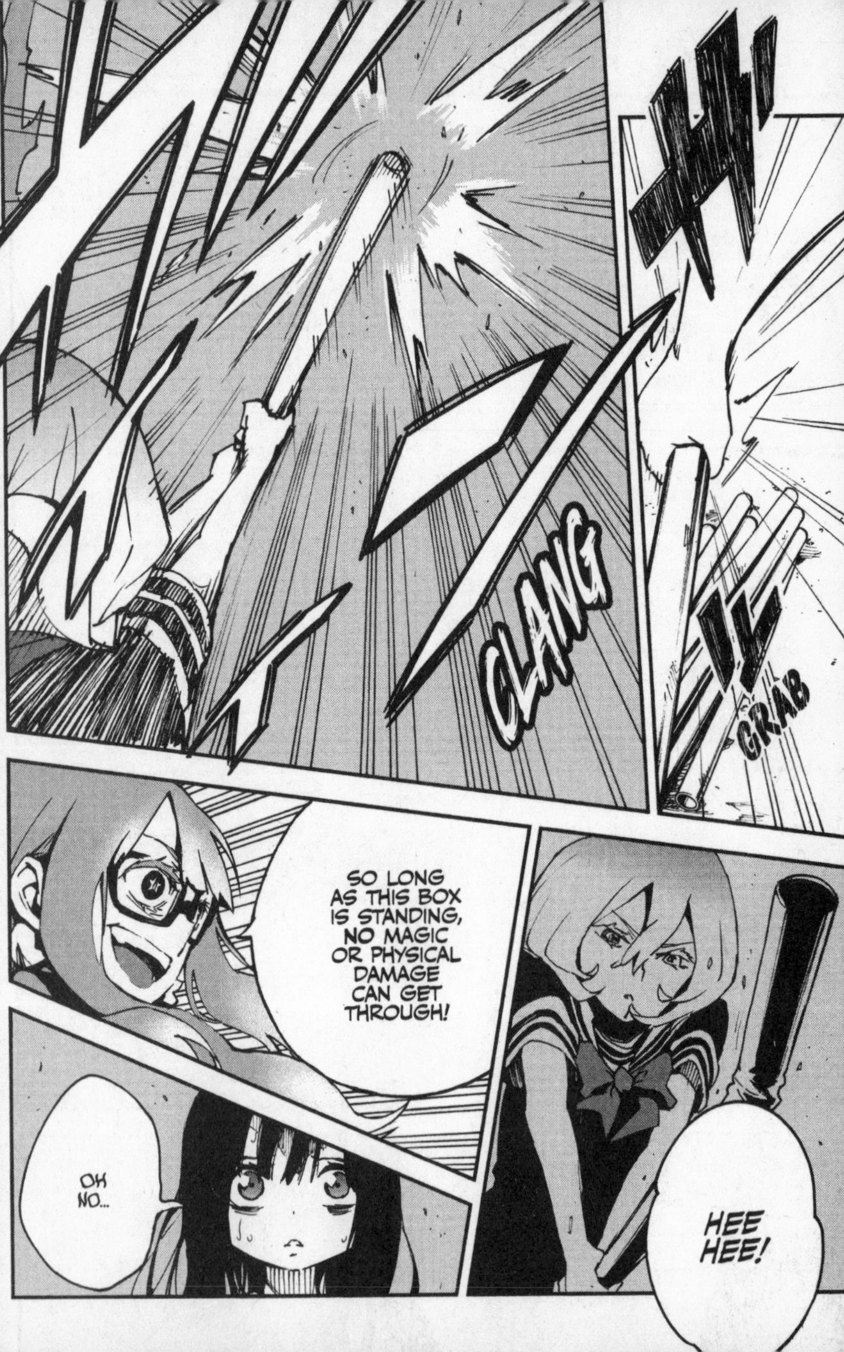
GRAB
CLANG
HEE HEE!
SO LONG AS THIS BOX IS STANDING, NO MAGIC OR PHYSICAL DAMAGE CAN GET THROUGH!
OH NO...

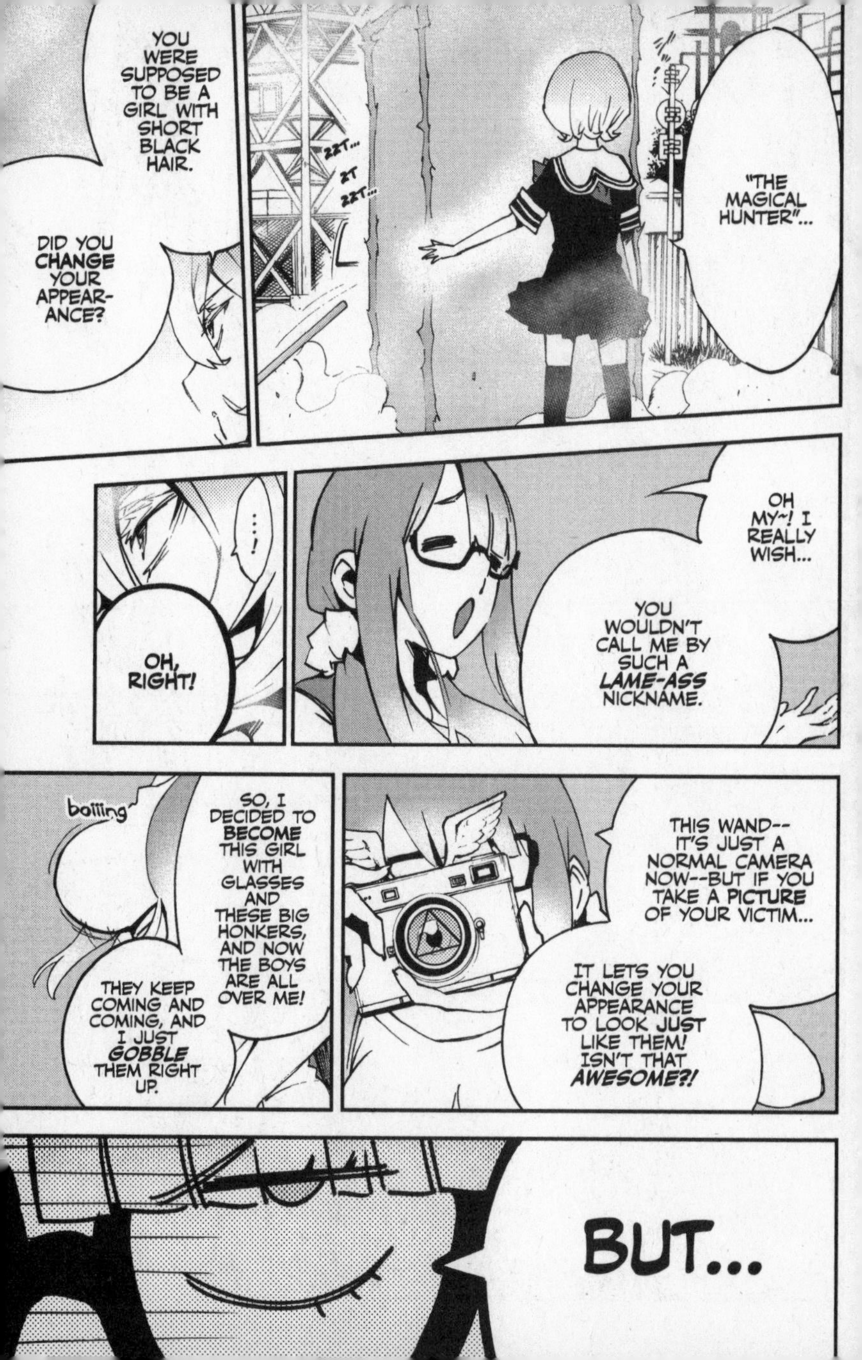
"THE MAGICAL HUNTER"...
ZZT... ZT ZZT...
YOU WERE SUPPOSED TO BE A GIRL WITH SHORT BLACK HAIR.
DID YOU CHANGE YOUR APPEARANCE?
OH MY~! I REALLY WISH...
YOU WOULDN'T CALL ME BY SUCH A LAME-ASS NICKNAME.
...!
OH, RIGHT!
THIS WAND--IT'S JUST A NORMAL CAMERA NOW--BUT IF YOU TAKE A PICTURE OF YOUR VICTIM...
IT LETS YOU CHANGE YOUR APPEARANCE TO LOOK JUST LIKE THEM! ISN'T THAT AWESOME?!
boiiing
SO, I DECIDED TO BECOME THIS GIRL WITH GLASSES AND THESE BIG HONKERS, AND NOW THE BOYS ARE ALL OVER ME!
THEY KEEP COMING AND COMING, AND I JUST GOBBLE THEM RIGHT UP.
BUT...

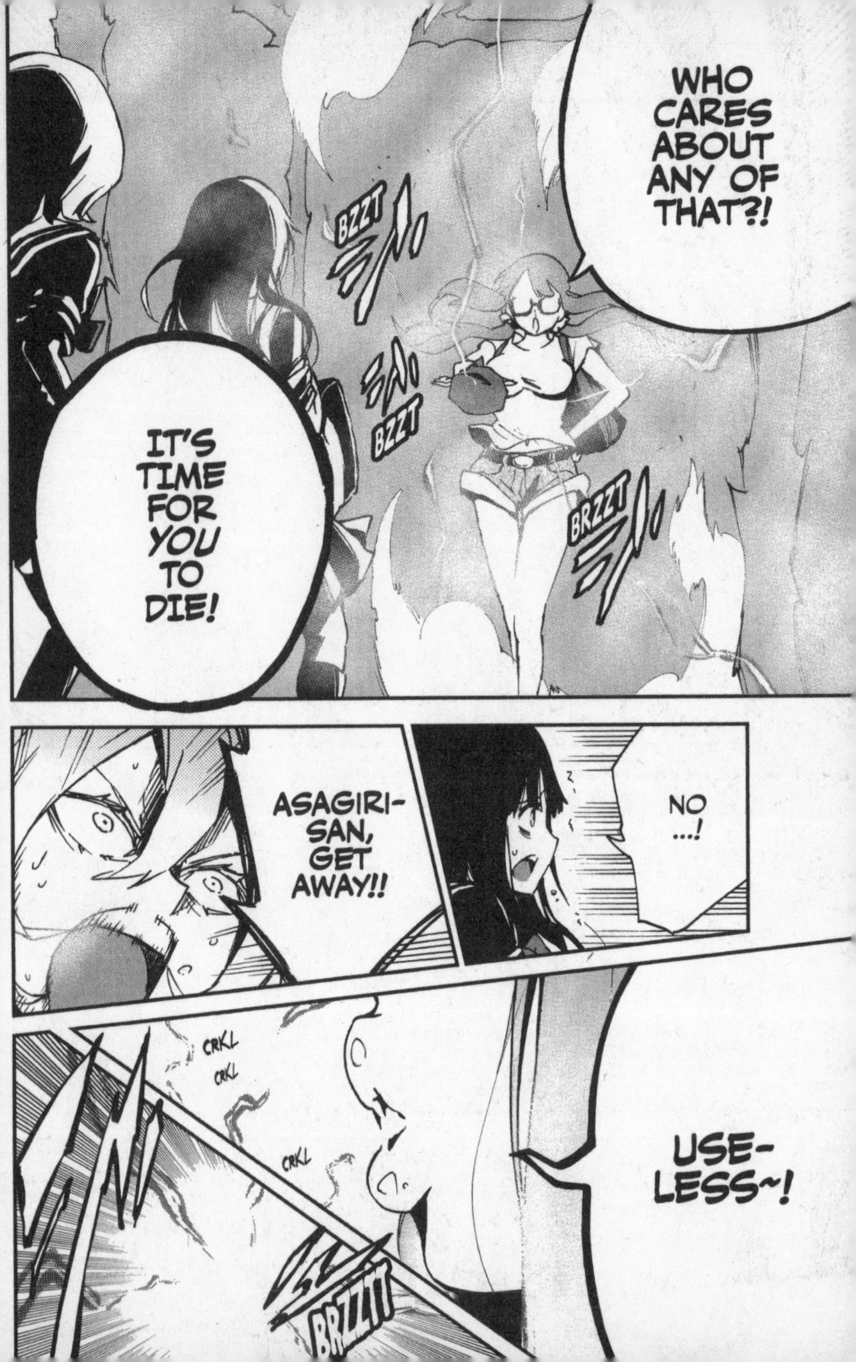

WHO CARES ABOUT ANY OF THAT?!
BZZT
BZZT
BRZZT
IT'S TIME FOR YOU TO DIE!
NO ...!
ASAGIRI-SAN, GET AWAY!!
USE-LESS~!
CRKL
CRKL
CRKL
BRZZTT

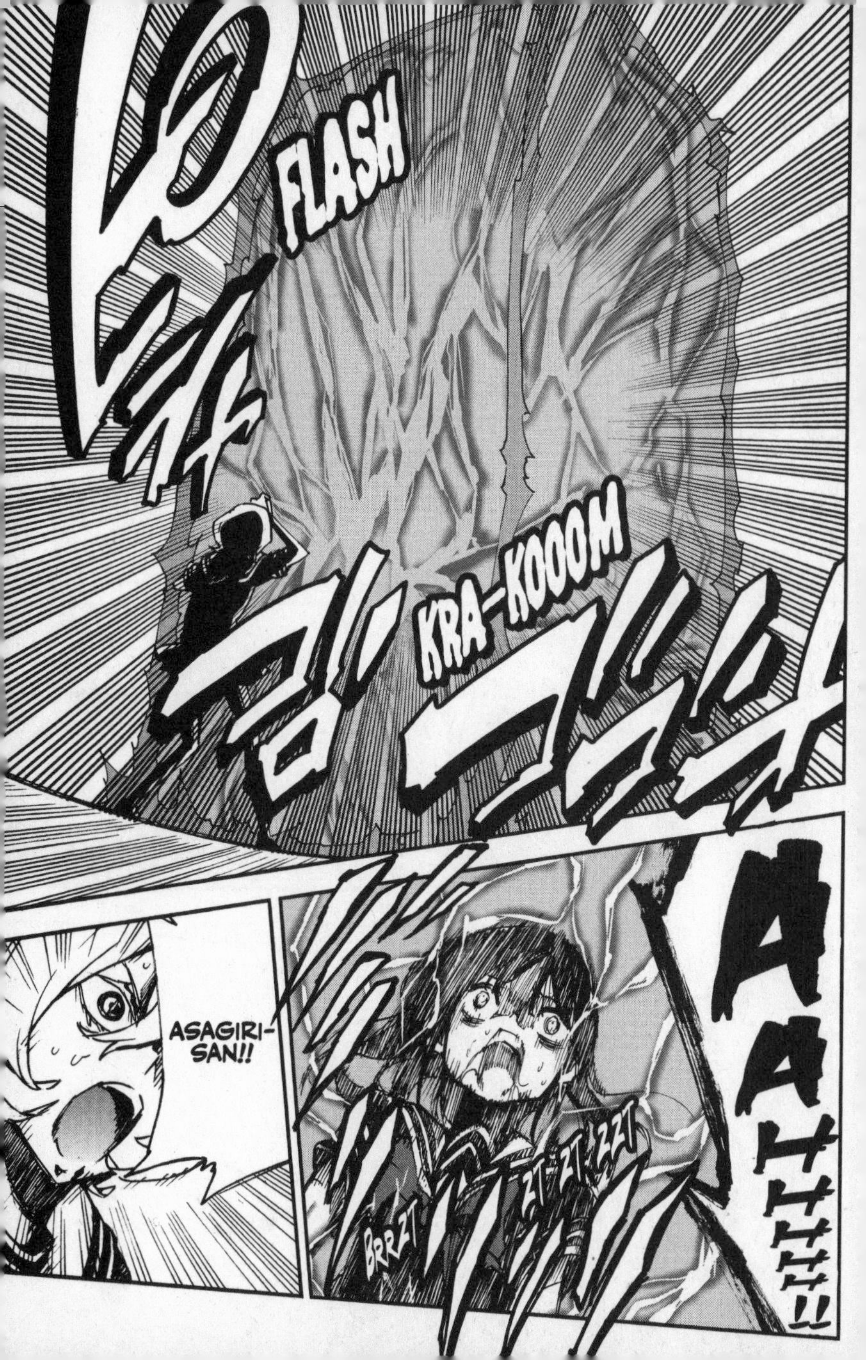
FLASH
KRA-KOOM
AAHHHHH!!
ZT-ZT-ZZT
BRRZT
ASAGIRI-SAN!!

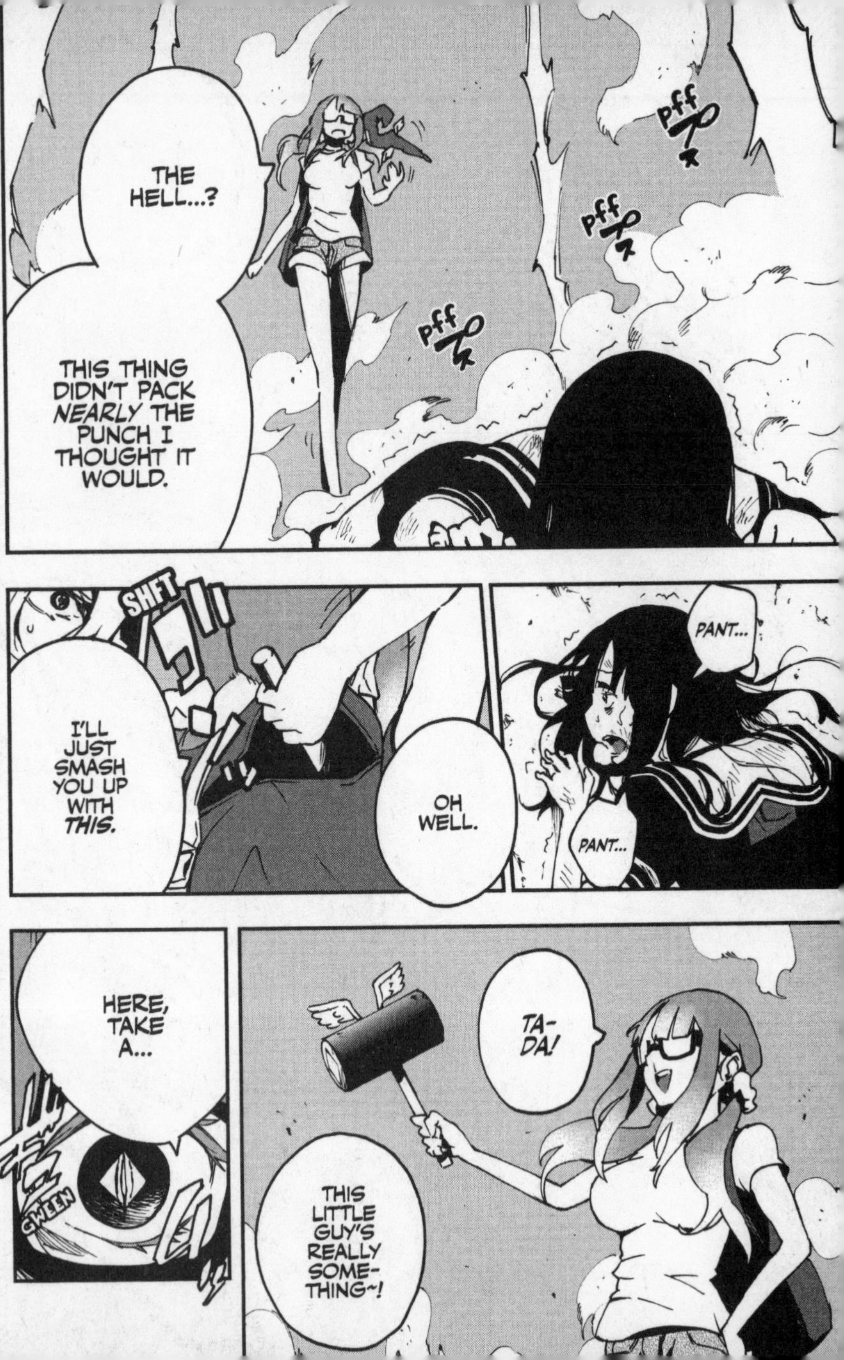
pff
pff
pff
THE HELL...?
THIS THING DIDN'T PACK *NEARLY* THE PUNCH I THOUGHT IT WOULD.
PANT...
PANT...
OH WELL.
SHFT
I'LL JUST SMASH YOU UP WITH *THIS.*
TA-DA!
THIS LITTLE GUY'S REALLY SOME-THING~!
HERE, TAKE A...
GWEEN

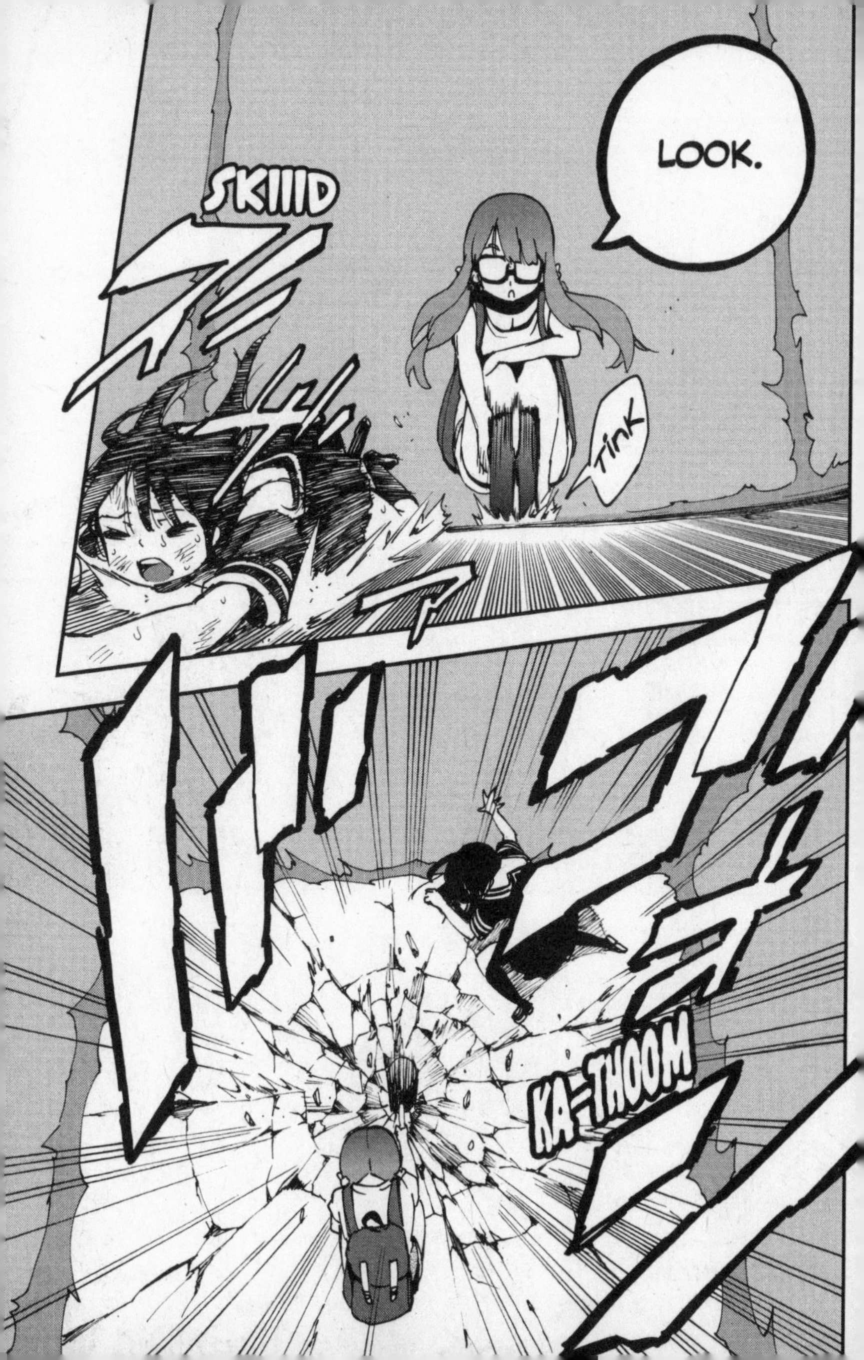
LOOK.
SKIIID
Tink
KA-THOOM

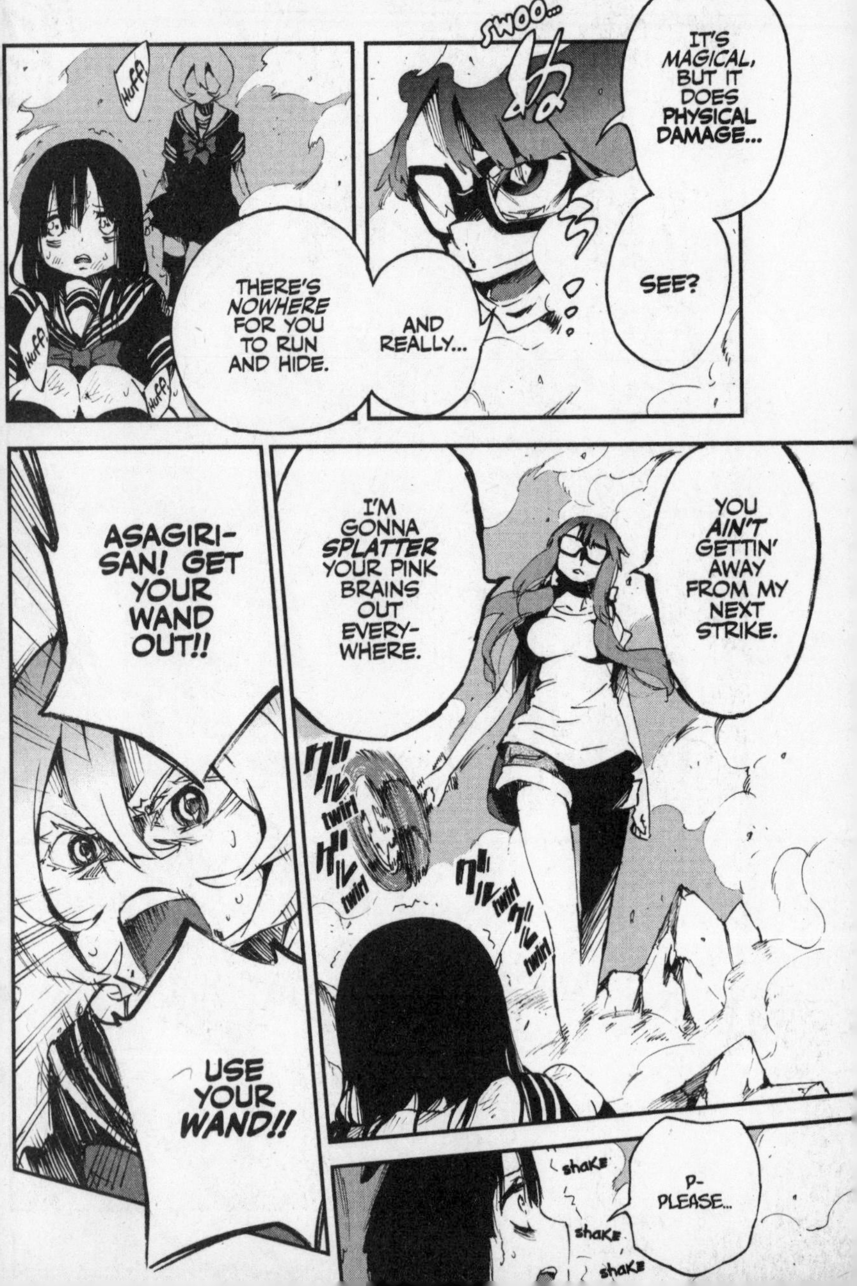
SWOO...
IT'S MAGICAL, BUT IT DOES PHYSICAL DAMAGE...
SEE?
AND REALLY...
HUFF
THERE'S NOWHERE FOR YOU TO RUN AND HIDE.
HUFF
HUFF
YOU AIN'T GETTIN' AWAY FROM MY NEXT STRIKE.
I'M GONNA SPLATTER YOUR PINK BRAINS OUT EVERY-WHERE.
twirl
twirl
twirl
twirl
shake
P-PLEASE...
shake
shake
ASAGIRI-SAN! GET YOUR WAND OUT!!
USE YOUR WAND!!

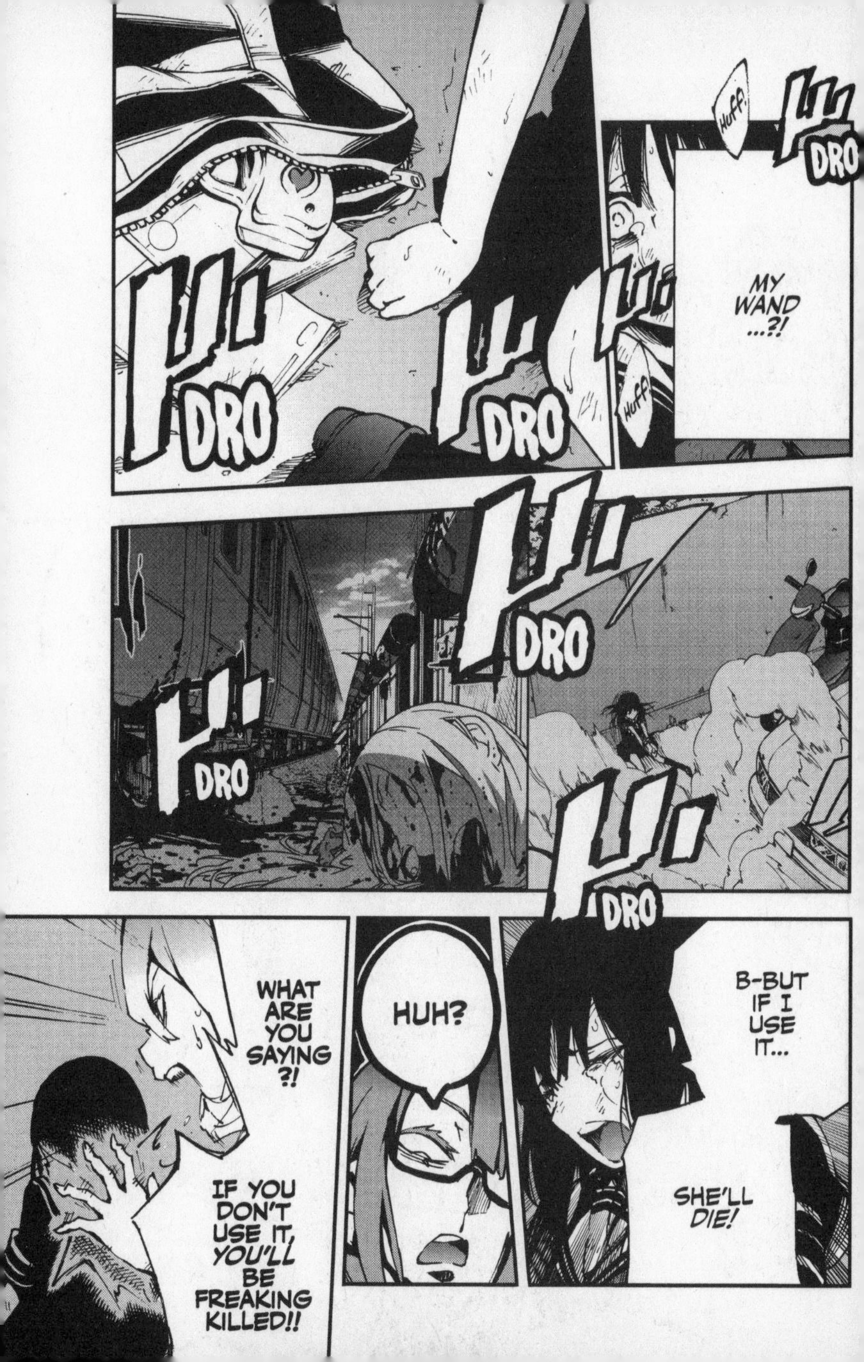
DRO
HUFF!
MY WAND ...?!
HUFF!
DRO
DRO
DRO
DRO
DRO
DRO
B-BUT IF I USE IT...
SHE'LL DIE!
HUH?
WHAT ARE YOU SAYING?!
IF YOU DON'T USE IT, YOU'LL BE FREAKING KILLED!!

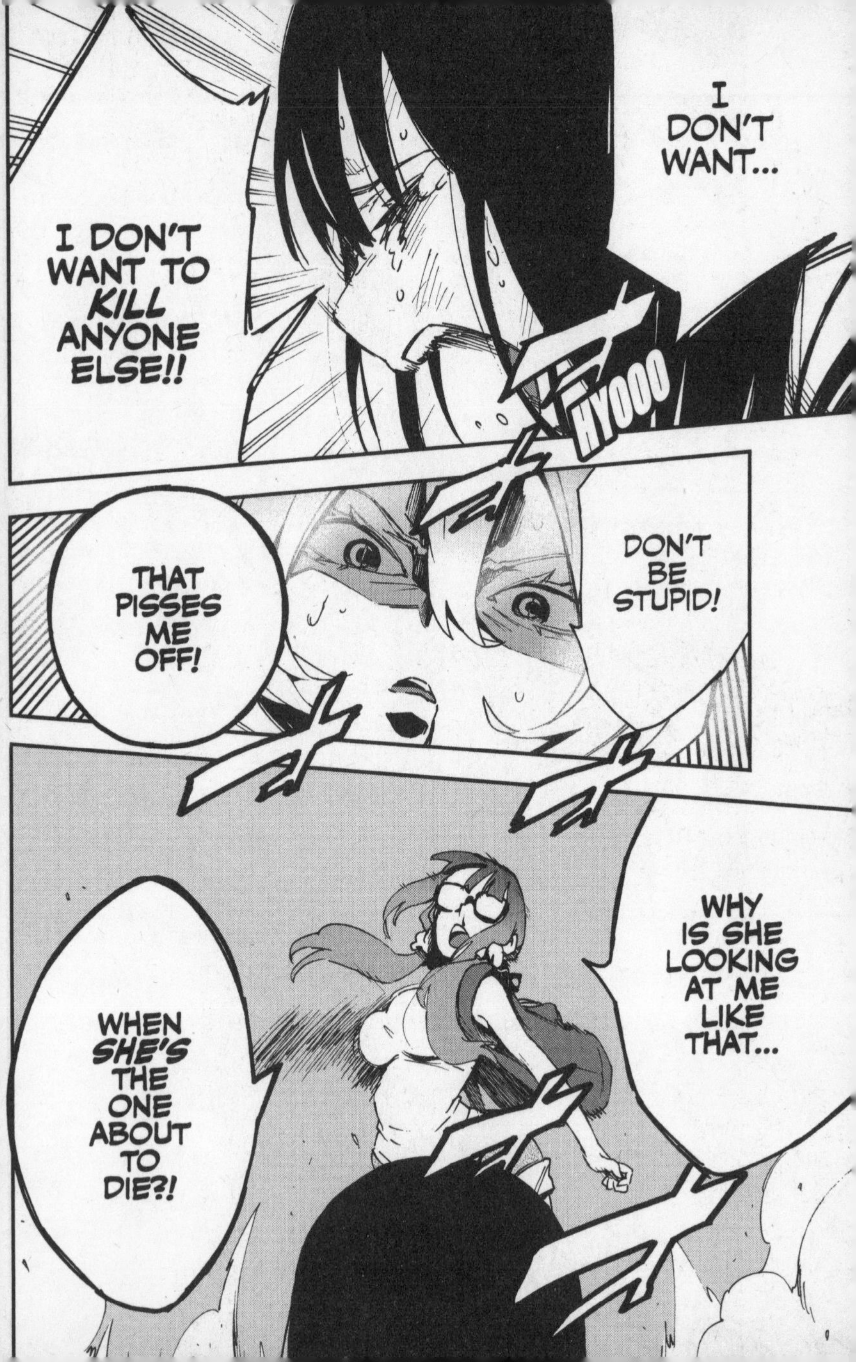
I DON'T WANT...
I DON'T WANT TO *KILL* ANYONE ELSE!!
HYOOO
DON'T BE STUPID!
THAT PISSES ME OFF!
WHY IS SHE LOOKING AT ME LIKE THAT...
WHEN *SHE'S* THE ONE ABOUT TO DIE?!

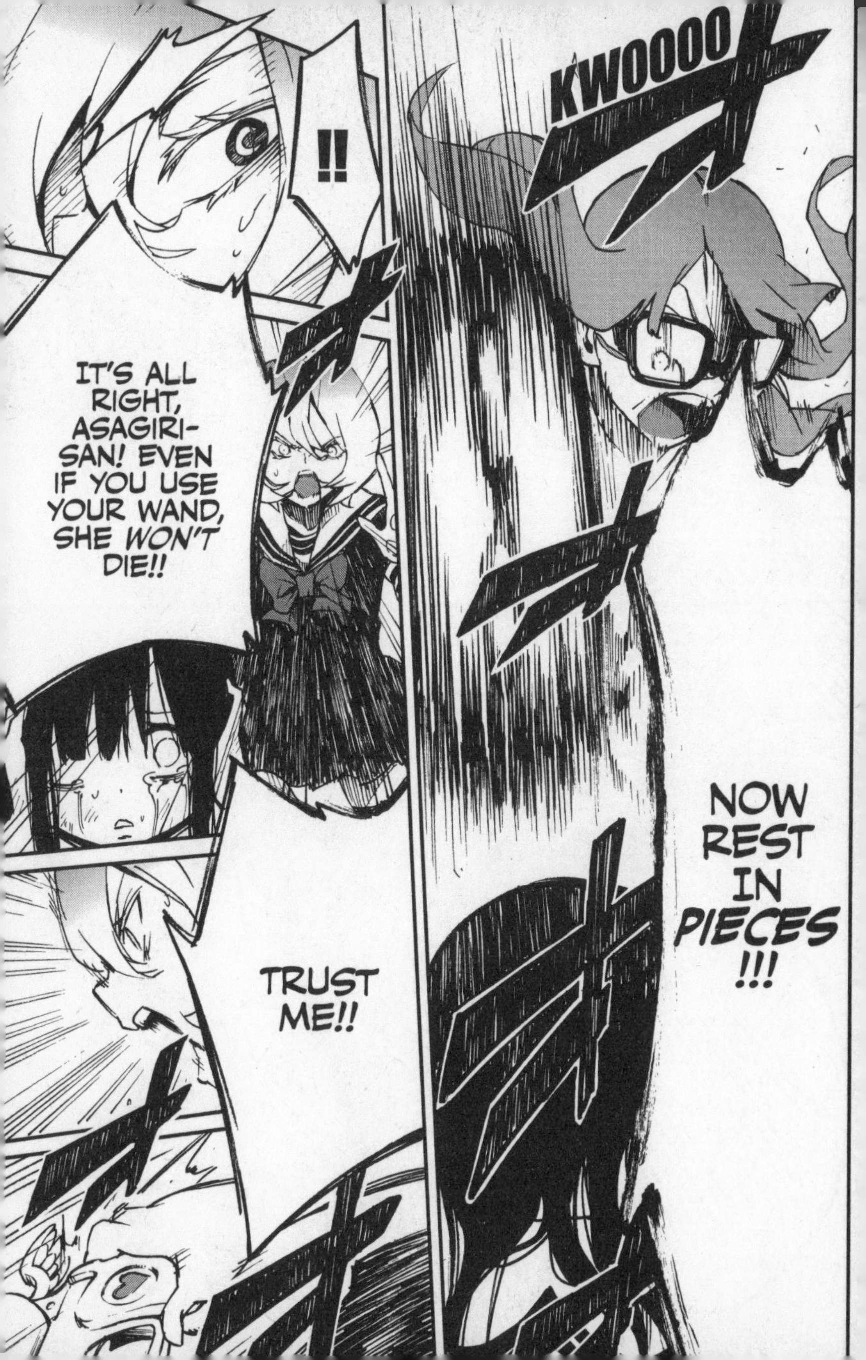
KWOOOO
NOW REST IN PIECES!!!
!!
IT'S ALL RIGHT, ASAGIRI-SAN! EVEN IF YOU USE YOUR WAND, SHE WON'T DIE!!
TRUST ME!!

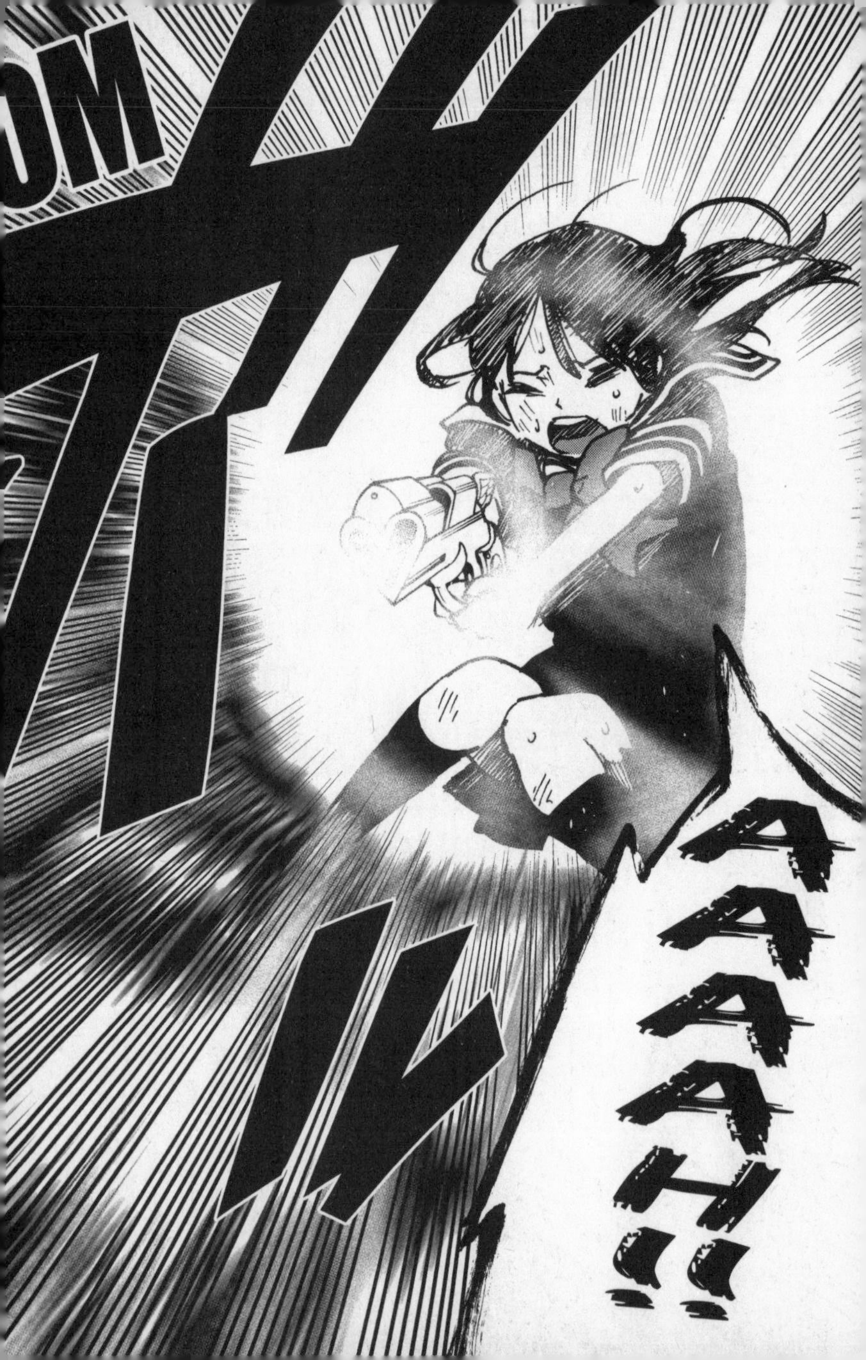
OM
AAAAH!!

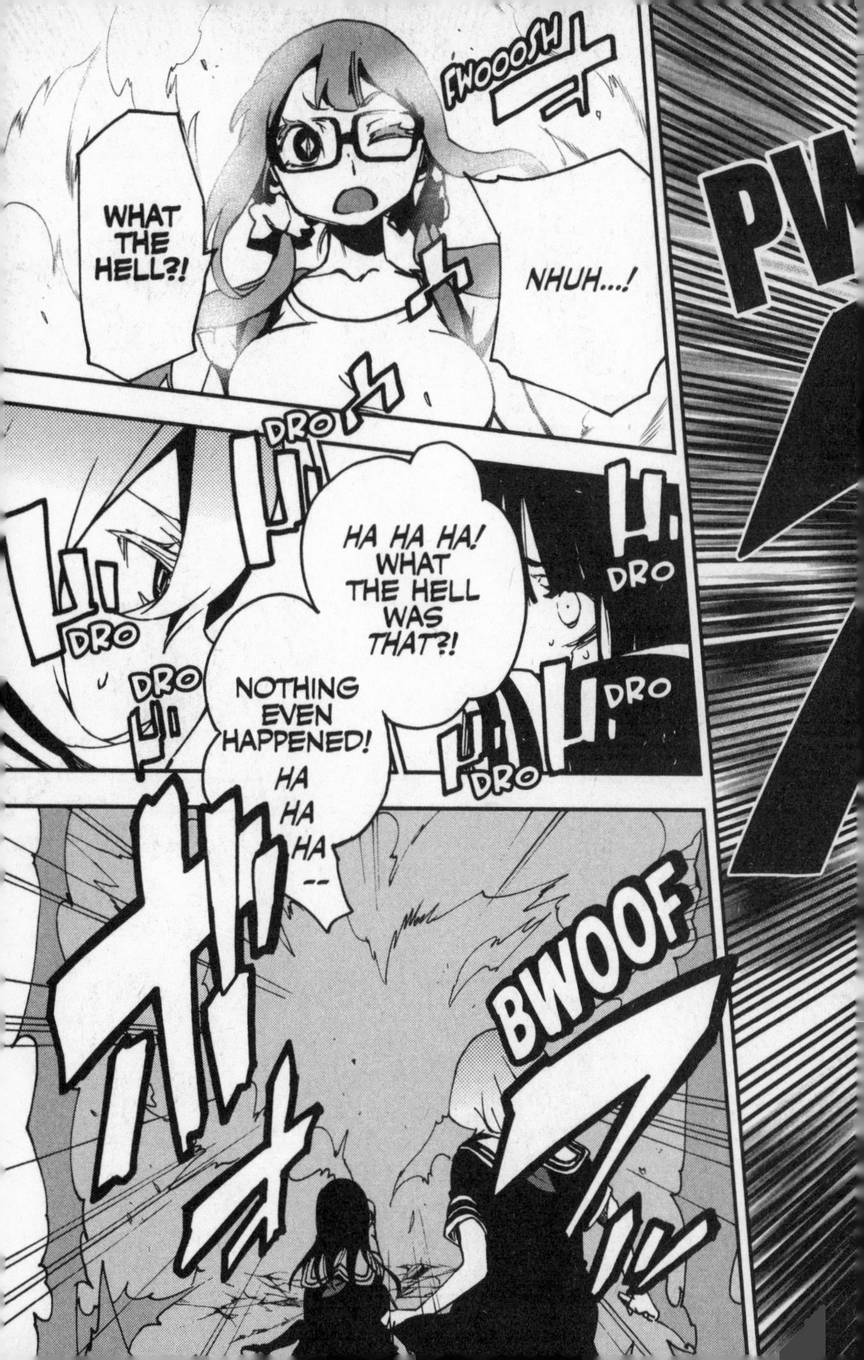
PW
FWOOOSH
NHUH...!
WHAT THE HELL?!
DRO
DRO
DRO
DRO
DRO
DRO
HA HA HA! WHAT THE HELL WAS THAT?!
NOTHING EVEN HAPPENED!
HA HA HA --
BWOOF

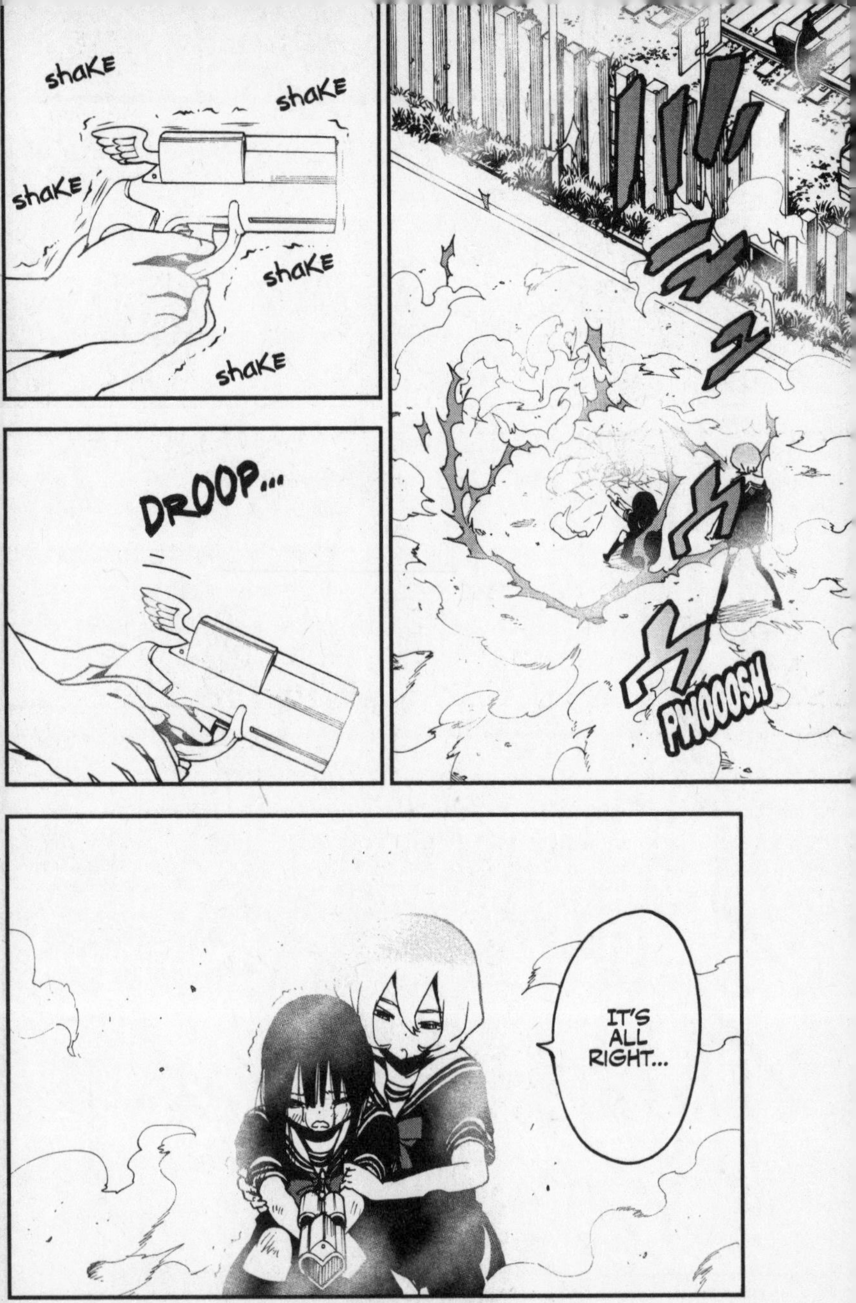
PWOOOSH
shaKE
shaKE
shaKE
shaKE
shaKE
DROOP...
IT'S ALL RIGHT...

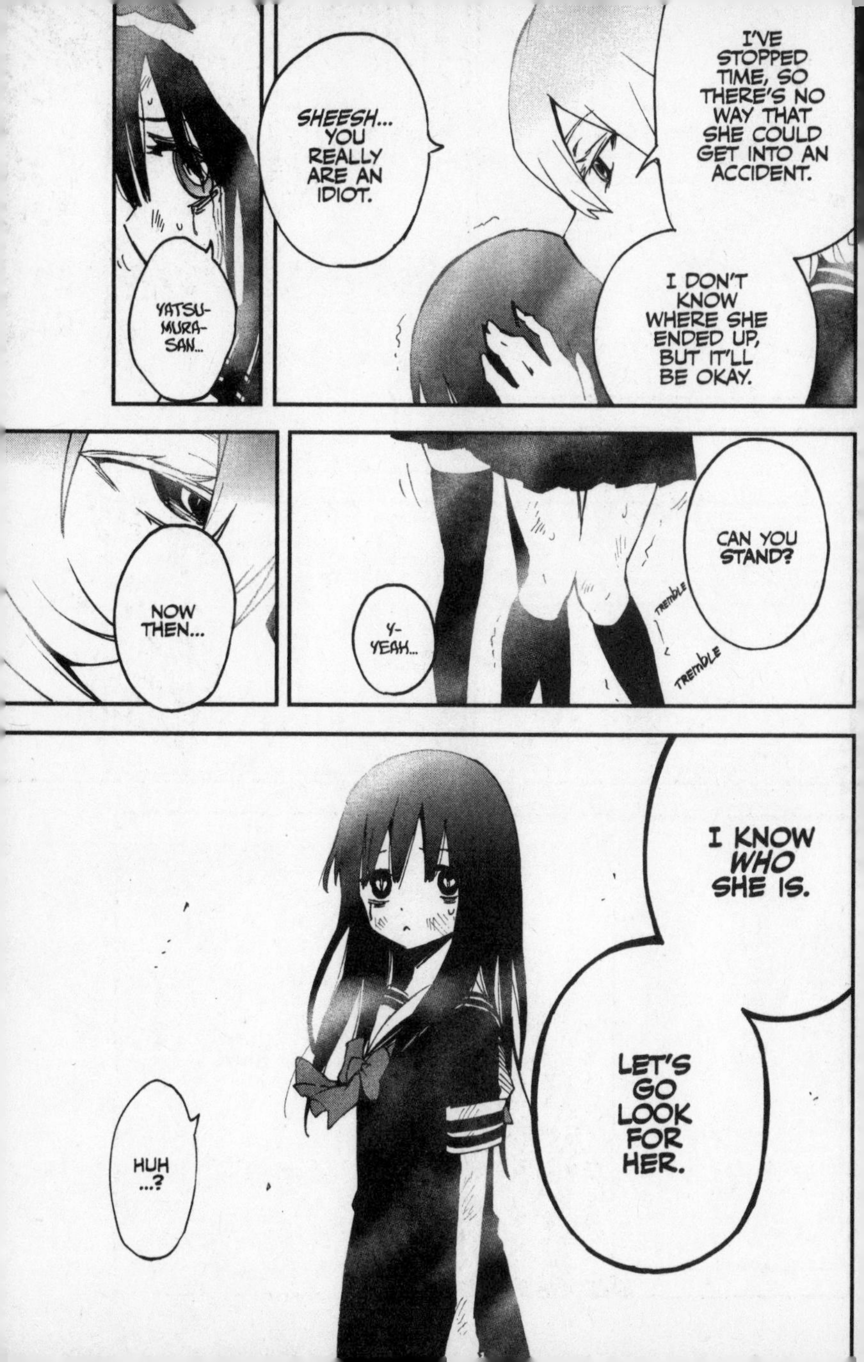
I'VE STOPPED TIME, SO THERE'S NO WAY THAT SHE COULD GET INTO AN ACCIDENT.
SHEESH... YOU REALLY ARE AN IDIOT.
I DON'T KNOW WHERE SHE ENDED UP, BUT IT'LL BE OKAY.
YATSU-MURA-SAN...
CAN YOU STAND?
TREMBLE
TREMBLE
Y-YEAH...
NOW THEN...
I KNOW *WHO* SHE IS.
LET'S GO LOOK FOR HER.
HUH ...?

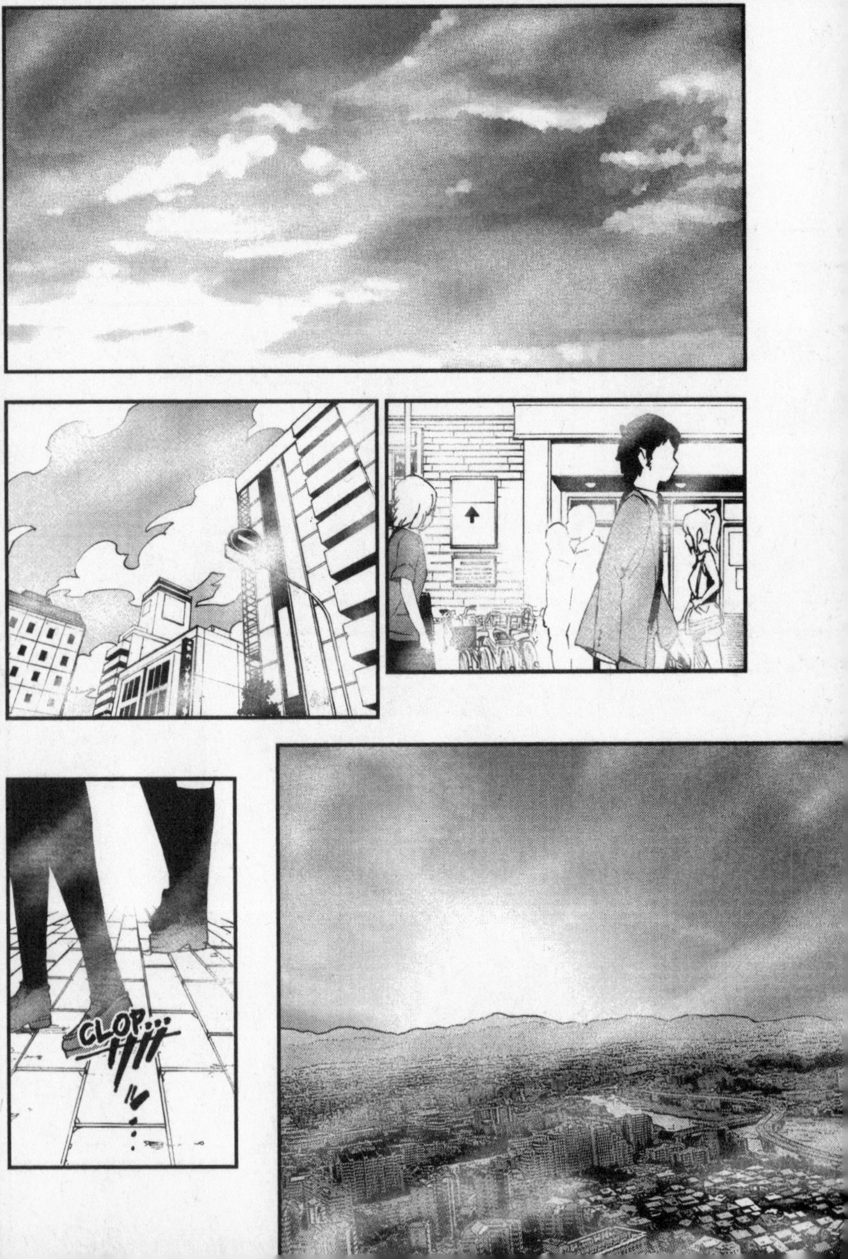
CLOP...

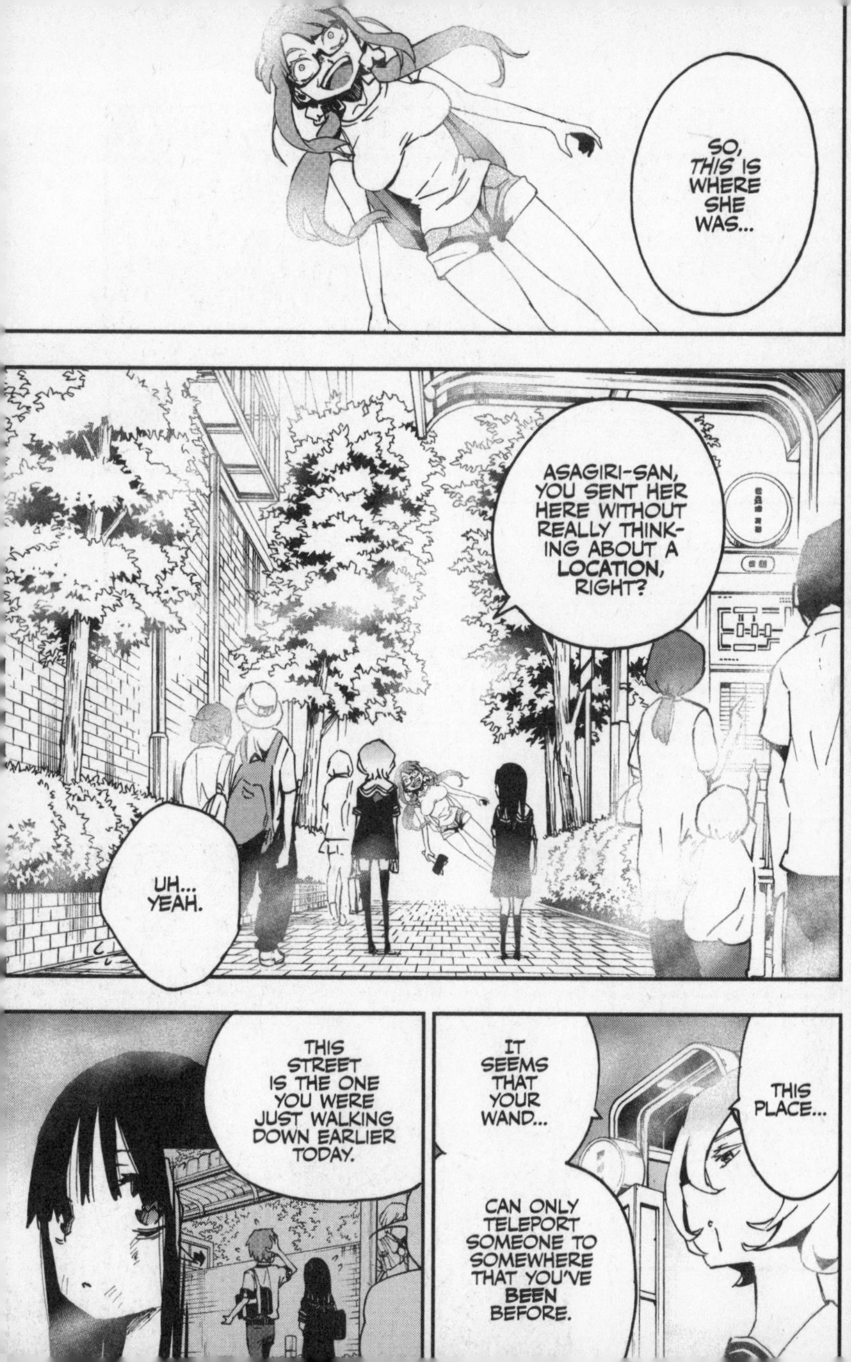
SO, *THIS* IS WHERE SHE WAS...
ASAGIRI-SAN, YOU SENT HER HERE WITHOUT REALLY THINKING ABOUT A LOCATION, RIGHT?
UH... YEAH.
THIS PLACE...
IT SEEMS THAT YOUR WAND...
CAN ONLY TELEPORT SOMEONE TO SOMEWHERE THAT YOU'VE BEEN BEFORE.
THIS STREET IS THE ONE YOU WERE JUST WALKING DOWN EARLIER TODAY.

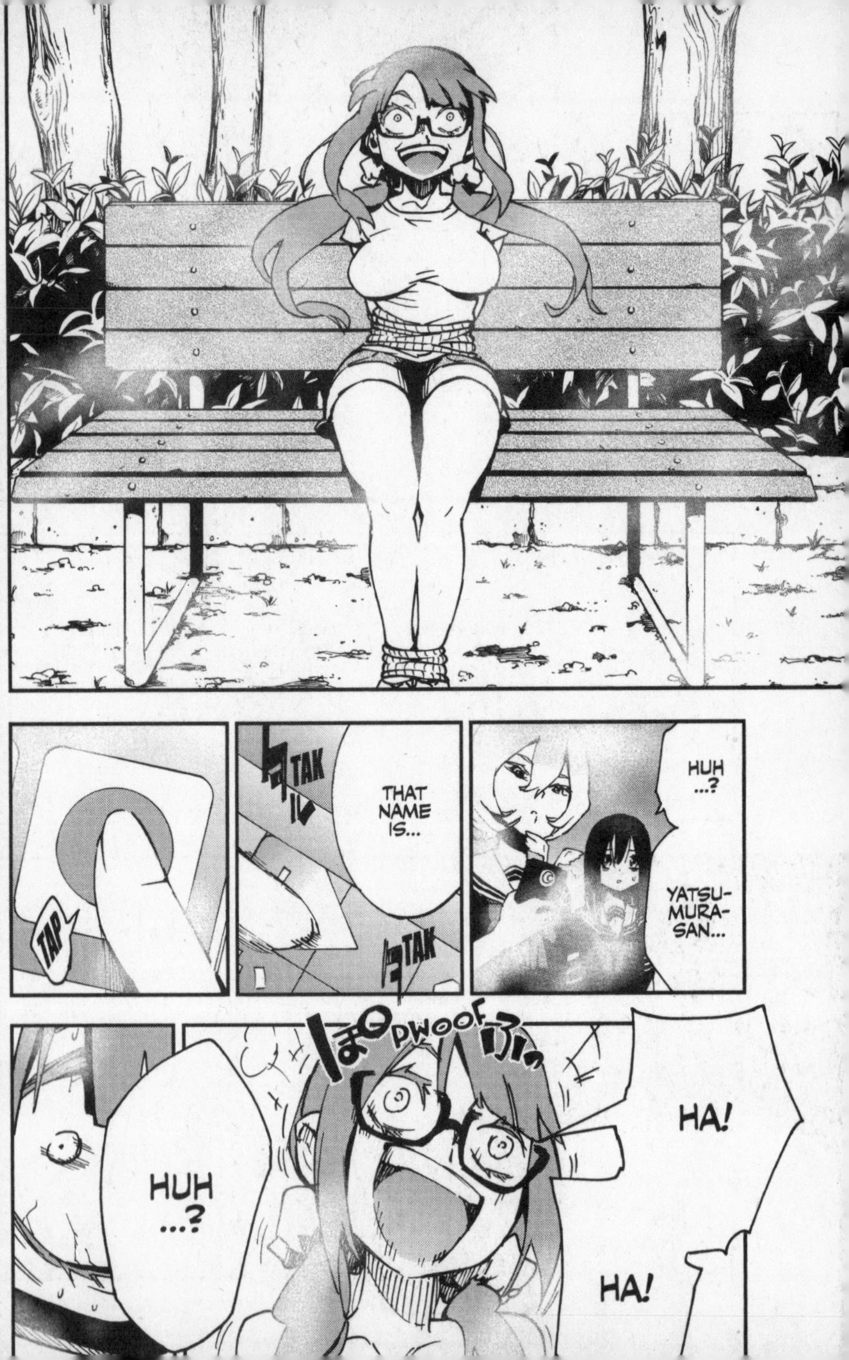
HUH ...?
YATSU-MURA-SAN...
TAK
THAT NAME IS...
TAK
TAP
PWOOF
HA!
HA!
HUH ...?

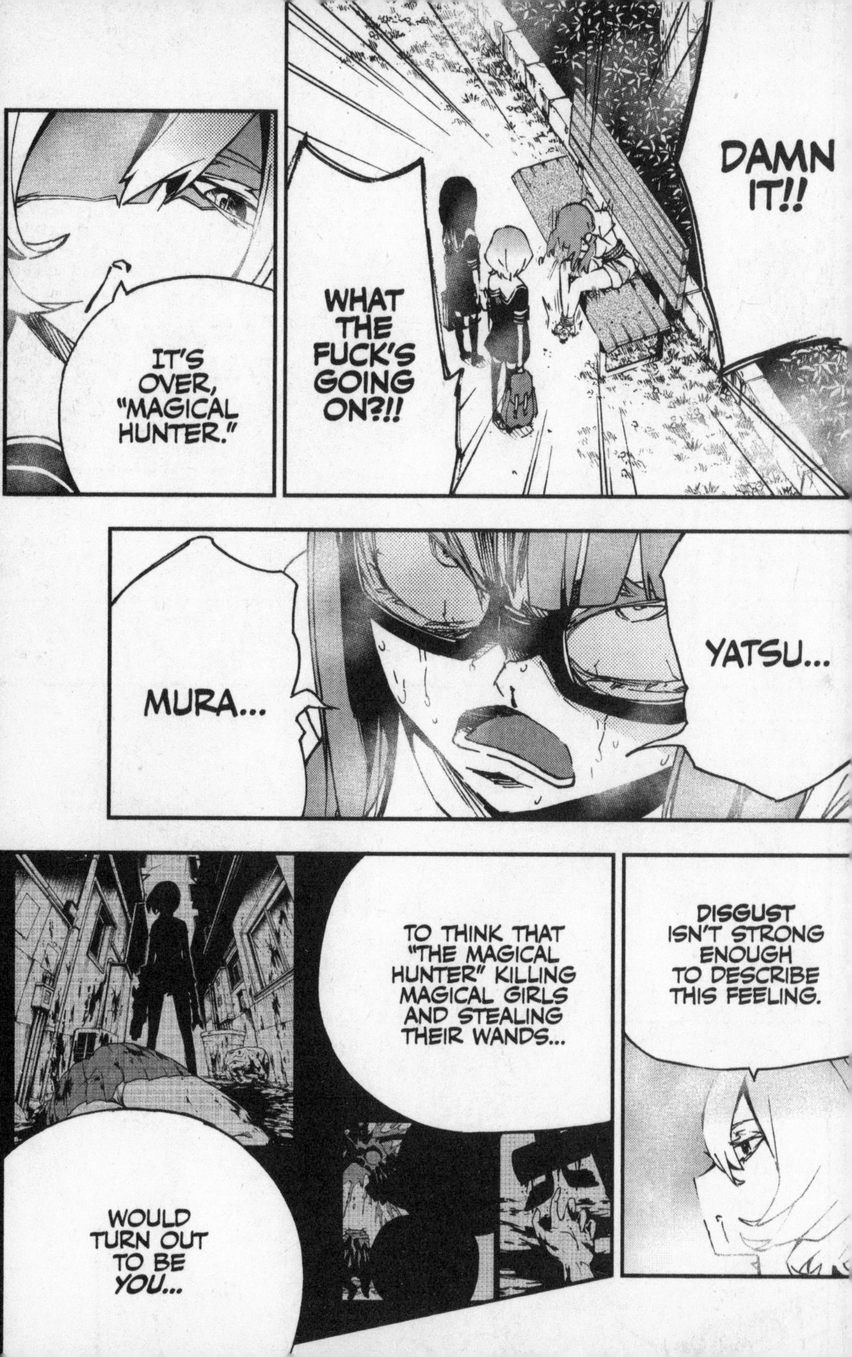
DAMN IT!!
WHAT THE FUCK'S GOING ON?!!
IT'S OVER, "MAGICAL HUNTER."
YATSU...
MURA...
DISGUST ISN'T STRONG ENOUGH TO DESCRIBE THIS FEELING.
TO THINK THAT "THE MAGICAL HUNTER" KILLING MAGICAL GIRLS AND STEALING THEIR WANDS...
WOULD TURN OUT TO BE *YOU*...

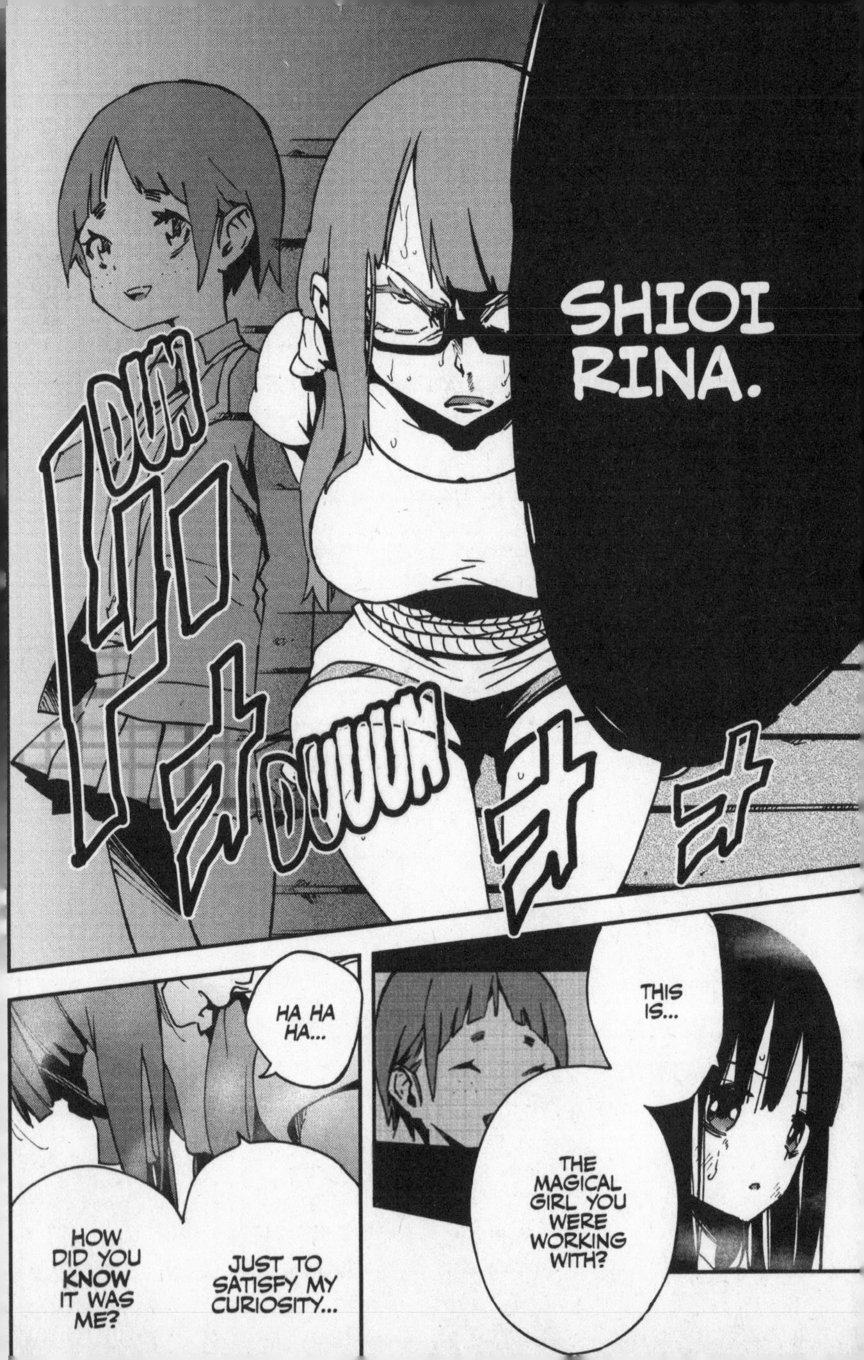
SHIOI RINA.
DUUUN
DUN
THIS IS...
THE MAGICAL GIRL YOU WERE WORKING WITH?
HA HA HA...
JUST TO SATISFY MY CURIOSITY...
HOW DID YOU KNOW IT WAS ME?

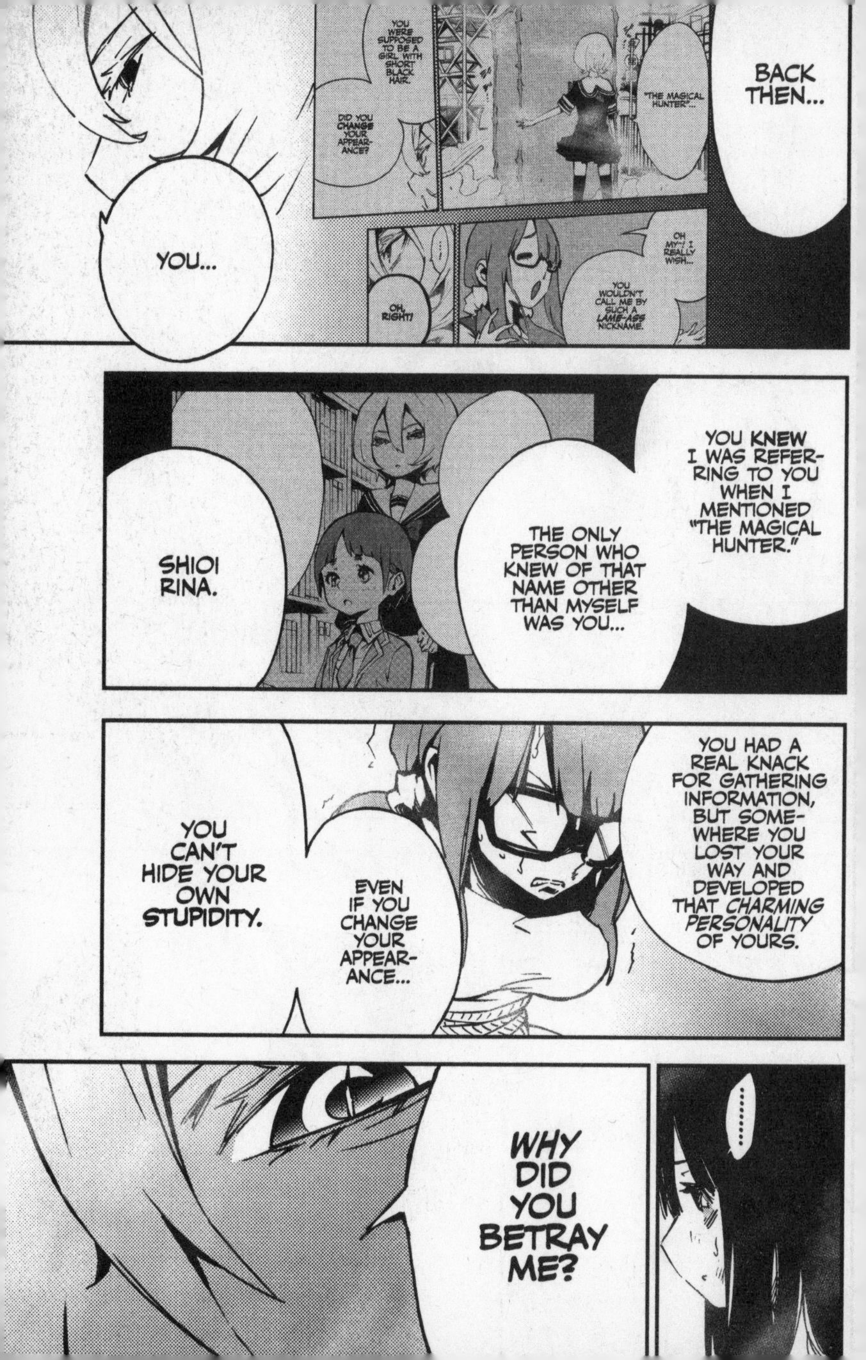
BACK THEN...
"THE MAGICAL HUNTER"...
YOU WERE SUPPOSED TO BE A GIRL WITH SHORT BLACK HAIR.
DID YOU CHANGE YOUR APPEARANCE?
OH MY~! I REALLY WISH...
YOU WOULDN'T CALL ME BY SUCH A *LAME-ASS* NICKNAME.
...!
OH, RIGHT!
YOU...
YOU KNEW I WAS REFERRING TO YOU WHEN I MENTIONED "THE MAGICAL HUNTER."
THE ONLY PERSON WHO KNEW OF THAT NAME OTHER THAN MYSELF WAS YOU...
SHIOI RINA.
YOU HAD A REAL KNACK FOR GATHERING INFORMATION, BUT SOMEWHERE YOU LOST YOUR WAY AND DEVELOPED THAT *CHARMING PERSONALITY* OF YOURS.
EVEN IF YOU CHANGE YOUR APPEARANCE...
YOU CAN'T HIDE YOUR OWN STUPIDITY.
......
WHY DID YOU BETRAY ME?

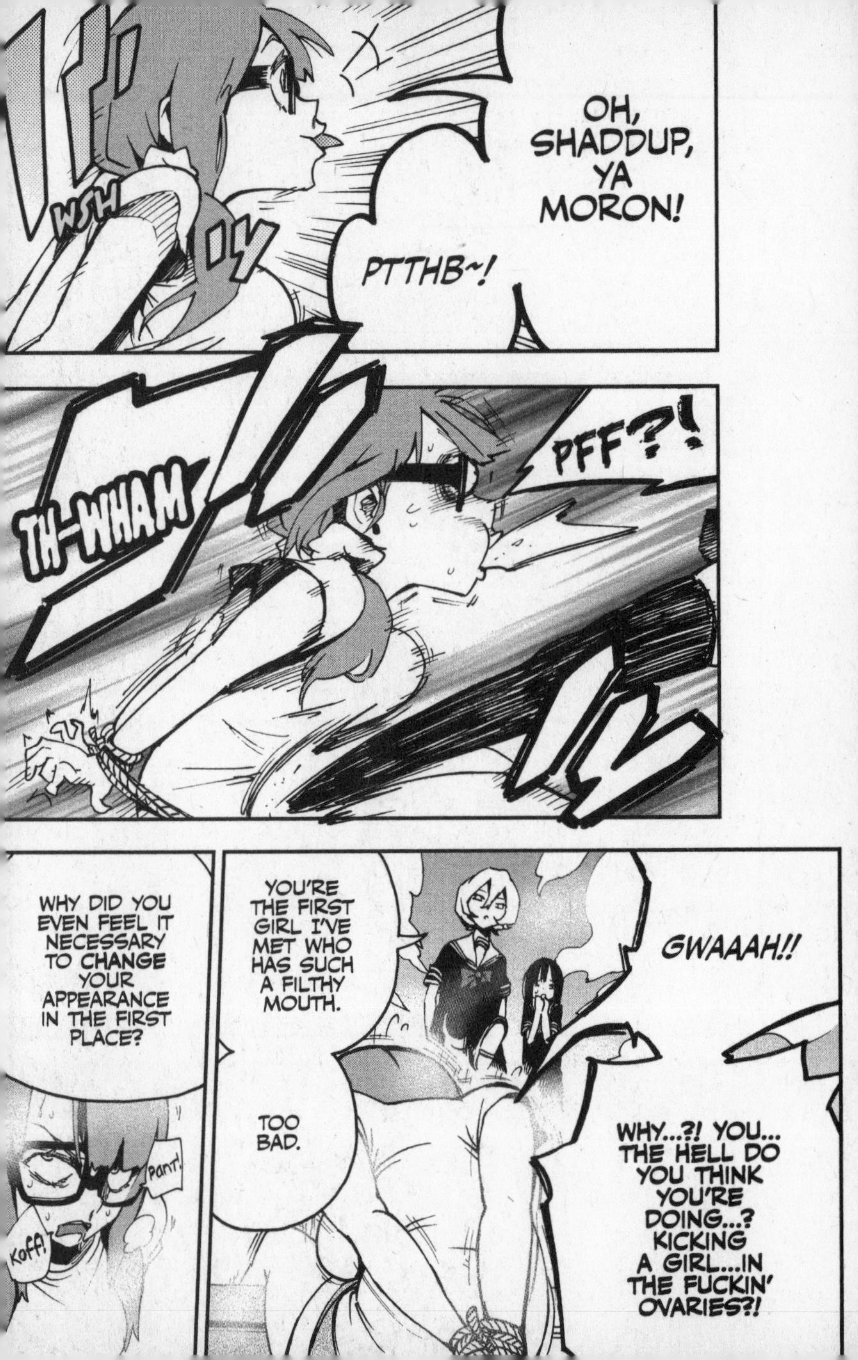
OH, SHADDUP, YA MORON!
PTTHB~!
WSH
PFF?!
TH-WHAM
GWAAAH!!
YOU'RE THE FIRST GIRL I'VE MET WHO HAS SUCH A FILTHY MOUTH.
WHY...?! YOU... THE HELL DO YOU THINK YOU'RE DOING...? KICKING A GIRL...IN THE FUCKIN' OVARIES?!
TOO BAD.
WHY DID YOU EVEN FEEL IT NECESSARY TO CHANGE YOUR APPEARANCE IN THE FIRST PLACE?
Pant!
Koff!

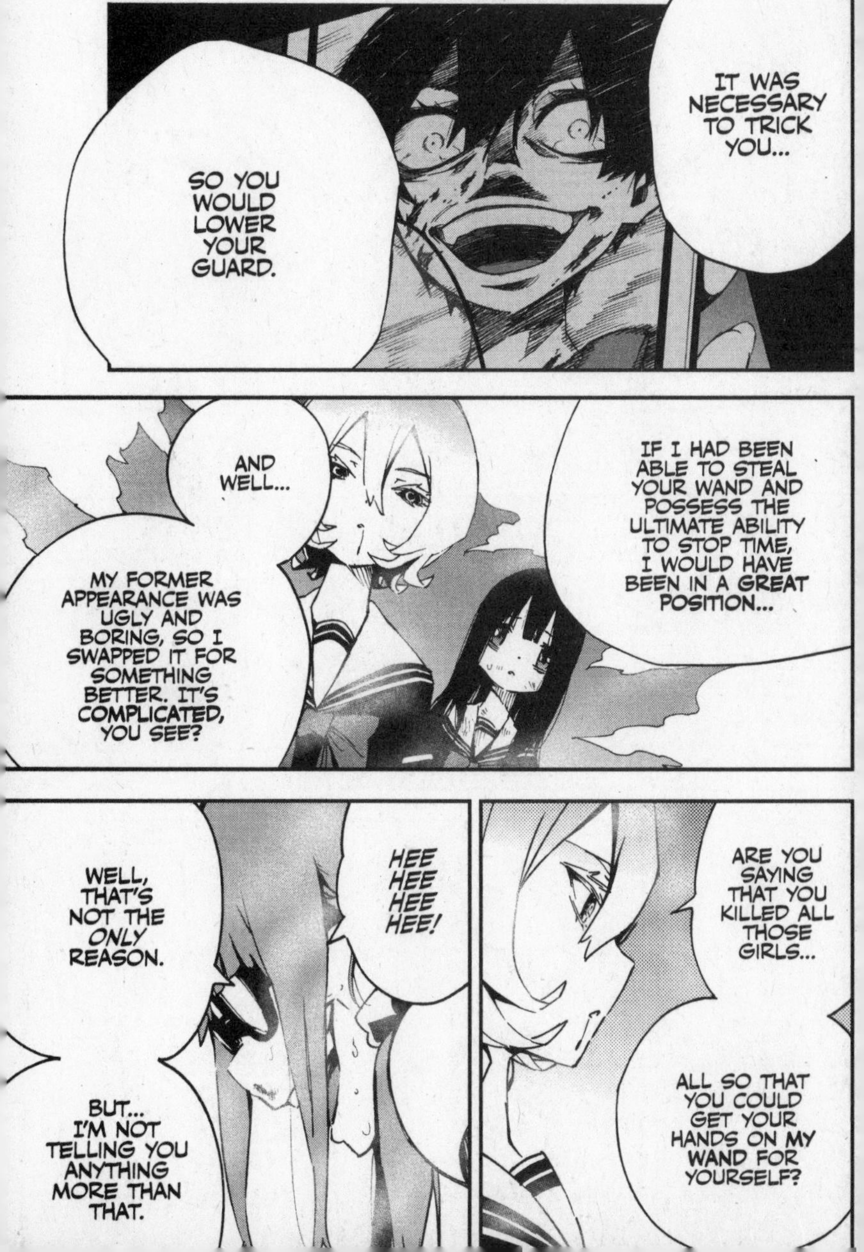
IT WAS NECESSARY TO TRICK YOU...
SO YOU WOULD LOWER YOUR GUARD.
IF I HAD BEEN ABLE TO STEAL YOUR WAND AND POSSESS THE ULTIMATE ABILITY TO STOP TIME, I WOULD HAVE BEEN IN A GREAT POSITION...
AND WELL...
MY FORMER APPEARANCE WAS UGLY AND BORING, SO I SWAPPED IT FOR SOMETHING BETTER. IT'S COMPLICATED, YOU SEE?
ARE YOU SAYING THAT YOU KILLED ALL THOSE GIRLS...
ALL SO THAT YOU COULD GET YOUR HANDS ON MY WAND FOR YOURSELF?
HEE HEE HEE HEE!
WELL, THAT'S NOT THE *ONLY* REASON.
BUT... I'M NOT TELLING YOU ANYTHING MORE THAN THAT.

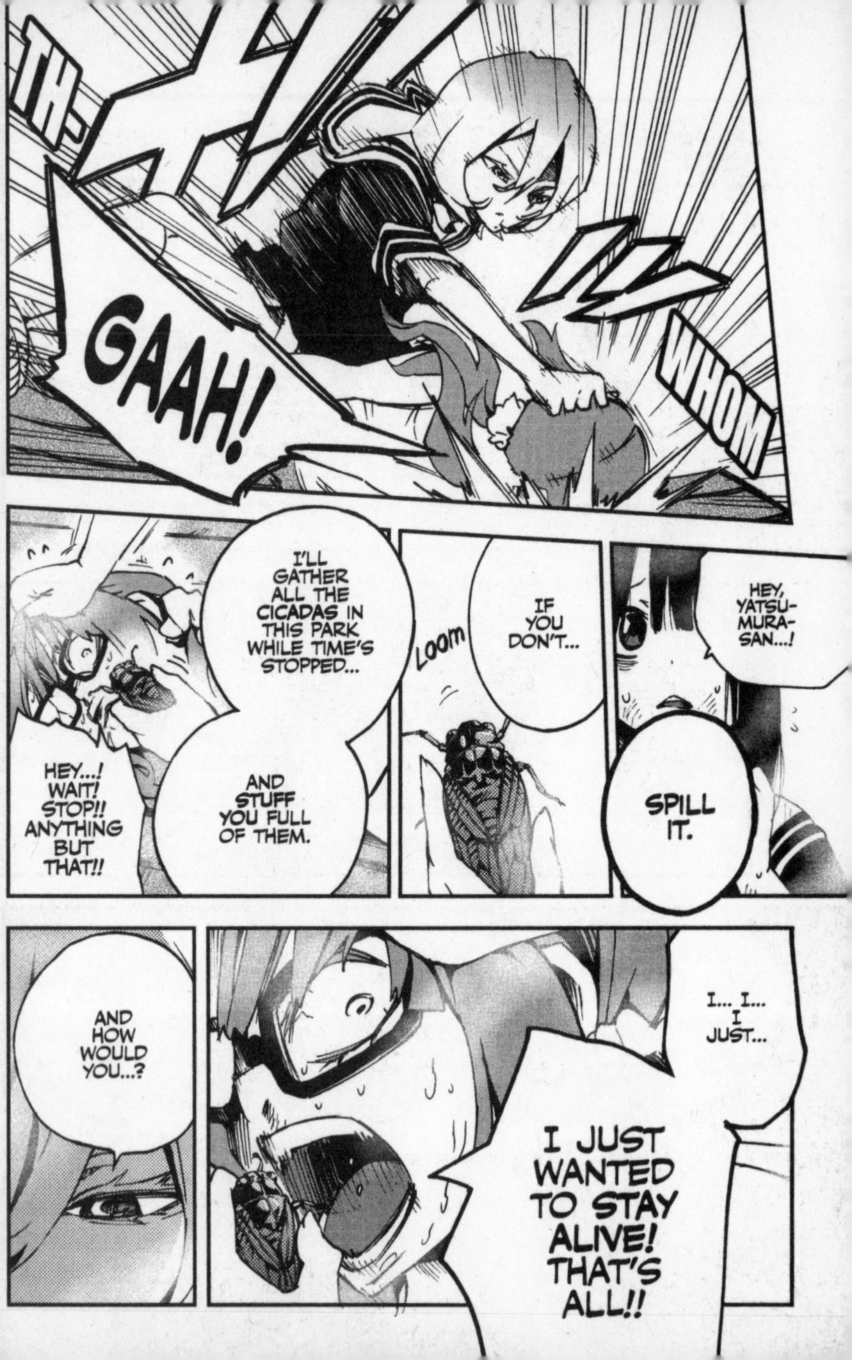
TH-
WHOM
GAAH!
HEY, YATSUMURA-SAN...!
SPILL IT.
IF YOU DON'T...
Loom
I'LL GATHER ALL THE CICADAS IN THIS PARK WHILE TIME'S STOPPED...
AND STUFF YOU FULL OF THEM.
HEY...! WAIT! STOP!! ANYTHING BUT THAT!!
I... I... I JUST...
I JUST WANTED TO STAY ALIVE! THAT'S ALL!!
AND HOW WOULD YOU...?

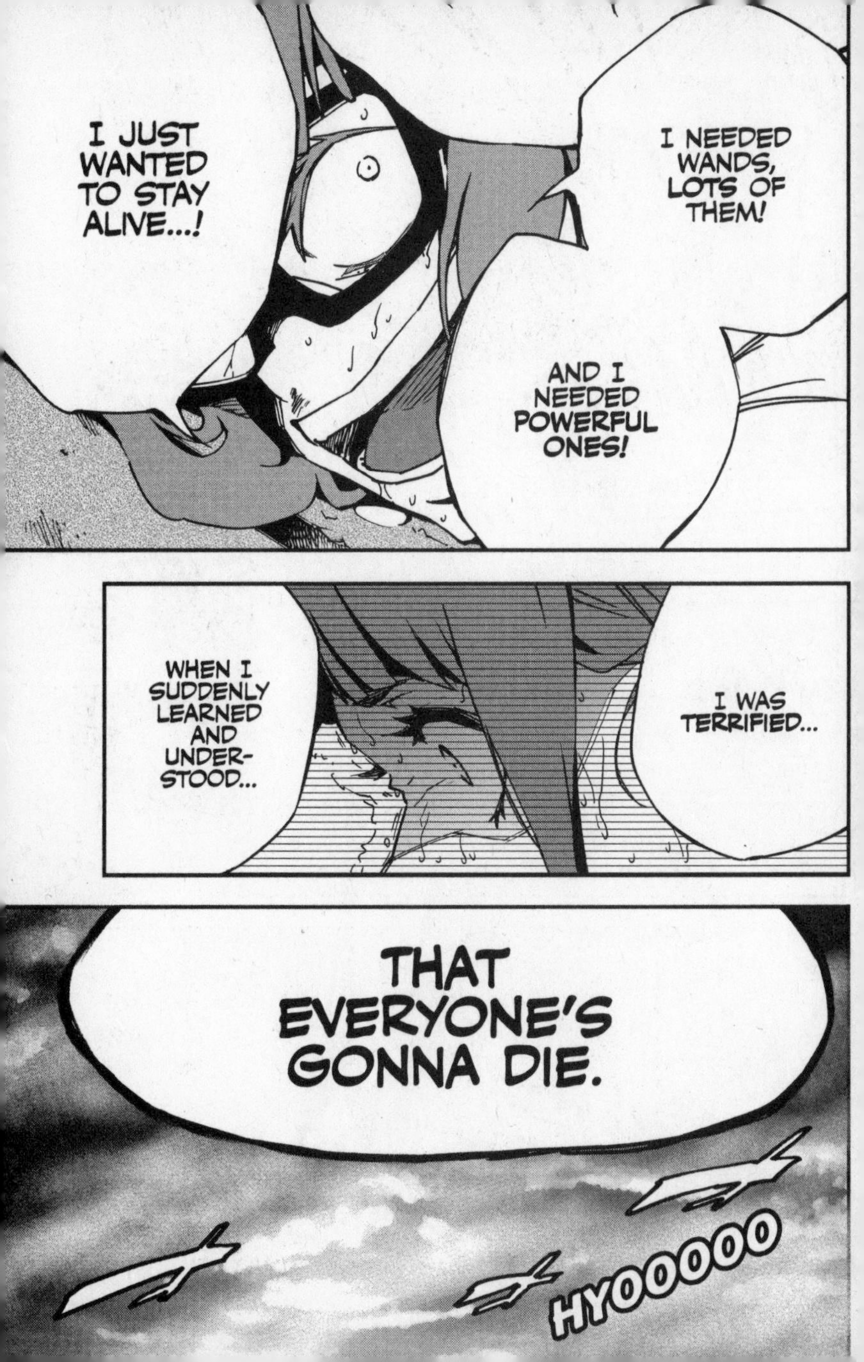
I NEEDED WANDS, LOTS OF THEM!
AND I NEEDED POWERFUL ONES!
I JUST WANTED TO STAY ALIVE...!
I WAS TERRIFIED...
WHEN I SUDDENLY LEARNED AND UNDER-STOOD...
THAT EVERYONE'S GONNA DIE.
HYOOOOOO

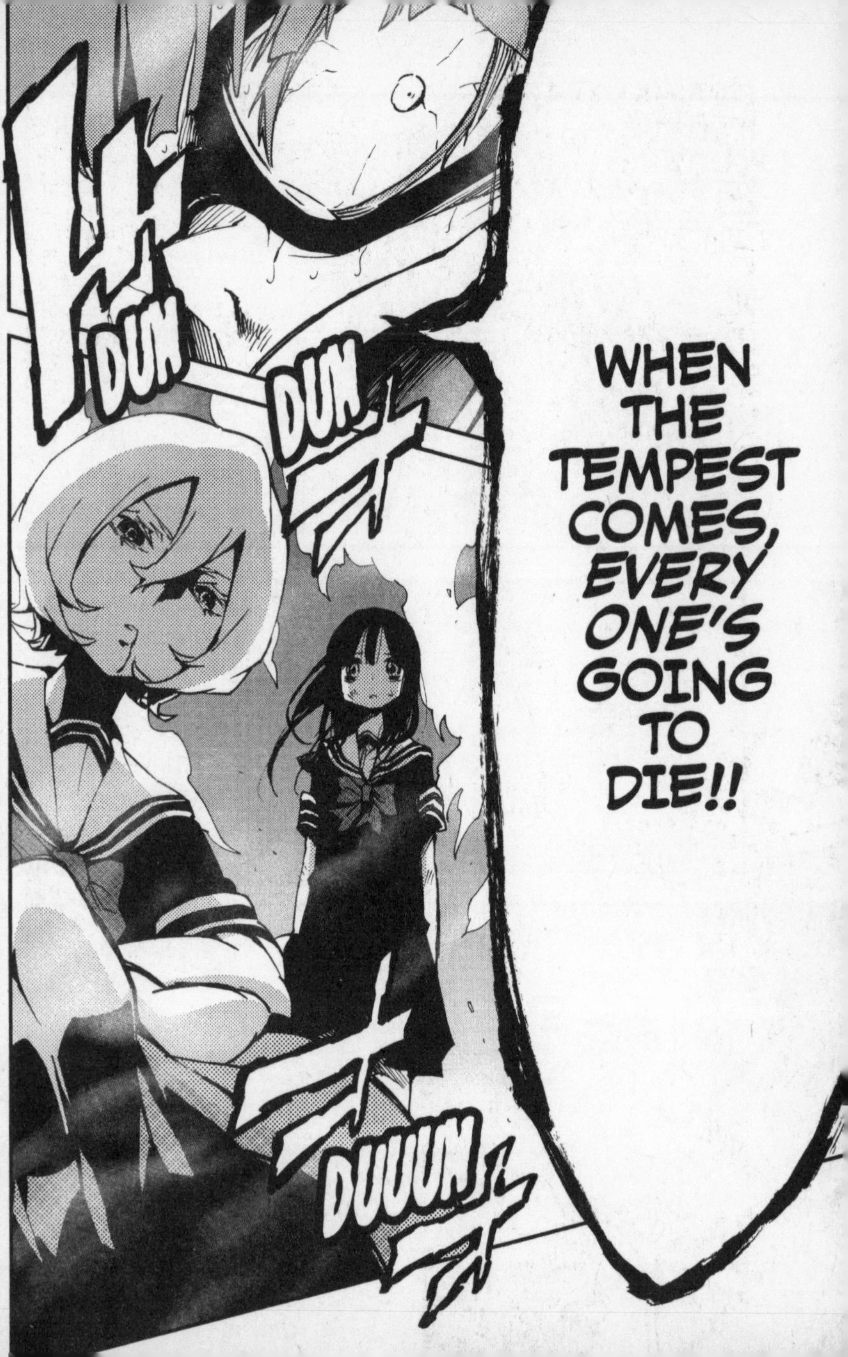
WHEN THE TEMPEST COMES, EVERY ONE'S GOING TO DIE!!
DUN
DUN
DUUUN

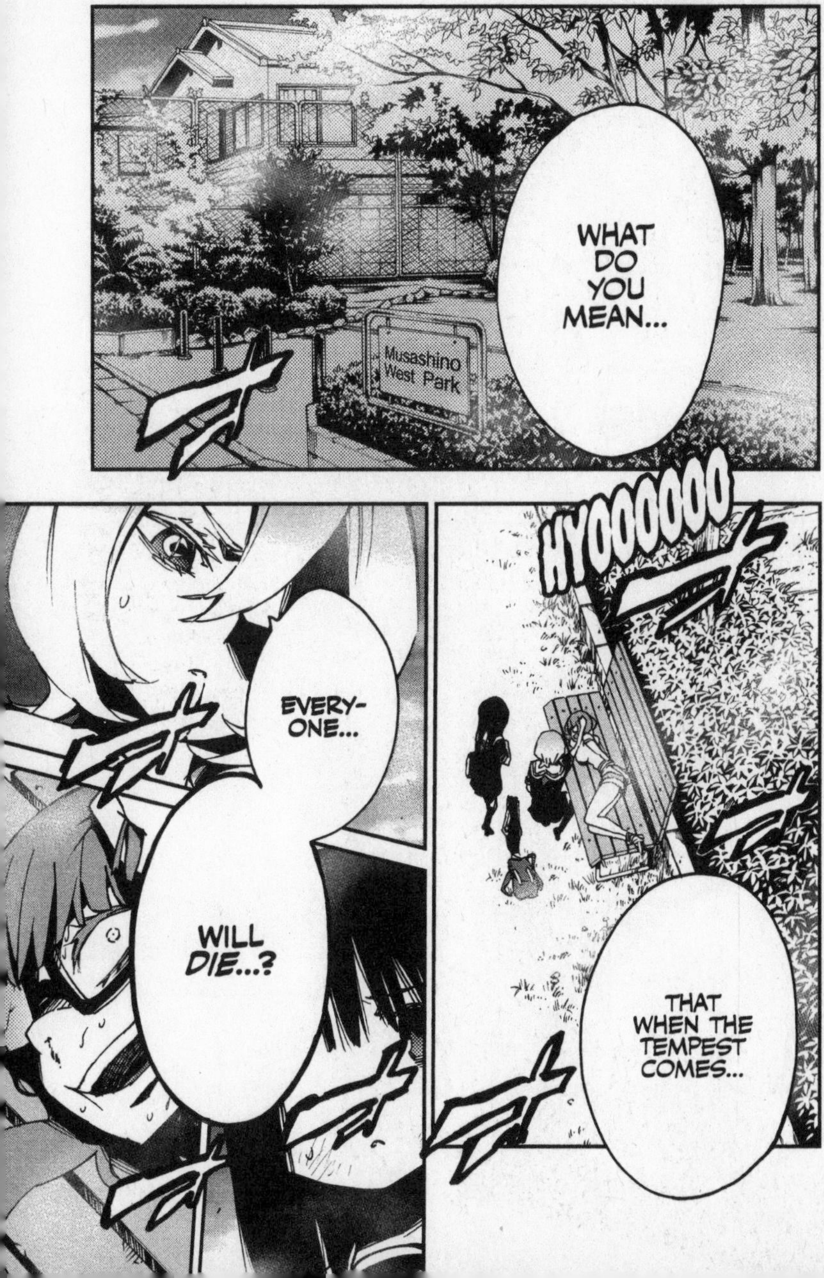
Musashino West Park
WHAT DO YOU MEAN...
HYOOOOOO
THAT WHEN THE TEMPEST COMES...
EVERY-ONE...
WILL DIE...?

SHORTLY BEFORE I BROKE CONTACT WITH YOU...

YATSU-MURA...

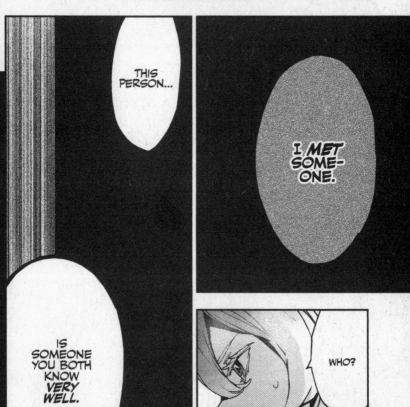

THIS PERSON...

I *MET* SOME-ONE.

IS SOMEONE YOU BOTH KNOW *VERY WELL*.

WHO?

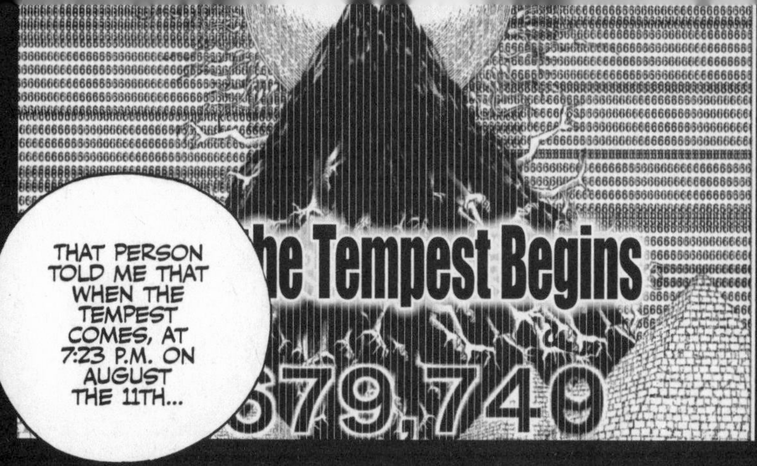
THAT PERSON TOLD ME THAT WHEN THE TEMPEST COMES, AT 7:23 P.M. ON AUGUST THE 11TH...
he Tempest Begins
379,740

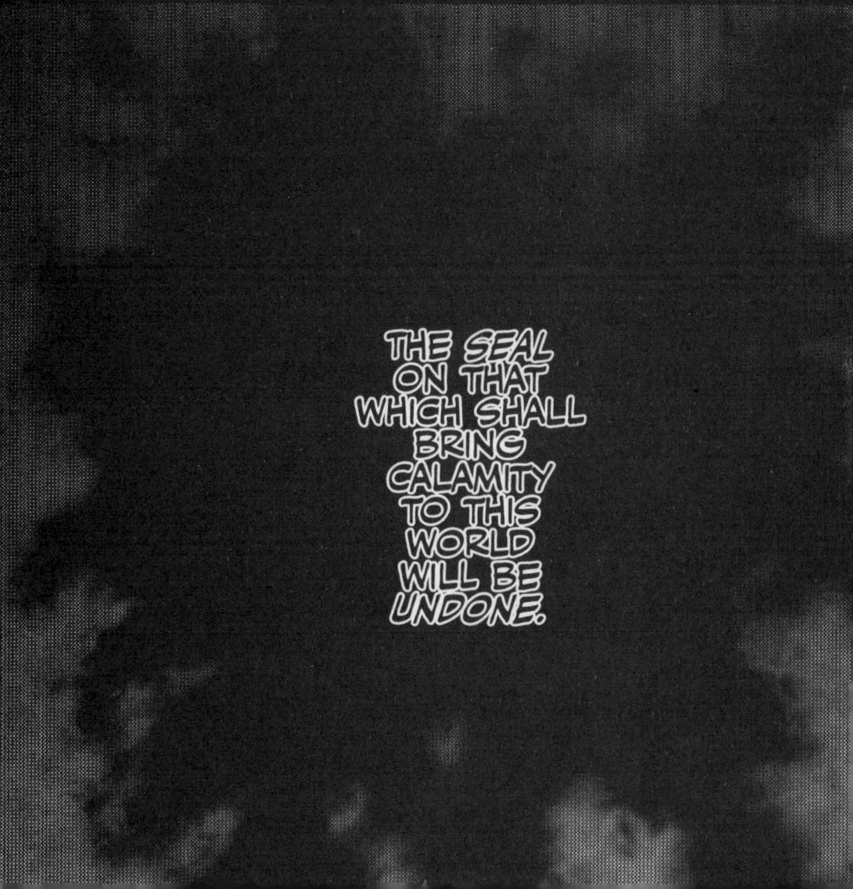
THE SEAL ON THAT WHICH SHALL BRING CALAMITY TO THIS WORLD WILL BE UNDONE.

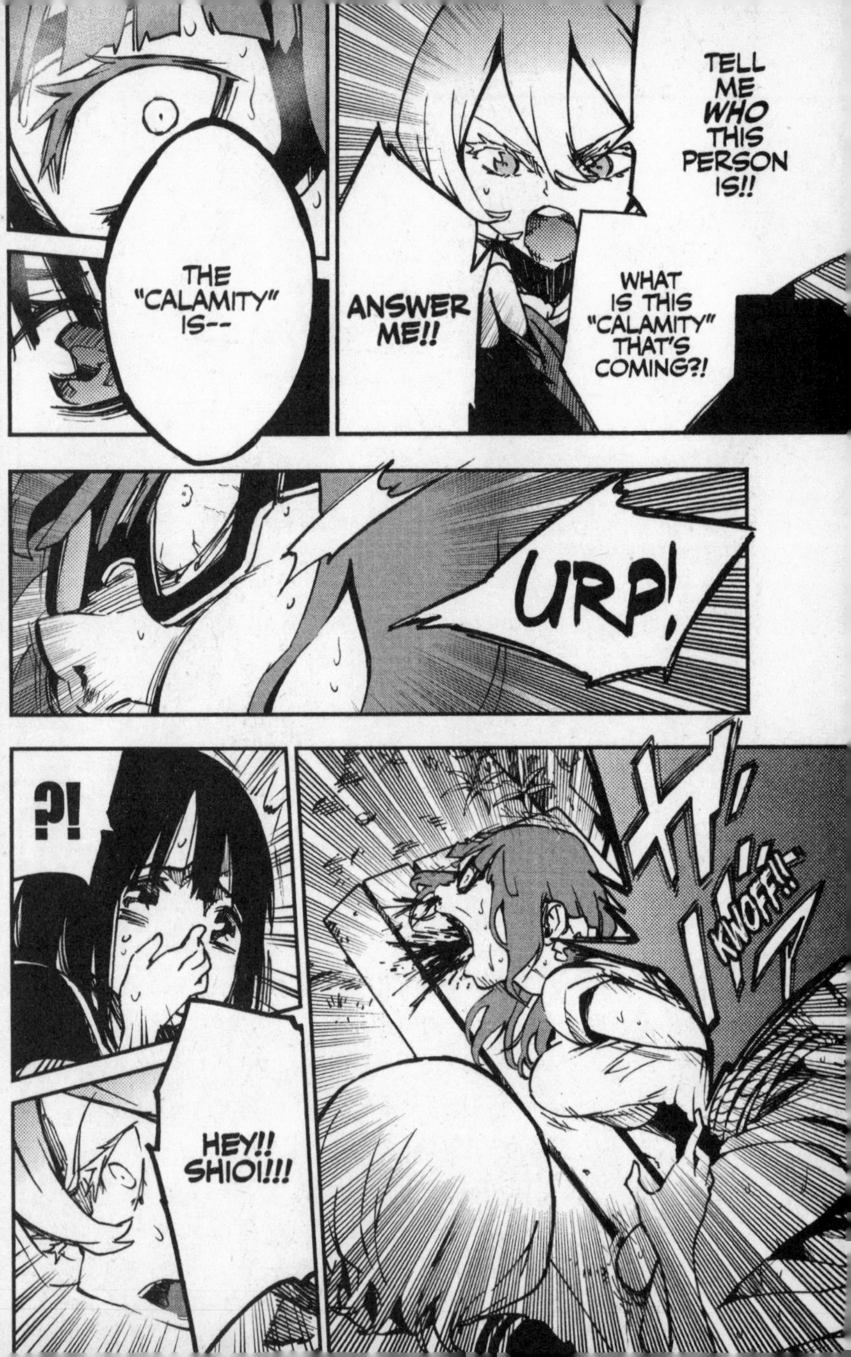
TELL ME WHO THIS PERSON IS!!
WHAT IS THIS "CALAMITY" THAT'S COMING?!
ANSWER ME!!
THE "CALAMITY" IS--
URP!
KNOFF!!
?!
HEY!! SHIOI!!!

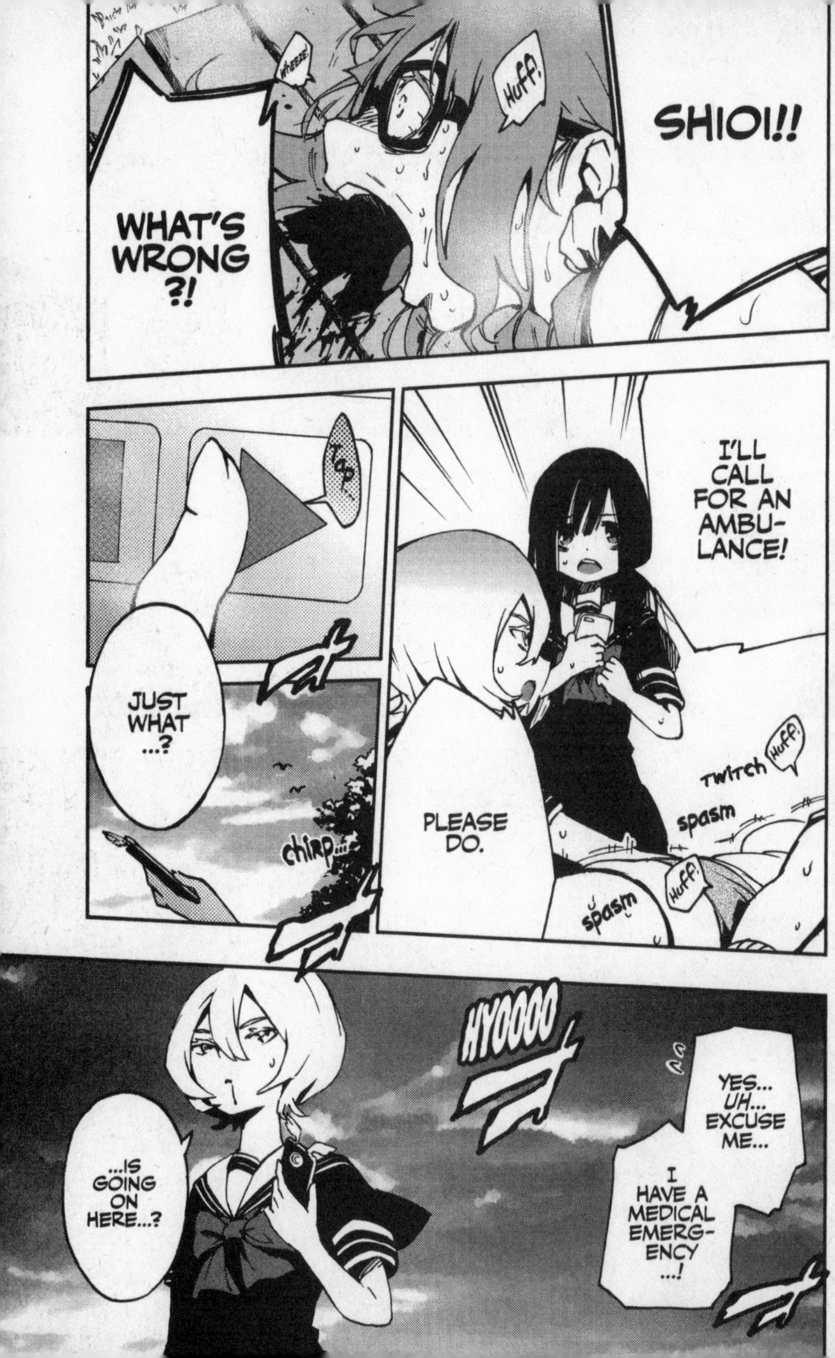
SHIOI!!
Huff!
WHEEZE!
WHAT'S WRONG ?!
I'LL CALL FOR AN AMBULANCE!
Huff!
TWITCH
spasm
Huff!
spasm
PLEASE DO.
Tap
JUST WHAT ...?
chirp...
HYOOOO
YES... UH... EXCUSE ME...
I HAVE A MEDICAL EMERGENCY ...!
...IS GOING ON HERE...?

MAGICAL GIRL SITE
ENTER 6

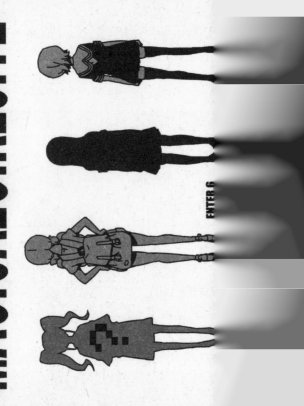

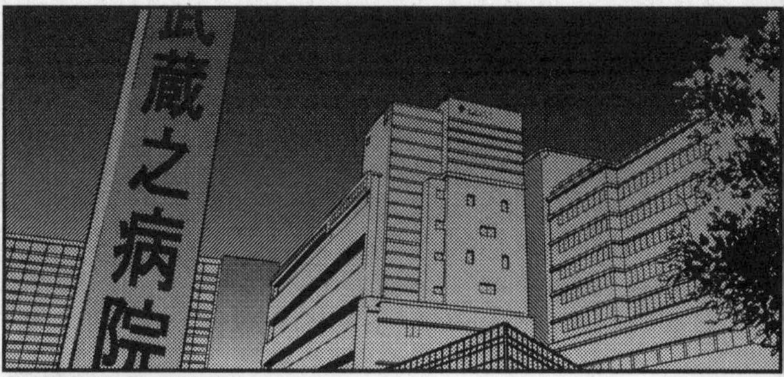
武藏之病院
Sign: Mushashino General Hospital

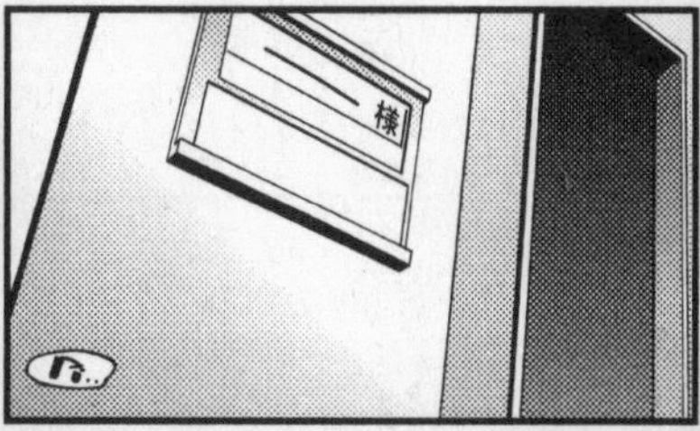
様
Pi...

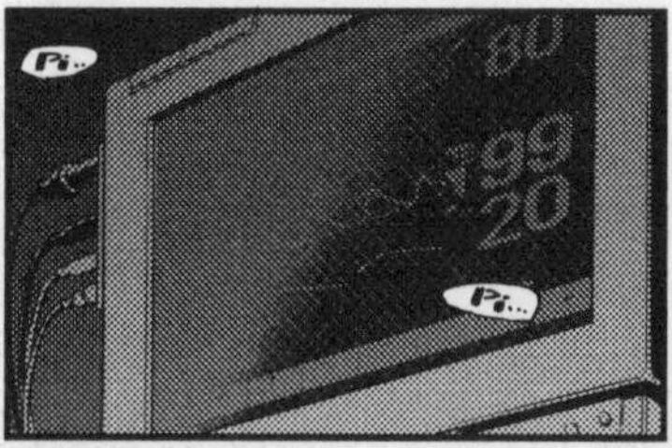
Pi...
80
99
20
Pi...

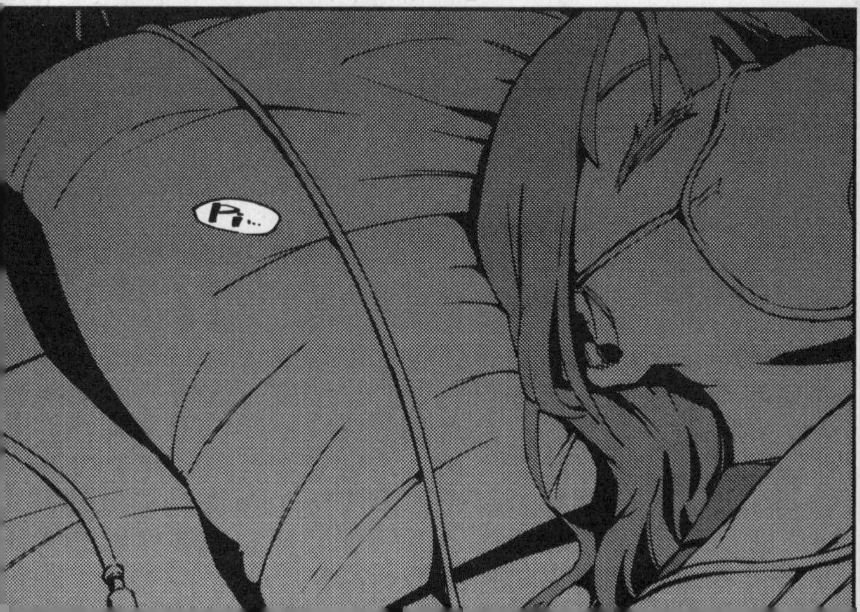
Pi...

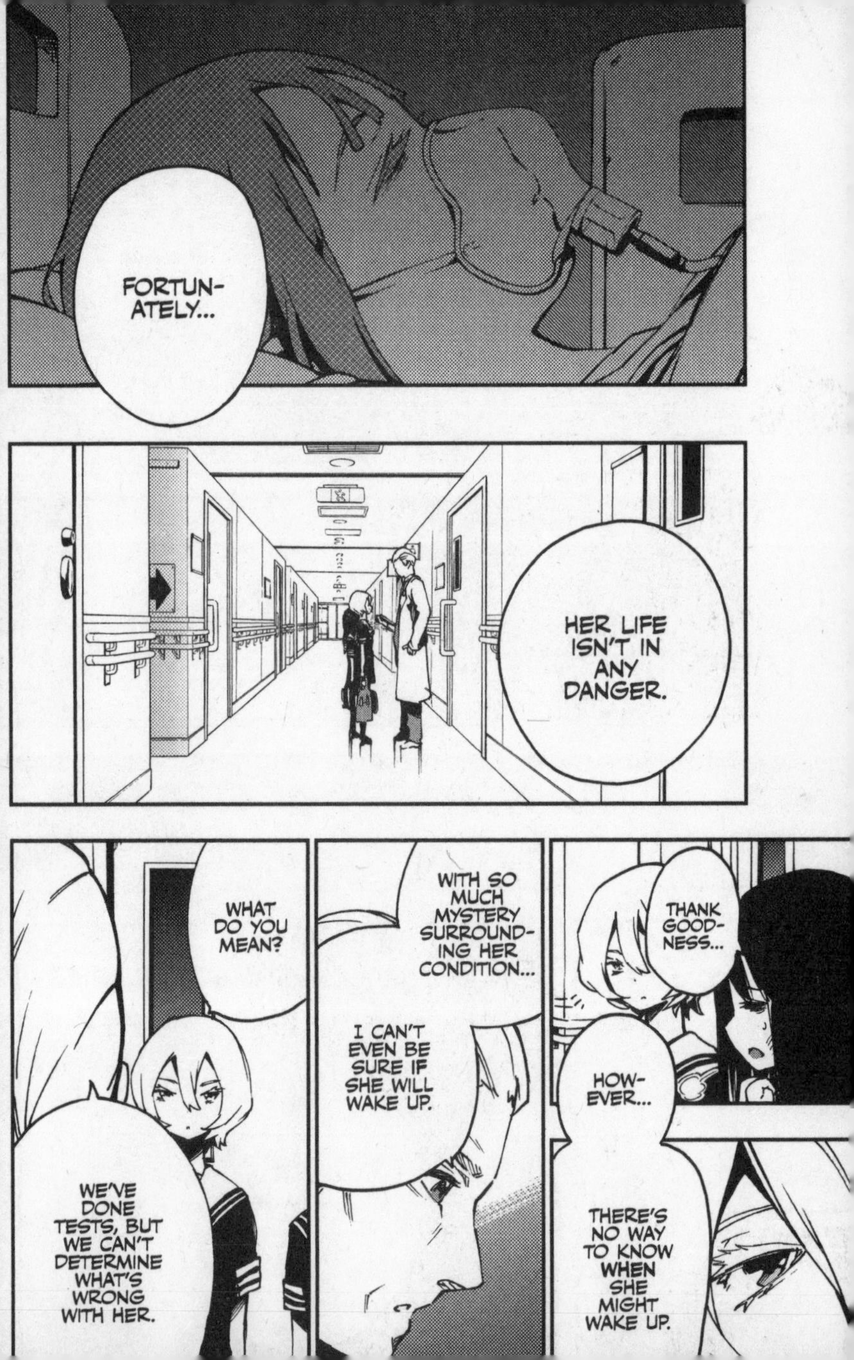
FORTUN-ATELY...
HER LIFE ISN'T IN ANY DANGER.
THANK GOOD-NESS...
HOW-EVER...
THERE'S NO WAY TO KNOW WHEN SHE MIGHT WAKE UP.
WITH SO MUCH MYSTERY SURROUND-ING HER CONDITION...
I CAN'T EVEN BE SURE IF SHE WILL WAKE UP.
WHAT DO YOU MEAN?
WE'VE DONE TESTS, BUT WE CAN'T DETERMINE WHAT'S WRONG WITH HER.

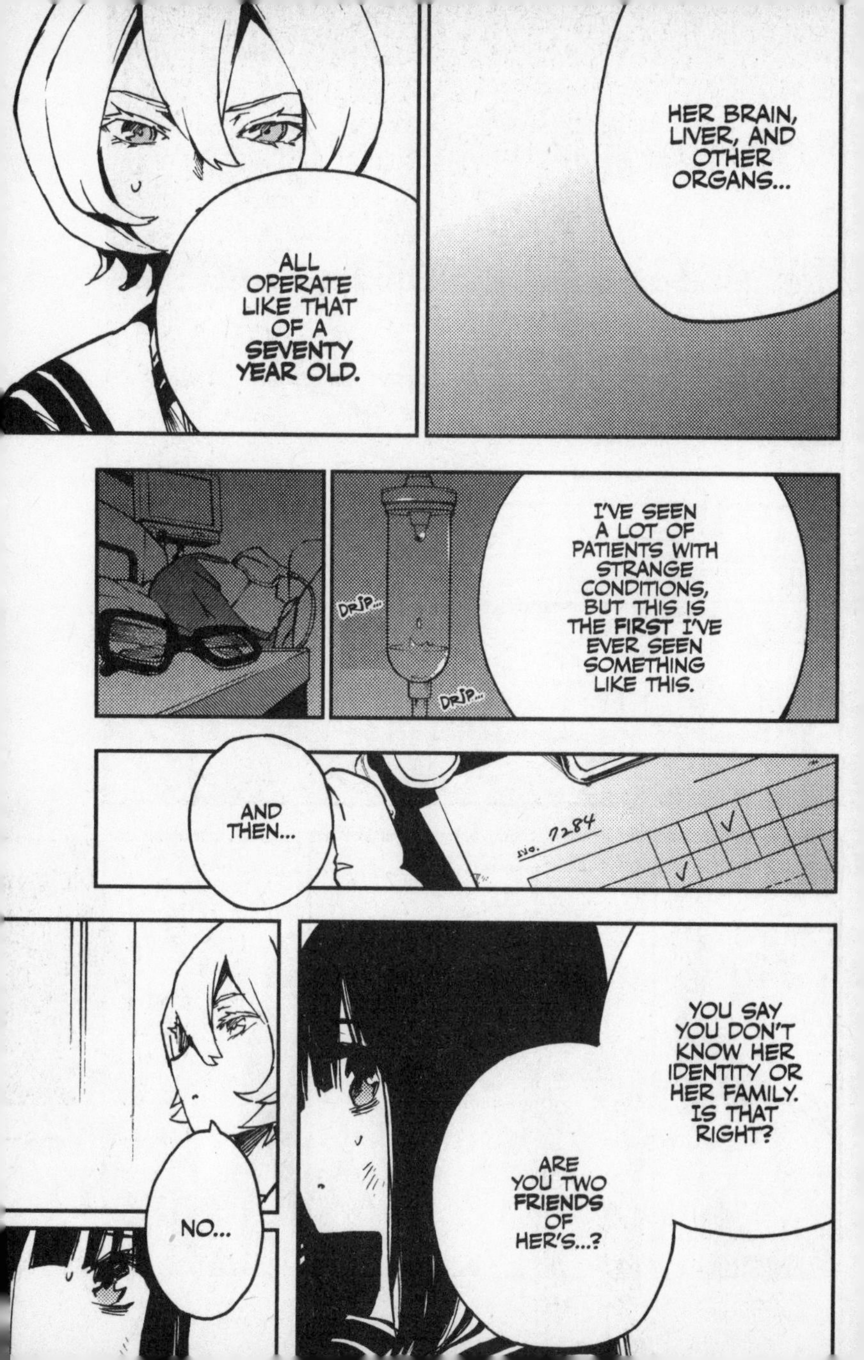
HER BRAIN, LIVER, AND OTHER ORGANS...
ALL OPERATE LIKE THAT OF A SEVENTY YEAR OLD.
I'VE SEEN A LOT OF PATIENTS WITH STRANGE CONDITIONS, BUT THIS IS THE FIRST I'VE EVER SEEN SOMETHING LIKE THIS.
DRIP...
DRIP...
No. 7284
AND THEN...
YOU SAY YOU DON'T KNOW HER IDENTITY OR HER FAMILY. IS THAT RIGHT?
ARE YOU TWO FRIENDS OF HER'S...?
NO...

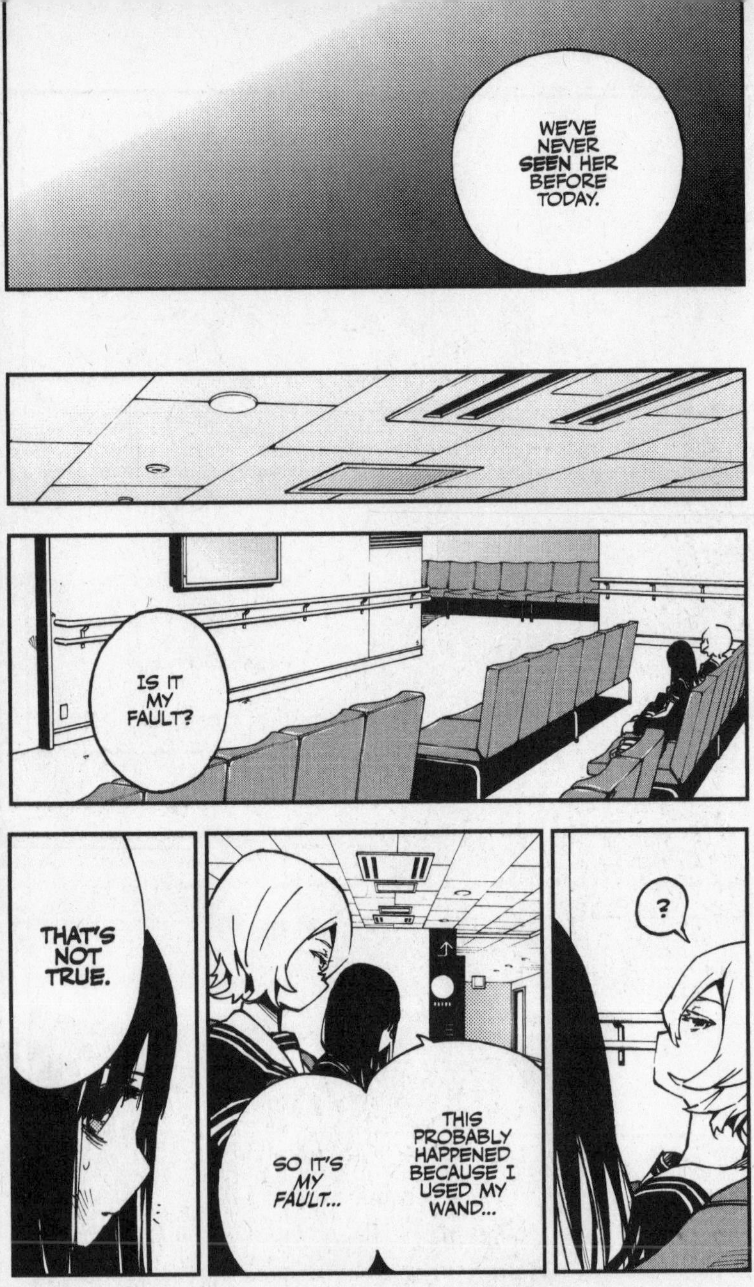
WE'VE NEVER SEEN HER BEFORE TODAY.
IS IT MY FAULT?
?
THIS PROBABLY HAPPENED BECAUSE I USED MY WAND...
SO IT'S MY FAULT...
THAT'S NOT TRUE.

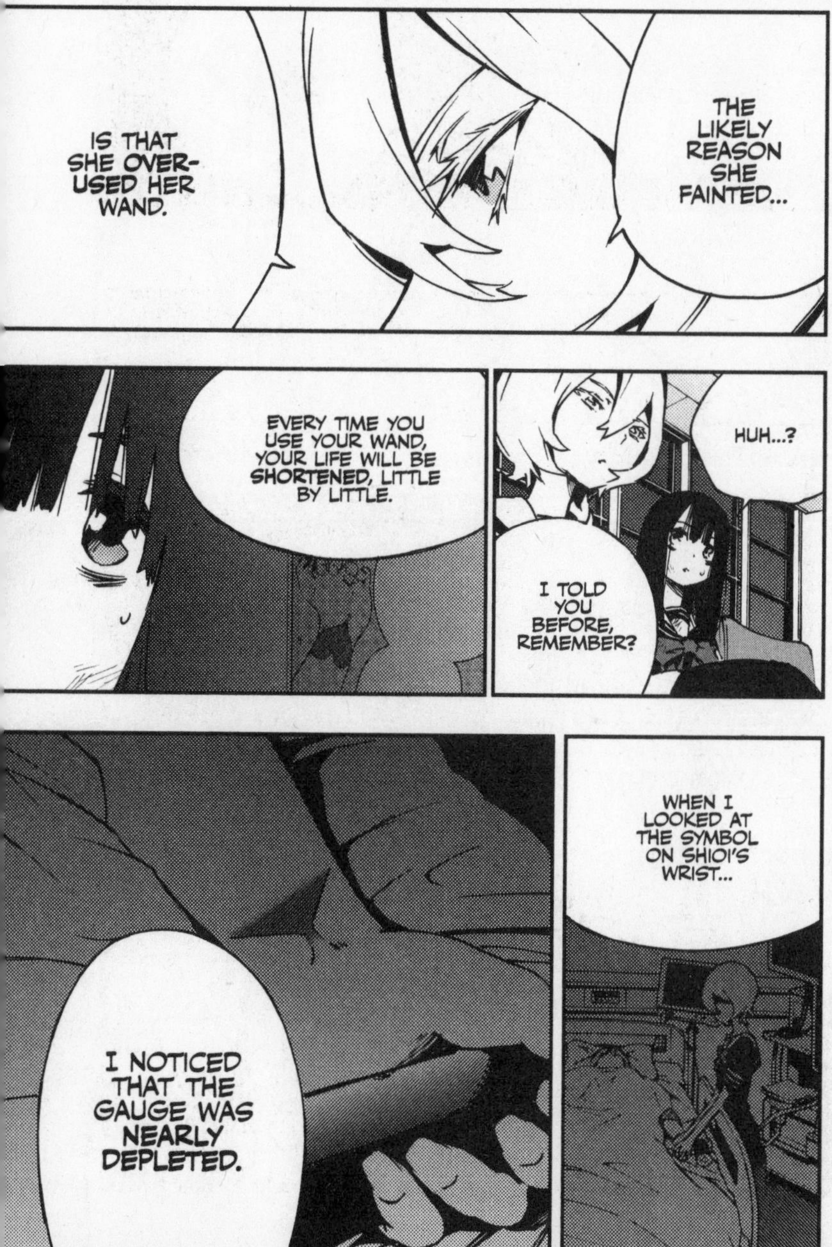
THE LIKELY REASON SHE FAINTED...
IS THAT SHE OVER-USED HER WAND.
HUH...?
I TOLD YOU BEFORE, REMEMBER?
EVERY TIME YOU USE YOUR WAND, YOUR LIFE WILL BE SHORTENED, LITTLE BY LITTLE.
WHEN I LOOKED AT THE SYMBOL ON SHIOI'S WRIST...
I NOTICED THAT THE GAUGE WAS NEARLY DEPLETED.

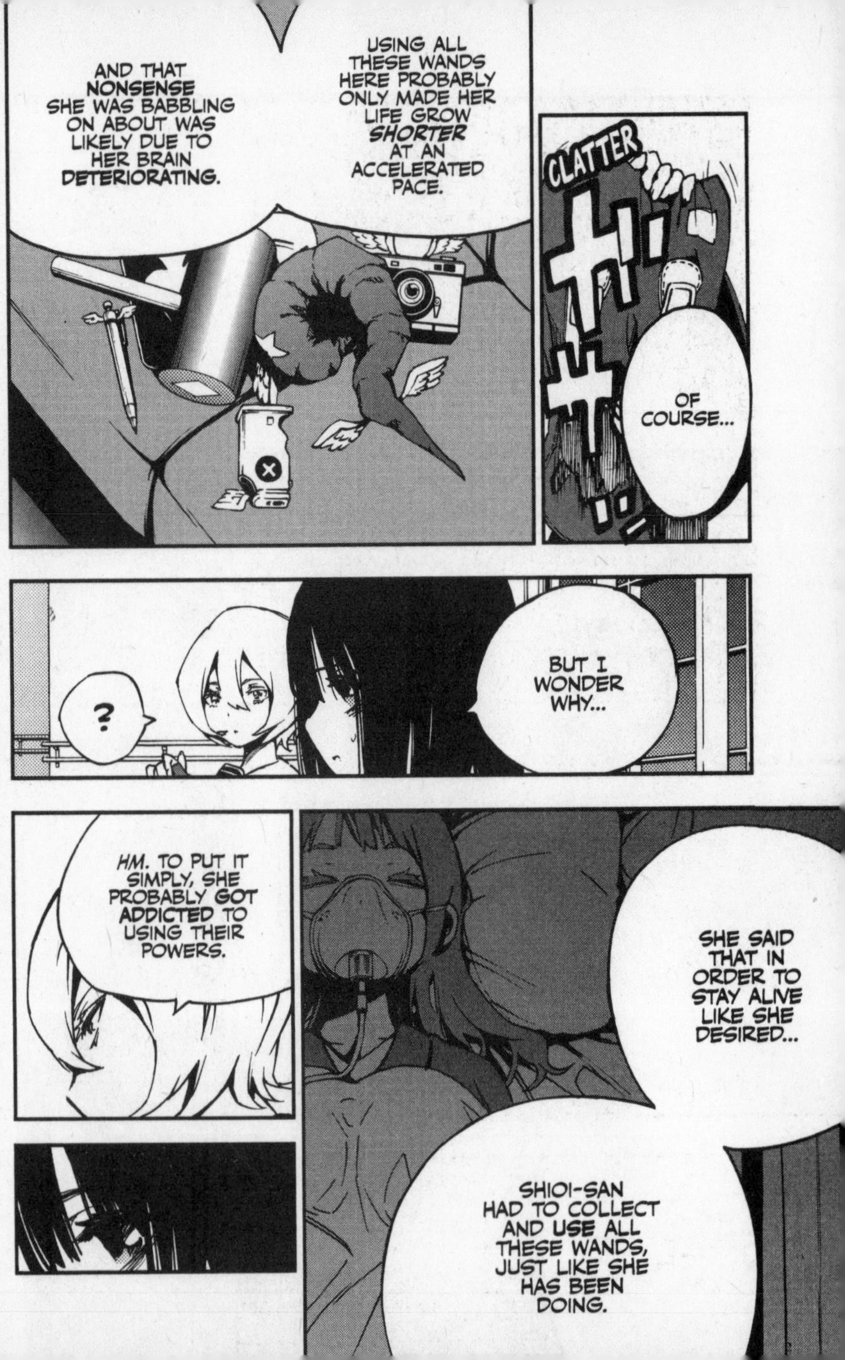
CLATTER
OF COURSE...
USING ALL THESE WANDS HERE PROBABLY ONLY MADE HER LIFE GROW *SHORTER* AT AN ACCELERATED PACE.
AND THAT **NONSENSE** SHE WAS BABBLING ON ABOUT WAS LIKELY DUE TO HER BRAIN DETERIORATING.
BUT I WONDER WHY...
?
SHE SAID THAT IN ORDER TO STAY ALIVE LIKE SHE DESIRED...
SHIOI-SAN HAD TO COLLECT AND **USE** ALL THESE WANDS, JUST LIKE SHE HAS BEEN DOING.
HM. TO PUT IT SIMPLY, SHE PROBABLY GOT ADDICTED TO USING THEIR POWERS.

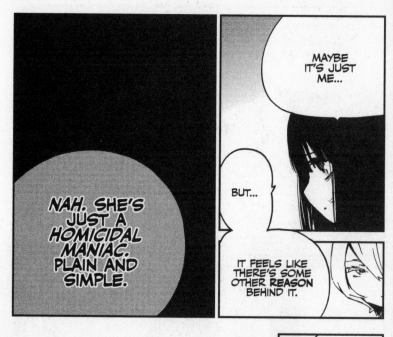

MAYBE IT'S JUST ME...

BUT...

IT FEELS LIKE THERE'S SOME OTHER REASON BEHIND IT.

NAH. SHE'S JUST A HOMICIDAL MANIAC. PLAIN AND SIMPLE.

CREAK...

AUGH...

THERE'S NOTHING MORE OR LESS TO IT.

WELL, SHIOI'S IN A COMA NOW.

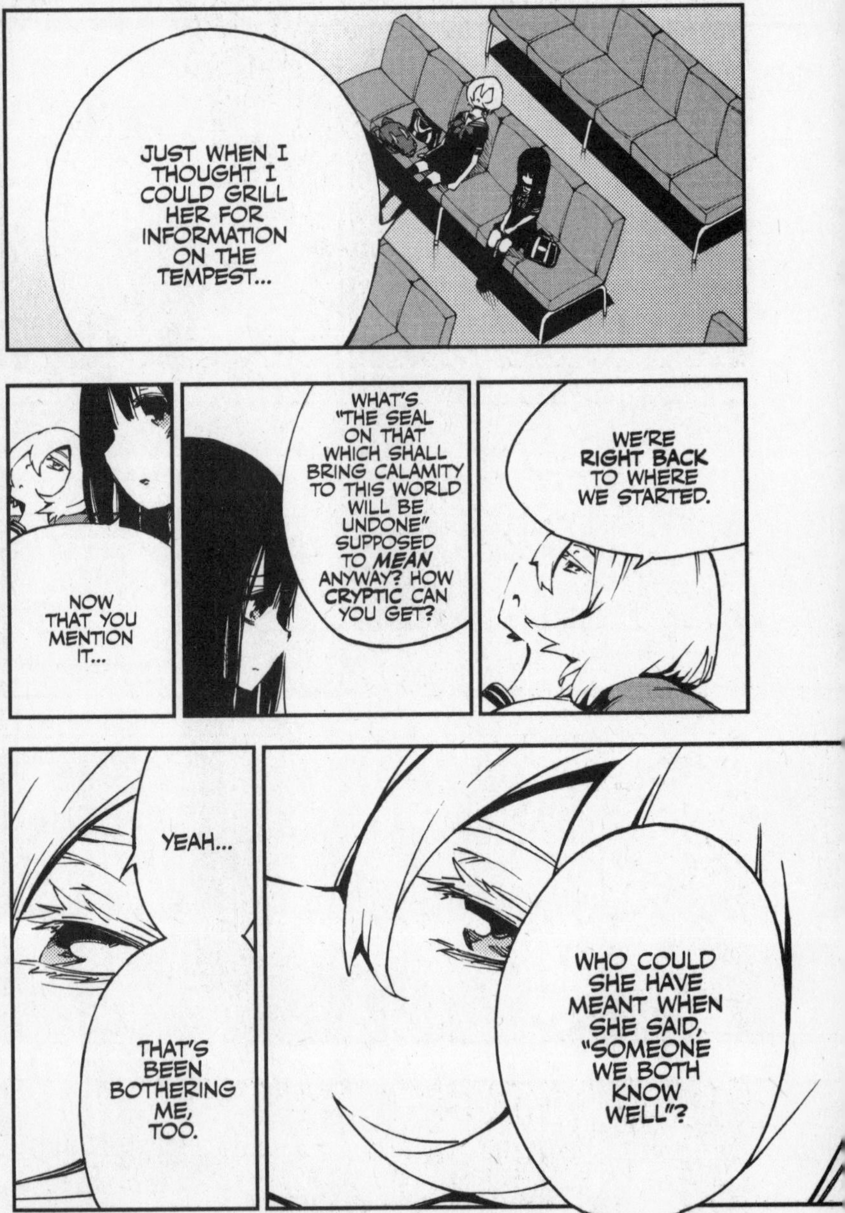
JUST WHEN I THOUGHT I COULD GRILL HER FOR INFORMATION ON THE TEMPEST...
WE'RE RIGHT BACK TO WHERE WE STARTED.
WHAT'S "THE SEAL ON THAT WHICH SHALL BRING CALAMITY TO THIS WORLD WILL BE UNDONE" SUPPOSED TO *MEAN* ANYWAY? HOW CRYPTIC CAN YOU GET?
NOW THAT YOU MENTION IT...
WHO COULD SHE HAVE MEANT WHEN SHE SAID, "SOMEONE WE BOTH KNOW WELL"?
YEAH...
THAT'S BEEN BOTHERING ME, TOO.

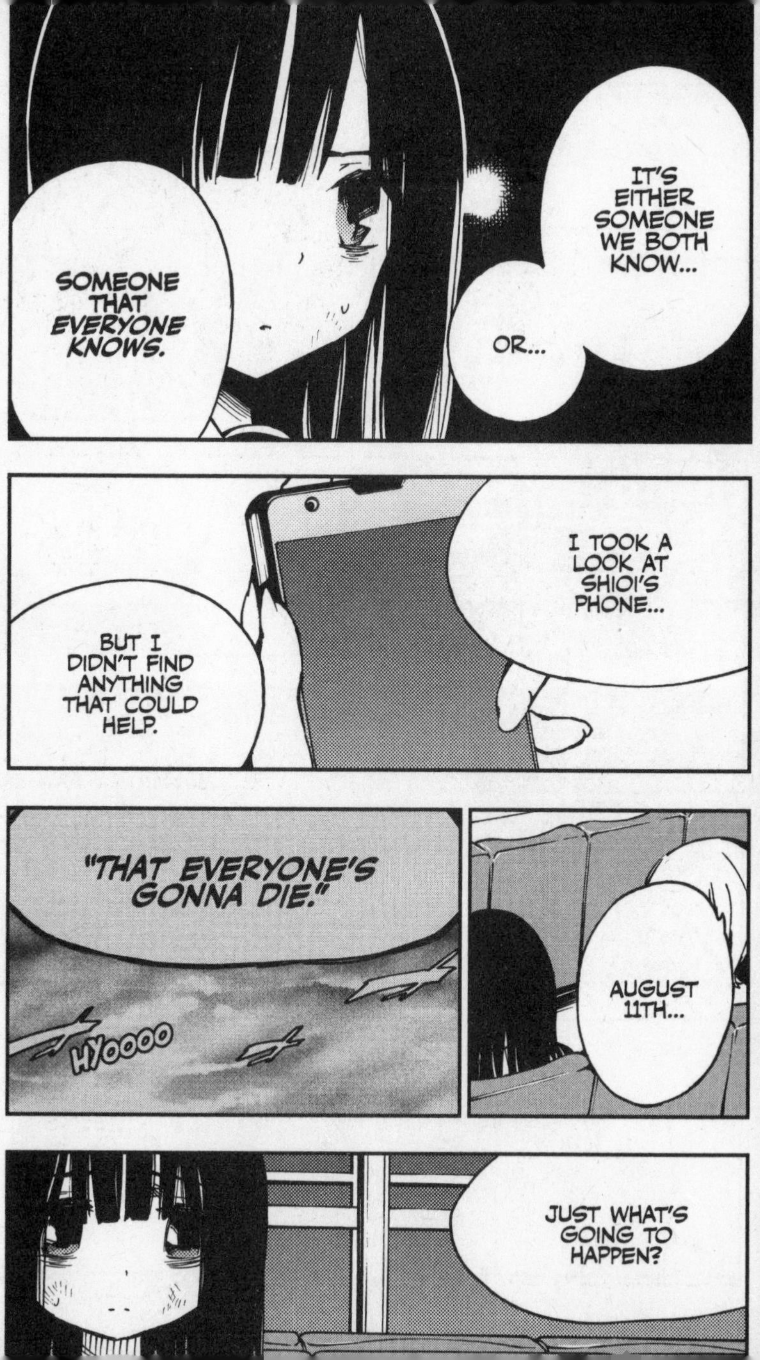
IT'S EITHER SOMEONE WE BOTH KNOW...
OR...
SOMEONE THAT EVERYONE KNOWS.
I TOOK A LOOK AT SHIOI'S PHONE...
BUT I DIDN'T FIND ANYTHING THAT COULD HELP.
AUGUST 11TH...
"THAT EVERYONE'S GONNA DIE."
HYOOOO
JUST WHAT'S GOING TO HAPPEN?

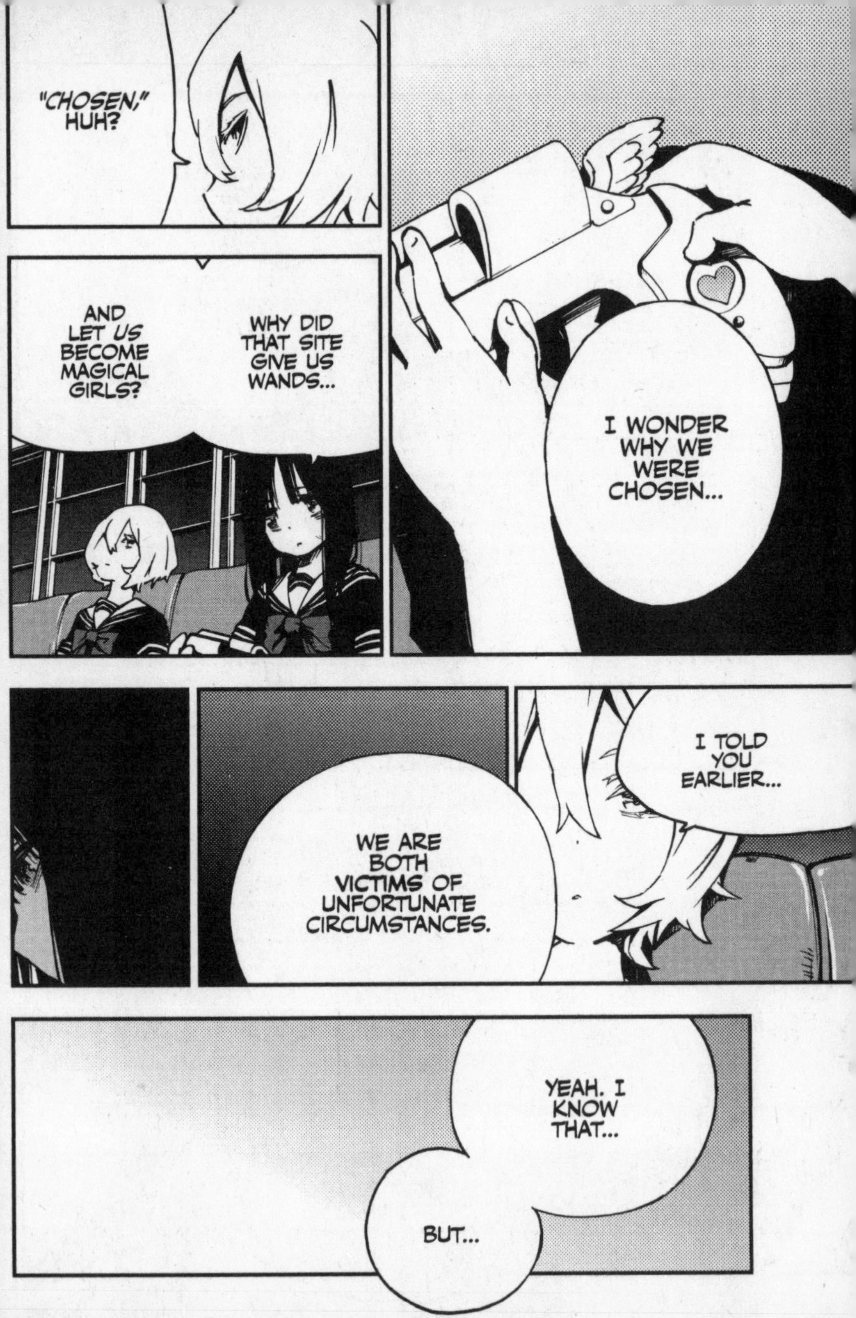
I WONDER WHY WE WERE CHOSEN...
"CHOSEN," HUH?
WHY DID THAT SITE GIVE US WANDS...
AND LET US BECOME MAGICAL GIRLS?
I TOLD YOU EARLIER...
WE ARE BOTH VICTIMS OF UNFORTUNATE CIRCUMSTANCES.
YEAH. I KNOW THAT...
BUT...

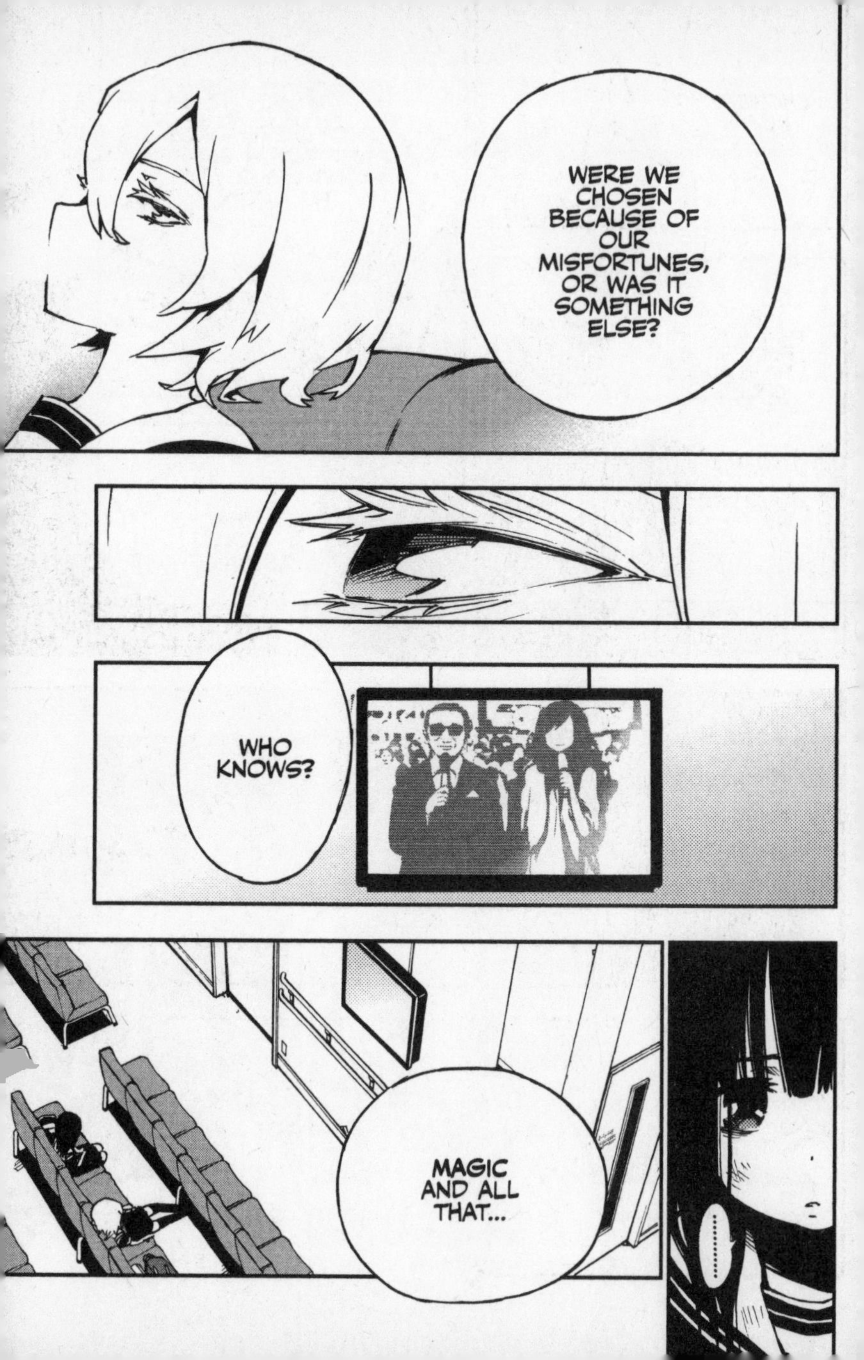
WERE WE CHOSEN BECAUSE OF OUR MISFORTUNES, OR WAS IT SOMETHING ELSE?
WHO KNOWS?
......
MAGIC AND ALL THAT...

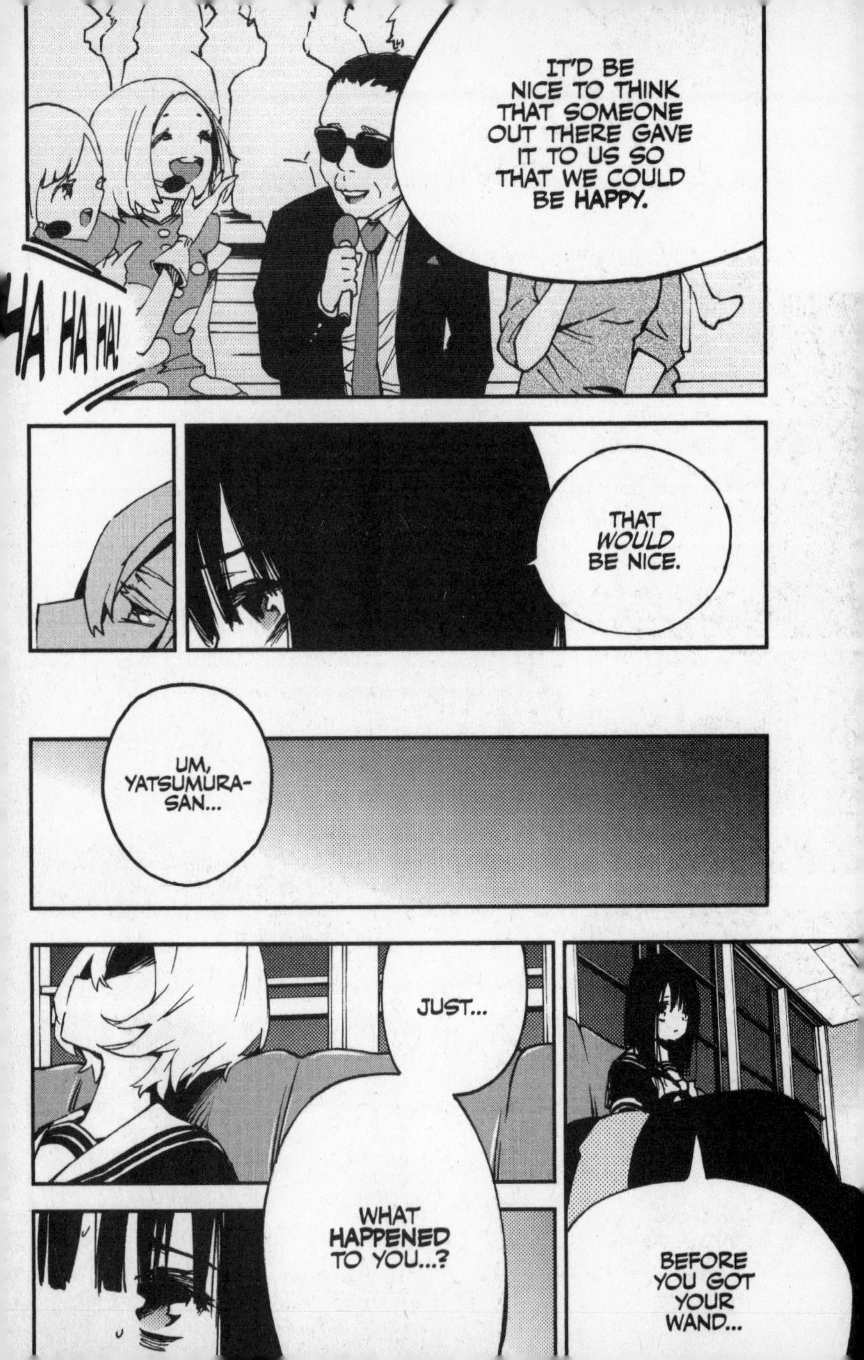
IT'D BE NICE TO THINK THAT SOMEONE OUT THERE GAVE IT TO US SO THAT WE COULD BE HAPPY.
HA HA HA!
THAT WOULD BE NICE.
UM, YATSUMURA-SAN...
JUST...
WHAT HAPPENED TO YOU...?
BEFORE YOU GOT YOUR WAND...

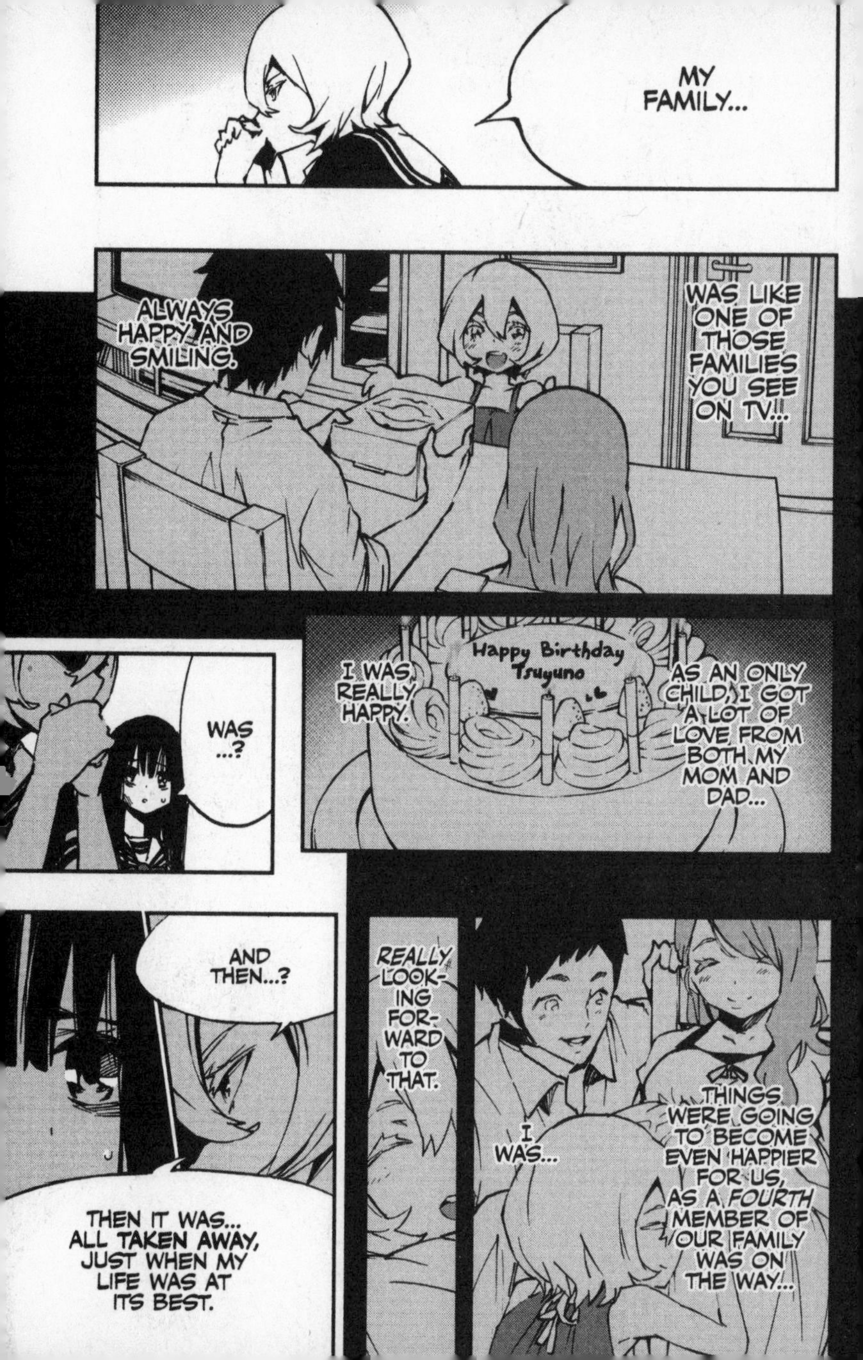
MY FAMILY...
WAS LIKE ONE OF THOSE FAMILIES YOU SEE ON TV...
ALWAYS HAPPY AND SMILING.
AS AN ONLY CHILD, I GOT A LOT OF LOVE FROM BOTH MY MOM AND DAD...
Happy Birthday Tsuyuno
I WAS REALLY HAPPY.
WAS ...?
THINGS WERE GOING TO BECOME EVEN HAPPIER FOR US, AS A *FOURTH* MEMBER OF OUR FAMILY WAS ON THE WAY...
I WAS...
REALLY LOOKING FORWARD TO THAT.
AND THEN...?
THEN IT WAS... ALL TAKEN AWAY, JUST WHEN MY LIFE WAS AT ITS BEST.

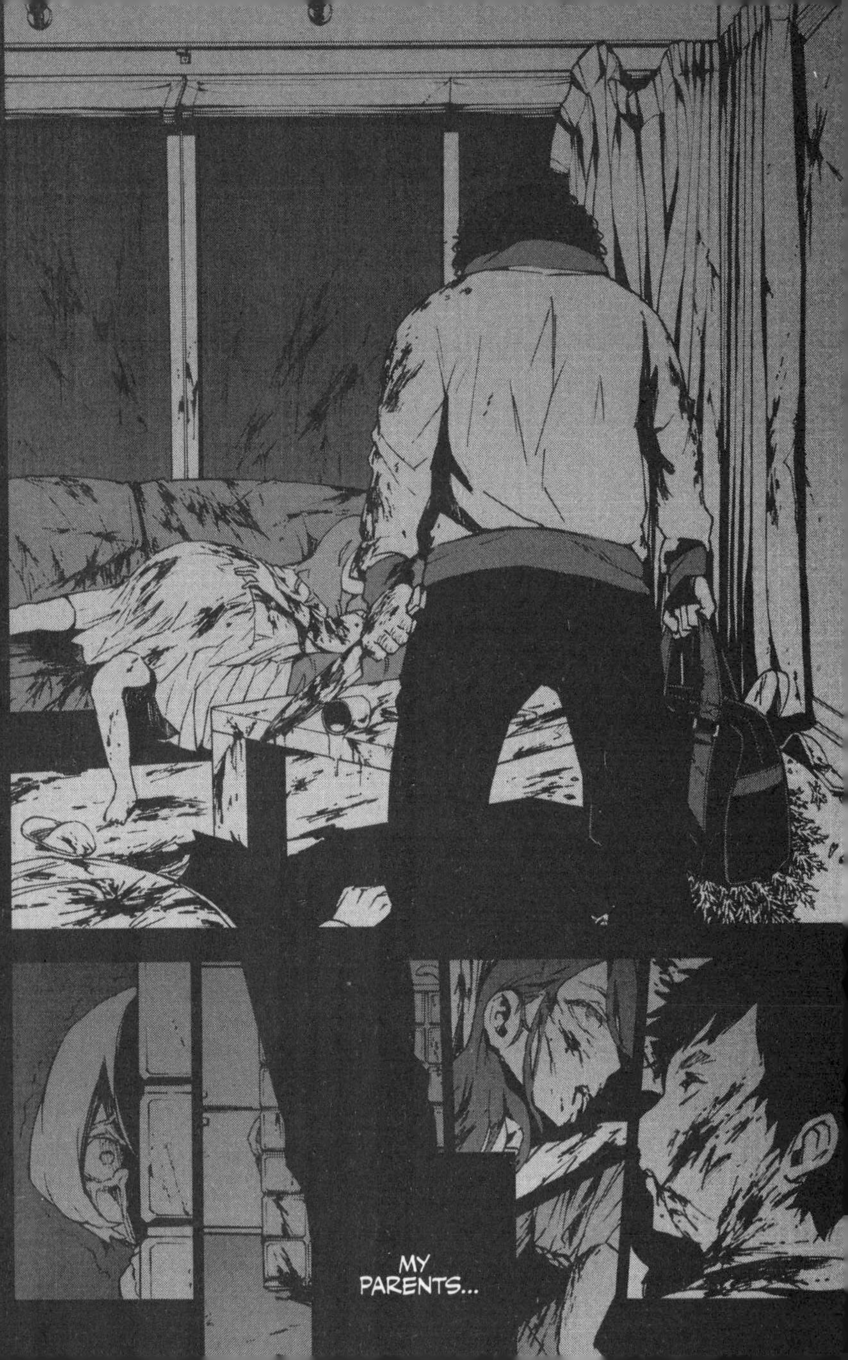
MY PARENTS...

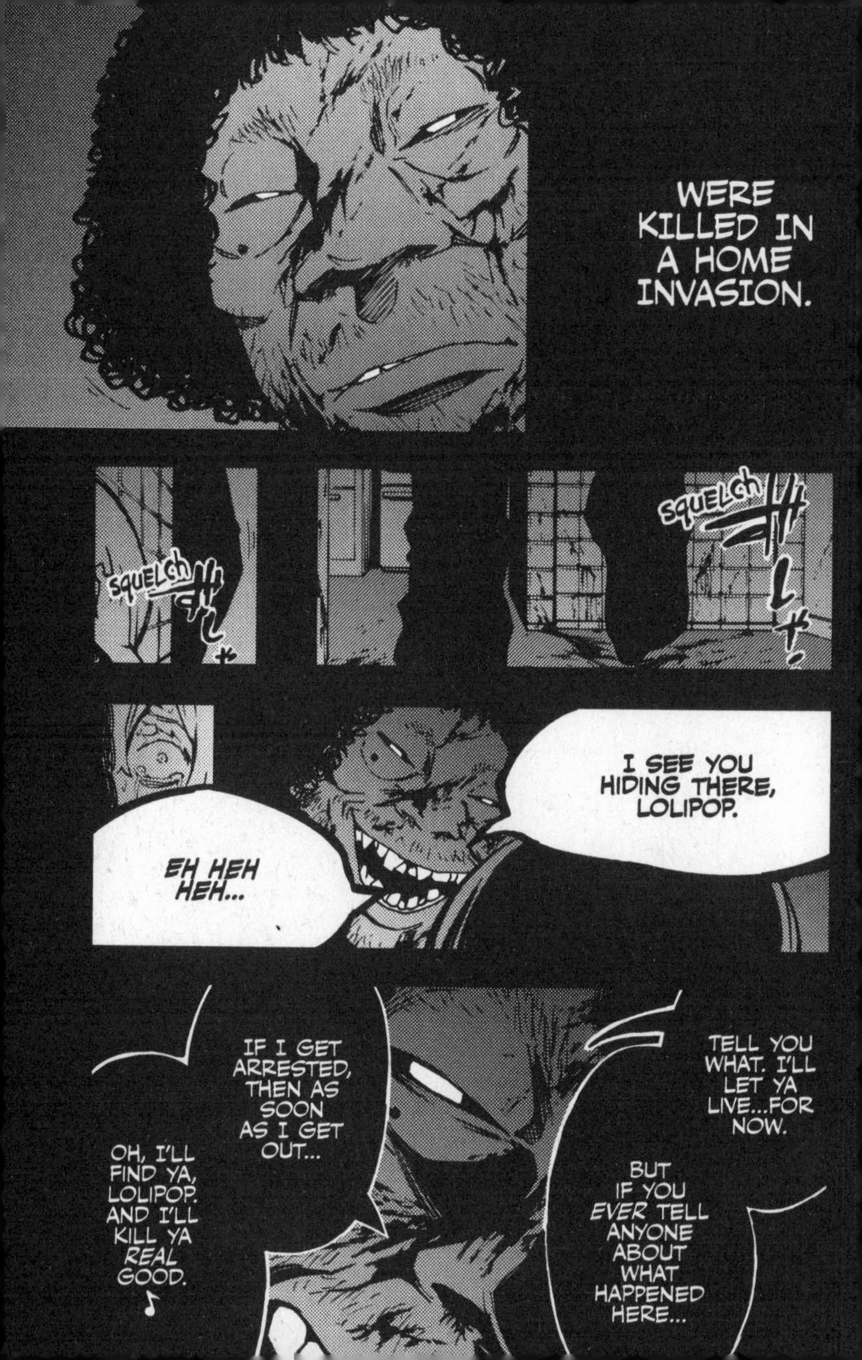
WERE KILLED IN A HOME INVASION.
squelch
squelch
I SEE YOU HIDING THERE, LOLIPOP.
EH HEH HEH...
TELL YOU WHAT. I'LL LET YA LIVE...FOR NOW.
BUT IF YOU *EVER* TELL ANYONE ABOUT WHAT HAPPENED HERE...
IF I GET ARRESTED, THEN AS SOON AS I GET OUT...
OH, I'LL FIND YA, LOLIPOP. AND I'LL KILL YA *REAL* GOOD. ♪

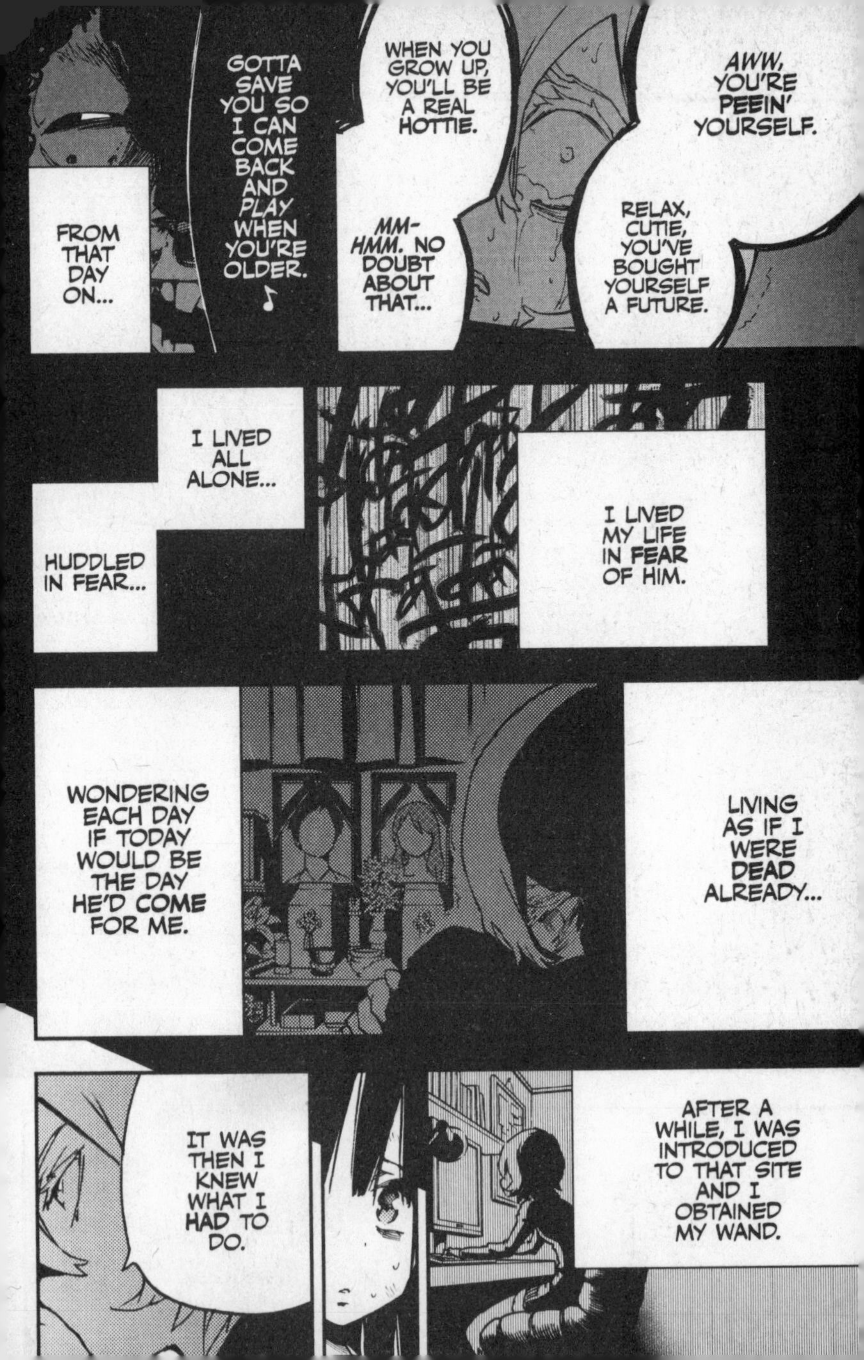
AWW, YOU'RE PEEIN' YOURSELF.
RELAX, CUTIE, YOU'VE BOUGHT YOURSELF A FUTURE.
WHEN YOU GROW UP, YOU'LL BE A REAL HOTTIE.
MM-HMM. NO DOUBT ABOUT THAT...
GOTTA SAVE YOU SO I CAN COME BACK AND *PLAY* WHEN YOU'RE OLDER. ♪
FROM THAT DAY ON...
I LIVED MY LIFE IN FEAR OF HIM.
I LIVED ALL ALONE...
HUDDLED IN FEAR...
LIVING AS IF I WERE DEAD ALREADY...
WONDERING EACH DAY IF TODAY WOULD BE THE DAY HE'D COME FOR ME.
AFTER A WHILE, I WAS INTRODUCED TO THAT SITE AND I OBTAINED MY WAND.
IT WAS THEN I KNEW WHAT I HAD TO DO.

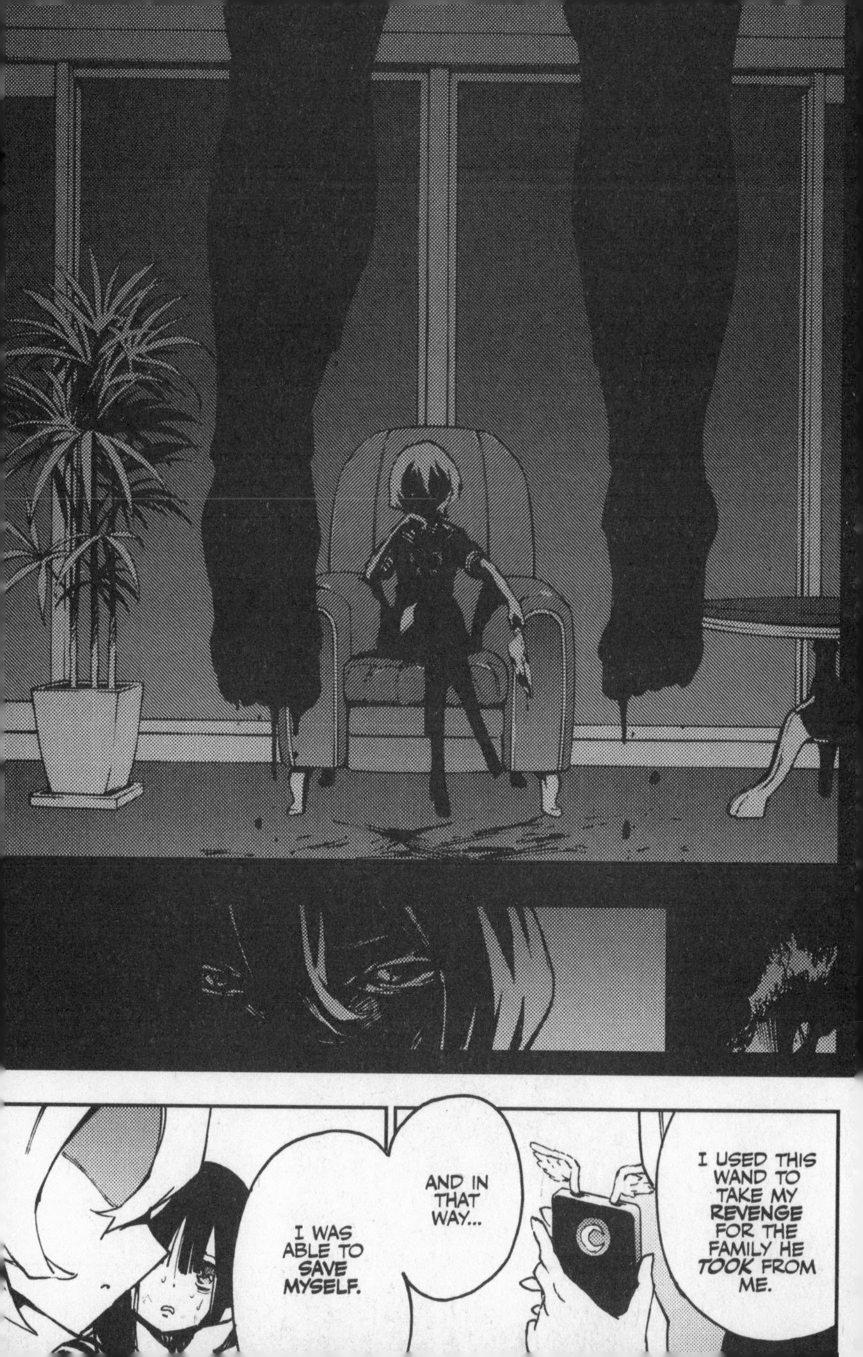
I USED THIS WAND TO TAKE MY REVENGE FOR THE FAMILY HE TOOK FROM ME.
AND IN THAT WAY...
I WAS ABLE TO SAVE MYSELF.

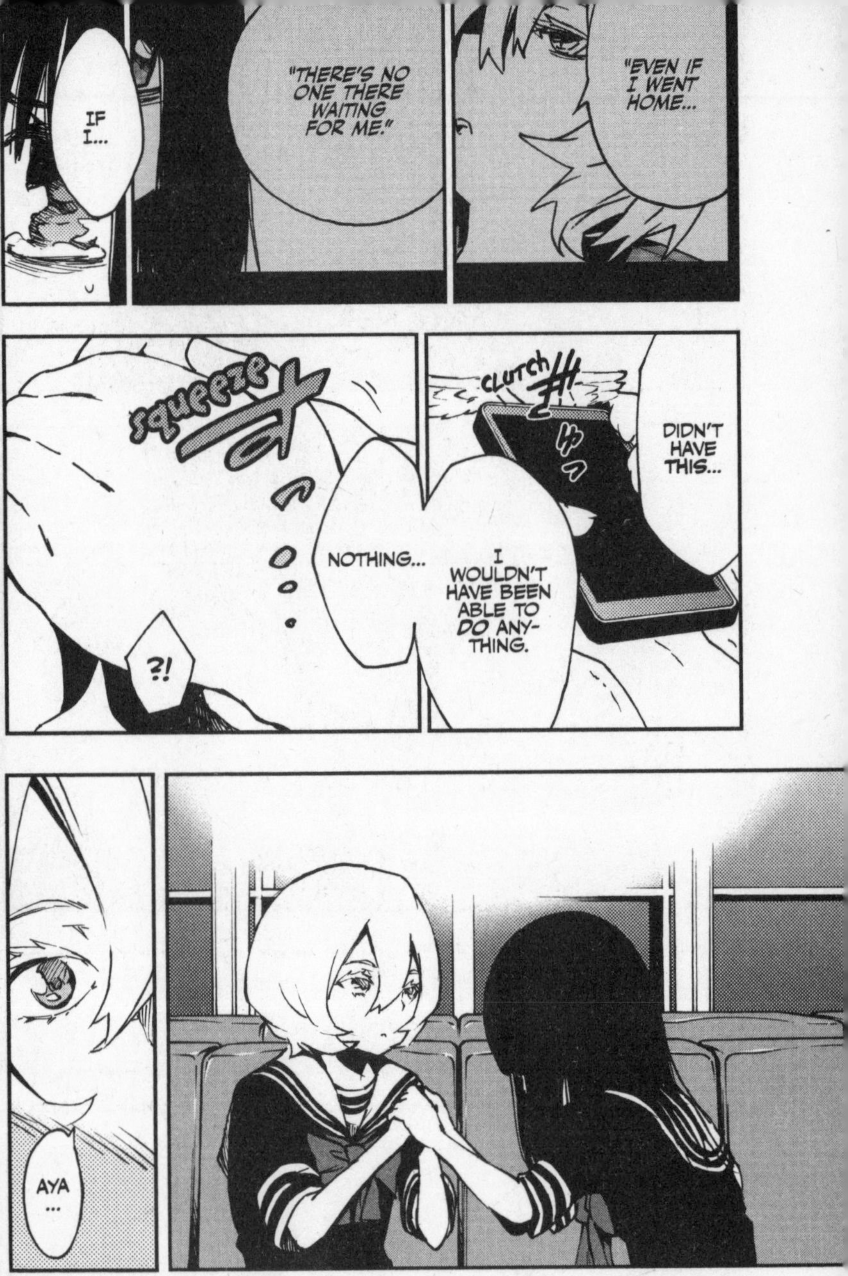
"EVEN IF I WENT HOME...
"THERE'S NO ONE THERE WAITING FOR ME."
IF I...
CLUTCH
DIDN'T HAVE THIS...
I WOULDN'T HAVE BEEN ABLE TO *DO* ANYTHING.
NOTHING...
squeeze
?!
AYA ...

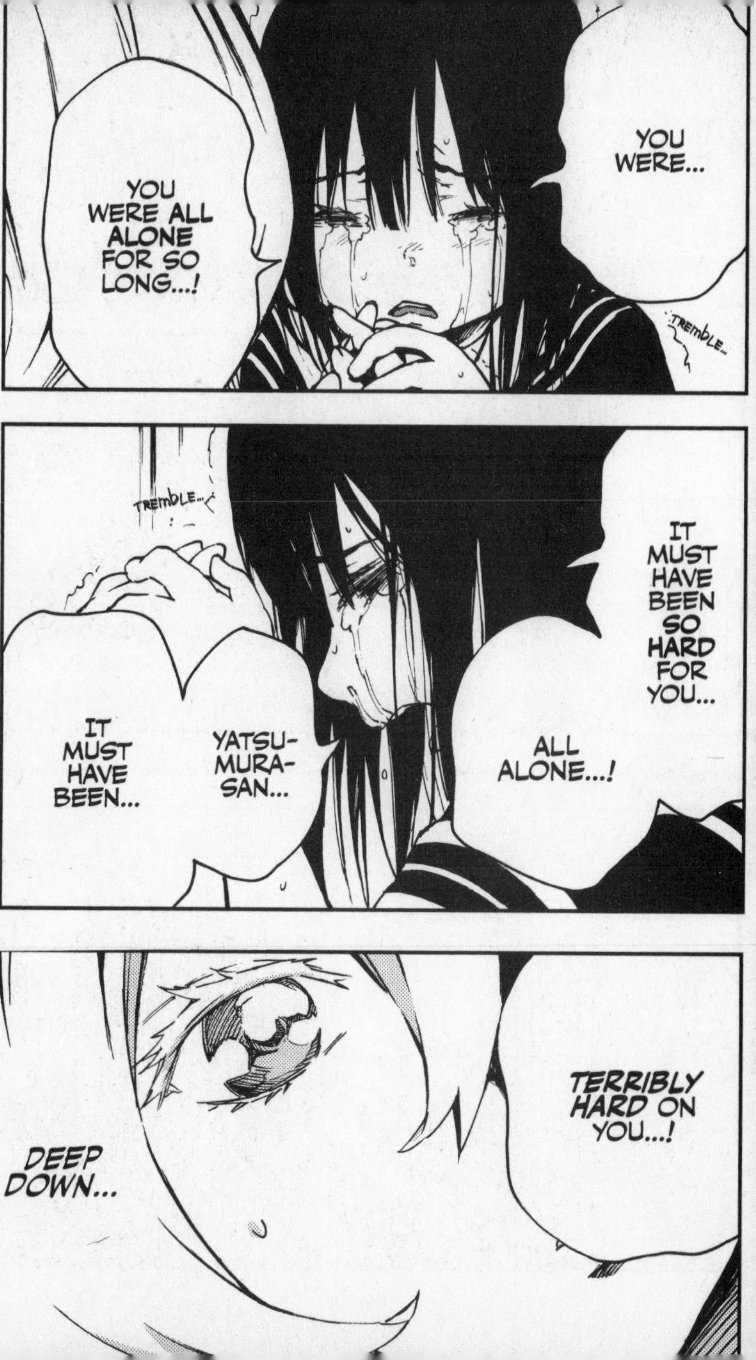
YOU WERE...
TREMBLE...
YOU WERE ALL ALONE FOR SO LONG...!
IT MUST HAVE BEEN SO HARD FOR YOU...
TREMBLE...
ALL ALONE...!
YATSU-MURA-SAN...
IT MUST HAVE BEEN...
TERRIBLY HARD ON YOU...!
DEEP DOWN...

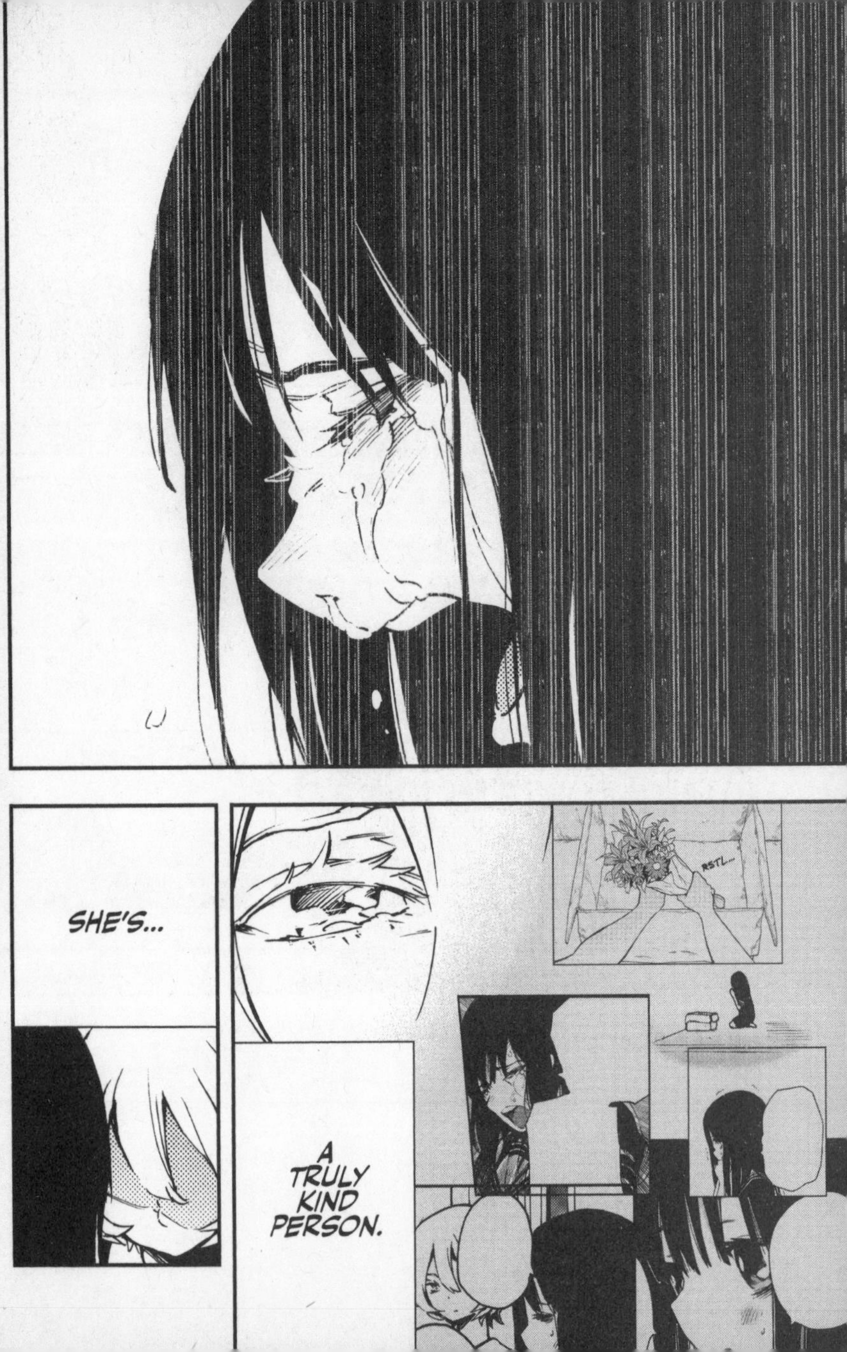
RSTL...
SHE'S...
A TRULY KIND PERSON.

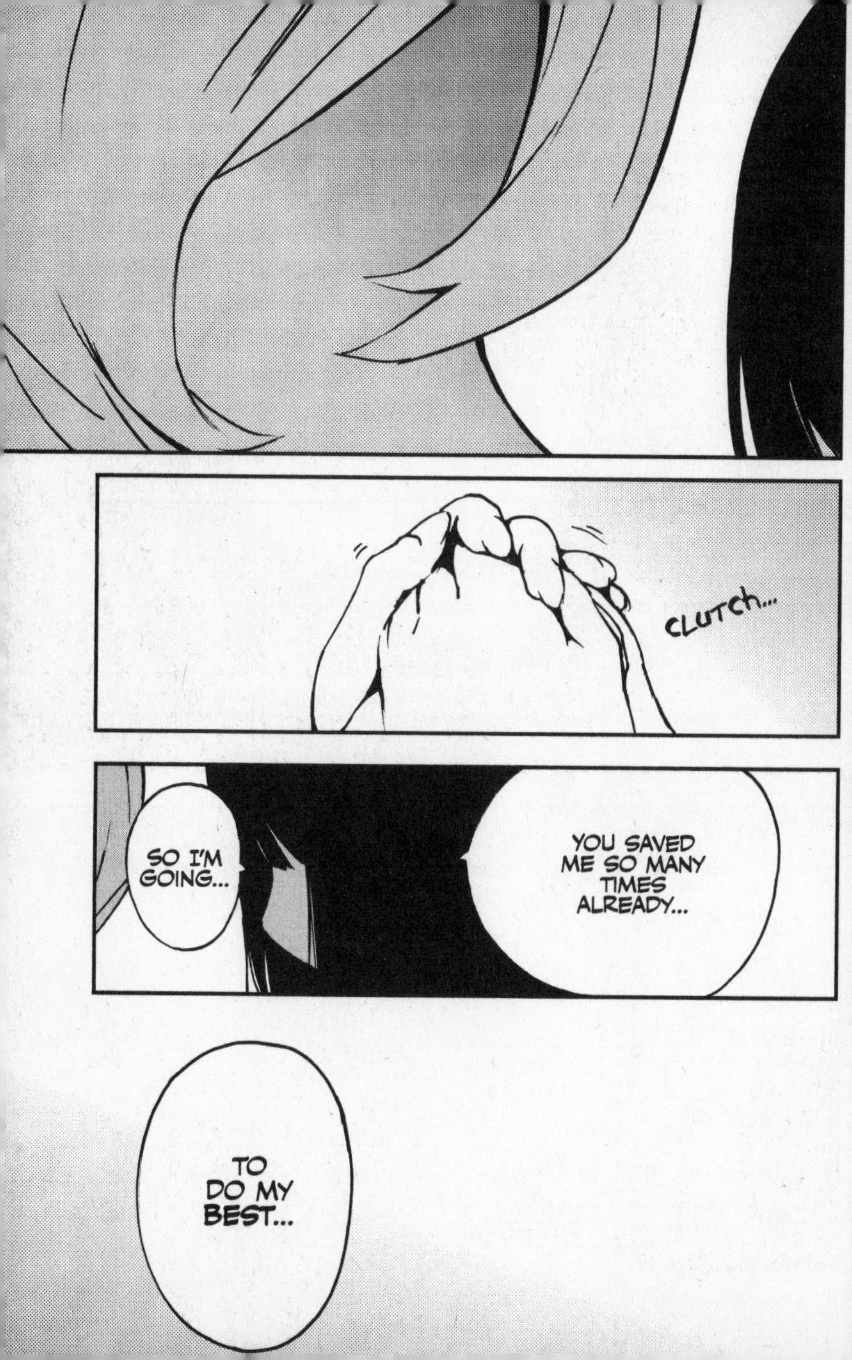
CLUTCH...
YOU SAVED ME SO MANY TIMES ALREADY...
SO I'M GOING...
TO DO MY BEST...

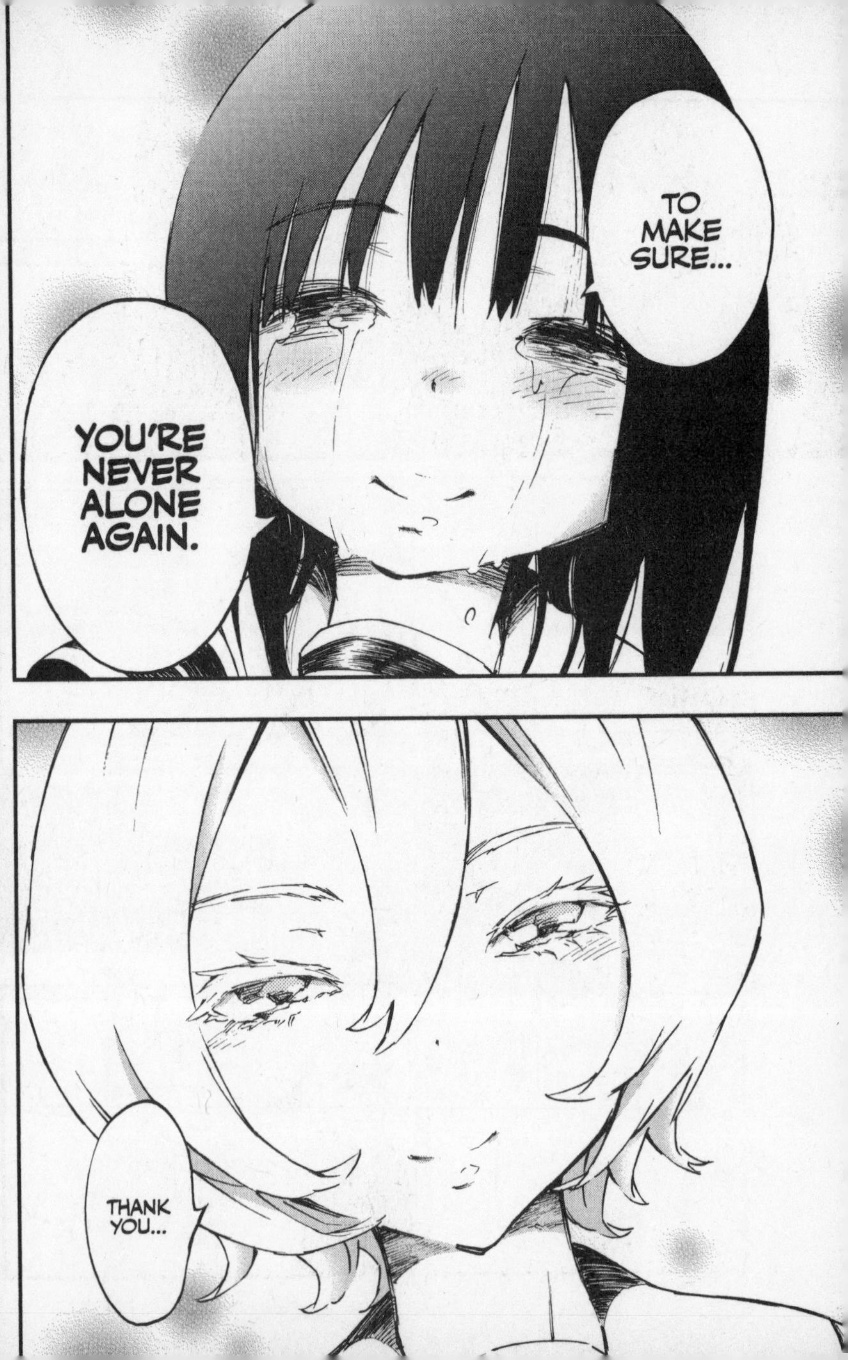
TO MAKE SURE...
YOU'RE NEVER ALONE AGAIN.
THANK YOU...

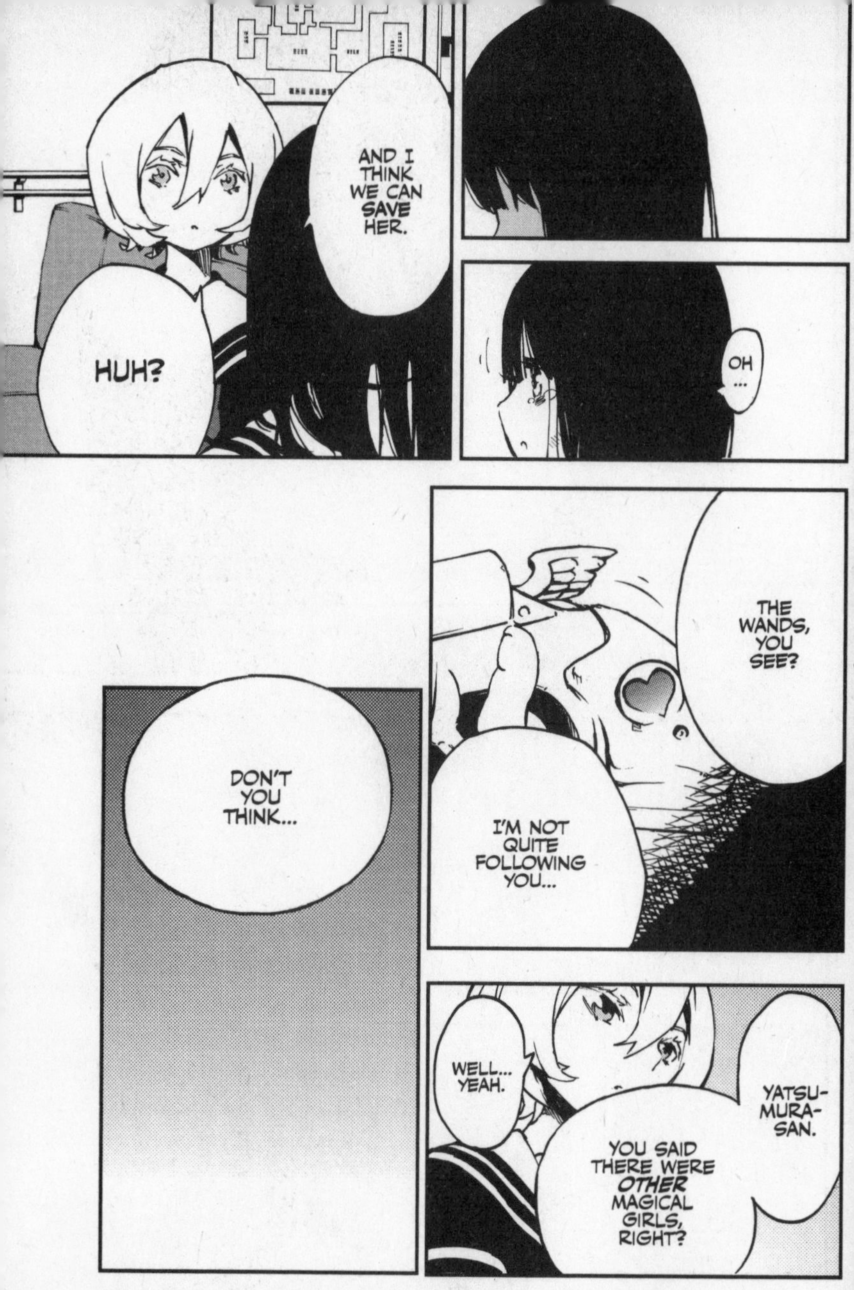
OH ...
AND I THINK WE CAN SAVE HER.
HUH?
THE WANDS, YOU SEE?
I'M NOT QUITE FOLLOWING YOU...
YATSU-MURA-SAN.
YOU SAID THERE WERE *OTHER* MAGICAL GIRLS, RIGHT?
WELL... YEAH.
DON'T YOU THINK...

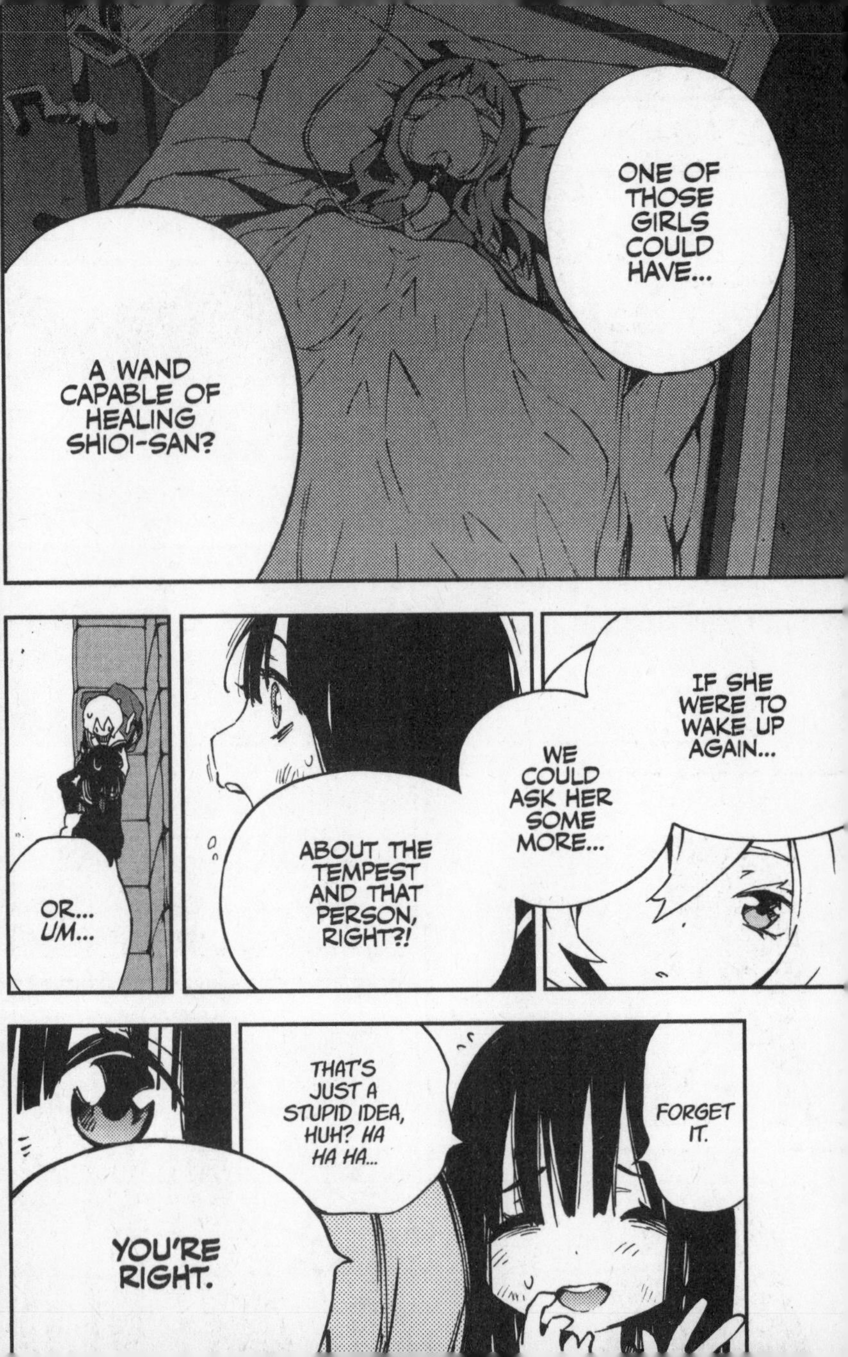
ONE OF THOSE GIRLS COULD HAVE...
A WAND CAPABLE OF HEALING SHIOI-SAN?
IF SHE WERE TO WAKE UP AGAIN...
WE COULD ASK HER SOME MORE...
ABOUT THE TEMPEST AND THAT PERSON, RIGHT?!
OR... UM...
FORGET IT.
THAT'S JUST A STUPID IDEA, HUH? HA HA HA...
YOU'RE RIGHT.

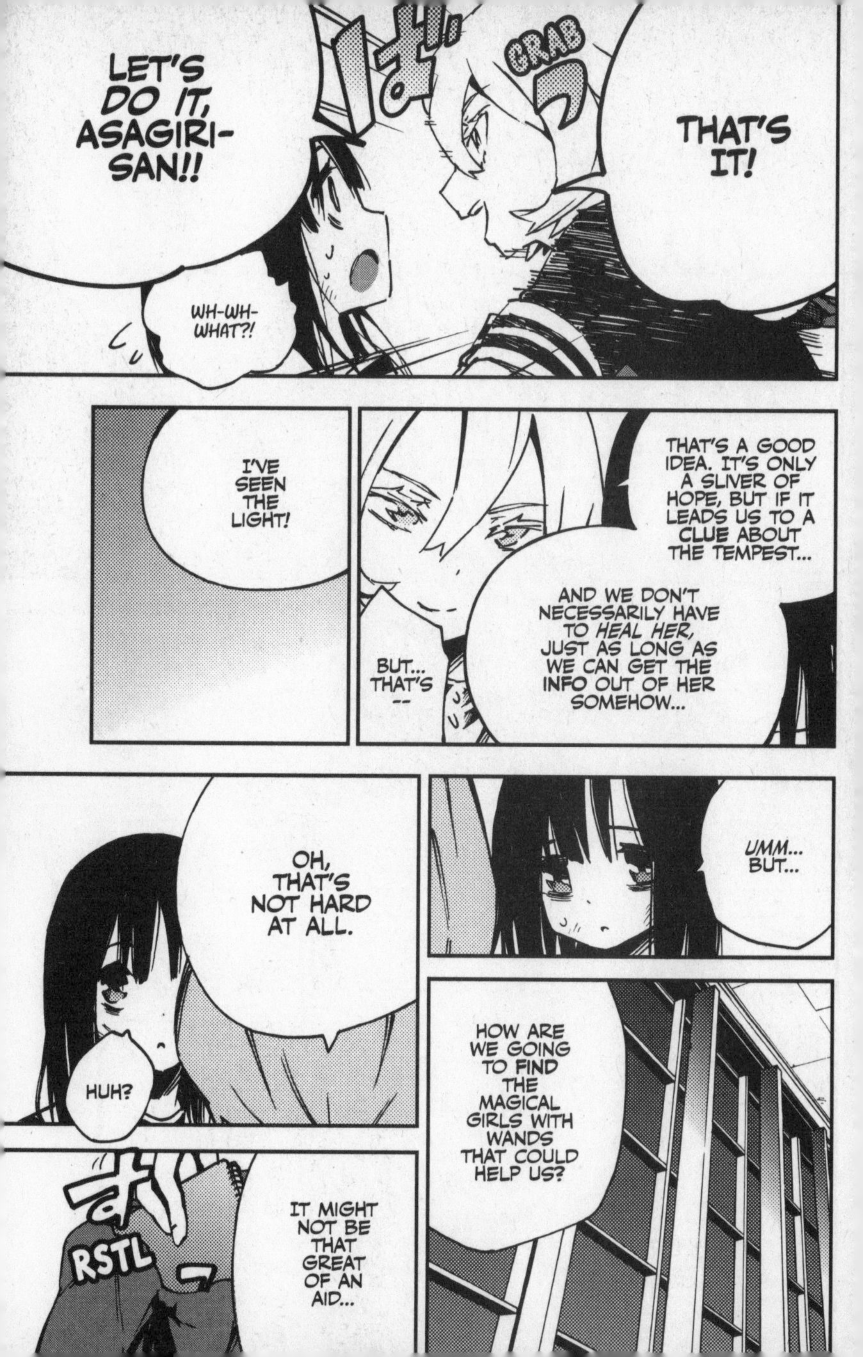
THAT'S IT!
CRAB
LET'S DO IT, ASAGIRI-SAN!!
WH-WH-WHAT?!
THAT'S A GOOD IDEA. IT'S ONLY A SLIVER OF HOPE, BUT IF IT LEADS US TO A CLUE ABOUT THE TEMPEST...
AND WE DON'T NECESSARILY HAVE TO HEAL HER, JUST AS LONG AS WE CAN GET THE INFO OUT OF HER SOMEHOW...
BUT... THAT'S --
I'VE SEEN THE LIGHT!
UMM... BUT...
HOW ARE WE GOING TO FIND THE MAGICAL GIRLS WITH WANDS THAT COULD HELP US?
OH, THAT'S NOT HARD AT ALL.
HUH?
IT MIGHT NOT BE THAT GREAT OF AN AID...
RSTL

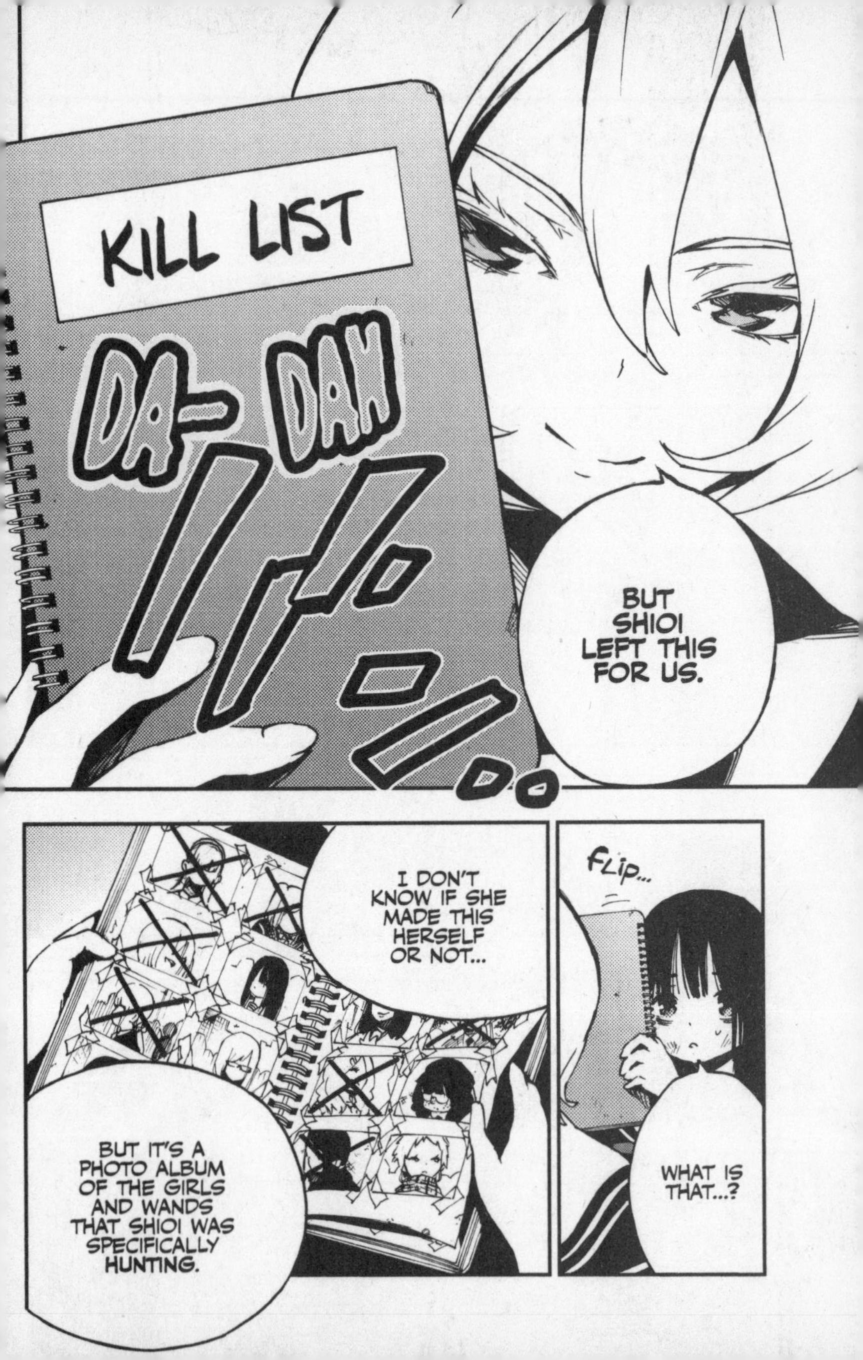
KILL LIST
DA-DAH
BUT SHIOI LEFT THIS FOR US.
FLIP...
WHAT IS THAT...?
I DON'T KNOW IF SHE MADE THIS HERSELF OR NOT...
BUT IT'S A PHOTO ALBUM OF THE GIRLS AND WANDS THAT SHIOI WAS SPECIFICALLY HUNTING.

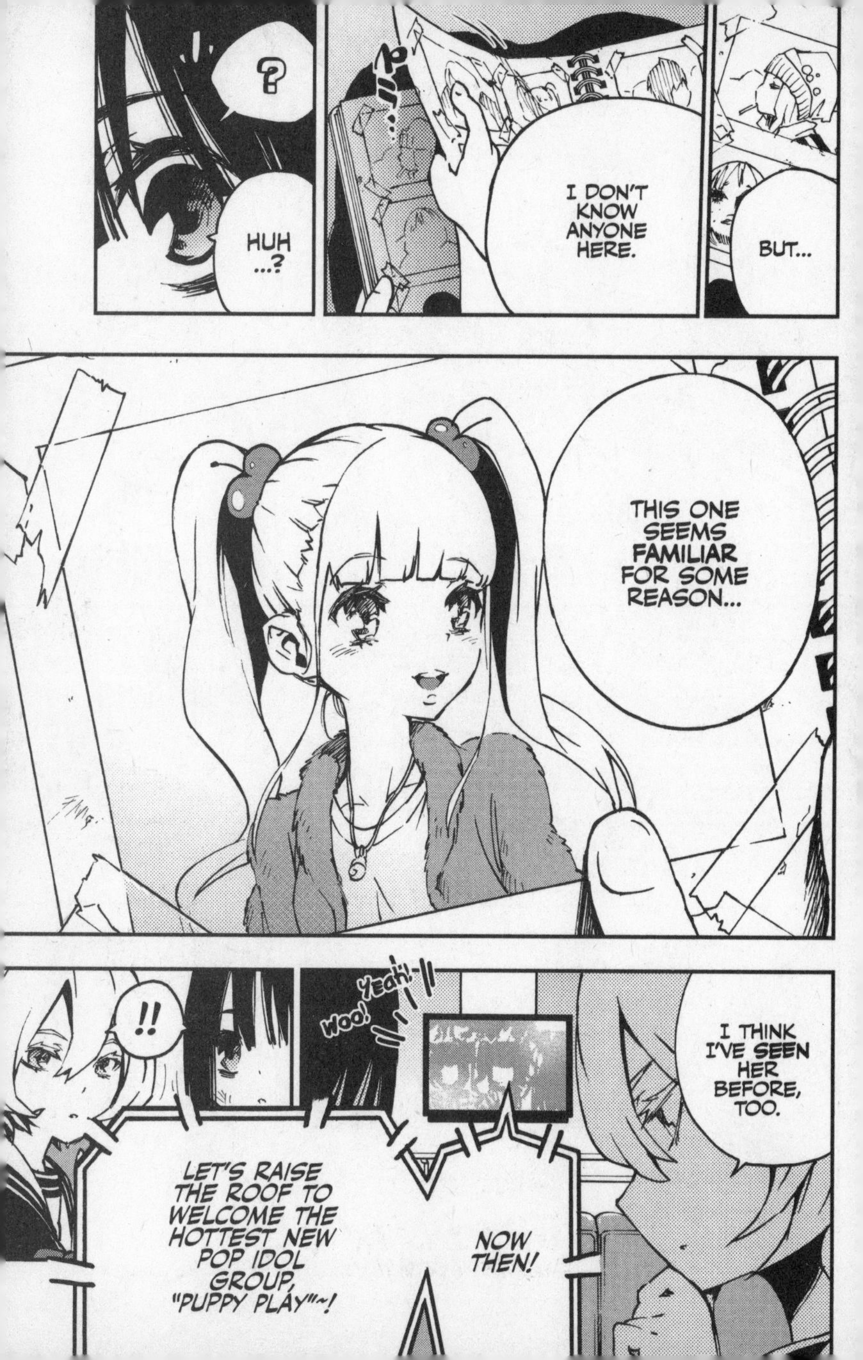
BUT...
I DON'T KNOW ANYONE HERE.
?
HUH ...?
THIS ONE SEEMS FAMILIAR FOR SOME REASON...
I THINK I'VE SEEN HER BEFORE, TOO.
Yeah!
Woo!
!!
NOW THEN!
LET'S RAISE THE ROOF TO WELCOME THE HOTTEST NEW POP IDOL GROUP, "PUPPY PLAY"~!

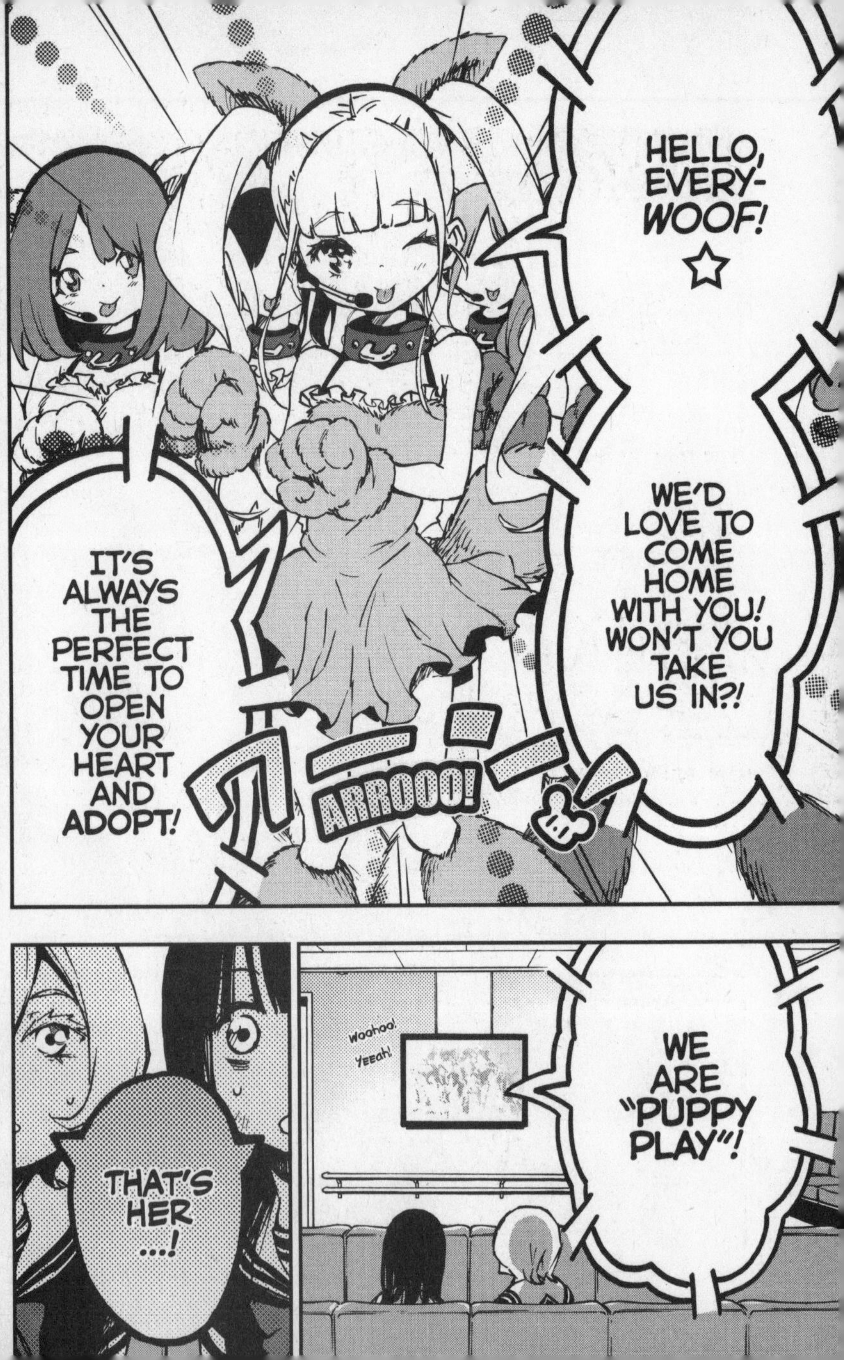
HELLO, EVERY-WOOF! ☆
WE'D LOVE TO COME HOME WITH YOU! WON'T YOU TAKE US IN?!
ARROOO!
IT'S ALWAYS THE PERFECT TIME TO OPEN YOUR HEART AND ADOPT!
WE ARE "PUPPY PLAY"!
Woohoo! YEEAH!
THAT'S HER ...!

ENTER. 6. 5
(SIDE STORY) REVENGE

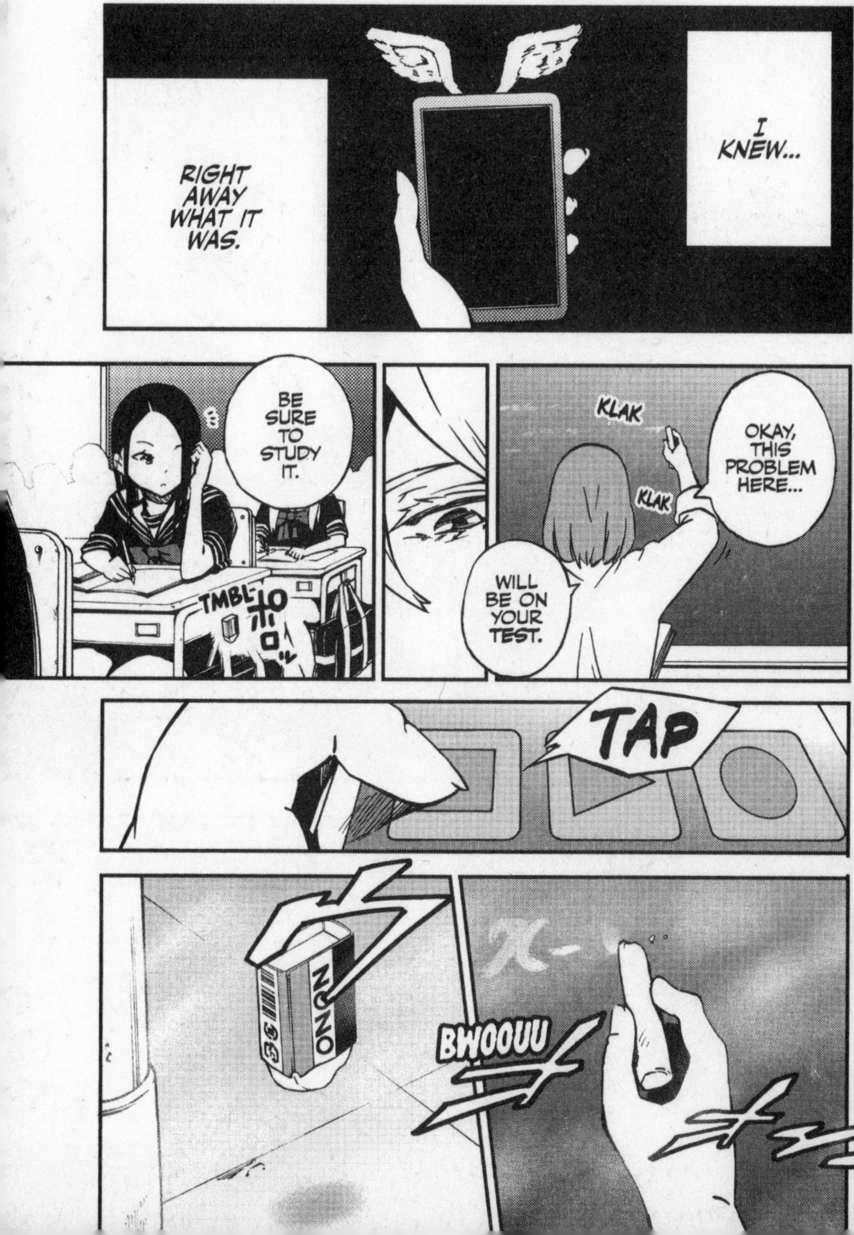

I KNEW...
RIGHT AWAY WHAT IT WAS.
KLAK
KLAK
OKAY, THIS PROBLEM HERE...
WILL BE ON YOUR TEST.
BE SURE TO STUDY IT.
TMBL-
ポロッ
TAP
NONO
BWOOUU

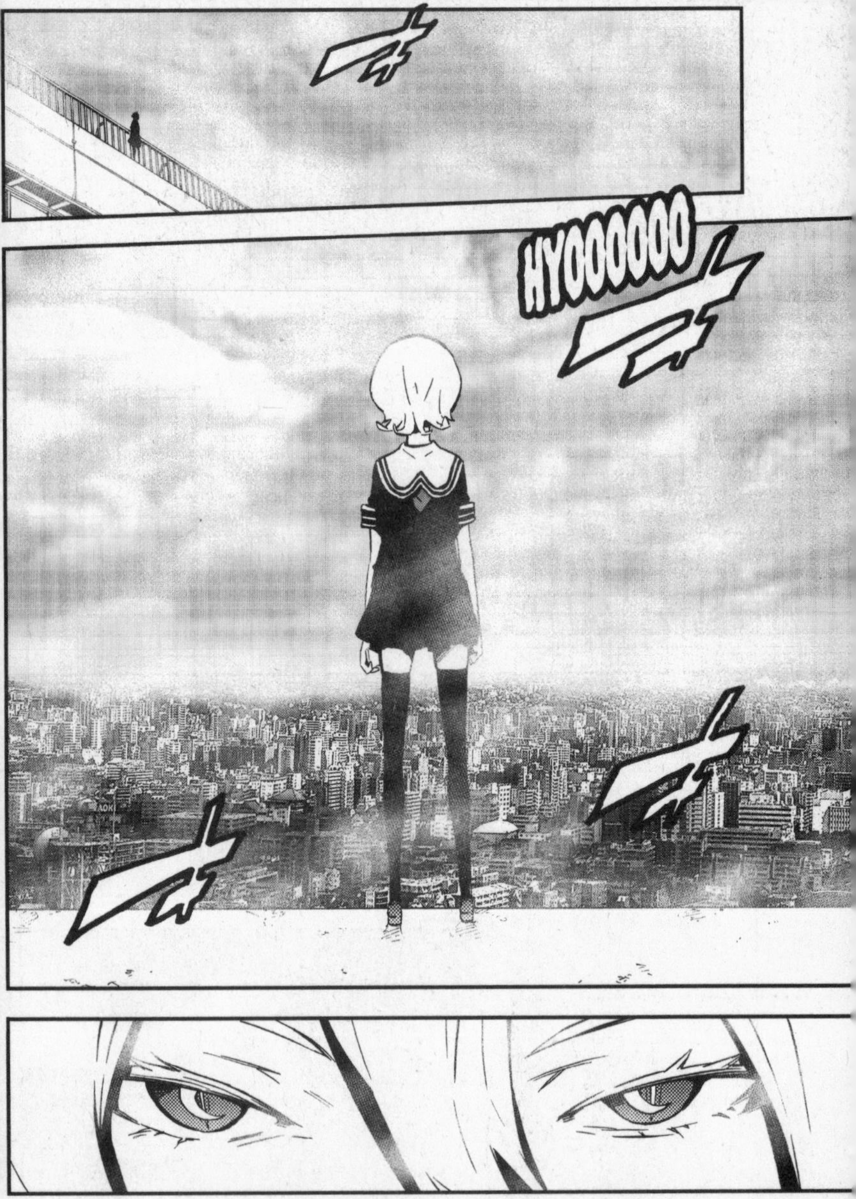
HYOOOOOO

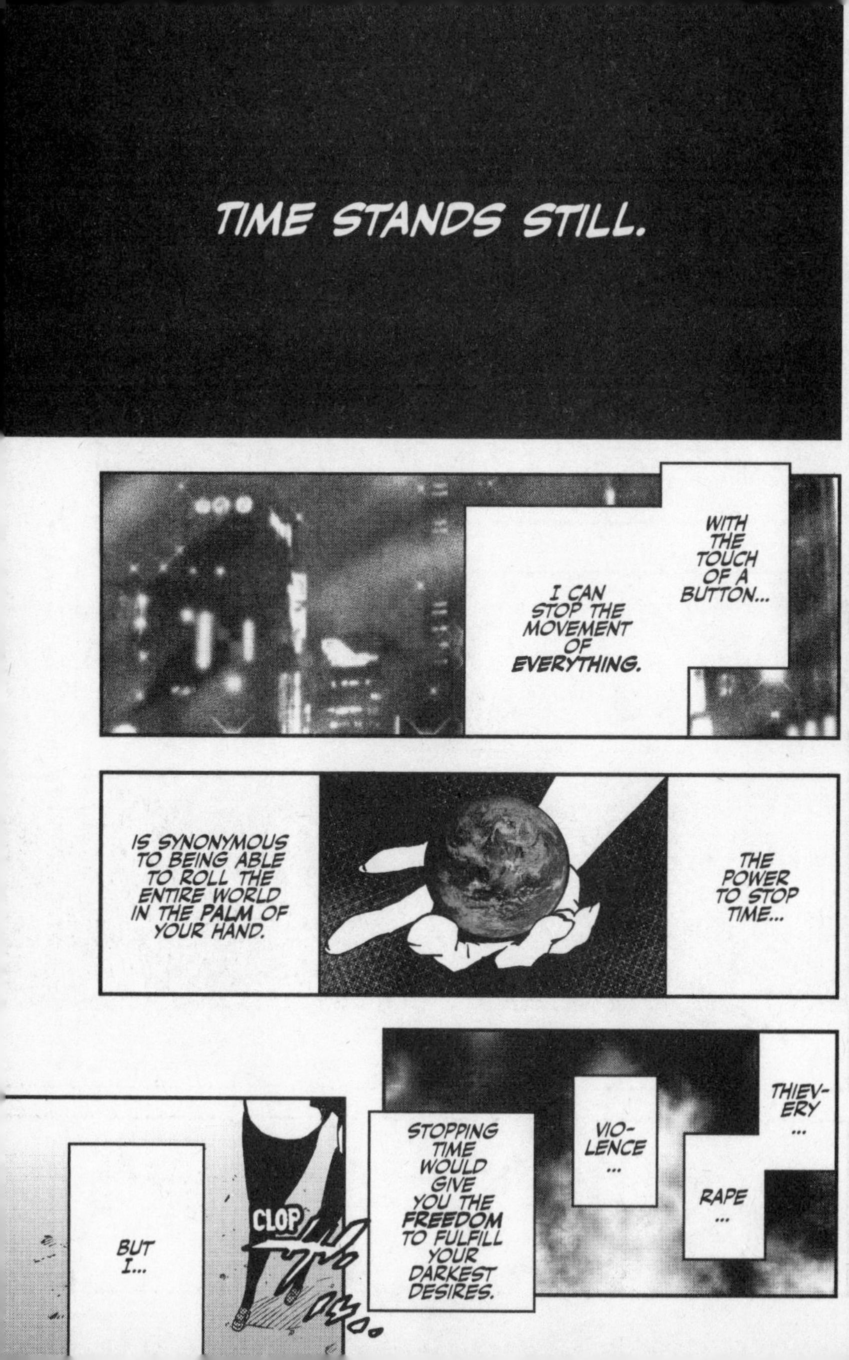
TIME STANDS STILL.
WITH THE TOUCH OF A BUTTON...
I CAN STOP THE MOVEMENT OF EVERYTHING.
THE POWER TO STOP TIME...
IS SYNONYMOUS TO BEING ABLE TO ROLL THE ENTIRE WORLD IN THE PALM OF YOUR HAND.
THIEVERY...
VIOLENCE...
RAPE...
STOPPING TIME WOULD GIVE YOU THE FREEDOM TO FULFILL YOUR DARKEST DESIRES.
CLOP
BUT I...

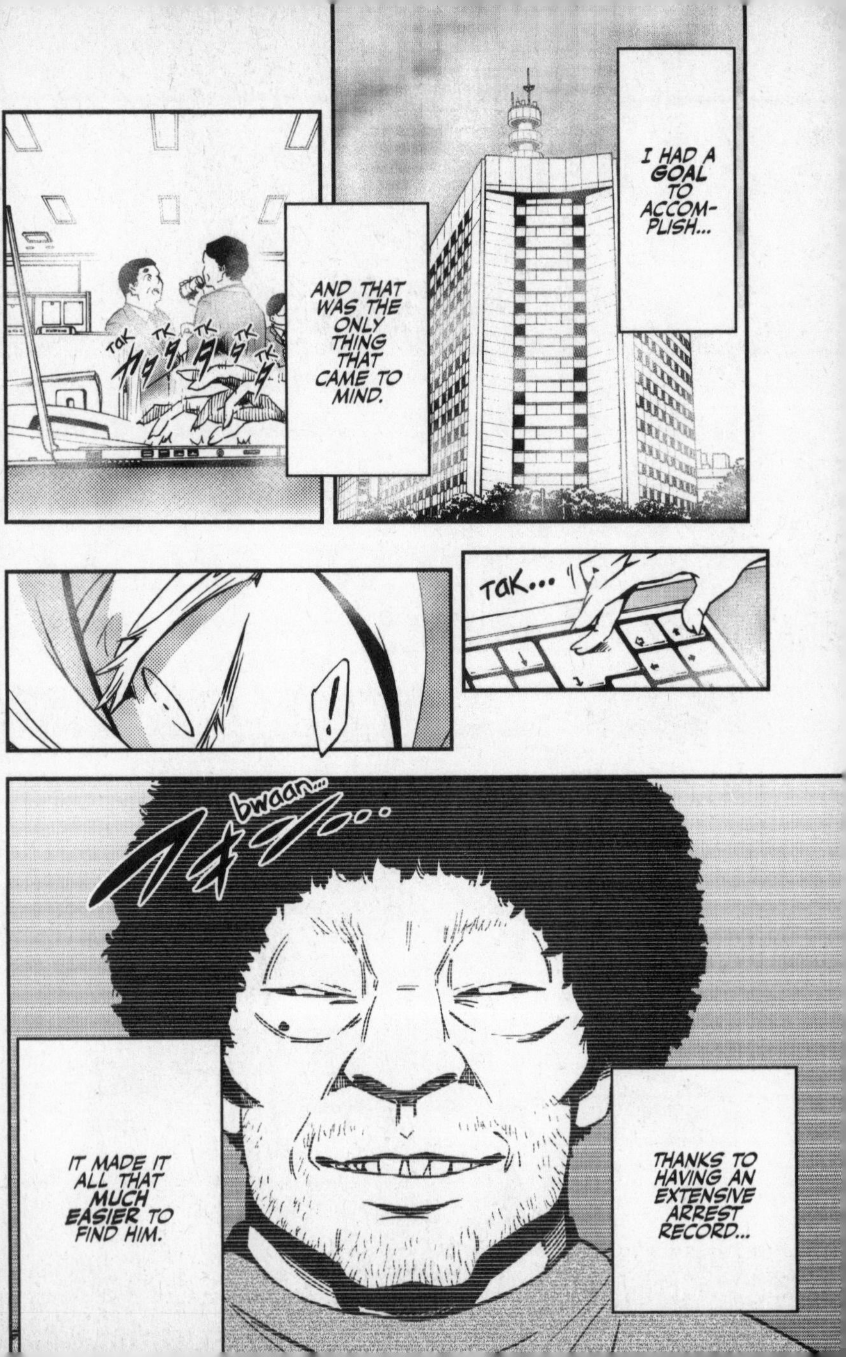
I HAD A GOAL TO ACCOMPLISH...
AND THAT WAS THE ONLY THING THAT CAME TO MIND.
TAK TK TK TK TK
TAK...
!
bwaan...
THANKS TO HAVING AN EXTENSIVE ARREST RECORD...
IT MADE IT ALL THAT MUCH EASIER TO FIND HIM.

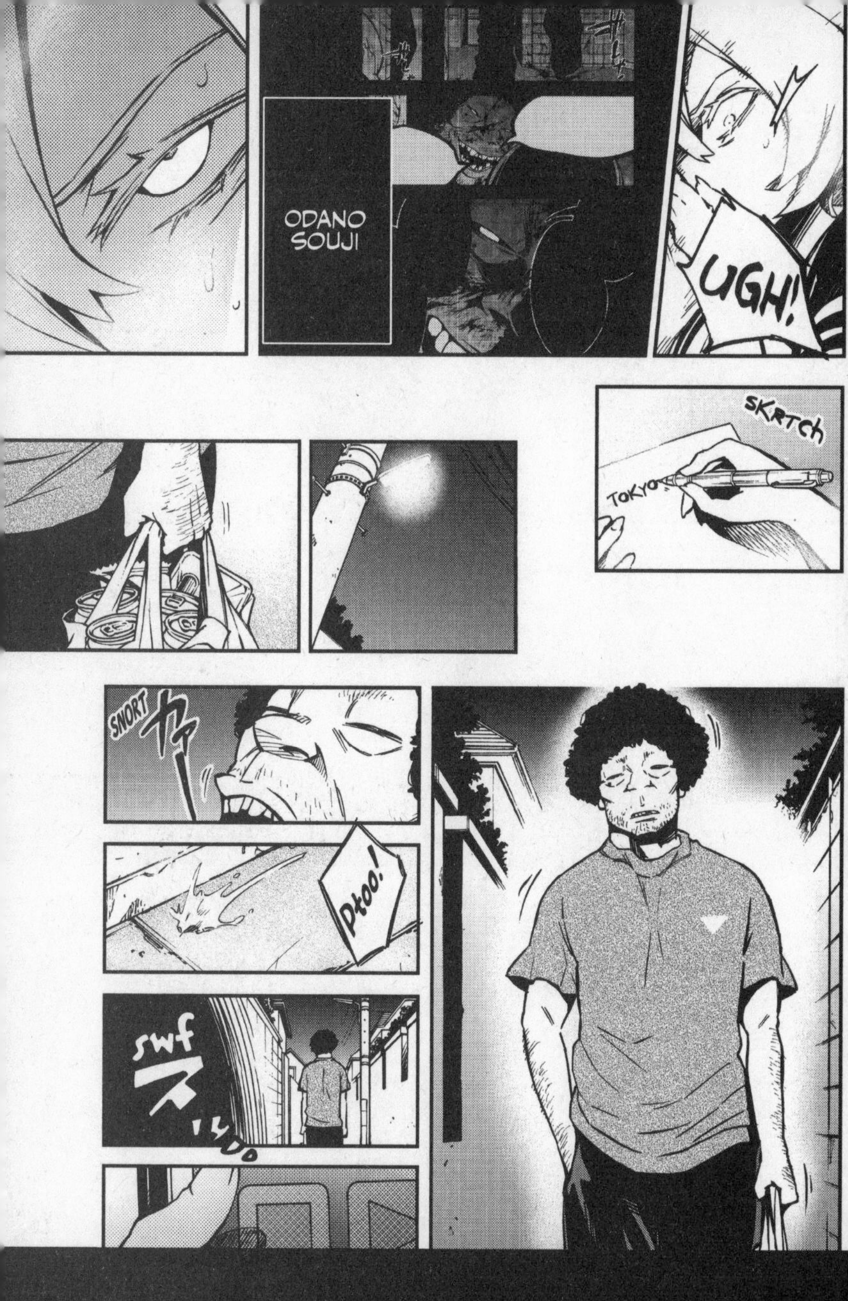
UGH!
ODANO SOUJI
SKRTCH
TOKYO
SNORT
Ptoo!
swf

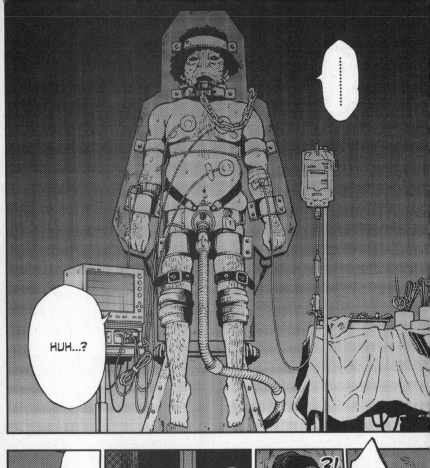

......

HUH...?

WHO'RE YOU, WIDDLE WADY?!

WHA'M I 'OIN ERE?!!

GOOD MORN-ING.

?!

MY TEETH ...?!!

WHA --?!

NAAH... AHHH?!!

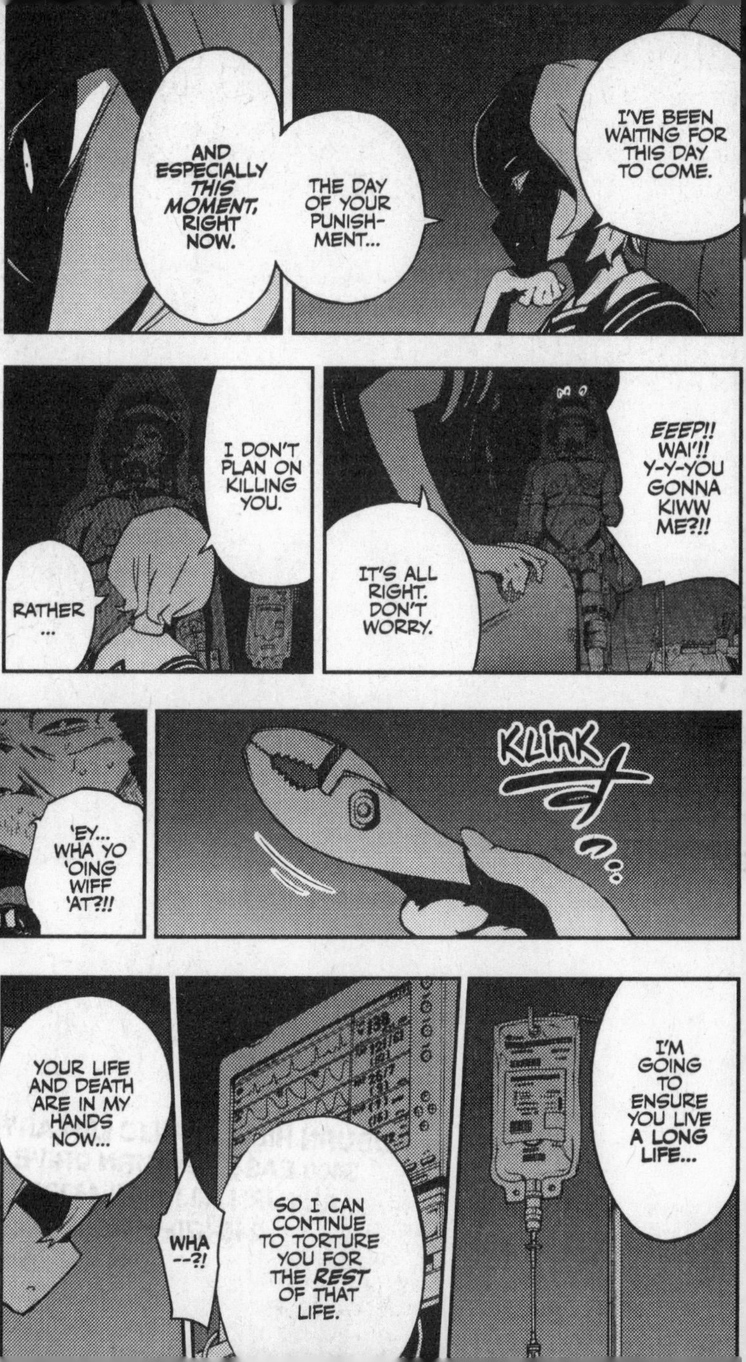
I'VE BEEN WAITING FOR THIS DAY TO COME.
THE DAY OF YOUR PUNISH-MENT...
AND ESPECIALLY *THIS MOMENT*, RIGHT NOW.
EEEP!! WAI'!! Y-Y-YOU GONNA KIWW ME?!!
IT'S ALL RIGHT. DON'T WORRY.
I DON'T PLAN ON KILLING YOU.
RATHER ...
KLINK
'EY... WHA YO 'OING WIFF 'AT?!!
I'M GOING TO ENSURE YOU LIVE A LONG LIFE...
SO I CAN CONTINUE TO TORTURE YOU FOR THE *REST* OF THAT LIFE.
WHA --?!
YOUR LIFE AND DEATH ARE IN MY HANDS NOW...

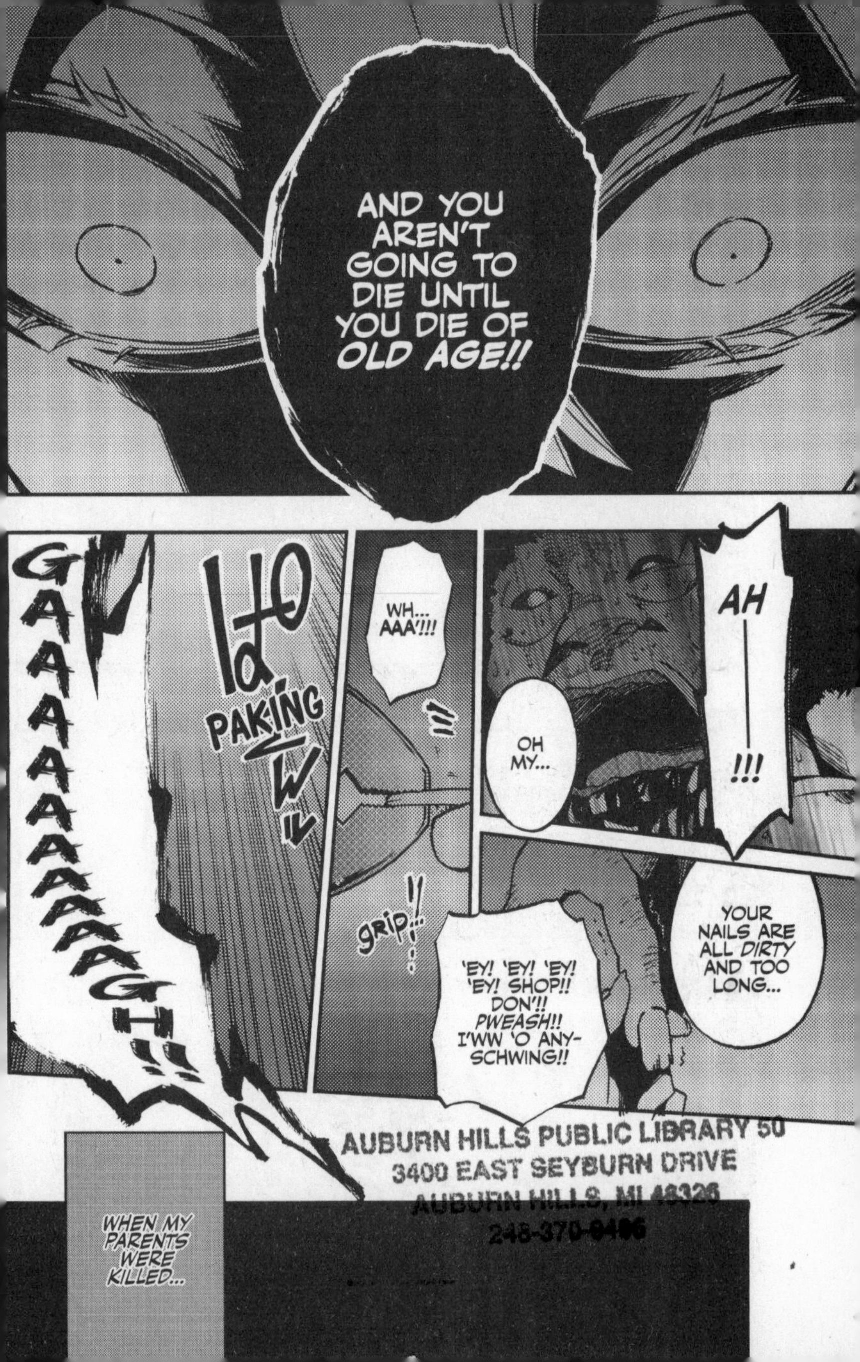
AND YOU AREN'T GOING TO DIE UNTIL YOU DIE OF OLD AGE!!
AH—!!!
OH MY...
YOUR NAILS ARE ALL DIRTY AND TOO LONG...
'EY! 'EY! 'EY! 'EY! SHOP!! DON'!! PWEASH!! I'WW 'O ANY-SCHWING!!
WH... AAA'!!!
grip!!
PAKING
GAAAAAAAAAAAAGH!!
WHEN MY PARENTS WERE KILLED...

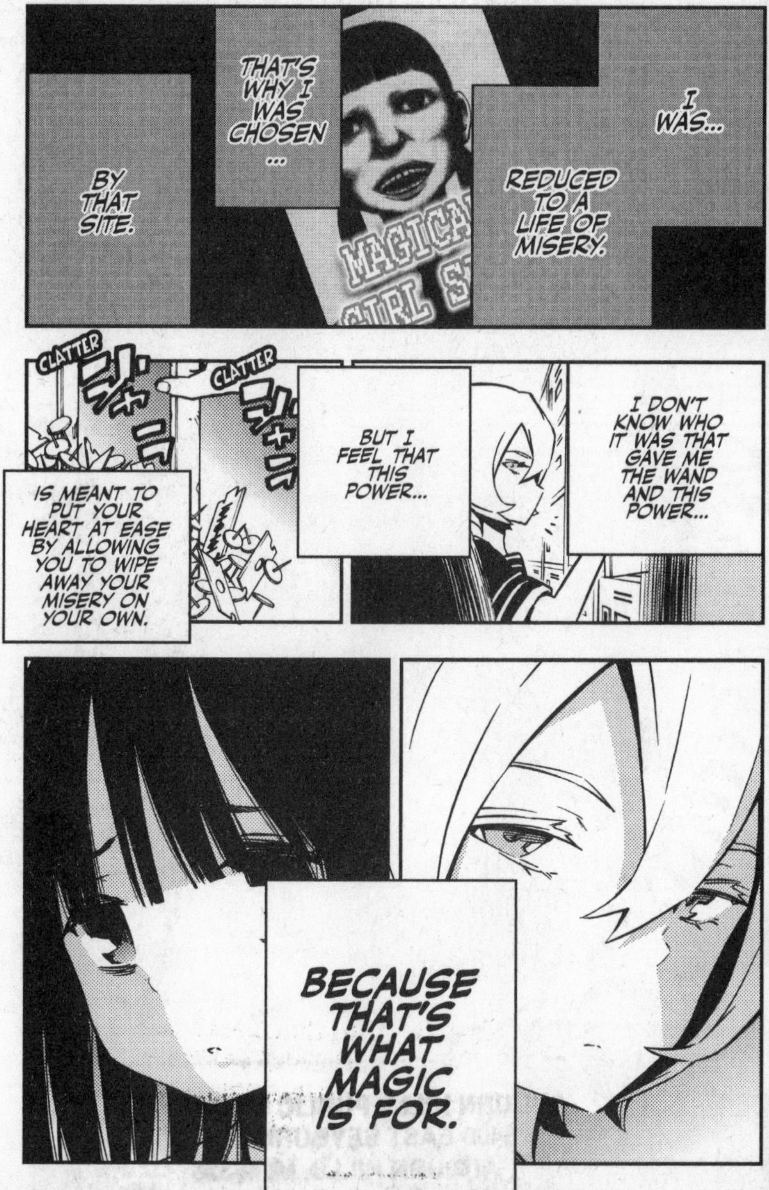
I WAS...
REDUCED TO A LIFE OF MISERY.
THAT'S WHY I WAS CHOSEN ...
BY THAT SITE.
I DON'T KNOW WHO IT WAS THAT GAVE ME THE WAND AND THIS POWER...
BUT I FEEL THAT THIS POWER...
CLATTER
CLATTER
IS MEANT TO PUT YOUR HEART AT EASE BY ALLOWING YOU TO WIPE AWAY YOUR MISERY ON YOUR OWN.
BECAUSE THAT'S WHAT MAGIC IS FOR.

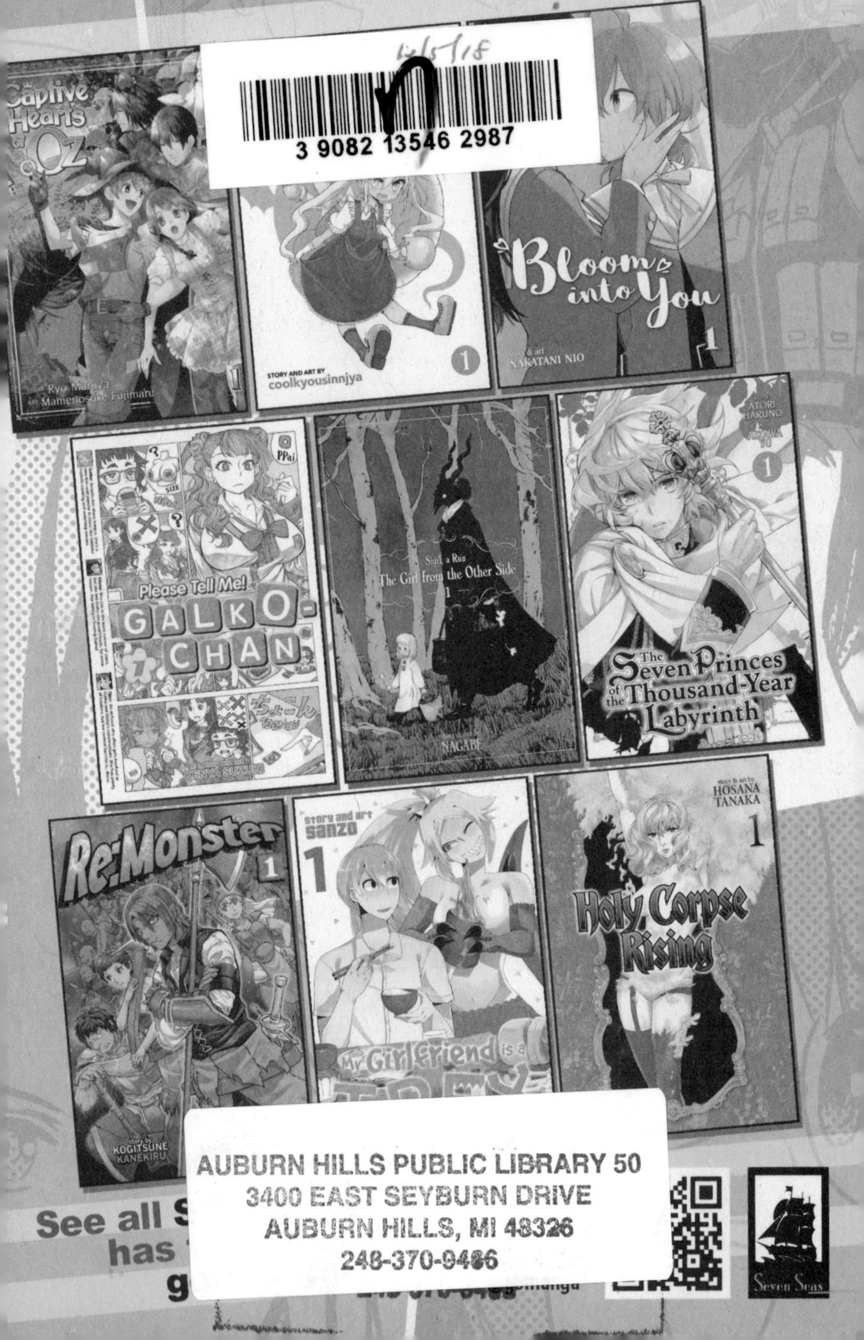
Captive Hearts of Oz
Ryo Maruya
Mamenosuke Fujimaru
1
STORY AND ART BY
coolkyousinnjya
1
Bloom into You
NAKATANI NIO
1
Please Tell Me!
GALKO-CHAN
KENYA SUZUKI
Siúil, a Rún
The Girl from the Other Side
NAGABE
ATORI HARUNO
1
The Seven Princes of the Thousand-Year Labyrinth
Re:Monster
1
KOGITSUNE KANEKIRU
story and art
sanzo
1
My Girlfriend is a
HOSANA TANAKA
1
Holy Corpse Rising